SAP S/4HANA® Business Process

SAP PRESS is a joint initiative of SAP and Rheinwerk Publishing. The know-how offered by SAP specialists combined with the expertise of Rheinwerk Publishing offers the reader expert books in the field. SAP PRESS features first-hand information and expert advice, and provides useful skills for professional decision-making.

SAP PRESS offers a variety of books on technical and business-related topics for the SAP user. For further information, please visit our website: www.sap-press.com.

Bardhan, Baumgartl, Choi, Dudgeon, Górecki, Lahiri, Meijerink, Worsley-Tonks
SAP S/4HANA: An Introduction (4th Edition)
2021, 648 pages, hardcover and e-book
www.sap-press.com/5232

Darío Franco, Jon Simmonds
SAP S/4HANA Sales Certification Guide: Application Associate Exam
2021, approx. 550 pp., paperback and e-book
www.sap-press.com/5308

Aditya Lal
SAP Activate Project Management Certification Guide:
Certified Associate Exam
2021, 530 pages, paperback and e-book
www.sap-press.com/5194

Stefanos Pougkas
SAP S/4HANA Financial Accounting Certification Guide:
Application Associate Exam (3rd Edition)
2021, 450 pages, paperback and e-book
www.sap-press.com/5310

Fabienne Bourdelle
SAP S/4HANA Sourcing and Procurement Certification Guide:
Application Associate Exam
2021, 452 pages, paperback and e-book
www.sap-press.com/5124

Murat Adivar

SAP S/4HANA® Business Process Integration Certification Guide

Application Associate Exam

Editor Megan Fuerst
Acquisitions Editor Emily Nicholls
Copyeditor Yvette Chin
Cover Design Graham Geary
Photo Credit iStockphoto.com: 1156318617/© Govindanmarudhai
Layout Design Vera Brauner
Production Graham Geary
Typesetting SatzPro, Krefeld (Germany)
Printed and bound in Canada, on paper from sustainable sources

ISBN 978-1-4932-2067-0

© 2021 by Rheinwerk Publishing, Inc., Boston (MA)
1st edition 2021

Library of Congress Cataloging-in-Publication data:
Names: Adivar, Murat, author.
Title: SAP S/4HANA business process integration certification guide : application associate exam / by Murat Adivar.
Description: 1st edition. | Bonn ; Boston : SAP Press ; Rheinwerk Publishing, 2021. | Includes index.
Identifiers: LCCN 2021014604 | ISBN 9781493220670 (hardcover) | ISBN 9781493220687 (ebook)
Subjects: LCSH: SAP HANA (Electronic resource)--Examinations--Study guides. | Management information systems--Examinations--Study guides. | Business--Data processing--Management. | Enterprise resource planning. | Database management--Certification--Study guides. | Database management--Examinations--Study guides.
Classification: LCC HD30.213 .A27 2021 | DDC 650.0285/53--dc23
LC record available at https://lccn.loc.gov/2021014604

All rights reserved. Neither this publication nor any part of it may be copied or reproduced in any form or by any means or translated into another language, without the prior consent of Rheinwerk Publishing, 2 Heritage Drive, Suite 305, Quincy, MA 02171.

Rheinwerk Publishing makes no warranties or representations with respect to the content hereof and specifically disclaims any implied warranties of merchantability or fitness for any particular purpose. Rheinwerk Publishing assumes no responsibility for any errors that may appear in this publication.

"Rheinwerk Publishing" and the Rheinwerk Publishing logo are registered trademarks of Rheinwerk Verlag GmbH, Bonn, Germany. SAP PRESS is an imprint of Rheinwerk Verlag GmbH and Rheinwerk Publishing, Inc.

All of the screenshots and graphics reproduced in this book are subject to copyright © SAP SE, Dietmar-Hopp-Allee 16, 69190 Walldorf, Germany.

SAP, ABAP, ASAP, Concur Hipmunk, Duet, Duet Enterprise, Expenselt, SAP ActiveAttention, SAP Adaptive Server Enterprise, SAP Advantage Database Server, SAP ArchiveLink, SAP Ariba, SAP Business ByDesign, SAP Business Explorer (SAP BEx), SAP BusinessObjects, SAP BusinessObjects Explorer, SAP BusinessObjects Web Intelligence, SAP Business One, SAP Business Workflow, SAP BW/4HANA, SAP C/4HANA, SAP Concur, SAP Crystal Reports, SAP EarlyWatch, SAP Fieldglass, SAP Fiori, SAP Global Trade Services (SAP GTS), SAP GoingLive, SAP HANA, SAP Jam, SAP Leonardo, SAP Lumira, SAP MaxDB, SAP NetWeaver, SAP PartnerEdge, SAPPHIRE NOW, SAP PowerBuilder, SAP PowerDesigner, SAP R/2, SAP R/3, SAP Replication Server, SAP Roambi, SAP S/4HANA, SAP S/4HANA Cloud, SAP SQL Anywhere, SAP Strategic Enterprise Management (SAP SEM), SAP SuccessFactors, SAP Vora, TripIt, and Qualtrics are registered or unregistered trademarks of SAP SE, Walldorf, Germany.

All other products mentioned in this book are registered or unregistered trademarks of their respective companies.

Contents at a Glance

1	SAP S/4HANA Basics	35
2	Core Finance: Financial Accounting	71
3	Core Finance: Management Accounting	125
4	Source-to-Pay Processing	183
5	Lead-to-Cash Processing	237
6	Design-to-Operate Processing	295
7	Enterprise Asset Management	359
8	Inventory, Warehouse, and Transportation Management	399
9	Project System	437
10	Hire-to-Retire Processing	477

Dear Reader,

In college, an upcoming exam meant three things: little sleep, lots of stress, and a very heavy bookbag.

As an English major, I often found that the books I needed to study exceeded the space on my desk. Between the stacks of novels, compendiums of literary theory, and collections of short stories and poetry, the reading material felt endless. It was often difficult to know exactly what would appear on a test—I remember one particular late-night study session spent agonizing over Shakespeare's 154 sonnets—and the test format itself could often be a mystery.

Luckily, when it comes to your SAP S/4HANA business process integration exam, this book is your one-stop shop. Instead of Dickens, Twain, and Tolstoy on your test, you'll review financial accounting, procurement, plant maintenance, and so on—all of which are covered within these pages. Plus, you'll find no better instructor than Murat Adivar, who will expertly prepare you for what to expect on exam day, teach you the core topics, and reinforce your knowledge with practice questions and answers. You'll be ready to make the grade with less stress, more sleep, and a much lighter bookbag!

What did you think about *SAP S/4HANA Business Process Integration Certification Guide: Application Associate Exam*? Your comments and suggestions are the most useful tools to help us make our books the best they can be. Please feel free to contact me and share any praise or criticism you may have.

Thank you for purchasing a book from SAP PRESS!

Megan Fuerst
Editor, SAP PRESS

meganf@rheinwerk-publishing.com
www.sap-press.com
Rheinwerk Publishing · Boston, MA

Contents

Preface 15
Introduction: The Path to Certification 19

1 SAP S/4HANA Basics   35

1.1	Objectives of This Portion of the Test	36
1.2	SAP S/4HANA Suite	37
	1.2.1 Motivators and Technology Enablers	37
	1.2.2 Components	39
	1.2.3 Key Characteristics	43
1.3	The Intelligent Enterprise	46
	1.3.1 The Intelligent Suite and Enhanced Business Processes	46
	1.3.2 Intelligent Technologies	48
	1.3.3 Industry Cloud	48
	1.3.4 SAP Business Technology Platform	48
1.4	SAP Fiori	50
	1.4.1 Design and Dimensions	50
	1.4.2 SAP Fiori Launchpad	52
	1.4.3 Application Types	54
1.5	System-Wide Concepts	54
	1.5.1 Data	55
	1.5.2 Client	57
	1.5.3 Transactions	57
	1.5.4 Documents	59
	1.5.5 Outputs	60
1.6	Business Process Integration	61
1.7	Important Terminology	61
1.8	Practice Questions	64
1.9	Practice Question Answers and Explanations	67
1.10	Test Takeaway	70

2 Core Finance: Financial Accounting — 71

- 2.1 Objectives of This Portion of the Test — 73
- 2.2 Data Structures for Financial Accounting — 73
  - 2.2.1 Organizational Data — 73
  - 2.2.2 Master Data — 75
  - 2.2.3 Data Assignments — 80
- 2.3 Key Processes of Financial Accounting — 81
  - 2.3.1 General Ledger Accounting — 81
  - 2.3.2 Accounts Payable — 98
  - 2.3.3 Accounts Receivable — 99
  - 2.3.4 Asset Accounting — 99
- 2.4 Integration with Other Modules — 108
  - 2.4.1 Integration via Cross-Module Data Assignments — 108
  - 2.4.2 Integration via Transactions — 109
- 2.5 Important Terminology — 111
- 2.6 Practice Questions — 114
- 2.7 Practice Question Answers and Explanations — 119
- 2.8 Test Takeaway — 124

3 Core Finance: Management Accounting — 125

- 3.1 Objectives of This Portion of the Test — 127
- 3.2 Data Structures for Management Accounting — 127
  - 3.2.1 Organizational Data — 128
  - 3.2.2 Master Data — 130
  - 3.2.3 Data Assignments — 133
- 3.3 Key Processes of Management Accounting — 133
  - 3.3.1 Cost Element Accounting — 134
  - 3.3.2 Cost Center Accounting — 136
  - 3.3.3 Activity-Based Costing — 146
  - 3.3.4 Internal Orders — 147
  - 3.3.5 Profitability Analysis and Sales Controlling — 151
  - 3.3.6 Product Cost Accounting — 155
  - 3.3.7 Profit Center Accounting — 158
- 3.4 Integration with Other Modules — 161
  - 3.4.1 Integration via Cross-Module Data Assignments — 161
  - 3.4.2 Integration via Transactions — 163

	3.5	Important Terminology	166
	3.6	Practice Questions	169
	3.7	Practice Question Answers and Explanations	175
	3.8	Test Takeaway	180

4 Source-to-Pay Processing 183

	4.1	Objectives of This Portion of the Test		185
	4.2	Data Structures for Source-To-Pay		185
		4.2.1	Organizational Data	186
		4.2.2	Master Data	188
		4.2.3	Data Assignments	201
	4.3	Key Processes of Source-to-Pay		204
		4.3.1	Determination of Requirements	205
		4.3.2	Source of Supply Determination	209
		4.3.3	Vendor Selection	211
		4.3.4	Purchase Order Handling	211
		4.3.5	Goods Receipt	215
		4.3.6	Invoice Verification	221
		4.3.7	Payment	223
	4.4	Integration with Other Modules		224
		4.4.1	Integration via Cross-Module Data Assignments	224
		4.4.2	Integration via Transactions	225
		4.4.3	SAP Ariba Integration	226
	4.5	Important Terminology		227
	4.6	Practice Questions		228
	4.7	Practice Question Answers and Explanations		233
	4.8	Test Takeaway		236

5 Lead-to-Cash Processing 237

	5.1	Objectives of This Portion of the Test		239
	5.2	Data Structures for Lead-to-Cash		240
		5.2.1	Organizational Data	240
		5.2.2	Master Data	243
		5.2.3	Data Assignments	249

5.3		**Key Processes of Lead-to-Cash**	251
	5.3.1	Order-to-Cash Overview	252
	5.3.2	Sales Order Handling	254
	5.3.3	Outbound Delivery Handling	265
	5.3.4	Billing	275
5.4		**Integration with Other Modules**	279
	5.4.1	Integration via Cross-Module Data Assignments	279
	5.4.2	Integration via Transactions	279
5.5		**Important Terminology**	281
5.6		**Practice Questions**	283
5.7		**Practice Question Answers and Explanations**	288
5.8		**Test Takeaway**	292

6 Design-to-Operate Processing 295

6.1		**Objectives of This Portion of the Test**	297
6.2		**Data Structures for Design-to-Operate**	297
	6.2.1	Organizational Data	298
	6.2.2	Master Data	298
	6.2.3	Data Assignments	312
6.3		**Key Processes of Design-to-Operate**	313
	6.3.1	Strategic Planning	314
	6.3.2	Demand Management	316
	6.3.3	SAP Integrated Business Planning	316
	6.3.4	Detailed Planning	317
	6.3.5	Manufacturing Control and Execution	327
6.4		**Integration with Other Modules**	341
	6.4.1	Integration via Cross-Module Data Assignments	341
	6.4.2	Integration via Transactions	342
6.5		**Important Terminology**	344
6.6		**Practice Questions**	346
6.7		**Practice Question Answers and Explanations**	352
6.8		**Test Takeaway**	356

7 Enterprise Asset Management 359

- **7.1** Objectives of This Portion of the Test 360
- **7.2** Data Structures for Enterprise Asset Management 361
  - 7.2.1 Organizational Data 361
  - 7.2.2 Master Data 363
  - 7.2.3 Data Assignments 371
- **7.3** Key Processes of Enterprise Asset Management 372
  - 7.3.1 Maintenance Notification 373
  - 7.3.2 Maintenance Planning 375
  - 7.3.3 Maintenance Control 379
  - 7.3.4 Maintenance Execution 380
  - 7.3.5 Maintenance Completion 381
- **7.4** Integration with Other Modules 386
  - 7.4.1 Integration via Cross-Module Data Assignments 386
  - 7.4.2 Integration via Transactions 387
- **7.5** Important Terminology 388
- **7.6** Practice Questions 390
- **7.7** Practice Question Answers and Explanations 395
- **7.8** Test Takeaway 398

8 Inventory, Warehouse, and Transportation Management 399

- **8.1** Objectives of This Portion of the Test 401
- **8.2** Inventory Management 402
  - 8.2.1 Organizational Data 402
  - 8.2.2 Goods Movements 403
  - 8.2.3 Documents for Goods Movements 410
- **8.3** Warehouse Management 411
  - 8.3.1 Organizational Data 412
  - 8.3.2 Centralized Warehouse Management 414
  - 8.3.3 Decentralized Warehouse Management 416
- **8.4** Extended Warehouse Management 417
- **8.5** Transportation Management 419

8.6	Integration with Other Modules	422
	8.6.1 Integration via Cross-Module Data Assignments	422
	8.6.2 Integration via Transactions	422
8.7	Important Terminology	424
8.8	Practice Questions	426
8.9	Practice Question Answers and Explanations	432
8.10	Test Takeaway	435

9 Project System 437

9.1	Objectives of This Portion of the Test	438
9.2	Data Structures for Project System	439
	9.2.1 Project Structuring Elements	439
	9.2.2 Data Assignments	451
9.3	Key Processes of Project System	452
	9.3.1 Project Planning	453
	9.3.2 Project Budgeting	456
	9.3.3 Project Execution	457
	9.3.4 Period-End Closing	461
9.4	Integration with Other Modules	463
	9.4.1 Integration via Cross-Module Data Assignments	463
	9.4.2 Integration via Transactions	465
9.5	Important Terminology	466
9.6	Practice Questions	467
9.7	Practice Question Answers and Explanations	471
9.8	Test Takeaway	474

10 Hire-to-Retire Processing 477

10.1	Objectives of This Portion of the Test	479
10.2	Data Structures for Hire-to-Retire	479
	10.2.1 Organizational Structures	479
	10.2.2 Master Data	485
	10.2.3 Data Assignments	489

10.3	**Key Processes of Hire-to-Retire**		490
	10.3.1	Hire-to-Retire Tasks	490
	10.3.2	Human Capital Management versus Human Experience Management	491
	10.3.3	SAP SuccessFactors Employee Central	495
	10.3.4	Self-Service Tools	496
10.4	**Integration with Other Modules**		497
	10.4.1	Integration via Cross-Module Data Assignments	497
	10.4.2	Integration via Transactions	498
10.5	**Important Terminology**		498
10.6	**Practice Questions**		500
10.7	**Practice Question Answers and Explanations**		503
10.8	**Test Takeaway**		505

The Author	507
Index	509

Preface

Welcome to the C_TS410 certification guide. This book is specifically written as support material for those preparing for the SAP Certified Application Associate – Business Process Integration with SAP S/4HANA (C_TS410_1809, C_TS410_1909, or C_TS410_2020) exam. We'll mainly focus on business processes and their integrations with the SAP S/4HANA intelligent enterprise suite. This book can also help application consultants, business process architects, program/project managers, and enterprise architects by providing a comprehensive overview of all business processes within SAP S/4HANA.

Using this book, you'll gain a thorough understanding of the exam's structure. You'll learn to navigate an SAP S/4HANA system, describe how various business transactions are performed in SAP S/4HANA, and explain the integration points between applications within the SAP S/4HANA intelligent enterprise.

How This Book Is Organized

This book's content is aligned with the SAP TS410 course syllabus and the C_TS410 certification exam structure. All the information provided in this book is relevant to what you'll need to know for the exam. We'll introduce you to SAP products and their supported business processes using real-world scenarios, figures, and straightforward language. Each chapter in this book ends with a section of practice questions to help test your knowledge of specific topic areas on the certification exam. We'll introduce you to several versions of the certification exam, test-taking techniques, and alternative ways to learn in the Introduction.

Now that you have an idea of how this book is structured, let's briefly look at the particular topics covered in each chapter:

- **Chapter 1: SAP S/4HANA Basics**
  In this chapter, we cover all basic certification-related concepts of SAP S/4HANA. We explain the technology enablers of and the motivation behind developing a new business suite that runs natively on SAP HANA. We outline the components of the intelligent enterprise framework and introduce SAP Fiori, SAP's next-generation user experience (UX). We conclude the chapter by highlighting some system-wide concepts (e.g., organizational data, master data, transactions, documents, outputs) that are essential for the certification exam.

- **Chapter 2: Core Finance: Financial Accounting**
  The focus of this chapter is to cover financial accounting in SAP S/4HANA. In particular, we concentrate on certification-related financial accounting topics and its key processes, such as general ledger accounting, accounts payable accounting, accounts receivable accounting, and asset accounting. We define the organizational and master data that support financial transactions and financial statements in SAP S/4HANA. We discuss the system-wide relationships between data and transactions that support the tasks of financial accounting. We highlight the touchpoints of integration between financial accounting and other business processes in the system.

- **Chapter 3: Core Finance: Management Accounting**
  This chapter prepares test takers for the coverage of management accounting in the exam. We focus on certification-related topics in management accounting and its key processes in SAP S/4HANA. We specifically cover cost element accounting, cost center accounting, activity-based costing, internal orders, profitability analysis and sales controlling, product cost accounting, and profit center accounting. We define the organizational data, master data, and controlling objects supporting tracking, management, and internal reporting capabilities in controlling. We discuss the cross-module relationships between management accounting and other system components and highlight the touchpoints of integration between the system modules and controlling.

- **Chapter 4: Source-to-Pay Processing**
  This chapter provides an overview of the source-to-pay business process in SAP S/4HANA integrated with SAP Ariba. We describe key source-to-pay tasks, such as determining requirements, source-of-supply determination, vendor selection, purchase order handling, goods receipt, invoice verification, and payment. We introduce the organizational and master data supporting source-to-pay processing in SAP S/4HANA and explain their relationships. We discuss the cross-module data assignments and highlight the touchpoints of integration between purchasing and other processes in the system.

- **Chapter 5: Lead-to-Cash Processing**
  This chapter focuses on the lead-to-cash business process enabled by SAP's intelligent enterprise framework. We comprehensively cover certification-related topics in the order-to-cash business process supported by SAP S/4HANA. We define the organizational and master data that support the sales and distribution transactions enabling the order-to-cash business process in SAP S/4HANA. We also explain the new master data approach of SAP S/4HANA, such as business partner roles and cross-module data assignments. We discuss the system-wide relationships between data and transactions that support the tasks of the order-to-cash business process. We end this chapter by highlighting the touchpoints of integration between the lead-to-cash processing and other business processes in the system.

- **Chapter 6: Design-to-Operate Processing**
  This chapter provides a comprehensive overview of the manufacturing process in the SAP S/4HANA intelligent enterprise. We cover the key processes of design-to-operate, including design, plan-to-produce, plan-to-deliver, and operate. We describe the organizational and master data in design-to-operate processing and explain how the production module integrates with other system modules during production planning and manufacturing execution. In particular, we discuss the roles of SAP Integrated Business Planning (SAP IBP) and embedded production planning and detailed scheduling (PP-DS) in the strategic and detailed planning of manufacturing.

- **Chapter 7: Enterprise Asset Management**
  This chapter prepares test takers for the exam's coverage of enterprise asset management. We focus on enterprise asset management's key processes, including inspection, preventive maintenance, breakdown maintenance, and corrective maintenance. We describe the organizational and master data in enterprise asset management and explain their roles in processing maintenance notifications and maintenance orders for technical objects. We discuss how SAP S/4HANA's plant maintenance module supports the maintenance planning, maintenance control, maintenance execution, and maintenance completion processes. We end the chapter by highlighting the touchpoints of integration.

- **Chapter 8: Inventory, Warehouse, and Transportation Management**
  This chapter focuses on the key topics of inventory management, warehouse management, and transportation management in SAP S/4HANA. We describe inventory management, warehouse management, and transportation management roles in enterprise management and explain the connections between them in SAP S/4HANA. In particular, we cover goods movements and describe the system documents generated by goods movements. We explain several warehouse management scenarios and discuss the key tasks of transportation management. We also clarify how each component integrates with each other and other system modules during stock movements and transportation.

- **Chapter 9: Project System**
  This chapter focuses on the Project System module in SAP S/4HANA. We describe project structuring elements in SAP S/4HANA and explain their relationships with the data and transactions of other system modules. We describe standard transactions in the planning, budgeting, execution, and period-end closing phases of a project and discuss how the Project System module integrates with other system modules during the project lifecycle.

- **Chapter 10: Hire-to-Retire Processing**
  This chapter covers the key topics in SAP SuccessFactors' hire-to-retire processing enhanced with SAP's human experience management (HXM) strategy. We

clarify the prominent differences between classic human capital management (HCM) and employee-centric HXM. We describe HXM structures and the structure of employee master records. We explain several employee master record maintenance processes in the system. We also introduce SAP SuccessFactors HXM Suite components, including SAP SuccessFactors Employee Central and SAP SuccessFactors Employee Central Payroll, and discuss cloud transition scenarios for core HCM processes.

Note
Notes will provide other resources to explore or additional detail that will help you with the topic under discussion.

Tip
Tips call out useful information, hints, and warnings to help you master each topic for exam day.

Example
Examples provide practical scenarios and explain how particular functions can be applied.

Acknowledgments

This book would not exist without the continuous encouragement of my family during unprecedented times. First, I would like to thank my beautiful wife Burcu Adivar and our terrific children Aliakin and Buket for their understanding, patience, and sincere support during my long working hours writing this book. Second, I would like to offer my sincere appreciation and thanks to Professor Pamela Jackson, who started the SAP consultant training initiative in Fayetteville, NC, and has changed many lives, including mine. I also thank Colleen Raftery, Heather Czech, and Constance Lightner for their invaluable support in establishing SAP Next-Gen Lab in Fayetteville, where we were able to develop a precious experience in TS410 training. Finally, I would like to thank Emily Nicholls and Megan Fuerst at SAP PRESS for their excellent professionalism that made this book possible.

Introduction: The Path to Certification

Techniques You'll Master

- Describe the scope and target audience of the C_TS410 certification
- Explain the question types and structure of the exam
- Understand the similarities and differences in topic areas covered by current versions of the certification exam
- Explain ways to learn the topic areas covered by the certification
- Learn techniques for taking the C_TS410 certification exam
- Identify helpful resources for the certification

In this introduction, we'll provide an overview of the scope, topic areas, and structure of the SAP Certified Application Associate – Business Process Integration with SAP S/4HANA (C_TS410) certification exam. In this introduction, we explain the scope of the certification and the learning path for preparing candidates for the certification exam.

Who This Book Is For

At the time of this writing, SAP offers more than 150 certifications focused on several business processes in SAP S/4HANA and other SAP solutions, including cloud solutions. These certifications are offered at the associate or professional levels and in several languages. The C_TS410 certification covers all business processes and their integrations in SAP S/4HANA.

This book is specifically designed for learners preparing for the 1809, 1909, or 2020 versions of the C_TS410 certification exam. However, since the core business processes in SAP S/4HANA are standard, this book's content should widely support future exam versions.

This book is also a good source of information for consultants who would like a comprehensive overview of business processes in SAP S/4HANA and to understand how SAP S/4HANA's components can be integrated to design a seamlessly integrated enterprise.

Note that the certification exam requires systematic exam preparation. Depending on your previous exposure to SAP systems and your knowledge of enterprise business processes, you may need to participate in some courses or training programs offered by SAP Training and Adoption and its officially sanctioned partners, such as SAP University Alliances institutions. Those programs provide access to SAP's training systems and official case study materials to develop your user skills on the software. This book is not intended to serve as a complete alternative to those education programs, although we comprehensively cover all the topic areas of the C_TS410 exam.

The C_TS410 Certification Exam

This section explains the technical details of the current versions of the C_TS410 certification exam, including a look at their similarities and differences.

Currently, SAP offers the following versions of the C_TS410 certification exam in the Certification Hub:

- C_TS410_1809
- C_TS410_1909
- C_TS410_2020

According to the SAP Training website, the certification is mainly intended for candidates who are currently working (or would like to work) in the following positions:

- Application consultant
- Business process architect
- Business process owner/team lead/power user
- Enterprise architect
- Program/project manager

Tip

The C_TS410 certification exam requires guided and systematic preparation. Your recent experience with SAP and basic knowledge of business processes in enterprise planning and management can significantly expedite your exam preparation process, but your prior knowledge alone may not be sufficient to pass the test.

You can take both exams either in the certification center or online through SAP's Certification Hub. Both exam versions have 80 questions (of equal weight) to answer in 3 hours (180 minutes).

The Certification Hub is a cloud-based platform that requires an annual subscription, providing six certification attempts for 12 months within the subscription date. A person who passes on the first try can potentially get six different certifications. Online certification exams in the Certification Hub are remotely proctored (by a real person) via webcam on your computer, and a proctoring software must be installed on your computer. You can use up to three tries for each certification type. In case of failure, you can try a previous version of the certification (if still available) or wait for the next version release, usually released in the first quarter of the new year.

Note

You can find more details about exam locations, exam rules, and learning materials for C_TS410 exams (and other SAP certification exams) at the SAP Training website at *https://training.sap.com/certification/*.

Note that SAP University Alliances institutions also offer C_TS410 bootcamps and onsite exams for their active students and recent graduates. You can perform a Google search to find a list of SAP University Alliances institutions in your country/area.

The following question types are standard in all SAP certification exams:

- **Multiple-choice questions**
  In a multiple-choice question, only one answer is correct.
- **Multiple-answer questions**
  In a multiple-answer question, out of four or five options, two or three answers may be correct. This type of question does not provide partial credit for partially correct selections. In other words, all of your selections must be correct to receive full credit.

Introduction: The Path to Certification

> **Tip**
> This book provides practice questions of both types at the end of each chapter to help you get familiar with the standard question types found in the C_TS410 certification exam.

Two main differences exist between the current versions of the exam:

- **Cut score**
  C_TS410_2020 requires at least 61% of your answers to be answered correctly, while the passing score in the C_TS410_1909 exam is 66% and the passing score in the C_TS410_1809 exam is 60%.

- **Topic areas**
  Table 1 summarizes the topic areas and their weights in the C_TS410 certification exam versions.

C_TS410_1809 Topic Area	Percentage	C_TS410_1909 Topic Area	Percentage	C_TS410_2020 Topic Area	Percentage
SAP S/4HANA Basics	8%–12%	SAP S/4HANA Basics	> 12%	SAP S/4HANA Basics	> 12%
Core Finance: Management Accounting	> 12%	Core Finance: Management Accounting	> 12%	Core Finance: Management Accounting	> 12%
Enterprise Asset Management	8%–12%	Enterprise Asset Management	8%–12%	Enterprise Asset Management	8%–12%
Order-to-Cash Processing	8%–12%	Lead-to-Cash Processing	8%–12%	Lead-to-Cash Processing	8%–12%
Plan-to-Produce Processing	8%–12%	Design-to-Operate Processing	8%–12%	Design-to-Operate Processing	> 12%
Purchase-to-Pay Processing	8%–12%	Source-to-Pay Processing	8%–12%	Source-to-Pay Processing	8%–12%
Project System	8%–12%	Project System	8%–12%	Project System	8%–12%
Core Finance: Financial Accounting	> 12%	Core Finance: Financial Accounting	< 8%	Core Finance: Financial Accounting	8%–12%
Warehouse Management	< 8%	Warehouse Management	< 8%	Warehouse and Inventory Management	< 8%
Human Capital Management	< 8%	Human Experience Management	< 8%	Hire-to-Retire Processing	< 8%

Table 1 Topic Areas in Versions 1809, 1909, and 2020

After passing the certification test, a successful candidate receives a digital badge issued by SAP, shown in Figure 1. This badge shows your demonstrated skills in the topic areas of the certification. Using the weblinks of your badge, you can electronically share this badge on social media or embed it in your digital resumes or emails.

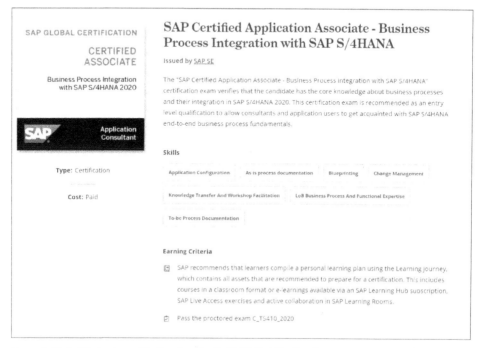

Figure 1 Digital Badge Issued by Passing the C_TS410 Certification Exam

> **Note**
> The digital badge for your C_TS410 certification, which is issued by SAP, does not include your test score in the C_TS410 exam but demonstrates your skills and earning criteria (see *http://s-prs.co/v523800*).

Ways to Learn

This section covers several ways to participate in official SAP Training and Adoption courses designed for the SAP Certified Application Associate – Business Process Integration with SAP S/4HANA (C_TS410) certification exam.

Face-to-Face Training

In-class training is one of the most effective ways to prepare for the certification exam. This type of training is usually offered either in a physical location or a virtual live classroom, requiring the trainee's active participation in live lectures. As for the training time, face-to-face training is offered in the form of an intense 10-day bootcamp run by an SAP-certified instructor. The certification exam is usually taken on the last day of the bootcamp. Official training materials and live software access are provided to students by SAP Training and Adoption and its partners officially authorized to offer TS410 training. Face-to-face training in the form of a 10-day TS410 bootcamp is recommended for candidates with recent experience of SAP S/4HANA software, and basic knowledge of business processes in enterprise planning and management can significantly expedite your exam preparation process. You can visit the SAP Training website at *https://training.sap.com/certification/* and search with the keyword "TS410" to find the current virtual or onsite training courses in your country and area, as shown in Figure 2.

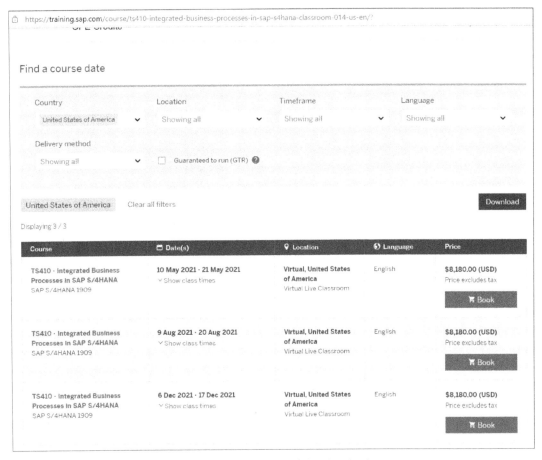

Figure 2 SAP Training Website for Training Search in a Country Area

Online Training

Online training is usually offered in the form of self-paced learning through SAP Learning Hub. This type of training is more flexible than in-class training in terms of time. This approach can be convenient for students who like using self-study materials, such as presentations, e-books, and videos, organized into SAP Learning Hub learning journeys. For instance, the learning journey titled "SAP S/4HANA – Scope and Business Process" is a collection of learning material for TS410. Online training requires a computer with a stable internet connection and multimedia system, as shown in Figure 3.

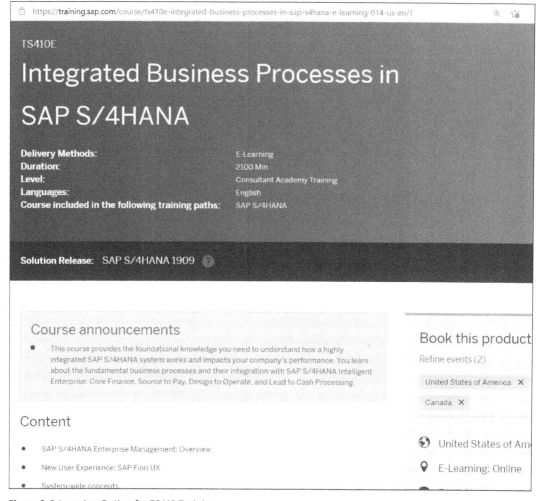

Figure 3 E-Learning Option for TS410 Training

SAP University Alliances Institutions

SAP University Alliances is a network of educational institutions offering courses and programs with SAP components. The courses and training resources offered in these institutions are supported by an SAP-owned initiative called SAP Next-Gen. SAP University Alliances institutions offer enterprise resource planning (ERP) courses or certification programs using SAP S/4HANA as the ERP software with hands-on practice and/or case studies designed by SAP. These programs are convenient for students who have no experience with ERP systems or business processes in SAP S/4HANA. At the SAP University Alliances website (*http://s-prs.co/v523801*), you'll find a list of SAP University Alliances institutions in your country and area, as shown in Figure 4.

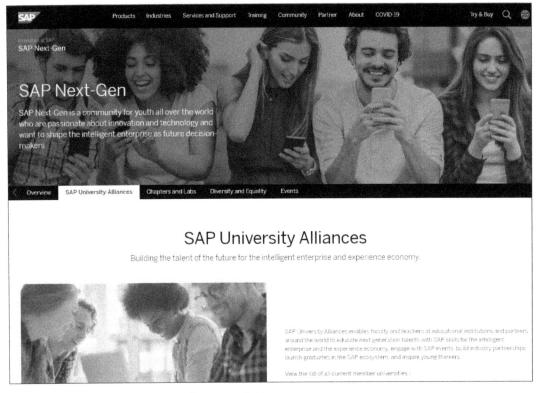

Figure 4 SAP University Alliances Institutions

Note that some SAP University Alliances institutions host SAP Next-Gen labs offering in-class TS410 bootcamps or online TS410 training courses for students, faculty, and recent graduates in the SAP University Alliances network. This option can be more cost-efficient compared to SAP Training and Adoption courses. You can find a list of these SAP Next-Gen labs and hubs on the SAP University Alliances website, as shown in Figure 5.

> **Note**
>
> SAP Training and Adoption and the Certification & Enablement Influence Council expend continuous effort to enhance the value of SAP certifications and their influence in the SAP ecosystem. Due to increased demand for certification, a growing number of people and websites may be trying to take advantage of people seeking SAP certification by offering resources and material not designed or created by SAP Training and Adoption. These resources can be severely misleading, costing time and money for exam candidates. The C_TS410 exam is only offered by SAP. We recommend checking the SAP Training and SAP University Alliances websites to verify SAP's approval before investing your time or financial resources in an education program.

> **Explore SAP Next-Gen Labs and hubs at campuses, partners and SAP locations**
>
> SAP Next-Gen Labs and hubs are opening around the world. Learn about some of the locations now available in your region:
>
> Asia Pacific and Japan   Europe, Middle East and Africa   **Americas**
>
> **Brazil**
> - Unisinos
> - SAP Next-Gen hub - São Paulo
> - SAP Next Gen hub - Sao Leopoldo
>
> **Canada**
> - Dalhousie University
>
> **Chile**
> - Universidad Santo Tomás
>
> **Columbia**
>
> **United States**
> - California State University, Chico
> - California State University, Los Angeles
> - Central Michigan University
> - Delaware State University
> - Drexel University
> - Fayetteville State University
> - Hawaii Pacific University
> - Pennsylvania State University (Penn State)
> - University of Illinois at Chicago
> - University of Southern California

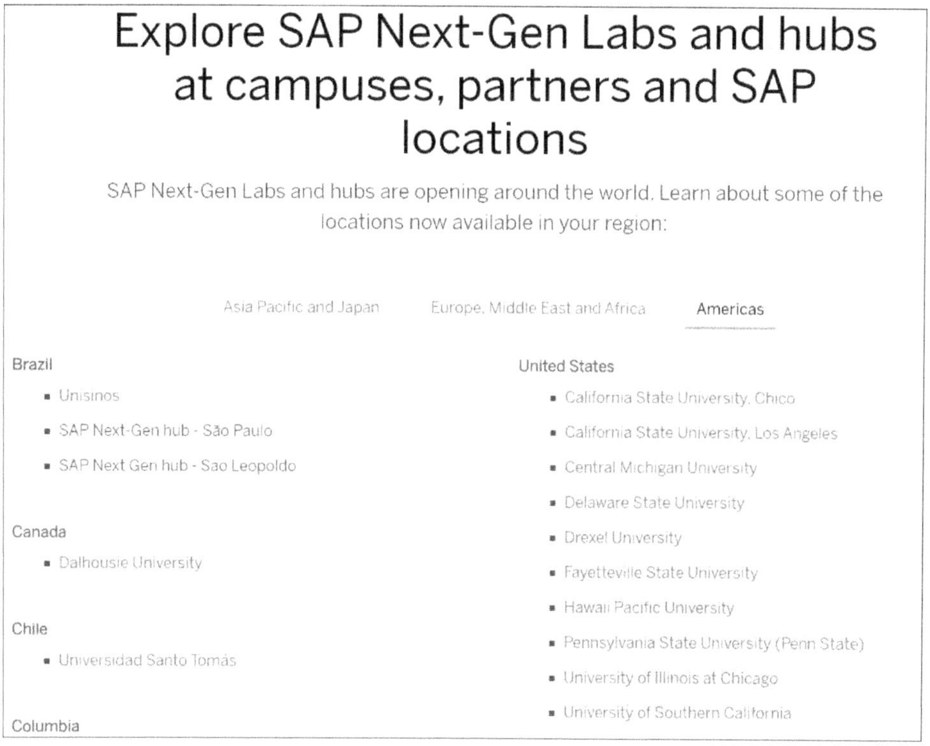

Figure 5 List of SAP Next-Gen Labs on the SAP University Alliances Webpage

Additional Learning Resources

In this section, we'll introduce some additional resources to help you build and maintain software skills in SAP S/4HANA.

SAP Learning Hub

SAP Learning Hub (*https://training.sap.com/learninghub*), shown in Figure 6, is SAP's web-based platform for a rich resource of learning materials that includes the following:

- **Learning content**
  Learning content is organized into collections of materials on a specific topic.
- **Learning rooms**
  A learning room is a community that brings you in touch with peers and SAP experts interested in common learning objectives.
- **Learning journeys**
  A learning journey is a learning path consisting of training sessions, learning room memberships, and learning content organized around a specific set of learning objectives.

You can request an SAP Learning Hub, discovery edition trial account to explore the available learning resources for a limited time.

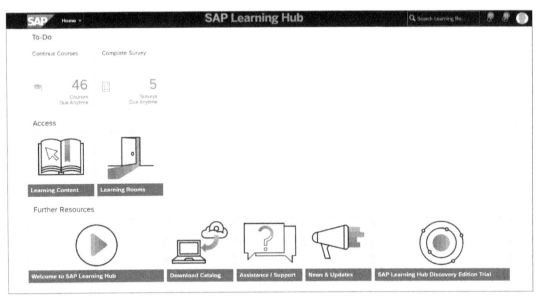

Figure 6 SAP Learning Hub

Based on your academic or professional affiliation, you may benefit from one of the following subscription-based editions of SAP Learning Hub:

- Professional edition
- Business edition
- Enhanced student edition
- Partner edition
- Academic edition

Note that the content at SAP Learning Hub varies based on the edition being used. SAP Live Access comes with an SAP Learning Hub subscription (or training purchase) and enables you to use the SAP S/4HANA training system for courses.

Figure 7 shows a learning journey that consists of various learning content to learn about the scope and integrated business processes of SAP S/4HANA; this learning journey also includes online training on TS410.

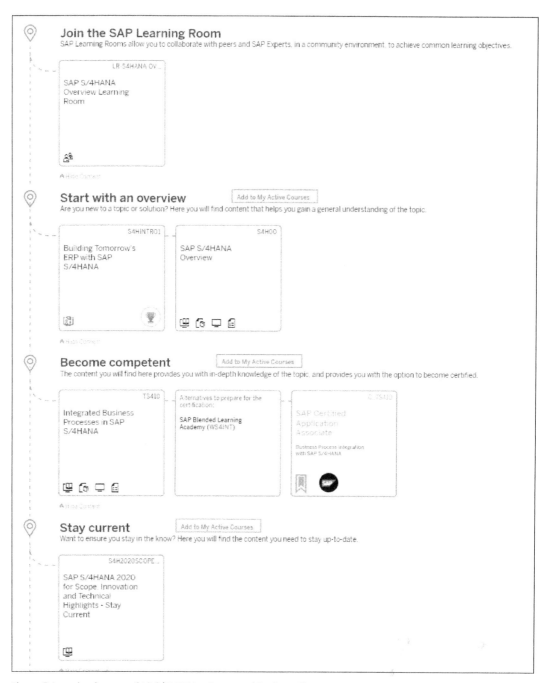

Figure 7 Learning Journey: SAP S/4HANA – Scope and Business Processes

SAP Help Portal

SAP Help Portal, shown in Figure 8, is a rich source of information that includes the following:

- A guide showing the available implementation options
- Product assistance providing more detailed information about processes and areas in SAP S/4HANA
- Information about SAP Best Practices and compatibility packs

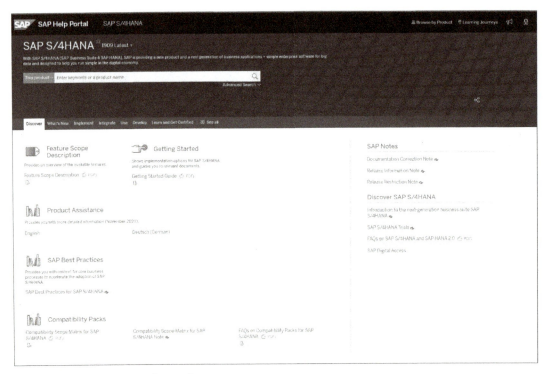

Figure 8 SAP Help Portal

You can reach the SAP Help Portal for SAP S/4HANA at the following link: *http://s-prs.co/v523802*.

Glossary

SAP's glossary (*https://help.sap.com/viewer/product/GLOSSARY*) is a web-based database that includes short descriptions of SAP terminology used in SAP applications and in SAP Help Portal, as shown in Figure 9.

Introduction: The Path to Certification 31

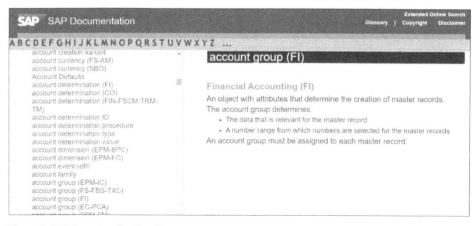

Figure 9 SAP Cross-Application Glossary

Application Helps

You can use F1 help in SAP GUI or SAP Fiori to get a technical description of a data field in a transaction of SAP S/4HANA. F4 help is another application help that shows a list of potential entries for a data field in a transaction of SAP S/4HANA. You can access these application help features by pressing F1 and F4 on your keyboard when you're logged on to the software, as shown in Figure 10.

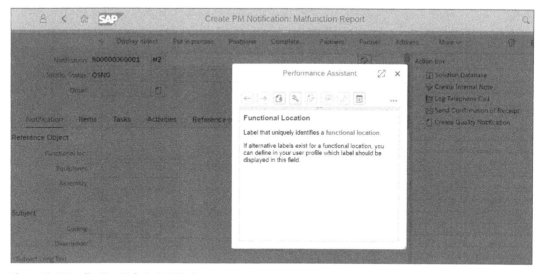

Figure 10 F1 Application Help in SAP Fiori

openSAP

openSAP (https://open.sap.com/) is a web-based learning environment that offers online courses made available by SAP over the internet free of charge for everyone. As shown in Figure 11, *openSAP Microlearning* includes self-contained videos that fit your individual learning goals. *openSAP Podcasts* includes podcasts on topics relevant to your business and personal interests. You can download or stream episodes with Apple Podcasts, Spotify, and TuneIn.

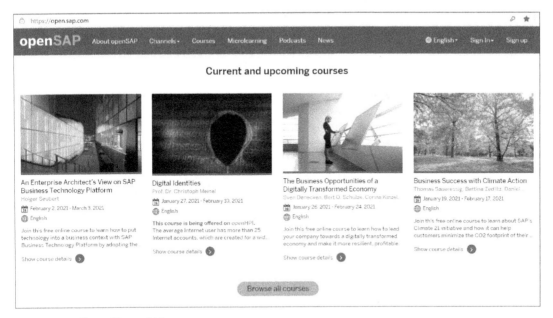

Figure 11 openSAP

Tips for Taking the C_TS410 Exam

In this section, we'll provide some tips for exam preparation and taking the exam.

Exam Preparation

This certification covers all business processes and their integrations in SAP S/4HANA. Because you'll review hundreds of course document pages, the exam entails systematic preparation. Thus, we recommend you start studying at least three months before the exam if you do not have any previous software and enterprise management experience. You may want to review the "Ways to Learn" section to find a learning program that suits your schedule. As for course materials, this book and the official SAP Training and Adoption documents should be sufficient to help you understand the exam's topic areas.

More than 88% of the questions relate to business processes and their integrations in the software. SAP S/4HANA provides organizational data, master data, and transactional data to map business process-relevant organizational structures and key tasks into the system. When you review a business process, make sure that you can explain the following points:

- Data structures (organizational data, master data, transaction data)
- Data assignments
- Key tasks of the business process
- Standard system transactions supporting the key tasks of the business process
- The sequence of transactions in the business process
- Touchpoints of integration
- Reporting tools

Try to answer the questions at the end of each chapter without any help from a course document. Compare your answers to correct answers and read the explanations for a better understanding. We recommend that you also review the sample questions available on the certification page, shown in Figure 12.

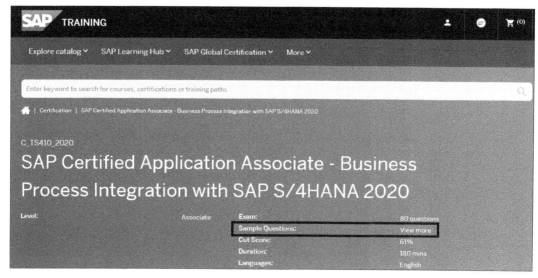

Figure 12 Link for Sample Questions on the Certification Exam Page

Everybody learns differently; you may want to create your own relatable figures, visuals, tables, and flashcards for efficient learning.

Taking the Exam

If you're taking the test at a certification center, someone will proctor you, and the test center fulfills the test's technical requirements.

If you're taking the test online through the Certification Hub (*https://sapcertification.questionmark.eu/*), your test session will be proctored remotely. In this case, you'll need a computer with the following technologies:

- Webcam
- Microphone or headset

- Broadband internet connection
- Proctoring software (e.g., Questionmark)

Ensure that your computer is up to date and will not system update or restart during the test. Visit the Certification Hub website, download and install the proctoring software, and test your internet connection before the exam.

The proctor will check your test environment before starting the test. Setting up an appropriate test environment is critical. Review the instructions about the test environment at the Certification Hub website.

The C_TS410 exam is a 180-minute (3-hour) test. You should physically and mentally prepare yourself for this intense experience. Avoid overthinking and trust your exam preparation process. You don't have to answer every question correctly. Remember that your test score will not be included in your digital badge. You just need to pass to get the badge.

Some questions will be easy to answer, and some of them will be challenging. Answer the easy ones in the first pass. Using the buttons in the exam platform, you can flag questions that require further review. You don't need to worry about the time; 180 minutes (about 3 hours) will be sufficient to have few passes on all questions.

Stay calm and focus on the questions; being unsure about several questions in a row is normal. All questions require you to think about the business processes, their transactions, and their connections with the other processes.

Choosing the correct option in a multiple-answer question may be easier if you focus on dropping options that are certainly wrong. Remember that you don't get partial credit for multiple-answer questions. On top of the question statement, the topic area of the question will be displayed. Considering that topic area may help you narrow down your focus to only potentially correct answers.

Test Takeaway

This part of the book introduced the certification options available and provided an overview of what to expect on the C_TS410 exam. We also discussed the learning methods and resources for exam preparation and shared some tips for studying the materials and taking the exam.

We're now ready to dive into the topics tested by the exam. In the next chapter, we'll cover some basics of SAP S/4HANA and the intelligent enterprise.

Chapter 1
SAP S/4HANA Basics

Techniques You'll Master

- Describe the components and the key aspects of SAP S/4HANA
- Explain the deployment options for SAP S/4HANA
- Identify the features of the intelligent enterprise and the technologies that support the intelligent enterprise framework
- Explain SAP Fiori and its user-centric design approach
- Describe the categories of SAP Fiori applications and the technologies underlying them

This chapter of the book covers all certification-relevant topics on the basics of SAP S/4HANA. We'll walk you through SAP S/4HANA's architecture, your deployment options, the intelligent enterprise, the SAP Fiori user interface (UI), and key system concepts.

> **Real-World Scenario**
>
> Intelligent technologies, significant advances in the computer hardware industry, and the exponential growth of business networks have significantly changed the business landscape and customer expectations. The core business processes are the same: Businesses still need to produce, sell, procure, and deliver their products or services. The way business organizations execute business processes, however, has changed profoundly. Companies in most industries are making considerable investments to transform their lines of business (LoBs). Transforming an LoB requires a transformation in terms of technologies, user experiences (UXs), and processes.
>
> As an SAP consultant, you must understand how SAP intelligent enterprise solutions can be implemented to enhance business processes with minimum cost and maximum business value. In particular, you should be knowledgeable about SAP S/4HANA deployment options, the functional scope of SAP S/4HANA, and LoB applications.

1.1 Objectives of This Portion of the Test

This portion of the certification covers the basics of SAP S/4HANA. In particular, motivators, technological enablers, components, and key aspects of the SAP S/4HANA suite are included. Consultants are expected to explain SAP S/4HANA deployment options and the differences between them. The design approach for SAP's next-generation UX and supporting technologies must also be known to answer this portion's questions.

For the certification exam, business process integration consultants must have a good understanding of the following topics:

- The SAP S/4HANA suite and business processes in SAP S/4HANA
- The intelligent enterprise and its LoB solutions
- The SAP Fiori UI
- System-wide concepts in SAP S/4HANA

Note
SAP S/4HANA basics cover more than 12% of the questions in the certification exam.

1.2 SAP S/4HANA Suite

In this section, we explain the components and the functional scope of the SAP S/4HANA suite. We also cover the technologies and the other SAP solutions that can enhance the core business processes and improve the UX in SAP S/4HANA.

Let's begin by explaining the motivators and enablers of SAP S/4HANA.

1.2.1 Motivators and Technology Enablers

For a moment, think about how mobile phones have evolved in the last decade. In the past, mobile phones served two core functions: audio calls and texts via short message service (SMS). Recent advances in cloud platforms, GPS technology, microchips, battery technology, touchscreens, memory, and Wi-Fi technology, as well as the exponential growth of social media, online shopping, and online banking, have driven smartphone development. Still, smartphones can perform the core functions of mobile phones. However, now, as shown in Figure 1.1, we use them for many other purposes, such as navigation, taking pictures, banking, shopping, traveling, and controlling the Internet of Things (IoT). The ways we interact with phone applications, even how we use the phone's core functions, have changed dramatically. For instance, we prefer video calls to audio calls, and we use messaging apps (e.g., WhatsApp, iMessage, Skype) or social media to text each other.

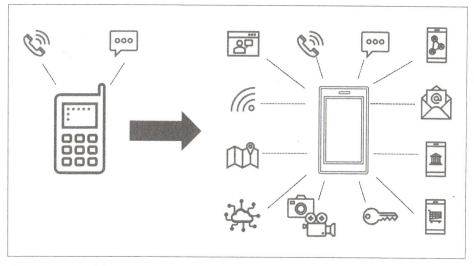

Figure 1.1 From Mobile Phone to Smartphone

As in phone technology, similar motivators and technology enablers have triggered an evolution in business applications software. Customers' expectations of an enterprise resource planning (ERP) system are way beyond executing core business transactions or integrating core business processes. Today's users need a business suite that can integrate with business networks; can exploit the full potential of multicore processors with big memories; and can support enhanced business processes powered by artificial intelligence (AI), machine learning, and cloud applications. Demand is also tremendous for new UIs providing a delightful and innovative UX that requires less training. More and more, users would like to use conversational AI and predictive decision support to execute routine business transactions.

The motivators and enablers of SAP S/4HANA can be categorized as follows:

- Changes and increased complexity in the business landscape
- Advances in hardware and cloud technologies

The business landscape has changed dramatically in recent years. The volume of digital information that must be processed by business software is increasing exponentially. Businesses would like to use social media data, the data flowing from mobile devices, and big data for a better customer experience. Developments in AI and machine learning increase the expectations for more intelligent and automated business systems. Globalization and the spread of business networks require ERP systems that can effectively collaborate with customers and suppliers. Another significant motivator for an advanced ERP system is the widespread usage of IoT in business processes. For instance, manufacturing companies are investing heavily in the Industrial Internet of Things (IIoT) for the digital transformation of manufacturing processes in the age of Industry 4.0. The seamless integration of IoT with business processes and handling of the data collected by IoT are other capabilities that businesses are expecting from business software.

Exponential advances in hardware and cloud technologies enable software developers to create smarter and more robust business applications. The most powerful technologies driving the development of a new business suite include:

- **Powerful multicore processors**
  The new powerful multicore processors enable parallelism and faster processing of many tasks.
- **Huge and affordable memory**
  Inexpensive and readily available memory enables completely in-memory databases and the simplification of data architectures.
- **Optimized onboard caches**
  Data is processed in CPUs, and the speed of data transfer between memory and CPU significantly impact the system's performance. Advances in the technology for onboard caches have enabled increases in system capacity by increasing CPU and memory capacity.
- **Cloud**
  Significant developments in cloud technologies enable software developers to design business applications fully deployable in the cloud. Cloud technologies help businesses reduce their IT costs; simplify their IT landscapes; and integrate heterogeneous systems, processes, and people in the cloud.

The software architecture of an existing SAP Business Suite on SAP HANA system could not exploit SAP HANA's full capabilities and the technologies we've listed. Thus, SAP decided to rewrite a new business suite from scratch, natively running on SAP HANA. This product is called SAP S/4HANA (i.e., SAP Business Suite for SAP HANA).

Figure 1.2 shows the preceding business application software, the motivating factors, and the technologies driving the development of SAP S/4HANA.

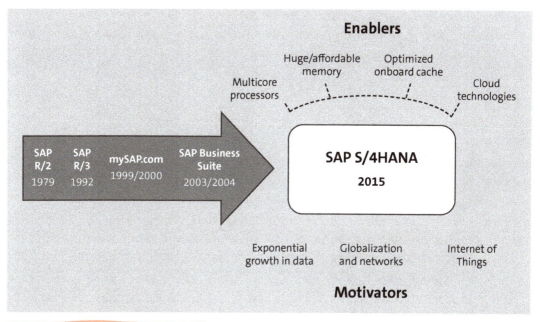

Figure 1.2 Evolution of SAP S/4HANA

1.2.2 Components

SAP S/4HANA, called the *digital core*, is not a single software but a suite of many applications. SAP S/4HANA consists of the following components:

- SAP S/4HANA Enterprise Management (simplified core)
- SAP's LoB products and solutions

SAP S/4HANA is the next generation of SAP Business Suite. SAP Business Suite consists of a central ERP component and its surrounding components, such as SAP Supplier Relationship Management (SAP SRM), SAP Supply Chain Management (SAP SCM), SAP Product Lifecycle Management (SAP PLM), and SAP Customer Relationship Management (SAP CRM), as shown in Figure 1.3.

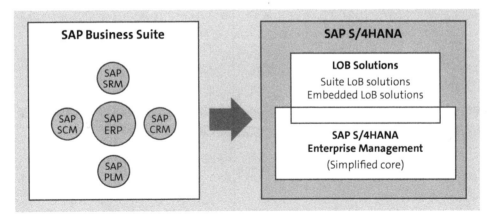

Figure 1.3 From SAP Business Suite to SAP S/4HANA

Enterprise Management

SAP S/4HANA has an entirely brand-new code that runs natively on SAP HANA, a digital platform component, and has all capabilities of SAP Business Suite. SAP S/4HANA Enterprise Management is the next generation of the central ERP component of SAP Business Suite, which is why SAP S/4HANA Enterprise Management is called the simplified core of SAP S/4HANA (suite). This simplified core includes applications that support standard ERP operational processes, such as order-to-cash processing, purchase-to-pay processing, plan-to-produce processing, finance, services, and human resources (HR).

Standard ERP operational processes have not changed significantly. However, the way we execute standard ERP operations has changed dramatically. For instance, customers use different channels to order products and services, and their expectations about the speed of delivery is not the same now. New disruptive technologies and production techniques drive the need for a broader ERP system with comprehensive capabilities. In addition to the standard business transactions supporting the standard ERP processes, SAP S/4HANA Enterprise Management provides some new functionalities that streamline, accelerate, and optimize business processes. For instance, SAP S/4HANA Enterprise Management provides a self-service requisitioning functionality so that employees can create, manage, and track their own purchase requisitions efficiently. This functionality enables employees to directly purchase goods and services from preferred vendors by using assigned catalogs, catalog-driven pricing, and approval workflows. Employees can use SAP Fiori apps for self-service requisitioning. Procurement analytics, another example of SAP S/4HANA Enterprise Management functionality, supports real-time monitoring and reporting. Using operational cards in SAP Fiori, the purchasing department can access an overview of the procurement process and see, for instance, which contracts are about to expire or which purchasing requisitions need to be assigned a source of supply. These new functionalities expedite the procurement process and help purchasing departments focus more on strategic purchasing decisions rather than on day-to-day purchasing transactions, such as creating purchase requisitions or orders.

> **Note**
> SAP S/4HANA Enterprise Management does not reinvent the purchase-to-pay business process but offers new solutions that improve its execution.

Combining simplifications and new functionalities, SAP S/4HANA Enterprise Management supports standard ERP operational processes (e.g., purchase-to-pay, order-to-cash, plan-to-produce, finance, services, and HR) with the following solutions, as shown in Figure 1.4:

- Streamlined procure-to-pay
- Accelerated plan-to-product
- Optimized order-to-cash
- Enhanced request-to-service
- Core finance activities
- Core HR activities

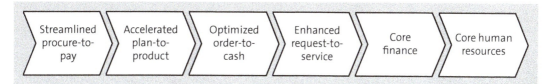

Figure 1.4 Enhanced Core Processes in SAP S/4HANA Enterprise Management

Line of Business Solutions and Products

The core functions of SAP S/4HANA Enterprise Management can be enhanced by adding LoB solutions.

The applications of SAP S/4HANA Enterprise Management and the LoB solutions for SAP S/4HANA are grouped into the following areas, as shown in Figure 1.5:

- Asset management
- Marketing
- Finance
- Manufacturing
- Research and development (R&D)/engineering
- Sales
- Sourcing and procurement
- Supply chain
- HR
- Service

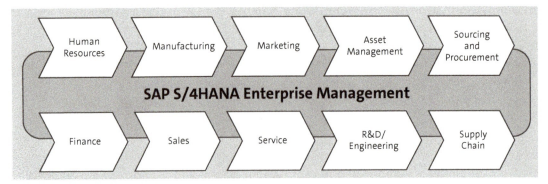

Figure 1.5 SAP S/4HANA Enterprise Management and LoB Solutions

There are three categories of LoB solutions: embedded LoB solutions, SAP S/4HANA LoB solutions, and suite LoB solutions. Embedded LoB solutions are included with a standard SAP S/4HANA Enterprise Management license, while SAP S/4HANA LoB solutions are available as add-ons requiring a separate license. For instance, operational procurement is an embedded LoB solution in sourcing and procurement and provides the following functionalities:

- Self-service requisitioning
- Requirements processing
- Purchase order processing
- Service purchasing
- Invoice processing

Central procurement is an example of an SAP S/4HANA LoB solution. With central procurement, you can integrate your other ERP systems with SAP S/4HANA, and your SAP S/4HANA system can act as a hub system unifying all purchasing activities in your enterprise. Central procurement can also integrate external procurement systems (e.g., SAP Ariba) with SAP S/4HANA. In this scenario, the purchasing department can control procurement operations in SAP S/4HANA centrally or decentrally in the integrated systems.

The suite LoB solutions and products are outside the shipment scope, and they require individual implementation projects. Suite LoB solutions are external solutions that can be integrated with SAP S/4HANA Enterprise Management through application programming interfaces (APIs). For instance, the following cloud LoB solutions are tightly integrated with SAP S/4HANA Enterprise Management and extend system functionality for more enhanced business processes:

- **SAP Ariba**
    SAP Ariba is a cloud-based application that provides a worldwide business commerce network connecting business-to-business (B2B) buyers and suppliers. SAP Ariba enables strategic sourcing and enhances the core procure-to-pay business process.

- **Concur Travel & Expense**
  SAP Concur offers some mobile and web-based solutions for travel and expense management.
- **SAP Fieldglass**
  SAP Fieldglass is a cloud-based vendor management system. SAP SuccessFactors provides a cloud-based human capital management (HCM) system, supporting talent management core HR and analytics.
- **SAP Customer Experience**
  SAP Customer Experience (formerly known as SAP C/4HANA) is a cloud solution supporting sales, marketing, services, and customer relationship management. This suite is made up of five cloud products: SAP Marketing Cloud, SAP Commerce Cloud, SAP Sales Cloud, SAP Service Cloud, and SAP Customer Data Cloud. SAP Customer Experience integrates with SAP S/4HANA to enhance the core order-to-cash business process and helps companies create customer experience-oriented lead-to-cash business processes.
- **SAP SuccessFactors**
  SAP SuccessFactors is cloud-based human experience management (HXM) software that supports the hire-to-retire business process, integrating with SAP Analytics Cloud and SAP S/4HANA.

1.2.3 Key Characteristics

In this section, we outline some critical aspects of SAP S/4HANA. We'll start with deployment, which is flexible with SAP S/4HANA. Based on your business requirements, you can choose one of the following deployment options for SAP S/4HANA:

- **On-premise**
  This deployment type offers a broader scope of business functions and greater flexibility for customization. New functions and innovations are delivered annually. Your organization would be responsible for maintenance and updates. In an on-premise deployment, you would purchase the hardware and software and operate both. SAP offers the on-premise edition with traditional licensing. On-premise users can access their systems by using SAP GUI or SAP Fiori.
- **Public cloud**
  The public cloud, known as SAP S/4HANA Cloud, is a multitenant software as a service (SaaS) solution. In SAP S/4HANA Cloud (also called a multitenant cloud), you'll share applications and the platform with other companies, reducing the total cost of ownership. A public cloud offers standard core process functionality, but its scope is not as broad as with an on-premise system. This version may be sufficient for many companies following standard business processes. The public cloud comes with limited ability for customization. Innovations and new functions are delivered quarterly. The hosting company takes care of updates and maintenance, reducing your direct IT costs.

- **Private cloud**
  SAP S/4HANA Cloud, private edition is a single-tenant cloud solution. In a private cloud, you do not share applications or the platform with other companies. In terms of functionality, scope, and customization, the private cloud edition is similar to the on-premise edition. Still, the hosting company carries out maintenance and updates. You may be able to choose when updates occur, but innovations are delivered annually. In a private cloud-type deployment, a cloud company provides the infrastructure. SAP offers all cloud editions with annual subscription-based pricing. All cloud solutions can be hosted in an SAP cloud infrastructure. Still, the private cloud can also be hosted on other (non-SAP) cloud infrastructures, such as Microsoft Azure or Amazon Web Services (AWS). Cloud customers can access their systems by using web GUI or SAP Fiori. Figure 1.6 shows a comparison of on-premise and cloud editions in terms of customization, governance (by owner), agility, and standardization of processes.

- **Hybrid (a combination of on-premise and cloud)**
  This deployment option is suitable if you want to carry out standard processes in the cloud (reducing the total cost of ownership) and benefit from the more profound customization capability of on-premise edition for specific applications running on your own servers. A hybrid deployment combines the SaaS model with an on-premise data infrastructure. Intense integration between on-premise and cloud applications is required in hybrid deployment.

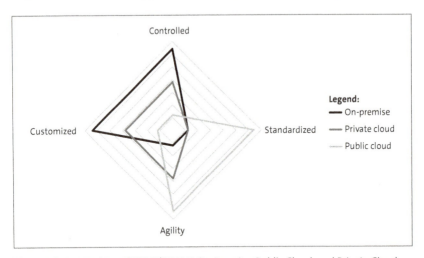

Figure 1.6 Comparison of SAP S/4HANA On-Premise, Public Cloud, and Private Cloud

Once you've chosen a deployment option and gotten your SAP S/4HANA system up and running, you can benefit from the following key characteristics of the suite:

- **Scalability**
  You can choose SAP S/4HANA Enterprise Management (simplified core) as an initial product and extend your system's functionality by adding LoB solutions and integrating cloud solutions and other business applications. SAP S/4HANA

can natively integrate with existing SAP cloud solutions, such as SAP Ariba, SAP Concur, SAP Customer Experience, SAP SuccessFactors, SAP Analytics Cloud, and SAP Sales Cloud/SAP Service Cloud.

- **Embedded analytics and reporting**
  The SAP S/4HANA code is written from scratch to run only on SAP HANA databases. This new system inherits all native capabilities of SAP HANA, such as reports, simulations, and (textual or predictive) analytics using real-time information. Many applications of SAP S/4HANA contain embedded analytics.
- **A new user experience**
  SAP S/4HANA comes with a new role-based interface, SAP Fiori, thus increasing productivity and improving the UX on any device.
- **Data footprint reduction and increased speed**
  SAP HANA is an entirely in-memory database with a columnar data structure and simplified data model that eliminates redundant tables in the system. SAP HANA's simplified data model significantly reduces the data footprint (from 593 GB to 8.4 GB) and accelerates business transactions in SAP S/4HANA. As a result, SAP S/4HANA comes with the following user benefits:

  – Lightweight code
  – Simplified applications that can run on any mobile device
  – Shorter response times
  – Faster backups and updates
  – Increased data throughput
  – Faster and real-time reports

The simplified architecture of SAP HANA streamlines your IT landscape, reduces maintenance costs and times, provides business agility, and increases data processing performance.

Figure 1.7 shows some key aspects of SAP S/4HANA and its native database SAP HANA.

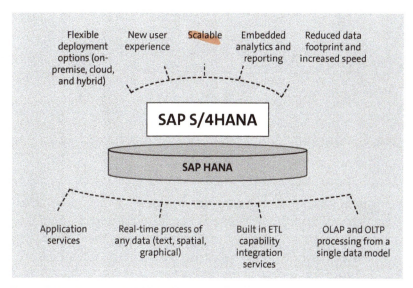

Figure 1.7 Key Aspects of SAP S/4HANA and SAP HANA

1.3 The Intelligent Enterprise

The intelligent enterprise represents SAP's innovative strategy to unlock the full potential of the intelligent suite. To become an intelligent enterprise, business organizations need to invest in four key areas, which we'll walk through in the following sections:

- The intelligent suite
- Intelligent technologies
- Industry cloud
- SAP Business Technology Platform (SAP BTP)

The intelligent enterprise's key characteristics include intelligent business processes empowered with intelligent technologies, analytics, experience management, and business networks, as shown in Figure 1.8.

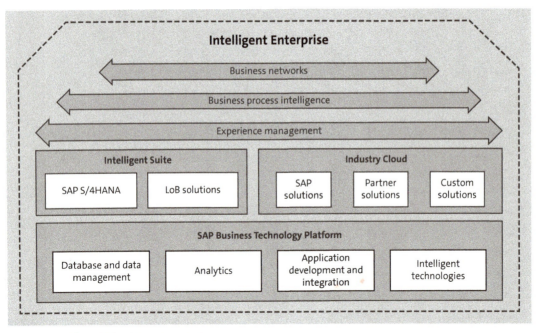

Figure 1.8 SAP's Intelligent Enterprise

1.3.1 The Intelligent Suite and Enhanced Business Processes

The intelligent suite is one of feature of an intelligent enterprise. The intelligent suite enhances business processes with intelligent technologies. Let's look at an example of an enhanced procurement process. The core procure-to-pay business process usually starts with a requisition, followed by creating an order, continuing with the receipt of goods and an invoice, and ending with a payment. Self-service requisitioning enables employees to create purchase requisitions and follow up on the progress. However, purchasing is not only about performing standard procurement transactions. As customers, employees may enjoy the collaborative and interactive shopping experience in their personal buying activities with online shopping platforms. As users, they expect to have a similar experience in the B2B procurement process. They would like to communicate with vendors, ask questions about products, or read other buyers' reviews to choose better products and supply sources. Ariba Network supports this requirement.

SAP S/4HANA's innovations, as well as its integration with business networks (i.e., Ariba Network) and cloud solutions, enable enhanced procure-to-pay processes by adding strategic sourcing to the process. This new core process is called *source-to-pay*. Another example of an enhanced business process is lead-to-cash, which is enabled by the SAP S/4HANA digital core along with the SAP Customer Experience suite. The lead-to-cash business process is the next level of the order-to-cash business process and includes lead management and opportunity management capabilities.

The intelligent suite represents the combination of SAP S/4HANA (suite) and cloud LoB solutions, all seamlessly integrated with SAP S/4HANA. Embedded machine learning technologies empower the business processes on the intelligent suite. The intelligent suite supports the following major end-to-end business processes as well as services (request-to-service) and core finance (record-to-report) activities:

- Source-to-pay
- Design-to-operate
- Lead-to-cash
- Hire-to-retire, including human experience management (HXM)

SAP's intelligent suite delivers intelligence across value chains. A *value chain* is a full range of activities a company must perform to create valuable products and services. The intelligent suite offers the following value chains:

- Customer experience
- Digital manufacturing and supply chain
- People management
- Network and spend management

Core business processes belong to these value chains. For instance, the lead-to-cash business process belongs to the customer experience value chain. The design-to-operate business process belongs to the manufacturing and supply chain value chain, and the source-to-pay business process belongs to the network and spend management value chain.

Figure 1.9 shows the value chains and LoB solutions in SAP's intelligent suite.

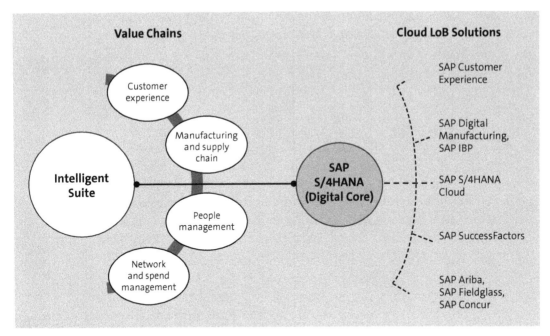

Figure 1.9 SAP Intelligent Suite: Value Chains and Cloud LoB Solutions

1.3.2 Intelligent Technologies

The intelligent suite's capabilities are enhanced by injecting intelligent technologies into business processes in the intelligent enterprise framework. These intelligent technologies include:

- AI
- IoT
- Machine learning
- Advanced analytics
- Blockchain

1.3.3 Industry Cloud

SAP's industry cloud provides an open business process and technology platform that extends SAP's intelligent suite and business processes with cross-industry cloud solutions built by SAP and its partners. The intelligent suite supports standardized end-to-end business processes designed according to best practices in all industries. SAP's industry cloud extends these end-to-end business processes, enabling industry-specific solutions (for example, SAP Cloud for Automotive) depending on the company's core business needs within the industry.

1.3.4 SAP Business Technology Platform

SAP BTP is the technology foundation on top of which the intelligent suite is built for an intelligent enterprise. Most organizations adopting SAP's intelligent suite or industry cloud will need a fundamental business technology layer consisting of the following components, as shown in Figure 1.10:

- Database component with SAP HANA at the center of a database foundation
- Analytics component enabling embedded analytics in the suite
- Intelligent technologies component integrating IoT with business processes and enhancing processes with conversational AI and RPA
- Application development and integration component delivered through the cloud-based platform

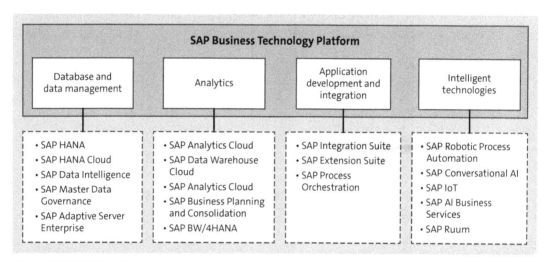

Figure 1.10 SAP BTP and its Components

The database and data management component has the following capabilities:

- **Application services**
  A full application development environment with productivity tools. This environment requires no application server but instead uses a web browser and SAP HANA.
- **Processing services**
  SAP HANA provides native in-memory engines that process any data (e.g., text, spatial, graph) in real time.
- **Integration services**
  Reads, synchronizes, and integrates multiple data sources and devices (IoT). SAP HANA has a built-in extract, transform, and load (ETL) capability that requires no separate software for data cleansing, profiling, or enrichment.
- **Database services**
  SAP HANA is a full in-memory database that can handle online transactional processing (OLTP) and online analytical processing (OLAP) from a single data model. Transactional data no longer needs to be transferred to another system for analytics. Analytical applications use the same copy of the data, and thus, real-time analysis of the data is possible.

Another essential building block of SAP BTP is the cloud application development and integration component, which is provided as an enterprise platform as a service (PaaS) that enables you to build, extend, and integrate business applications in the cloud.

SAP BTP components can be deployed on many cloud services, including AWS, Microsoft Azure, Google Cloud, and SAP.

Note

The C_TS410_1809 and C_TS410_1909 certification exams still refer to SAP Cloud Platform. The cloud platform combines SAP API Business Hub and SAP Cloud Platform, SAP's application development and integration platform. SAP Cloud Platform has evolved into SAP BTP, and its extension and integration services are available on SAP BTP as SAP Integration Suite and SAP Extension Suite. Application development and integration capabilities are now available on SAP BTP as cloud services.

1.4 SAP Fiori

SAP Fiori provides a browser-based and mobile-enabled UI for SAP applications across different LoBs. It is based on design thinking principles focusing more on UX than on functionality. The tradeoff between UX and functionality is meaningful as UX comes with the following business values:

- More productivity
- Better user adoption
- Fewer user errors
- Less training costs

Note that SAP Fiori is not a replacement or upgrade for SAP GUI, SAP Enterprise Portal, or SAP Business Client. It is an entirely new product enhancing the UX for SAP customers. On-premise users can benefit from SAP Fiori apps' simplicity and mobility while still using SAP GUI for certain transactions. Cloud users need to use SAP Fiori. You don't have to be on SAP S/4HANA to be able to use SAP Fiori. SAP Fiori can also connect users to the applications on SAP Business Suite.

Let's take a closer look at the SAP Fiori UX, including its design, dimensions, launchpad, and applications.

1.4.1 Design and Dimensions

In terms of their expectations of a business application software, three types of users in the system can be identified:

- Occasional users
  These users prefer to use device-independent (browser-based) interfaces and require that transactions be simple (perhaps a single step), clear, and fast.

- **Expert users**
  These users prefer to use desktop-based graphical UIs and expect transactions to provide maximum functionality on multiple systems.
- **Developers**
  These backend-oriented users do not require any specific UI but do require overall authorization in the system.

In software design, UI and UX represent two different approaches. A UI approach aims to develop applications with maximum functionality for all user roles on the software. Maximum functionality is like having all the control buttons on your car's dashboard for all roles, such as driver and mechanic. UX is a user-centric software design approach with the objective of achieving the best UX. SAP Fiori represents SAP's next-generation UX, providing the best UX along with maximum role-based functionality.

The SAP Fiori design approach is organized into three dimensions:

1. **Concept**
   SAP Fiori offers a new UX built on five conceptual pillars:
   - **Role-based**
     SAP Fiori puts users and their business roles at the center of everything. Without losing integration, SAP Fiori decomposes multifunctional SAP transactions into several discrete apps suited to user roles. In SAP Fiori launchpad, every user sees role-based apps and the information essential for their daily tasks in the organization. In this sense, SAP Fiori is different than classic UIs with functional-based applications.
   - **Adaptive**
     SAP Fiori is adaptive to multiple use cases and devices, including desktop computers, laptops, or smartphones.
   - **Coherent**
     In all applications, SAP Fiori provides consistent interaction screens along with an intuitive experience that requires less training.
   - **Simple**
     SAP Fiori offers a role-based simplification of business processes. SAP Fiori includes what is necessary, but no more.
   - **Delightful**
     Enabling you to do your daily tasks simply, SAP Fiori results in efficient work and creates a delightful connection between the user and the software.

2. **Design**
   SAP Fiori's design principles are structured into visual design, information architecture, and interaction patterns. SAP regularly updates design guidelines to empower organizations to design their own applications.

3. **Technology**
   The majority of SAP Fiori apps are built using SAPUI5 as UI technology, and they

use SAP Gateway or core data services (CDS) views. SAPUI5 is based on HTML5 and compatible with any device using a web browser, such as Edge, Chrome, Firefox, and Safari. SAP Fiori also supports apps developed in native languages, such as Apple Xcode (for iOS devices) or Java in Android Studio (for Android devices). SAP Fiori also supports conversational AI apps in SAP Conversational AI (formerly SAP CoPilot).

1.4.2 SAP Fiori Launchpad

SAP Fiori launchpad offers end users a single point of access to a collection of apps across the different functionalities (modules) and LoB solutions of SAP. Figure 1.11 shows SAP Fiori launchpad with tiles representing several business applications in SAP S/4HANA. By using SAP Fiori launchpad, end users can access on-premise SAP S/4HANA apps, SAP S/4HANA Cloud apps, custom-built apps, and third-party software.

Figure 1.11 Application Tiles in SAP Fiori Launchpad

Based on your job role, the system admin determines the set of apps your SAP Fiori launchpad can access. End users can customize the following options in SAP Fiori launchpad:

- Select a design theme and colors
- Activate user profiling

- Define the appearance and the behavior of notifications
- Determine the default values for certain apps

> **Tip**
> SAP S/4HANA has generally moved away from the term *module* in favor of *functionality*. The term *module* was more apt in the SAP ERP era, when functionalities were provided as individual components rather than embedded within the system. However, for the purposes of this exam, the terms *module* or *application component* are still used to refer to a group of transactions supporting a business process, so we'll follow suit in this book to best reflect the terminology you'll see on exam day.

In addition to serving as a single point of entry and personalization options, SAP Fiori launchpad offers the following features:

- Enterprise search
- Notifications
- Analytical cards
- Integration with SAP Conversational AI (formerly SAP CoPilot)
- Embedded analytics
- Mobile-enabled
- Digital assistant with fully integrated conversational UX

Figure 1.12 shows the result of the app search in SAP Fiori launchpad. You can also see an analytical card for invoice processing in the top-left corner.

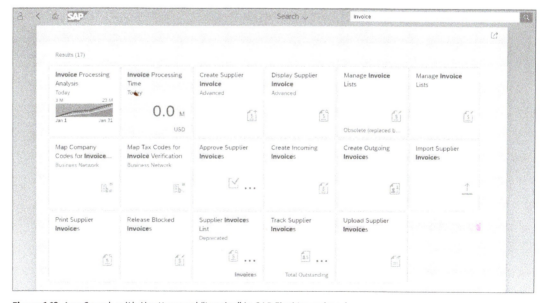

Figure 1.12 App Search with the Keyword "Invoice" in SAP Fiori Launchpad

1.4.3 Application Types

Thousands of applications are available on SAP Fiori launchpad. SAP Fiori apps can be grouped into three categories in terms of their functionality and their usage of other technologies, as shown in Figure 1.13:

- **Transactional applications**
  These applications use ABAP to provide task-based access to SAP S/4HANA or SAP Business Suite functions on any database. The Create Sales Order app and the Create Material Master Record app are examples of transactional SAP Fiori apps.

- **Analytical applications**
  These applications provide real-time information on a large volume of data by using SAP HANA's analytical capabilities. Analytical apps help users to monitor key performance indicators (KPIs) and to gain insight into business data in SAP S/4HANA or SAP Business Suite on SAP HANA. For instance, a warehouse clerk can view and analyze a specific range of material documents in SAP S/4HANA.

- **Fact sheet applications**
  Fact sheet applications use SAP HANA's enterprise search capabilities to display essential facts and contextual information about the objects in SAP S/4HANA and SAP Business Suite on SAP HANA. Fact sheet apps are available for SAP S/4HANA and SAP Business Suite on SAP HANA. For instance, from a sales document, you can navigate to the business partner master record.

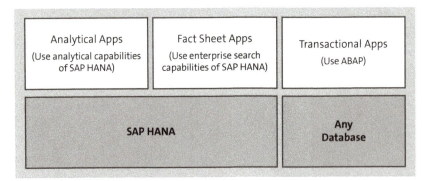

Figure 1.13 Categorization of SAP Fiori Apps by Usage of Additional Technologies

1.5 System-Wide Concepts

SAP S/4HANA is a business process management system that integrates business processes using a massive amount of data stored in a central database called SAP HANA. In the system, you can create, change, and process data using business transactions, resulting in documents and (optionally) outputs. This section describes system data categories and explains the relationship between transactions, documents, and outputs.

1.5.1 Data

Your data is essential to map the enterprise and business processes into the system. Data is a foundation for all business transactions in the system. Three categories of data exist in SAP S/4HANA:

- **Organizational data**
  This data in SAP S/4HANA represents the organizational structure and areas of responsibilities in the real-world enterprise. The SAP system has two main areas: the application area and the Customizing area, or the SAP Implementation Guide (IMG). This type of data can be created and maintained in Customizing (in the IMG) by a person authorized with configuration roles. Organizational data in the system does not change very often. The hierarchical structure and the areas of responsibilities in a real-world enterprise structure are mapped into the system by assigning organizational data to each other. For instance, a company code is organizational data in SAP S/4HANA, representing the enterprise's legal entity responsible for legal (external) reporting, such as balance sheets and income statements. A sales organization is organizational data in the system representing the enterprise's highest level of selling entity. You can create sales organizations for all regional selling entities and assign them to a single company code for financial accounting and legal reporting. Understanding organizational data and organizational data assignments are of vital importance for mapping your enterprise into SAP S/4HANA.

- **Master data**
  This data in SAP S/4HANA represents the goods, services, objects, lists, locations, information, persons, business partners, and relations in real-world business processes. Master data is essential for the execution of business transactions in the system. Material master records, routings, purchasing info records, customer/vendor master records, general ledger accounts, equipment master records, functional location master records, condition master records, and work center master records are examples of master data in different system modules. Based on system preferences, you can use numbers, character strings, or alphanumeric codes (a combination of letters and numbers) to identify master data in SAP S/4HANA. During transactions, you enter the alphanumeric code to call the master data from the system. For instance, when you create a sales order, you'll need to enter the material number. The system automatically copies the pricing conditions and storage location information from the material master record to the sales order. The master data can often change based on business dynamics and market conditions. You can maintain master data using standard user-level transactions (application area) or Customizing (IMG). Cross-module master data assignments and master data-to-organizational data assignments are essential to understand the integrations between business processes in SAP S/4HANA.

- **Transactional data** *Procurement*

This data in SAP S/4HANA is the data created during system transactions. You cannot execute system transactions without using organizational data, master data, and transaction-specific user inputs. For instance, when you create a purchase order (a transaction in purchasing), you must enter a purchasing organization (organizational data in purchasing), a material number (belongs to a material master record), a required delivery date, and quantities (transaction-specific user inputs).

Table 1.1 summarizes the organizational and master data in some core processes.

Core Process	Organizational Data	Master Data
Order-to-cash	Client, company code, sales area (sales organization, distribution channel, division), plant, shipping point, storage location	Material master record, customer master record, conditions, output master record
Purchase-to-pay	Client, company code, plant, storage location, purchasing organization, purchasing group	Material master record, vendor master record, purchasing info record
Plan-to-produce	Client, company code plant, storage location	Material master data, bills of materials (BOMs), routings, production versions, production resources and tools (PRTs), work center
Enterprise asset management	Client, company code, plant, maintenance plant, maintenance planning plant, maintenance work center	Functional location master record, equipment master record, serial numbers, BOMs
Financial accounting	Client, company code, business area, segment	General ledger accounts (balance sheet, profit and loss [P&L], reconciliation) and subledger accounts (customer, vendor, asset, contract accounts receivable)
Management accounting	Client operating concern, controlling area	Cost element, revenue element, activity type, statistical key figure, cost center, profit center, internal order

Table 1.1 Organizational and Master Data in Core Business Processes

Core Process	Organizational Data	Master Data
HCM *(Human Capital Management)*	Organizational structure (organizational unit, jobs, positions, persons), enterprise structure (client, company code, personnel area, personnel subarea), personnel structure (employee group, employee subgroup, payroll areas)	Employee master record (personnel file, infotypes)

Table 1.1 Organizational and Master Data in Core Business Processes (Cont.)

We'll explain the relationships between organizational data and master data in great detail in further chapters.

1.5.2 Client

A *client* represents the highest level of organizational data in the SAP organizational hierarchy. This organizationally, technically, and transactionally self-contained unit has its own master records and tables. Thus, the client keeps its data and transactions separate from other clients on the database. To log on to the SAP system, you must enter the client number and your user credentials defined for that client. Then, you can execute business transactions, process data, and analyze system data within the client.

1.5.3 Transactions

Transaction Code = TCode

Transactions are the indivisible system operations performed on system data. Each transaction consists of a series of screens with data fields and buttons. SAP is a multilingual and multicurrency system. Transaction names can differ based on the language you choose. However, each transaction is uniquely identified by a transaction code (also referred to as a "T-Code") in the system. Create Sales Order (Transaction VA01), Balance Sheet (Transaction F01), and Assign Company Code to Controlling Area (Transaction OX19) are examples of transactions in SAP S/4HANA. Depending on your system deployment, you can access SAP S/4HANA transactions using UIs, such as SAP GUI (the graphical UI for desktops) or SAP Fiori launchpad (browser-based interface). In SAP UIs, transactions are grouped into functional and technical categories, such as **Materials Management**, **Sales and Distribution**, **Accounting**, **Human Resources**, **ABAP Workbench**, and **Information Systems**. SAP GUI provides the SAP Easy Access screen where system transactions are grouped into folders (also called SAP S/4HANA modules) based on their business functionalities, as shown in Figure 1.14.

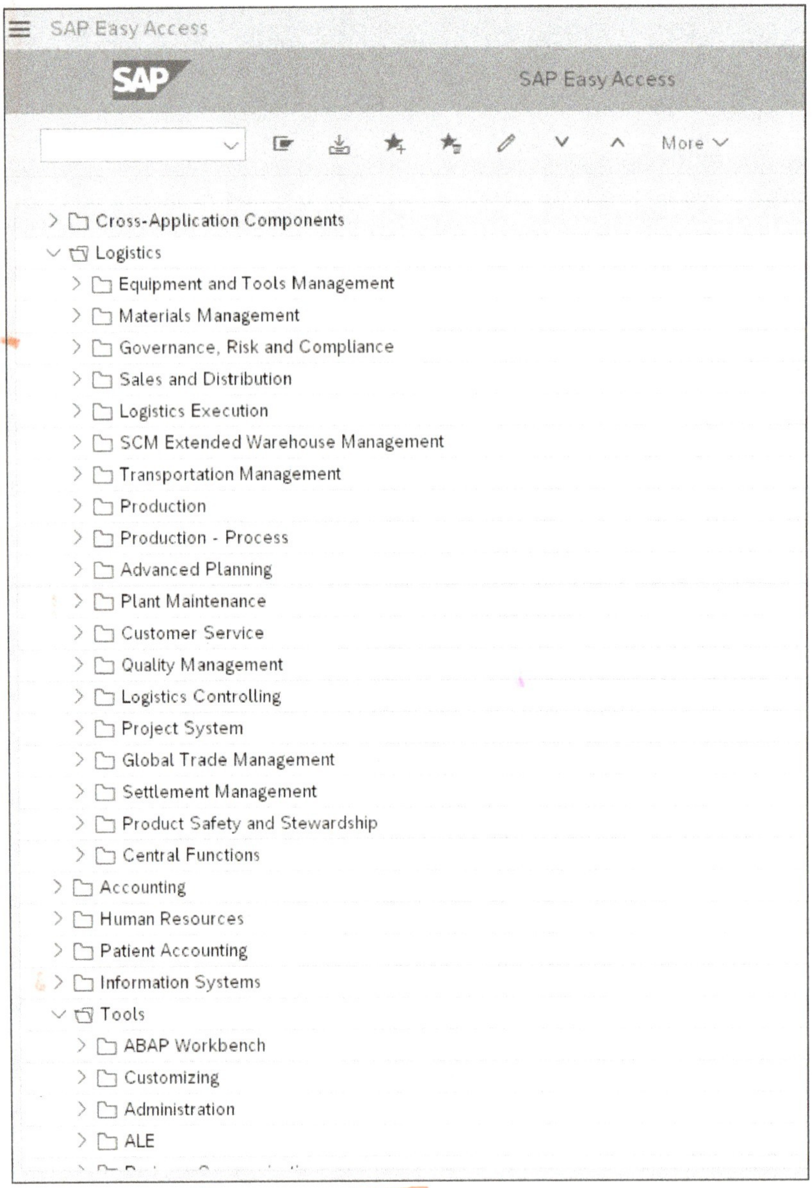

Figure 1.14 SAP Easy Access Screen in SAP GUI

Table 1.2 outlines the relationship between the system components of the SAP Easy Access screen and supported core processes.

Module	Core Process
Purchasing (part of materials management)	Purchase-to-pay
Sales and distribution	Order-to-cash

Table 1.2 SAP S/4HANA Modules and Supported Processes

Module	Core Process
Production	Plan-to-produce
Inventory management (part of materials management)	Inventory management
Plant maintenance	Enterprise asset management
HR	HCM
Financial accounting	Financial accounting
Controlling	Management accounting
Project System	Project management
Logistics execution	Warehouse management
Quality management	Quality management

Table 1.2 SAP S/4HANA Modules and Supported Processes (Cont.)

1.5.4 Documents

At the end of every successful transaction, a document is created and archived in the SAP system. Every document is assigned a unique number. You can call or display documents by entering their document numbers in transactions. Documents play three crucial roles in the system:

- Recording a change in the system data
- Integrating business processes (or connecting modules) in SAP S/4HANA
- Creating a data source for subsequent transactions

For instance, when you receive goods in purchasing, you'll post a goods receipt, and then the material and accounting documents are created in the system to record the change in stock quantity and stock value. The next step is invoice verification. The material document for goods receipt and the purchase order document constitute a data source for invoice verification.

Once the document is created in the system, you have limited ability to change the document. For instance, you can add a reference or comment to the original document. To reverse the transaction for that document, you must start a new transaction, which will create another document.

Every document in the system consists of a document header and document items. The data in the document header is valid for the entire document. Each document item contains data specific to that item. For instance, Figure 1.15 shows a material document with vendor information and document number at the header level and the material received for a purchase order.

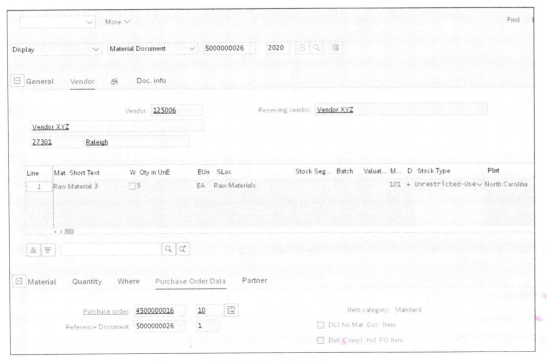

Figure 1.15 Material Document for Goods Receipt Posting

1.5.5 Outputs

Outputs in SAP S/4HANA include the messages, confirmations, and notifications your business partners or other users receive upon competition of business transactions. You can define output generation time; the transmission medium (for instance, fax/electronic data interchange [EDI], or email); and the language in the output master data. Sales order confirmations, shipping notifications, and customer invoices (in sales and distribution) are examples of outputs.

To illustrate the relationship between transaction, document, and output, let's consider the billing process in sales and distribution. When you successfully complete Transaction VF01/VF04 (Create Billing Document), a billing document is created in billing. This document connects the sales process to financial accounting and prepares the system to receive a customer payment. As an output of the billing process, a customer invoice is created and sent to the customer.

SAP S/4HANA output management supports the following printing channels:

- Email
- Printout
- XML

SAP S/4HANA output management supports the following print technologies:

- Smart forms
- Adobe forms
- Adobe forms using fragments

1.6 Business Process Integration

Business process integration is a broad topic that includes the digital core, LoB solutions, and cloud platforms. This book focuses on the integration of core business processes in SAP S/4HANA as relevant for the certification exam. The core business processes in SAP S/4HANA can integrate in several ways. Throughout this study guide, we explain the integration of system modules in three categories:

- **Cross-module data assignments**
  Cross-module organizational/master data assignments link the modules supporting different business processes in SAP S/4HANA. For instance, assigning a reconciliation account to a customer in its master record links the customer in sales and distribution to general ledger accounting. Another example is assigning a cost center to a work center in the work center master record, which links the work center in production to management accounting.
- **Transactions triggering other transactions in different modules**
  Completing a transaction in one module can trigger a transaction in another module, which creates an integration between the business processes supported by different system modules. For instance, in production, material requirements planning (MRP) can generate purchase requisitions automatically and link production to the procurement process.
- **Documents**
  In the system, the successful completion of a business transaction results in the creation of a document. Documents record data changes into other modules. For instance, the goods movements in key logistics processes (purchasing, sales and distribution, and production) may generate accounting, controlling, and Material Ledger documents, thus integrating accounting with key logistics processes.

1.7 Important Terminology

In this chapter, the following terminology we use is important to know for the exam:

- **Business process**
  A sequence of related and structured activities serving a particular business goal, such as purchasing, producing, sales, services, and finance. Purchase-to-pay, order-to-cash, and plan-to-product are examples of core processes in SAP

S/4HANA. Source-to-pay, lead-to-cash, and design-to-operate are examples of enhanced end-to-end business processes supported by LoB solutions in the intelligent suite.

- **Intelligent enterprise**
  The intelligent enterprise represents SAP's core solution supporting all mission-critical processes for a given company, including a combination of intelligent suite, industry cloud, intelligent technologies, and SAP BTP.

- **Intelligent suite**
  The intelligent suite represents SAP's core solution with a combination of the digital core (SAP S/4HANA suite) and all cloud LoB solutions, supporting the enhanced processes such as source-to-pay, lead-to-cash, design-to-operate processes.

- **Intelligent technologies**
  The digital technologies, such as artificial intelligence (AI), the Internet of Things (IoT), machine learning, and advanced analytics, enabling the intelligent enterprise.

- **Line of business (LoB) solutions**
  Set of SAP solutions or applications supporting business process management in SAP S/4HANA and the intelligent suite. SAP Customer Experience (suite), SAP Ariba, SAP SuccessFactors, and SAP Concur are some examples of cloud LoB solutions.

- **SAP Ariba**
  A business network that brings buyers and suppliers together. A cloud-based solution that can seamlessly integrate with SAP S/4HANA to enhance the procurement process.

- **SAP Business Technology Platform (SAP BTP)**
  Foundation for the intelligent enterprise, SAP BTP consists of a database component, analytics component, intelligent technologies component, and application development and integration component.

- **SAP Cloud Platform**
  SAP's application development and integration platform on the cloud. It has evolved into SAP BTP.

- **SAP Concur**
  An SAP solution that provides mobile and web-based applications for travel and expense management.

- **SAP Customer Experience**
  A suite of cloud applications for sales, marketing, services, and customer relationship management. SAP Customer Experience integrates with SAP S/4HANA and supports the lead-to-cash business process. SAP Customer Experience was formerly known as SAP C/4HANA.

- **SAP Fieldglass**
  A cloud-based vendor management system that supports external talent and contingent workforce management.
- **SAP Fiori**
  SAP's design language for next-generation user experience (UX) and business applications.
- **SAP Fiori application types**
  Three types of SAP Fiori applications exist in terms of the technology they use: transactional apps, analytical apps, and fact sheet apps.
- **SAP Fiori launchpad**
  A collection of applications that provides browser-based access to SAP S/4HANA transactions.
- **SAP HANA**
  In-memory platform on which SAP S/4HANA is built. Online analytical processing (OLAP) and online transactional processing (OLTP) environments are together on SAP HANA.
- **SAP S/4HANA Enterprise Management**
  The simplified core of SAP S/4HANA (suite) and the next generation of the ERP component of SAP Business Suite, SAP S/4HANA Enterprise Management includes core transactions and embedded LoB solutions for SAP S/4HANA, supporting enhanced core processes, such as streamlined purchase-to-pay, accelerated plan-to-product, and optimized order-to-cash processes.
- **SAP S/4HANA suite**
  The digital core of the intelligent suite, SAP S/4HANA (suite) includes all functions of SAP S/4HANA Enterprise Management and suite LoB solutions that may require additional licenses.
- **SAP SuccessFactors**
  SAP's cloud-based solution for human experience management (HXM).
- **System deployment**
  Three deployment options are available for SAP S/4HANA: on-premise, in the cloud, or hybrid, a combination of both.
- **System module**
  A group of system transactions supporting a specific business process. For instance, the sales and distribution module in SAP S/4HANA supports the order-to-cash business process.
- **Value chain**
  A full range of activities a company needs to perform to create valuable products and services. For instance, SAP's intelligent suite offers the following value chains: customer experience, manufacturing and supply chain, people engagement, and network and spend management.

1.8 Practice Questions

These practice questions will help you evaluate your understanding of the topics covered in this chapter. The questions shown are similar to those found on the certification examination. Although none of these questions will be found on the exam itself, they will allow you to review your knowledge of the subject. Select the correct answers and then check the completeness of your answers in the next section. Remember that you must select all correct answers on the exam and select only correct answers to receive credit for the question.

1. Which of the following are technology enablers of SAP S/4HANA? (There are two correct answers.)
   - ☒ A. Huge affordable memory
   - ☐ B. Touchscreen technology
   - ☒ C. Optimized onboard cache
   - ☐ D. Business networks

2. Which of the following are motivators of the development of a next-generation business suite on SAP HANA? (There are three correct answers.)
   - ☒ A. Exponential growth in data
   - ☒ B. Growth in business networks
   - ☒ C. Widespread use of IoT
   - ☐ D. Multicore processors
   - ☐ E. Database with OLAP and OLTP environments together

3. Which of the following are the components of SAP S/4HANA (suite)? (There are two correct answers.)
   - ☐ A. SAP Ariba
   - ☐ B. SAP HANA
   - ☒ C. SAP S/4HANA Enterprise Management
   - ☒ D. LoB solutions and applications

4. Which of the following is correct about SAP S/4HANA?
   - ☐ A. SAP S/4HANA can run on any database
   - ☐ B. All LoB solutions come with the standard shipment and don't require an extra license
   - ☒ C. SAP S/4HANA can run only on SAP HANA
   - ☐ D. SAP S/4HANA is still in progress does not support all core business processes covered by SAP Business Suite

5. Which of the following is correct about the deployment of SAP S/4HANA?

☐ A. It can be deployed either on-premise or in the cloud but not both
☒ B. Public and private cloud deployment options are possible
☐ C. Only the LoB solutions can be deployed in the cloud
☐ D. SAP S/4HANA Enterprise Management must be deployed on-premise, but LoB solutions can be deployed in the cloud

6. Which of the following provides a business network that enables strategic sourcing in procurement and enhances the procure-to-pay business process?

☐ A. SAP SuccessFactors
☐ B. SAP Customer Experience
☐ C. SAP Fieldglass
☒ D. SAP Ariba

7. Which value chains does the intelligent enterprise offer? (There are three correct answers.)

☒ A. Customer experience
☐ B. Supplier relationship management
☐ C. Core finance
☒ D. Network and spend management
☒ E. Manufacturing and supply chain

8. Which of the following best describes the major components of the intelligent enterprise framework? (There are three correct answers.)

☐ A. Digital core
☒ B. Intelligent suite
☐ C. SAP Fiori
☒ D. Industry cloud
☒ E. SAP BTP

9. What does SAP BTP consist of? (There are two correct answers.)

☐ A. SAP S/4HANA
☒ B. Database and data management component
☒ C. Application development and integration
☐ D. SAP Fiori

10. Which of the following represents the new SAP S/4HANA UX?

    ☐ A. SAP HANA
    ☐ B. SAP Fiori
    ☐ C. The cloud platform
    ☐ D. The digital platform

11. Which of the following is correct about SAP Fiori?

    ☐ A. Functionality is more important than the UX
    ☐ B. Uniqueness: All users have the same level of access to applications
    ☐ C. Multiple transactions are combined to provide more functionality
    ☐ D. Provides a single point of access to SAP S/4HANA apps and cloud solutions

12. Which of the following are types of SAP Fiori apps available only on SAP HANA? (There are two correct answers.)

    ☐ A. Analytical apps
    ☐ B. Educational apps
    ☐ C. Transactional apps
    ☐ D. Fact sheet apps

13. Which of the following are system-wide concepts in SAP S/4HANA? (There are two correct answers.)

    ☐ A. Organizational data and master data form the foundation for the execution of the system transactions
    ☐ B. The successful completion of a business transaction results in the generation of a document
    ☐ C. Organizational data in the system changes more often than master data
    ☐ D. System documents are used to inform business partners and other users

14. Which of the following are examples of outputs? (There are two correct answers.)

    ☐ A. Billing documents
    ☐ B. Customer invoices
    ☐ C. Sales documents
    ☐ D. Shipping notifications

15. Which of the following are correct about the system documents? (There are two correct answers.)

    ☐ A. Documents consists of header-level and item-level data
    ☐ B. Document number is part of item-level data
    ☐ C. Documents record changes in the system data
    ☐ D. Documents are for information purposes only and cannot be used as an origin of data for another transaction

16. Which of the following is *not* one of the ways business processes are integrated in SAP S/4HANA?

    ☐ A. Transactions
    ☐ B. Outputs
    ☐ C. Documents
    ☐ D. Cross-module (organizational and master) data assignments

17. Which of the following are the printing technologies that SAP S/4HANA output management supports? (There are two correct answers.)

    ☐ A. Adobe forms using fragments
    ☐ B. Smart forms
    ☐ C. Microsoft Powerpoint
    ☐ D. Adobe Document Designer

1.9 Practice Question Answers and Explanations

1. Correct answers: **A and C**

   Huge affordable memory, powerful multicore processors, cloud technologies, and optimized onboard cache are technology drivers for the development of smarter business applications.

2. Correct answers: **A, B, and C**

   Exponential growth in data, growth in business networks, and widespread use of IoT are motivators of SAP S/4HANA. Multicore processors and databases are the technologies underlying SAP S/4HANA.

3. Correct answers: **C and D**

   SAP Ariba is a business network that brings suppliers and buyers together into a single platform. Although it can natively integrate with SAP S/4HANA, SAP Ariba is not a component of SAP S/4HANA. SAP HANA is the database on which SAP S/4HANA runs, not a component. SAP S/4HANA consists of SAP S/4HANA Enterprise Management and LoB solutions.

4. Correct answer: **C**

    SAP S/4HANA is built to run optimally only on SAP HANA, which reduces the data footprint of SAP S/4HANA and makes it significantly faster than other business application software. Some LoB solutions are embedded in SAP S/4HANA Enterprise Management. However, some suite LoB applications and cloud LoB solutions may require additional licenses. SAP S/4HANA is broad in scope and, in particular, supports all core ERP processes previously available from its predecessor, SAP Business Suite.

5. Correct answer: **B**

    SAP S/4HANA provides flexible deployment options to meet customer requirements optimally. SAP S/4HANA can be deployed on-premise, in the cloud, or a combination of both. Not all LoB solutions are cloud applications; some LoB solutions are embedded in SAP S/4HANA Enterprise Management, while some LoB applications are available as add-ons.

6. Correct answer: **D**

    SAP Ariba provides a business network that brings vendors and purchasers together. SAP SuccessFactors is a cloud-based solution for HXM. SAP Customer Experience is a suite of cloud solutions for sales, marketing, services, and customer experience management. SAP Fieldglass is a vendor management system that supports external talent and contingent workforce management.

7. Correct answers: **A, D, and E**

    SAP S/4HANA offers the following value chains: customer experience, manufacturing and supply chain management, people management, and network and spend management. Core finance is a process in SAP S/4HANA. Supplier relationship management is the external module interfacing with the ERP component of the former suite, i.e., SAP Business Suite.

8. Correct answers: **B, D, and E**

    The intelligent enterprise framework represents a core solution that features the following major components: the intelligent suite, industry cloud, and SAP BTP. SAP Fiori is the design language that enables the new UX for SAP S/4HANA applications. SAP S/4HANA is the digital core of the intelligent suite.

9. Correct answers: **B and C**

    SAP BTP is the foundation and horizontal technology layer for the intelligent enterprise and industry cloud. It consists of a database component, an analytics component, an intelligent technologies component, and an application development and integration component.

10. Correct answer: **B**

    SAP Fiori represents the next generation of the SAP S/4HANA UX. SAP Fiori provides a single access point for the applications of SAP S/4HANA and SAP Business Suite. SAP HANA is the database on which SAP S/4HANA natively runs. SAP BTP is part of the digital platform and represents SAP's development and integration platform.

11. Correct answer: **D**

    The UX is at the center of SAP Fiori's design approach. SAP Fiori provides role-based applications that suit the needs of users in their business transactions. In SAP Fiori launchpad, multistep applications are decomposed for the user roles to provide a simple and productive UX. SAP Fiori launchpad can serve as a single point of access to all SAP S/4HANA and cloud apps.

12. Correct answers: **A and D**

    In terms of the other technologies they use, three types of SAP Fiori apps exist: analytical apps, transactional apps, and fact sheet apps. Analytical and fact sheet applications are based on the analytical and enterprise search capabilities of SAP HANA, which means these apps are available only on SAP HANA. Transactional apps use ABAP and thus are available on any database.

13. Correct answers: **A and B**

    Organizational data and master data form the foundation for the execution of the system transactions. Successful completion of a business transaction results in the generation of a document. Documents record changes in system data and can serve as the origin of data for further business transactions. System outputs (not documents) are used to inform business partners.

14. Correct answers: **B and D**

    In the system, documents are different from outputs. Outputs represent the messages, notifications, and confirmations sent to business partners. Customer invoices and shipping notifications are examples of system outputs.

15. Correct answers: **A and C**

    Documents record the system data changes, and they can be the origin of data for other transactions. For instance, a sales order document is a basis for outbound delivery and billing. Documents consist of header-level data and item-level data. The data at the header level of the document is valid for the entire document. Each document is assigned a document number that resides in the header level of the document.

16. Correct answer: **B**

    Business processes in SAP S/4HANA are integrated via transactions, documents, and cross-module data assignments. Outputs are mostly used as external messages and confirmations sent to customers and suppliers.

17. Correct answers: **A and B**

    SAP S/4HANA output management supports email, printout, and XML printing channels and supports the following printing technologies: smart forms, Adobe forms, and Adobe forms using fragments.

1.10 Test Takeaway

In this chapter, you learned the certification-relevant basics of SAP S/4HANA, SAP's intelligent enterprise, and SAP Fiori, the next-generation SAP UX. A good understanding of the concepts in this chapter will enable you to explain the following topics in detail:

- SAP Business Suite was unable to exploit the full capabilities of SAP HANA. Some motivators and technology enablers drove the development of a new business suite for SAP HANA, called SAP S/4HANA.
- SAP S/4HANA consists of SAP S/4HANA Enterprise Management (simplified core) and LoB solutions. Some LoB solutions are embedded in SAP S/4HANA Enterprise Management, and some are provided externally in the cloud. The intelligent suite represents the combination of SAP S/4HANA (suite) and all cloud LoB solutions. The intelligent suite supports the enhanced end-to-end processes, such as source-to-pay, lead-to-cash, and design-to-operate processes.
- Supporting all mission-critical processes of an enterprise, the intelligent enterprise features the following key components: the intelligent suite, industry cloud, intelligent technologies, and SAP BTP.
- SAP Fiori represents the new SAP UX. SAP Fiori launchpad is the browser-based interface for SAP S/4HANA applications and serves as a single access point for system transactions and cloud applications.
- Organizational data, master data, and transactional data are the foundation for the execution of system transactions. Successful completion of transactions leads to document generation and outputs (optional messages and confirmations that go to business partners and other users).

In the next chapter, we provide an overview of the financial accounting process in SAP S/4HANA.

Chapter 2
Core Finance: Financial Accounting

Techniques You'll Master

- Describe the key processes in financial accounting and the scope of these key processes
- Explain the master and organizational data that support the transactions of financial accounting
- Understand and fulfill the requirements of financial transactions and perform transactions
- Identify the touchpoints of integration between the financial accounting module in SAP S/4HANA and other system modules

This chapter of the book covers all certification-relevant topics related to financial accounting with SAP S/4HANA. We'll describe the master data, organizational data, and system transactions that support financial accounting and also explain potential integration scenarios.

SAP S/4HANA provides financial accounting and controlling application components (modules) to support two specialized accounting branches: financial accounting and management accounting. Financial accounting is externally focused. The purpose of financial accounting is to enable legal reporting according to the country's legal requirements, track the financial impact of business processes, and provide financial reports for investors. Laws and regulations define the content of financial accounting. However, management accounting is internally focused, and its purpose is to manage the company concerning costs and revenues. The internal reports in management accounting are intended to monitor and improve business operations and optimize their costs and revenues. Management requirements define the content and principles of management accounting.

Some essential tasks in financial accounting include the following:

- Posting all financial transactions, revenues, and expenses
- Keeping past postings unchanged in the system for reporting purposes
- Recording monetary and value flows
- Inventory evaluation

> **Real-World Scenario**
>
> Financials is the backbone of any company. Financial accounting is responsible for tracking all business process-related financial impacts, providing summaries, and creating external reporting. Companies periodically issue financial reports and statements to inform their owners, stockholders, tax authorities, and lenders about the company's financial value and financial performance in compliance with legal requirements.
>
> As an SAP consultant, you should clearly understand how business processes are connected to financial accounting in the real world and how you can map those connections into the system. In particular, you should be able to explain in simple terms how the system enables the administration and monitoring of business partner and asset financial records during business transactions and how those records are reconciled and summarized in general ledgers for financial reporting at any time. Finally, you must be able to simply describe how global companies can perform parallel accounting in SAP S/4HANA to meet various reporting standards.

2.1 Objectives of This Portion of the Test

This portion of the certification aims to test your knowledge of key financial accounting processes. In particular, the certification exam includes questions about the organizational data, master data, and standard transactions of financial accounting. SAP consultants are expected to understand financial accounting functions and all touchpoints of integration between the financial accounting module and other system modules.

For the certification exam, business process integration consultants must have a good understanding of the following topics:

- Master data and organizational data assignments in financial accounting
- Scope of financial accounting and its key processes
- Financial statements and external reporting
- Potential integration scenarios between financial accounting and other system modules

Note
The topic of financial accounting covers 8%–12% of the questions in the certification exam.

2.2 Data Structures for Financial Accounting

In this section, we explain certification-relevant topics of financial accounting. We'll introduce you to organizational data and master data in financial accounting and explain the relationships (and assignments) between organizational and master data. We also cover the key processes in financial accounting.

2.2.1 Organizational Data

In this section, we'll focus on organizational data in financial accounting. To map the organizational structure of your enterprise into the system, you'll need the following organizational data:

- Client
- Company code
- Segment
- Business area

Client

A *client* is the highest-level unit of all organizational elements in an SAP system. A client represents the enterprise or headquarters group in real business. In SAP S/4HANA, the organizational data, master data, and transactional data are maintained at the client level. The technical role of the client in SAP S/4HANA is to keep this data separate from other clients.

> **Tip**
> We usually use the words *client* and *customer* interchangeably in daily life. However, those words refer to different data in SAP terminology. The client in an SAP system defines the highest level of hierarchical organizational data. The transactions performed and data stored at the client level are valid and applicable to all company codes in the enterprise structure. However, a customer is master data in the sales and distribution module. Customer master data is maintained at different organizational levels, such as client, company code, and sales organization (see Chapter 5).

Company Code

A *company code* is organizational data representing an independent legal entity that enables the modeling of a business organization based on financial reporting requirements, such as balance sheets, income statements, and profit and loss (P&L) statements. This entity is the smallest SAP entity supporting a fully legal set of books. The company code is the highest organizational unit in external (legal) reporting and is usually created based on geographic considerations. Every business process relevant to financial accounting (e.g., sales, procurement, production, human resources [HR], maintenance) uses a company code as organizational data. An enterprise must have at least one company code. You can define multiple company codes in a client if you want to manage the financial accounting of several independent companies. In the system, you can use a four-character alphanumeric key to identify a company code.

Segment

A *segment* represents a division of a company for which you can create financial statements for legal reporting. A segment is organizational data that you can use as a dimension for reporting purposes in the system. Segment reporting is used to meet reporting requirements determined by several accounting principles such as International Financial Reporting Standards (IFRS) and Generally Accepted Accounting Principles (GAAP). In particular, GAAP defines a segment as a part of a company with its own financial data concerning profits and consumption.

Segment reporting can also help companies monitor economic performance, assess risks and opportunities, and effectively forecast a company's sales and financial reserves. Based on your reporting needs, you can define two types of segments:

- Business segments
- Geographical segments

These segments can be used in document splitting (if active) as well as in financial statements. Segments are created at the client level. In Customizing, you can define a segment and assign multiple profit centers to that segment. Profit centers are highly integrated with other objects in the system (i.e., products, cost centers, assets, projects, and orders). In document splitting, the system derives the segments automatically from the profit centers. You do not need to set a segment manually.

Business Area

A *business area* is organizational data that represents a separate operational and responsibility area in the organization. You can use business areas in external segment reporting based on significant operation areas (e.g., product lines, branches) across company codes. You can define a business area if you would like to create financial statements (balance sheets and income statements) for internal areas, in addition to for company codes. In Customizing, you can create a business area and activate it for several company codes; as a result, you can activate several business areas for a single company code or activate a single business area for several company codes. Once you activate a business area for a company code, you can manually enter that business area in business transactions to post items in that business area.

Business areas can also be automatically derived from other account assignments, such as from cost centers and assets. You can assign cost centers and assets to business areas in their master records.

2.2.2 Master Data

In financial accounting, the following kinds of master data are used:

- **Master data in general ledger accounting**
  Includes general ledger accounts and profit center master records.
- **Master data in subledger accounting**
  Includes customer accounts, vendor accounts, asset accounts, and business partner master records.

In this section, you'll learn certification-relevant details about these types of master data.

Master Data in General Ledger Accounting

This section introduces the master data that serves as a foundation for transactions in general ledger accounting. Let's begin with a look at general ledger accounts.

General Ledger Accounts

In Section 2.3.1, you'll learn how to create and maintain general ledger accounts. For now, we'll only introduce some essential facts about general ledger accounts.

General ledger accounts are master records in general ledger accounting. General ledger accounts include the cumulative financial data required for generating financial statements. Three categories of general ledger accounts exist:

- **Balance sheet accounts**
  These accounts record postings from business transactions.
- **Profit and loss (P&L) or income statement accounts**
  These accounts record expenses or revenues from operating and nonoperating expenses.
- **Reconciliation accounts**
  These accounts connect subledger accounts (customer, vendor, asset, contract accounts receivable/accounts payable) to the general ledger. In the master record of a subledger account, you'll assign a reconciliation account. The reconciliation between subledgers and the general ledger is guaranteed because reconciliation accounts are closed for direct posting; they simply fetch the data from the assigned subledger accounts simultaneously when posted. Reconciliation accounts enable you to create income statements or balance sheets any time you want.

Profit Center Master Record

The profit center master record consists of profit centers and a standard hierarchy of profit centers. To define profit centers in the system, you must create a profit center hierarchy assigned to a controlling area and then assign the profit center to the hierarchy. A profit center can be assigned to a segment and a company code in its master record, as shown in Figure 2.1.

> **Note**
> Profit centers were formerly part of profit center accounting in controlling. You can use profit centers both in financial accounting and controlling in parallel. However, if you use profit centers as a document splitting characteristic in the new general ledger, you must use profit centers only in the new general ledger accounting.

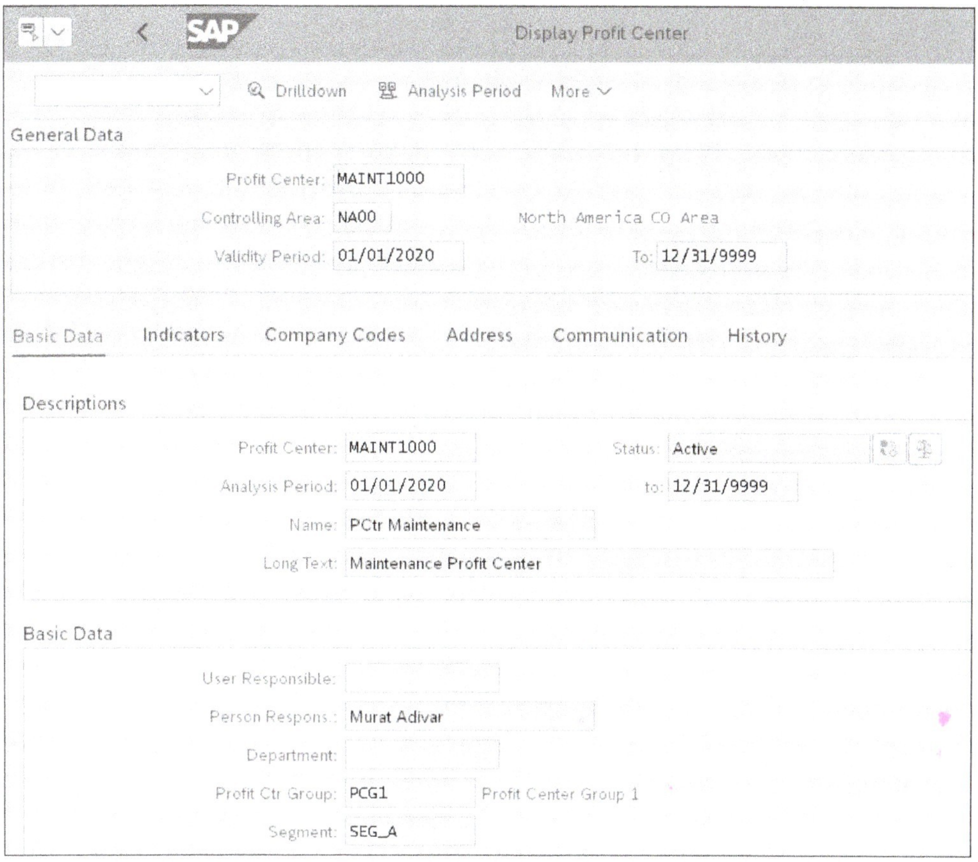

Figure 2.1 Profit Center Master Record

Master Data in Subledger Accounting

This section introduces master data that serves as a foundation for transactions in accounts receivable accounting, accounts payable accounting, asset accounting, and bank ledger accounting. Let's begin with subledger accounts.

Subledger Accounts

General ledger accounts record the cumulative accounting data of financial transactions and subledger accounts. Subledger accounts are used to record the financial details of all business transactions. For instance, a general ledger accounts receivable account includes all financial records for receivables, but they don't show how much each customer owes the company. You would need to look at the subledger account for the customer to see customer-specific financial details. Subledger accounts are generally categorized in the following way:

- **Customer accounts**
  A customer in financial accounting is also a customer in sales and distribution. The customer master record is called a customer account when relevant to accounting. A customer account is master data in accounts receivable accounting.

- **Vendor accounts**
  A vendor in financial accounting is also a vendor in purchasing. The vendor master record is called a vendor account when relevant to accounting. A vendor account is master data in accounts payable accounting.

- **Asset accounts**
  For each fixed asset of the company, you'll need to create an asset account in the system. An asset account is master data in asset accounting.

- **Contract accounts receivable and accounts payable**
  These accounts are held by business partners where posting data for contracts is recorded.

Subledger accounts are connected to the general ledger through reconciliation accounts.

Business Partner Master Record *(used to be customers +/or vendors)*

Business partners represent persons, organizations, and groups with which your company does business. In SAP S/4HANA, you cannot create customer and vendor master records directly. Instead, you first create a business partner master record centrally and then assign the desired roles (vendor or customer) to the business partner; this two-step method is called the *new business partner approach* in SAP S/4HANA. Three structural objects are essential for the creation of a business partner master record:

- Business partner category
- Business partner roles
- Business partner grouping

To create a *business partner master record*, you must choose one of the following business partner categories, as shown in Figure 2.2:

- **Person**
  Enter the first and last name of the person and add the other details (e.g., gender and title).

- **Organization**
  Enter the name of the organization (company), legal form and entity, and the industry.

- **Group**
  Enter at least two names (e.g., names of a married couple).

Figure 2.2 Business Partner Category Required First When Creating a Business Partner Master Record

Master data is a foundation of business transactions in the system. To support the various requirements of business processes, business partner master data is structured into *business partner roles* maintained at the following organization levels:

- **Business partner general role**
  After choosing the business partner category, you need to maintain the data in the business partner general role (**Business Partner (Gen.)**) data. This role is maintained at the client level and contains generic information about the business partner, such as an address, language, and bank information.

- **Financial accounting customer and customer roles**
  Customers in accounting are also customers in sales and distribution, which means using two different data types might be helpful to support transactions in financial accounting as distinct from sales and distribution transactions. The system supports this requirement by providing customer and vendor roles for business partners. For instance, the financial accounting customer (**FI Customer**) role for a business partner stores the data relevant for accounts receivable transactions, while the customer role includes sales-relevant data. The financial accounting customer role data is maintained at the company code level. If the customer does business with multiple company codes, you'll need to create a financial accounting customer role for each company code. Customer role data is maintained at the sales organization level.

- **Financial accounting vendor and vendor roles**
  Similarly, vendors in accounting are also vendors in purchasing, and you need different types of vendor data for both processes. The financial accounting vendor (**FI Vendor**) role for a business partner includes accounts payable-relevant

data, while the vendor role contains data relevant to transactions in purchasing. Financial accounting vendor role data is maintained at the company code level, while you'll maintain vendor role data at the purchase organization level.

We'll discuss customer and vendor roles in more detail for source-to-pay in Chapter 4 and lead-to-cash in Chapter 5.

When you create a business partner master record, an internal business partner number is assigned. This number uniquely identifies the business partner within the enterprise (the client). When you extend a business partner with a customer role, the system assigns an external customer number to the customer. This number uniquely identifies the customer among your company's customers. The customer number also identifies the customer's subledger account in accounts receivable. The system asks for this customer number when you want to use a customer master record in any transaction, such as creating a customer's sales order and displaying the balances in a customer's account. If the customer is also a vendor for your company, you can extend that business partner with a vendor role. In this case, an external vendor number is assigned to the business partner. Thus, based on roles, a business partner may have three different numbers in the system: a business partner number, a customer number, and a vendor number. The intervals for external and internal numbering are defined by maintaining *business partner groupings* in Customizing. Each business partner in the system must be assigned to a business partner grouping.

2.2.3 Data Assignments

By assigning organizational data in financial accounting, you can map your enterprise structure in accounting into SAP S/4HANA. The following organizational data assignments are possible within financial accounting:

- Several company codes can be assigned to a client. A company code can be assigned to only one client.
- Segments are created at the client level, and a client may have several segments.
- Several profit centers can be assigned to a segment. A profit center can be assigned to only one segment.
- Several business areas can be activated for a single company code. A business area can be activated for several company codes.

The following master data assignments are possible within financial accounting:

- General ledger accounts are managed at the company code level. A general ledger account can belong to only one company code. Company code-specific data for a general ledger account master record are defined in the company code segment.
- Customer and vendor accounts are subledger accounts, and they must be assigned to reconciliation accounts. A customer (or vendor) can be assigned to

only one reconciliation account. Several customers can be assigned to a single reconciliation account.

- Asset accounts are subledger accounts, but an asset account can be assigned to multiple general ledger accounts, such as reconciliation accounts, accumulative depreciation accounts, and depreciation expense accounts. Multiple assets can be assigned to these general ledger accounts. An *account determination key* is the mechanism connecting an asset to various general ledger accounts. The account determination key is defined in Customizing and linked to various general ledger accounts. Then account determination key is assigned to the asset via the asset class in the asset master record.
- A profit center must be assigned to a company code if several company codes exist in the controlling area.
- You can assign profit centers indirectly to fixed assets using the cost center stored in the asset master record.
- A company code must be assigned to an operational chart of accounts. Multiple company codes can use the same chart of accounts. In this case, the general ledgers of these company codes will have an identical structure.

2.3 Key Processes of Financial Accounting

In this section, we cover the following key processes of financial accounting:

- General ledger accounting
- Accounts receivable accounting
- Accounts payable accounting
- Asset accounting
- Bank ledger accounting

2.3.1 General Ledger Accounting

The crucial task of general ledger accounting is to enable a full representation of external accounting and a comprehensive overview of general ledger accounts, which record summary totals of subledger accounts and financial transactions. In particular, the central role of general ledger accounting is to support external reporting via financial statements available at any time. In the system, the general ledger accounting application component is fully integrated with all other modules and synchronously records all accounting-relevant system updates of business transactions (e.g., the primary postings and settlements from internal accounting).

A general ledger is a central record-keeping ledger used to sort, store, and summarize accounting data that flows from subledgers and business transactions. Your company's financial statements are generated from the summary totals calculated in general ledgers. In the system, you can use multiple (general) ledgers to perform parallel accounting, which is vital for multinational companies with multiple company codes in different countries so they can meet the different accounting principles and reporting standards in each country. One of these ledgers must be the leading ledger, which will be based on the accounting principles (e.g., IFRS) expected for consolidated financial statements. You can define only one leading ledger in the system, which must be integrated with all parallel (nonleading) ledgers. When the leading ledger receives a posting, parallel ledgers are automatically updated. Parallel ledgers can be based on different accounting principles (e.g., UK GAAP for the United Kingdom, US GAAP for the US, and HGB for Germany) to meet different countries' local reporting standards, as shown in Figure 2.3. Note that parallel ledgers are not subsidiary ledgers.

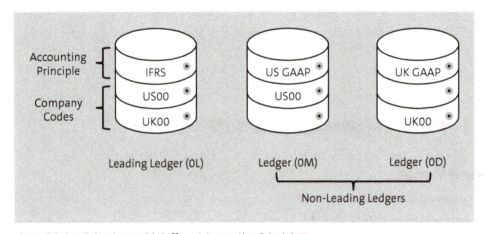

Figure 2.3 Parallel Ledgers with Different Accounting Principles

To configure general ledger accounting, you'll first create your company codes and controlling areas and make the settings for fiscal year posting periods and currencies. You can define fiscal years and their posting periods in the form of fiscal year variants and assign variants to company codes. A fiscal year is a period for which your company creates financial statements. The fiscal year resides in the header part of all accounting documents in the system. Currency is the legal means of payment in a country and is assigned to a company code. The next step is to create and configure the general ledgers. For parallel accounting, the system allows you to create multiple general ledgers, but one of these ledgers must be designated the leading ledger. Company codes are assigned to various ledgers (for different accounting principles), but you must assign all company codes to the leading ledger. For each company code, the system must know which currency is used to manage the assigned ledger. Figure 2.4 shows some example company codes with their currencies, assigned to the leading ledger **0L**.

Key Processes of Financial Accounting Section 2.3

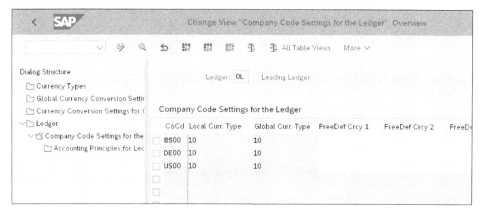

Figure 2.4 Company Code Settings for the Leading Ledger

Finally, you must assign one accounting principle to each combination of ledger and company code, as shown in Figure 2.5.

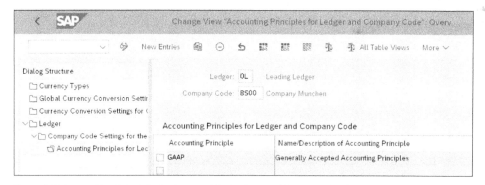

Figure 2.5 Accounting Principle Assignment for Ledger and Company Code

Now, let's dive more deeply into the specific objects and associated processes that fall within general ledger accounting.

General Ledger Accounts

In Customizing, you must define the following structural objects before creating a general ledger account master record:

- List of charts of accounts
- Charts of accounts
- Account groups

You can use the *list of all charts of accounts* to quickly manage, create, and define charts of accounts that will be used in the client, as shown in Figure 2.6.

84 Chapter 2 Core Finance: Financial Accounting

Chart of Accts	Chart of Accounts Description
CASK	Chart of accounts - Slovakia
CATR	Sample chart of accounts - Turkey
CATW	Chart of accounts - Taiwan
CAUA	Chart of accounts - Ukraine
GKR	German Joint Standard Accounting System
☑ GL00	Global Chart of Accounts
IKR	Chart of accounts - industry
INT	Sample chart of accounts
SNC	Plano Oficial de Contabilidade (PT)valid from 2010
WEG	Sample Chart of Accounts WEG

Figure 2.6 List of All Charts of Accounts

A *chart of accounts* is an ordered list of all general ledger accounts used by one or more company codes. A chart of accounts does not include any balances or transactions from the general ledger accounts. For each general ledger account, the chart of accounts includes an account number, account name (definition), and the type of general ledger account (P&L account or balance sheet account). In the financial accounting information system, you can use Transaction S_ALR_87012333 (G/L Account List) to display a chart of accounts. For example, Figure 2.7 shows a global chart of accounts in the system.

ChAc	G/L accoun	CoCd	Long Text	D	D
GL00	100000	US00	Bank Account		
GL00	101000	BS00	Alternate Bank Account		
GL00	101000	DE00	Alternate Bank Account		
GL00	101000	US00	Alternate Bank Account		
GL00	110000	BS00	Trade Accounts receivables		
GL00	110000	DE00	Trade Accounts receivables		
GL00	110000	US00	Trade Accounts receivables		
GL00	110050	BS00	Allowance for Bad Debt		
GL00	110050	DE00	Allowance for Bad Debt		
GL00	110050	US00	Allowance for Bad Debt		
GL00	110100	BS00	Miscellaneous Accounts Receivable		
GL00	110100	DE00	Miscellaneous Accounts Receivable		
GL00	110100	US00	Miscellaneous Accounts Receivable		
GL00	110200	BS00	Interest Receivable		
GL00	110200	DE00	Interest Receivable		
GL00	110200	US00	Interest Receivable		
GL00	200000	BS00	Inventory-Raw Materials		
GL00	200000	DE00	Inventory-Raw Materials		
GL00	200000	US00	Inventory-Raw Materials		
GL00	200100	BS00	Inventory-Finished Goods		

Figure 2.7 Global Chart of Accounts

General ledger accounts are managed at the company code level and structured according to the chart of accounts. You can assign a company code to a chart of accounts in Customizing, as shown in Figure 2.8. Each company code must be assigned to a chart of accounts.

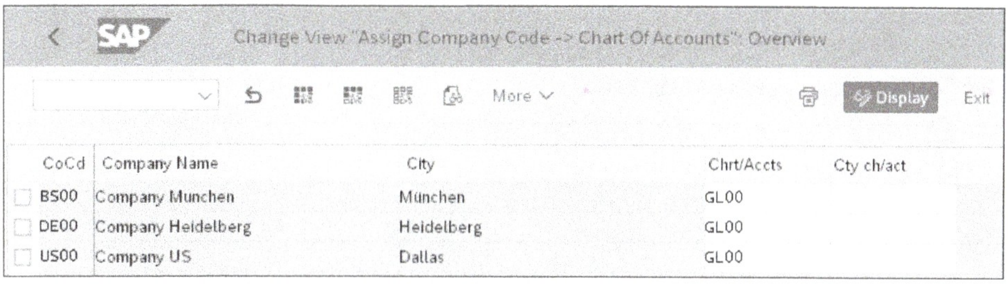

Figure 2.8 Company Codes Assigned to the Global Chart of Accounts

If you have multiple company codes in a client, you can either assign all company codes to the same operating chart of accounts or use two additional charts of accounts. Assigning all company codes to the same operating chart of accounts means you'll use identically structured general ledger accounts (with similar accounting requirements) in all company codes. You might prefer this approach if all company codes operate in the same country. If you have company codes in different countries, you may need general ledger accounts with different accounting requirements. In this case, you can assign up to two additional charts of accounts to your company codes.

In the system, in terms of their functions, three types of charts of accounts exist:

- **Operating chart of accounts**
  This kind of chart of accounts lists the general ledger accounts a company code uses in its daily postings. The assignment of one operating chart of accounts is mandatory for each company code.
- **Group chart of accounts**
  This kind of chart of accounts includes the general ledger accounts used by the entire corporate group and enables group reporting.
- **Country-specific chart of accounts**
  This kind of chart of accounts contains the general ledger accounts used to meet a country's legal reporting requirements.

When you create a general ledger account, you must select an *account group* in the chart of accounts segment of the general ledger account master record. Each general ledger account must belong to an account group. Account groups categorize your general ledger accounts into user-defined segments. You can create account groups in Customizing for each chart of accounts. Fixed asset accounts, material accounts, cash accounts, bank accounts, reconciliation accounts, and P&L accounts are examples of account groups common in the system. Account groups are identified by four-digit codes in the system. The account group determines the characteristics that control how the general ledger account can be created. When you create an account group, you can specify the following options:

- **The number range**
  The allowed range from which an account number can be selected. For instance, Figure 2.9 shows that a number interval from **220000** to **300000** is valid for accounts in the **Fixed Assets** account group.

- **The screen layout (field status)**
  You can select an account group and define field statuses for different data field categories, such as account control, account management, document entry, and bank/financial details. By defining a field status for each field group, you can specify which fields are required, optional, suppressed, and displayed when a general ledger account is being created in that account group, as shown in Figure 2.10.

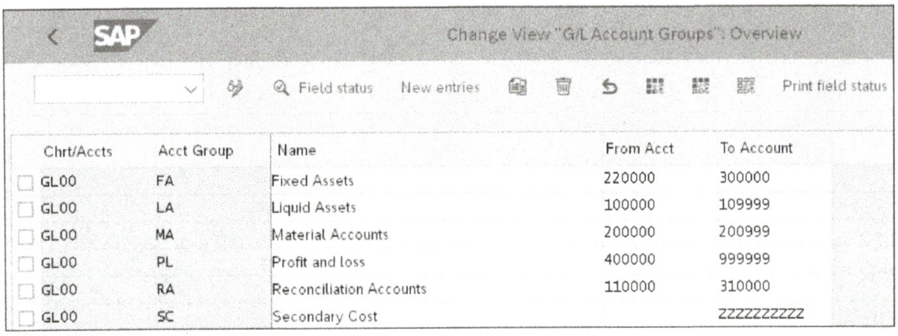

Chrt/Accts	Acct Group	Name	From Acct	To Account
GL00	FA	Fixed Assets	220000	300000
GL00	LA	Liquid Assets	100000	109999
GL00	MA	Material Accounts	200000	200999
GL00	PL	Profit and loss	400000	999999
GL00	RA	Reconciliation Accounts	110000	310000
GL00	SC	Secondary Cost		ZZZZZZZZZZ

Figure 2.9 Account Groups and Number Intervals

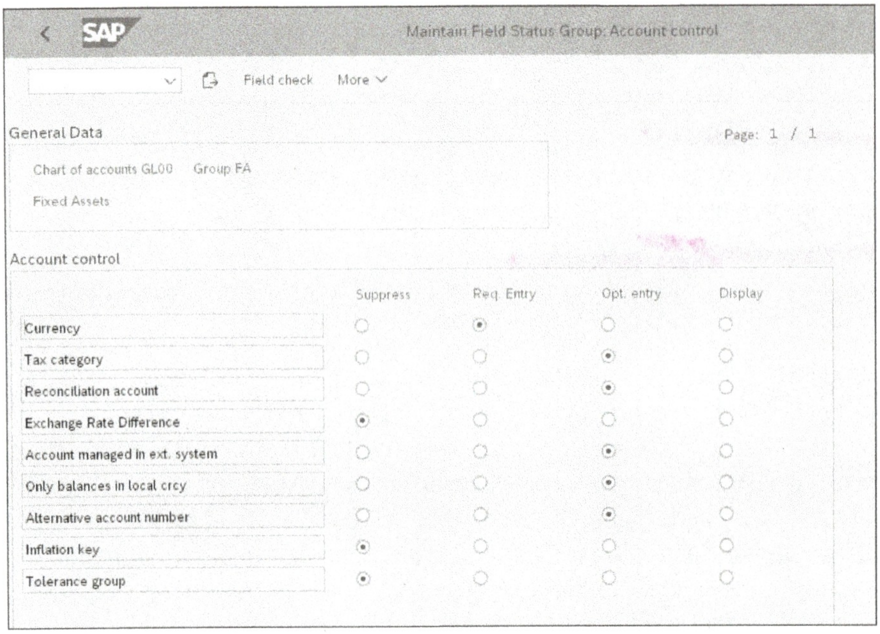

Maintain Field Status Group: Account control

General Data
Chart of accounts GL00   Group FA
Fixed Assets

Page: 1 / 1

Account control

	Suppress	Req. Entry	Opt. entry	Display
Currency	○	●	○	○
Tax category	○	○	●	○
Reconciliation account	○	○	●	○
Exchange Rate Difference	●	○	○	○
Account managed in ext. system	○	○	●	○
Only balances in local crcy	○	○	●	○
Alternative account number	○	○	●	○
Inflation key	●	○	○	○
Tolerance group	●	○	○	○

Figure 2.10 Fixed Assets Account Group: Field Status for the Fields in the Account Control Category

Figure 2.11 shows the relationships among charts of accounts, account groups, company codes, accounting principles, and ledgers.

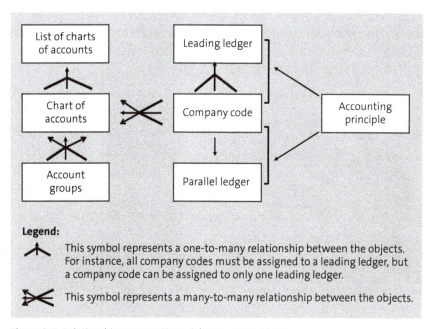

Figure 2.11 Relationships among Financial Accounting Objects

Data in General Ledger Accounts

The company codes assigned to the same chart of accounts can use identically structured general ledger accounts (not necessarily identical transactions). However, different company codes should also have some company code-specific settings in their general ledger accounts. General ledger account master data is structured into several segments to support this requirement (i.e., chart of accounts segment, company code segment, and controlling area segment). To create and edit a general ledger account master record, you must maintain data at these segments.

From a financial accounting point of view, general ledger account master data has two important data segments:

- Chart of accounts segment
- Company code segment

Figure 2.12 shows sample data in two different general ledger accounts (with identical chart of accounts, account type, and account number) managed by two different company codes. Notice that the accounts are assigned to the same chart of accounts and share the same data in the chart of accounts segment.

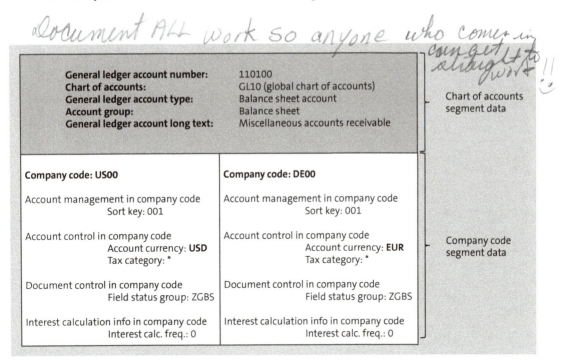

Figure 2.12 Data in Chart of Accounts and Company Code Segments in a General Ledger Account Master Record

Let's first take a closer look at the *chart of accounts segment*, where you'll define data at the chart of accounts level. The data in this segment is shared by all company codes sharing the same chart of accounts. To create a general ledger account, you must first provide some information in the chart of accounts segment: the general ledger account type (**G/L Account Type**), an account group (**Account Group**), descriptions for the general ledger account (**Short Text** and **G/L Acct Long Text**), and a consolidation account number (**Trading partner**), as shown in Figure 2.13. Note that the account group, which controls the status of the data fields in the company code segment, was described in more detail earlier in this section.

Your selection in the **G/L Account Type** dropdown list in the chart of accounts segment plays a crucial role in determining the connection between the general ledger account and its financial statements (e.g., balance sheets and income statements). In particular, the **G/L Account Type** specifies whether the account is one of the following types of general ledger accounts:

- **Balance sheet accounts**
  These accounts are the accounts posted from business transactions. For instance, Figure 2.13 shows the accounts receivable account, which receives postings from sales and distribution.

- **Primary cost and revenue accounts**
  These accounts are income statement accounts that reflect a company's operating expenses, such as payroll, labor expenses, and administration costs. Primary cost and revenue accounts are integrated with controlling.

- **Secondary cost accounts**
 These accounts are used in controlling to record internal value flows in the organization, such as internal activity cost allocations and settlements.

- **Nonoperating expense or income accounts**
 These accounts are income statement accounts that reflect gains and losses from activities not relevant to the company's primary businesses. For instance, if your company's primary business is manufacturing, then income from an asset's sale or profit from a financial investment is regarded as nonoperating income. A donation to a charity is an expenditure but not an operational cost. Nonoperating expense or income accounts reflect expenses that were never associated with any controlling object before, such as cost center, order, or profitability segment. Thus, these accounts are not linked to controlling.

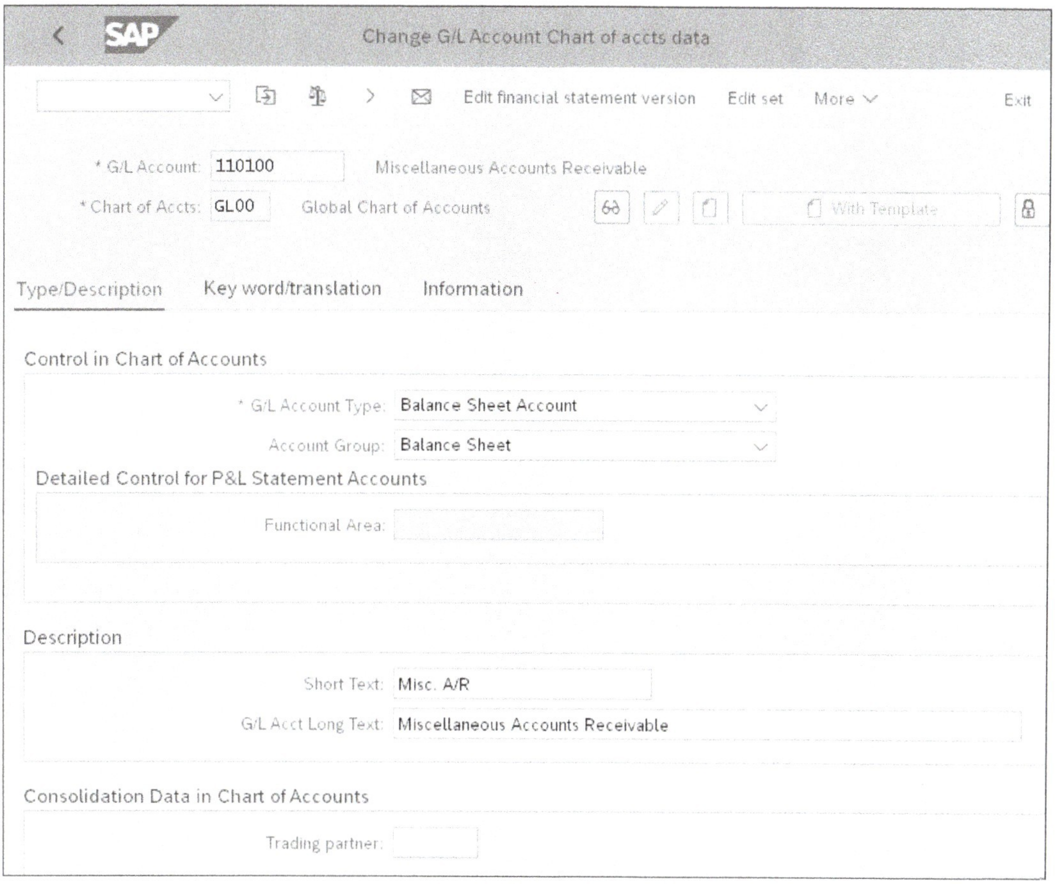

Figure 2.13 Chart of Accounts Segment of the General Ledger Account Master Record

Now, let's consider the *company code segment*. Data at the company code segment varies from one company code to another. In this segment, you can define how a specific company code manages the account. The data fields you must maintain in the company code segment are determined by the account group you select in the chart of accounts segment. For instance, if you choose the **Reconciliation Account** option from the **Account Group** dropdown list, you must make a selection in the **Recon. Account for Acct Type** dropdown list in the **Control Data** view, as shown in Figure 2.14. Otherwise, this field will not be visible. Using this field, you can determine which type of subledger accounts (vendor, customer, asset, or contract accounts receivable) can be assigned to this reconciliation account.

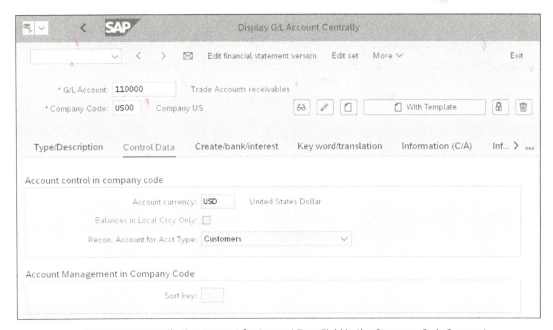

Figure 2.14 Reconciliation Account for Account Type Field in the Company Code Segment

Other data you can maintain in the company code segment include the account currency, tax category, bank data, interest data, account control, and account management data, as shown in Figure 2.15.

The income statement (P&L) accounts are integrated with controlling. From a controlling perspective, the master record of general ledger accounts for cost and revenue has an additional segment: the *controlling area segment*.

Both primary costs/revenue accounts and secondary cost accounts are created like other general ledger accounts. If you choose the account group as **Profit and Loss**, then you must maintain some controlling area-specific data in addition to chart of accounts-specific and company code-specific data. The cost element category (**CElem category**) and internal unit of measure (**Internal UoM**) are examples of controlling area-specific data, as shown in Figure 2.16. The system provides the cost element categories to classify the primary and secondary cost elements and determine the controlling transactions through which cost elements can be posted directly or indirectly.

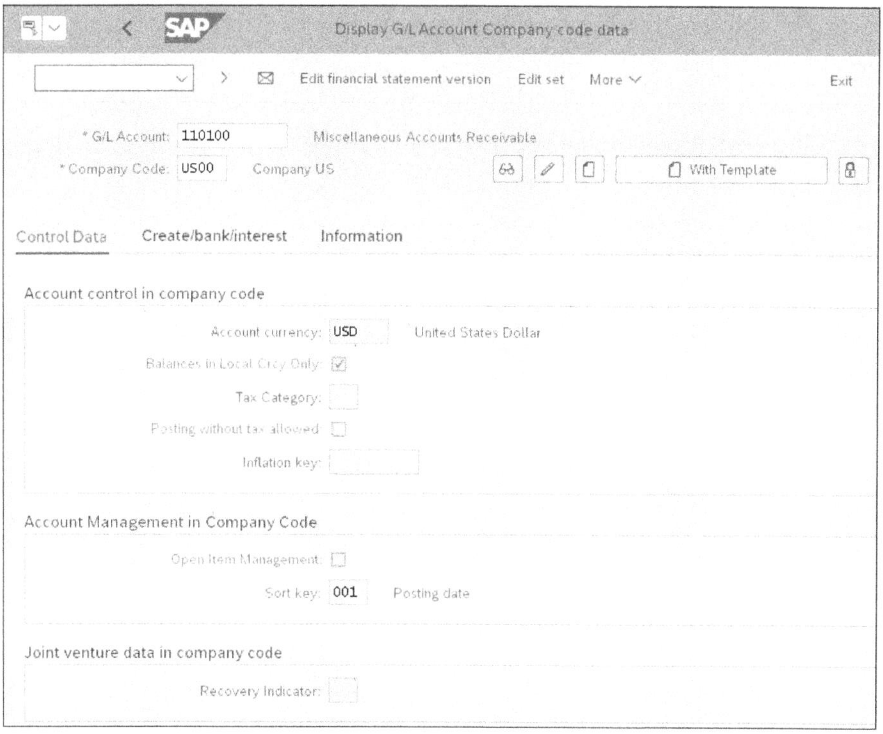

Figure 2.15 Company Code Segment of the General Ledger Account Master Record

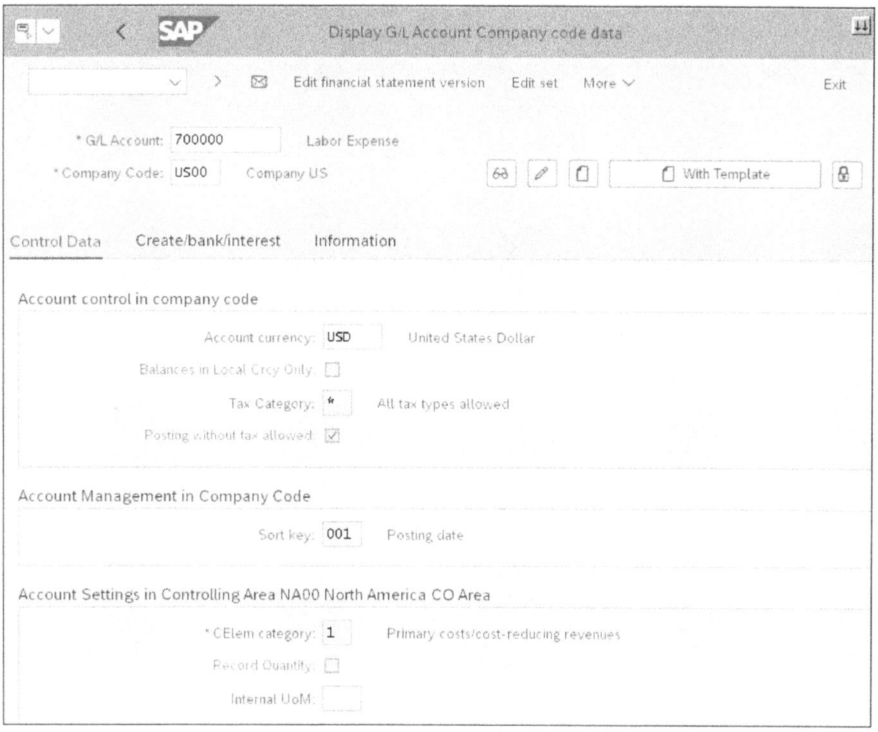

Figure 2.16 Controlling Area-Specific Data in a General Ledger Account Master Record

Posting a General Ledger Account Document

A general ledger is managed at the company code level. To post a general ledger account document, you must first choose a company code and then maintain the following data at the header and item levels, as shown in Figure 2.17:

- **Header-level data**
  Includes the document date, posting date, reference, currency, header text, and cross-company code number (to create multiple documents in different company codes).

- **Item-level data**
  Includes the general ledger account number, debit/credit, amount in document currency, tax category, tax jurisdiction code, business area, and other assignment objects such as orders, project work breakdown structure (WBS) elements, cost centers, and profit centers.

Figure 2.17 General Ledger Document Entry Screen

The information you must enter at the item level varies depending on the type of general ledger account you're posting. For instance, a document item for a bank account may not require a tax category, or you must enter a cost center when posting to an expense account.

When you complete the general ledger document entry, an accounting document is created. Many documents exist in the system, but as shown in Figure 2.18, you can quickly identify an accounting document from the following fields in the header:

- **Document Number**
- **Company Code**
- **Fiscal Year**
- **Currency**

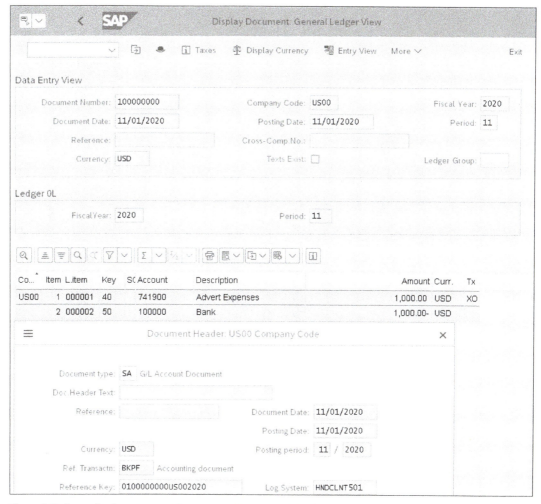

Figure 2.18 General Ledger Account Document with Header Details

You'll see the document type in the general ledger account document's header details, in the **Document type** field. In the system, a document type is identified using a two-character key, and each document is assigned a document type. For instance, as shown in Figure 2.18, the document type **SA** stands for general ledger account document.

Another important key in the general ledger account document is the *posting key*, which can be seen in the general ledger account document's item-level data (the **Key** column shown in Figure 2.18). When you post a general ledger account document, the system automatically assigns each line a posting key. The posting key controls the following item-level settings:

- The account type (general ledger account or subledger account) you're posting
- Type of posting (debit or credit)
- The field status of additional details

Note

You do not need to enter the posting key manually in the line items during the general ledger account document entry. You only need to enter a general ledger account number and choose a debit/credit indicator, and the system generates the posting key from these entries.

In the system, the posting key is identified by a two-digit number. For instance, posting keys **40** and **50** post debits and credits, respectively, to general ledger accounts. In Customizing, you can define document types (and document number ranges) and the posting keys (the left and right sides of Figure 2.19, respectively).

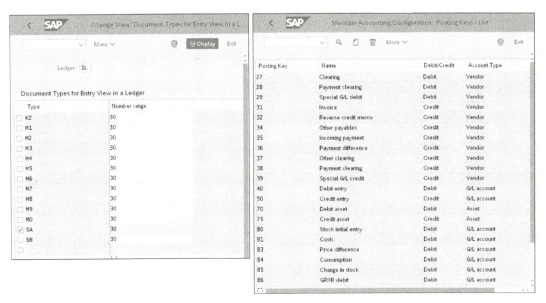

Figure 2.19 Document Types and Posting Keys in Customizing

Document Splitting

Document splitting is a function of general ledger accounting in SAP S/4HANA. Document splitting enables you to create complete financial statements for several dimensions, including the following:

- Segments
- Profit centers
- Business areas
- Custom-defined segments

To use document splitting, you must activate the functionality in Customizing. You can activate document splitting at the client level. To avoid using document splitting in some company codes within a client, you can deactivate document splitting for specific company codes, as shown in Figure 2.20.

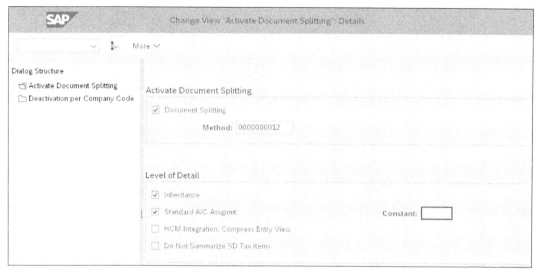

Figure 2.20 Document Splitting Activation in Customizing

To activate document splitting, you must choose a document splitting method, which includes document splitting rules describing which items in a document the system should split and how. Document splitting rules are defined by the item categories assigned to general ledger accounts for which the system split postings.

When you display accounting documents, you can choose two view options: **Entry View** or **General Ledger View**. If document splitting is active for your company code, you'll see the segment-level split of the line items you entered during the accounting document posting.

If you enter expense accounts in a document posting, you also must enter a cost object, for instance, a cost center. Cost centers are assigned to profit centers linked to segments in the system. Thus, the derivation of segment splits for the line items posted to expense accounts is straightforward. However, for the line items posted to balance sheet accounts, the system uses splitting rules defined in Customizing. Based on the proportions predefined in Customizing, the system splits a line item into segments.

The following example shows how the document splitting works in the invoice verification step of procurement. Assume that you have a vendor's invoice with the items shown in Table 2.1.

Posting Key	Account	Cost Center	Profit Center	Segment	Amount
31	Vendor XYZ				1000
40	Expense	CCA	PCA	Seg A	400
40	Expense	CCB	PCB	Seg B	600

Table 2.1 Vendor's Invoice Line Items

When you verify the invoice, the system creates an accounting document with the line items in the general ledger view, as shown in Table 2.2.

Document No: 1999000	Document Date: 11/01/2020	Posting Date: 11/01/2020	Company Code: US00	Fiscal Year: 2020	
Posting Key	Account	Cost Center	Profit Center	Segment	Amount
31	Acct Payable			Seg A	400
31	Acct Payable			Seg B	600
40	Expense	CCA	PCA	Seg A	400
40	Expense	CCB	PCB	Seg B	600

Table 2.2 Invoice Document Line Items: General Ledger View

Notice that the first line item in Table 2.1 has been split into two line items in Table 2.2. Now, we have four line items in the accounting document.

Our example shows the splitting of an invoice document. In Customizing, you can designate other document types for splitting, such as contract settlements, vendor documents, and more, as shown in Figure 2.21.

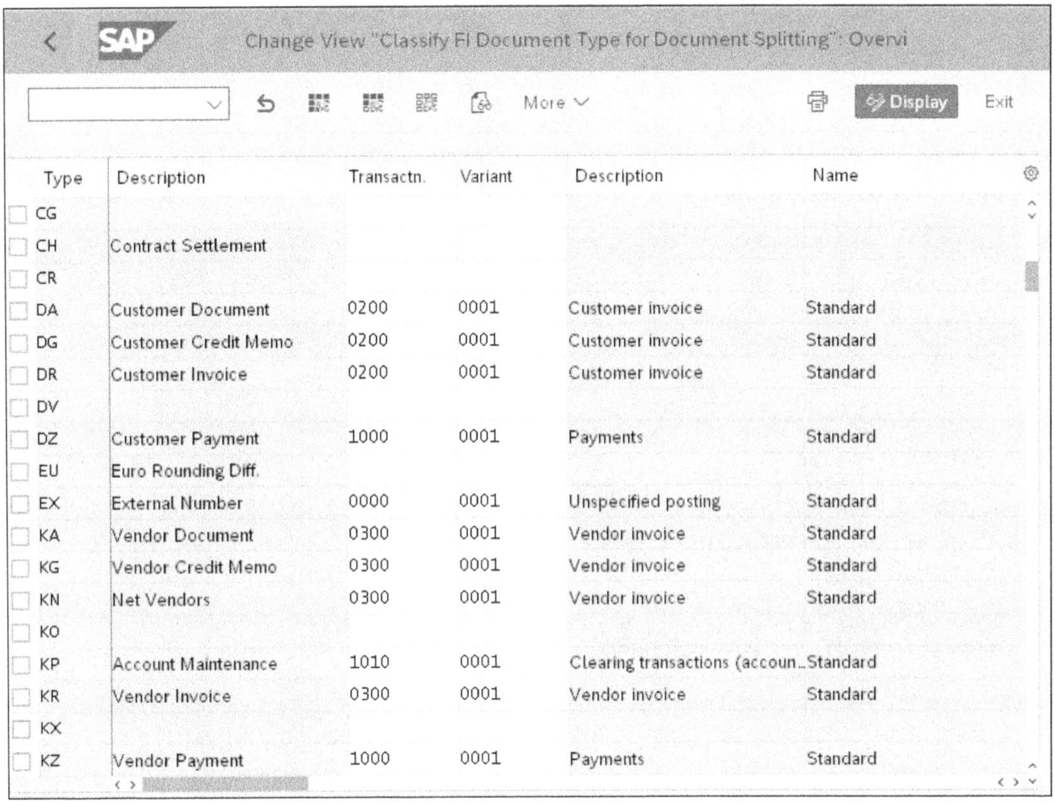

Figure 2.21 Classification of Documents for Splitting

Financial Statements

A *financial statement* is an official report that outlines the balances of the general ledger accounts (balance sheet and income statement accounts) in a structure. During year-end closing, every company prepares the following basic financial statements, according to local reporting standards:

- **Balance sheet**
  A balance sheet provides a comparison of assets and liabilities. Fixed assets, materials in inventory, receivables of the company, and cash in the bank are examples of items reported in the balance sheet's assets section. Loans and payables to vendors are examples of items reported in the liabilities section.

- **Profit and loss (P&L) (income) statement**
  A P&L statement, or income statement, provides a comparison of the company's revenues and expenditures relevant to the company's core business operations.

Financial statements are created at the company code level. The structure of financial statements and the general ledger accounts that inform the financial statements are defined in the form of a *financial statement version*. You must define financial statement versions in Customizing to structure and print out financial statements, as shown in Figure 2.22.

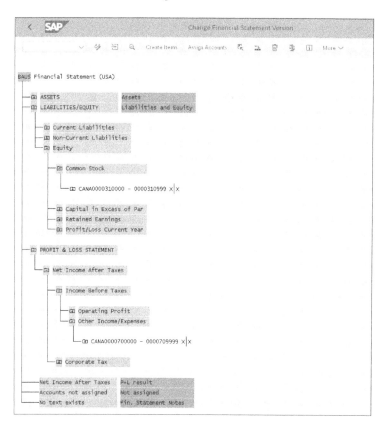

Figure 2.22 Financial Statement Version for the US

2.3.2 Accounts Payable

funds owed BY company

Concerned with accounting records for vendors, accounts payable involves subledger (vendor) accounts to track money owed or paid to individual vendors and general ledger accounts such as accounts payable reconciliation accounts and goods receipt/invoice receipt clearing accounts (also referred to as GR/IR accounts).

The accounting data for all your vendors is administered and recorded in the system's accounts payable application component. Vendor accounts are subledger accounts connected to the general ledger through reconciliation accounts. In the vendor master record, you must assign an accounts payable reconciliation account to each vendor. Accounts payable is fully integrated with the general ledger. All updates/postings to accounts payable are synchronously recorded in the general ledger. The accounts payable receives most of its data from the transactions of the purchase-to-pay business process. For instance, the GR/IR account receives data from goods receipt postings. The accounts payable reconciliation account is updated when a vendor account is posted during invoice verification and payment. Vendor invoices are entered into the system using Transaction FB70 (Document Entry). You can pay out payables in purchasing manually or by using the payment program, a part of the accounts payable application component.

Figure 2.23 shows synchronous debit and credit postings in general ledger and subledger accounts during goods receipt, invoice verification, and payment processing in the purchase-to-pay business process.

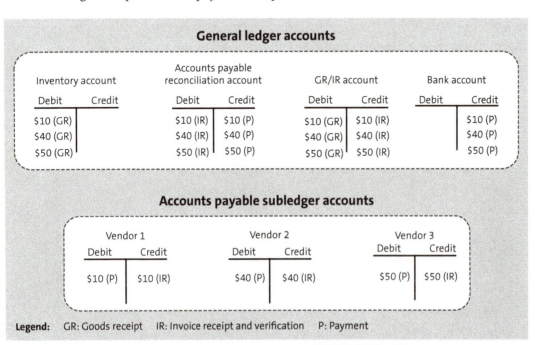

Figure 2.23 Data Flow between Accounts Payable Subledger Accounts and General Ledger Accounts during Transactions in a Purchase-to-Pay Process

More detailed explanations of the vendor master data and payment process are available in Chapter 4.

2.3.3 Accounts Receivable

[handwritten: funds owed to company]

Accounts receivable is concerned with accounting records for customers and involves subledger (customer) accounts to track the money owed or paid by individual customers and general ledger accounts, such as accounts receivable reconciliation accounts and other miscellaneous accounts receivable accounts.

Accounting data for all your customers is administered and recorded in the system's accounts receivable application component. Customer accounts are subledger accounts connected to the general ledger through reconciliation accounts. In the customer master record, you must assign an accounts receivable reconciliation account to each customer. Accounts receivable is fully integrated with the general ledger. All updates/postings to accounts receivable are synchronously recorded in the general ledger. Accounts receivable accounts receive most of their data from the transactions of the order-to-cash business process. For instance, an accounts receivable reconciliation account is updated during the billing and payment. The general ledger accounts integrated with accounts receivable also get updates from order-to-cash transactions. For instance, the cost of goods sold (COGS) and inventory-trading goods accounts are updated when you post goods issues for customer orders in sales and distribution.

More detailed explanations of the customer master data and billing process are available in Chapter 5.

2.3.4 Asset Accounting

Asset accounting is a key financial accounting process that mainly focuses on monitoring and managing fixed tangible assets, such as manufacturing plants, buildings, land, machinery, office furniture, equipment, and vehicles. A *fixed tangible asset* is a piece of physical property that a company owns for the long term and uses in its core business operations. SAP S/4HANA provides asset accounting as a submodule of the financial accounting module. The asset accounting module supports the entire lifecycle of fixed tangible assets, from initial acquisition to asset retirement.

> **Tip**
>
> Do not confuse fixed (long-term) tangible assets with current tangible assets, which are either in cash form or can be sold for cash if needed in liquidation, such as cash in the bank, cash equivalents, inventory, and accounts receivable. Your current and fixed (long-term) assets are reported in different sections of your company's balance sheet. Accounts receivable, bank ledger, and inventory accounts record the financial value of your current tangible asset and update the balance sheet's totals. Asset accounts in SAP are subledger accounts for fixed/tangible assets.

You can also manage intangible assets (e.g., patents, copyrights) in the asset accounting module. Intangible assets do not retire or depreciate.

The asset accounting module is fully integrated with the other system modules and supports all asset posting and legal reporting requirements for a company's assets.

We'll unpack asset accounting objects and processes in the following sections.

Asset Master Data

From a financial accounting perspective, asset accounts are subledger accounts connected to the general ledger through a reconciliation account. From the plant maintenance point of view, assets are technical objects (equipment/functional location) that must be maintained. In Customizing, you can set up the system to create/edit an asset master record in asset accounting and an equipment master record in plant maintenance synchronously.

To create an asset master record, you must enter a company code and an asset class. Each asset belongs to only one company code, and every asset in the system must be assigned to an asset class. Asset classes can be defined in Customizing. Buildings, vehicles, office equipment, assets under construction, and low-value assets are examples of asset classes, which control asset accounts and structure them according to user requirements.

An asset class controls certain features important for managing fixed assets in the system, such as the following:

- Determines the default values in the asset master record
- Controls the asset numbers that can be assigned to an asset within the asset class
- Defines the screen layout and field characteristics (required/optional/suppressed) in the asset master record
- Triggers separate balance sheet line items in which a different class of assets is reported
- Provides an account determination key that connects the asset to several balance sheet and depreciation accounts, as shown in Figure 2.24

Asset master data is structured into two segments, as shown in Figure 2.25:

- General master data: Includes views for general information, time-dependent information, account assignment information, inventory, and origin data.
- Data for asset valuation: Includes a view for depreciation areas.

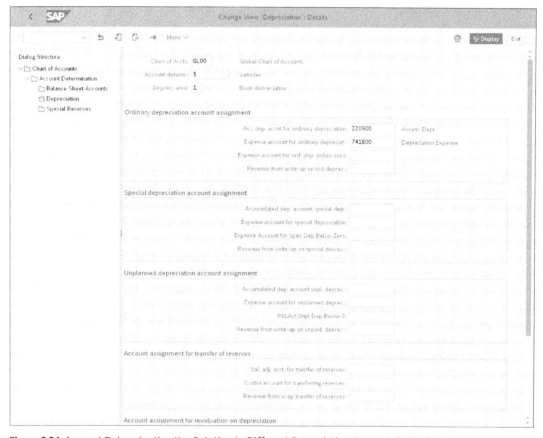

Figure 2.24 Account Determination Key Pointing to Different Depreciation Accounts in the System

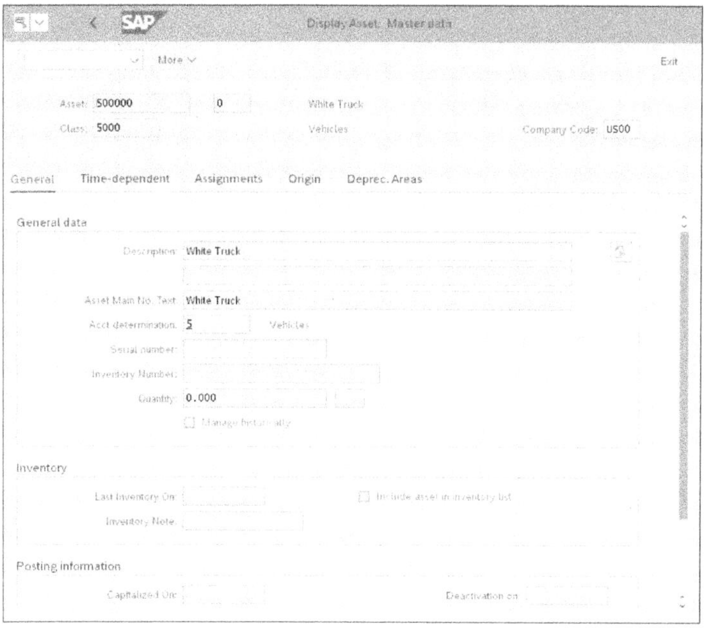

Figure 2.25 Asset Master Record for a Vehicle

Asset Posting

The following asset postings are possible in asset accounting:

- Purchasing and selling
- Depreciation and appreciation
- Acquisition from internal activity (production)
- Credit memos
- Asset retirement
- Adjustment postings

During an asset posting, the system creates postings to several general ledger and subledger accounts. In addition to company code, currency, account numbers, and the amounts you're posting, two crucial keys must be used in all asset postings:

- Transaction type
- Posting key

The transaction type (**TType**) classifies the type of asset posting (e.g., acquisition, retirement, or transfer) and determines where (in which column) the transaction is listed on the asset history sheet. The posting key (**PstKy**) is a two-digit numerical key that determines the account type you're posting to, the type of posting (debit/credit), and the layout of entry screens, as shown in Figure 2.26.

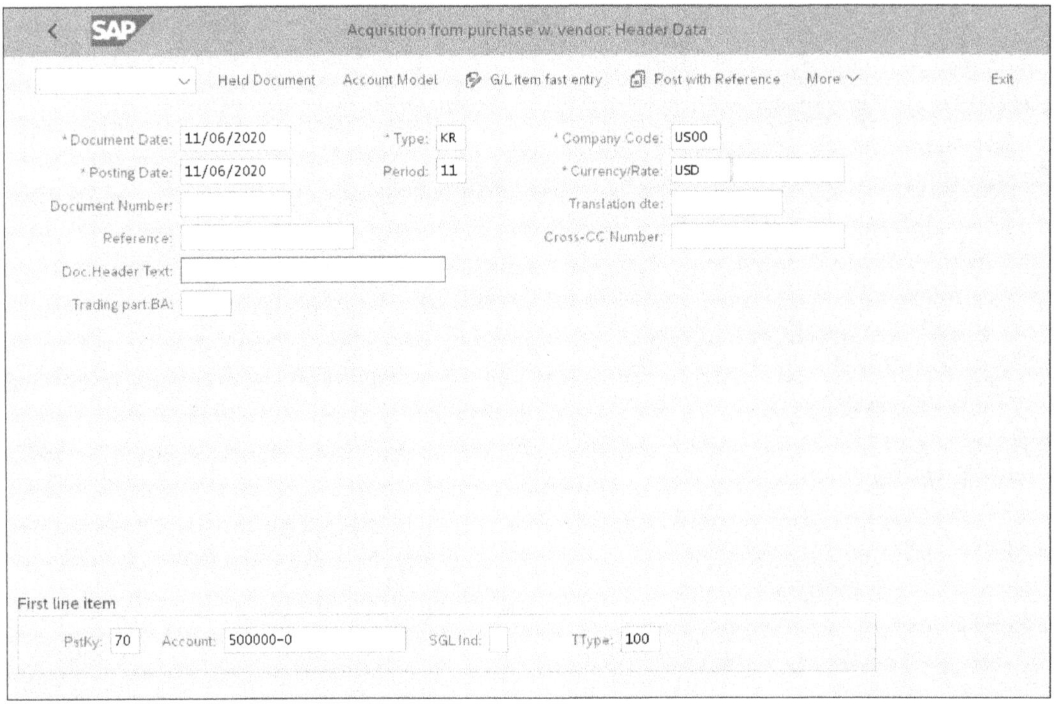

Figure 2.26 Acquisition Posting with the Vendor

Asset Acquisition

The following asset acquisition methods are supported by the system:

- External acquisition
- Acquisition from internal activity

Let's begin with *external acquisition*. You can buy an asset using standard functions of purchasing, such as a purchase order (for a vendor), a goods receipt, or an invoice receipt. When you create a purchase order item for an asset, you can create an asset master record and use it as an account assignment object. (You must choose the account assignment category **A**.) In this case, the system capitalizes the asset during the invoice receipt.

The system also supports external asset acquisitions within asset accounting by using postings integrated (or not integrated) with accounts payable accounting in the following ways:

- **Integrated asset acquisition posting**
  You can buy an asset by posting an asset acquisition in asset accounting with the vendor but without reference to a purchase order. A prerequisite to this method is to define a *technical clearing account for integrated asset acquisition* as a reconciliation account. In this method, you can use the asset posting Transaction F-90 with the following entries:
  - A debit to the asset clearing account with the posting key **70**, transaction type **100** (acquisition)
  - A credit to the vendor account with the posting key **31**

- **Nonintegrated asset acquisition posting**
  You can buy an asset without using the vendor master record or without reference to a purchase order. In this case, you can post the acquisition of a purchased asset to a clearing account rather than using integrated posting to accounts payable. You can use Transactions ABZON and F-91 for nonintegrated asset acquisition.

With integrated asset acquisition posting, the system creates two documents:

- **Operational document**
  This document includes the following information:
  - Includes a line item (debit) (posting key **70**) posted to the technical clearing account for integrated asset acquisition
  - Includes a line item (credit) (posting key **31**) posted to accounts payable
  - Does not include line items for specific accounting principles

- **Valuation document**
  For each accounting principle assigned to the company code, the system generates a separate valuation document that includes the following:
  - A line item (credit) (posting key **75**) posted to the technical clearing account for integrated asset acquisition
  - A line item (debit) (posting key **70**) posted to the asset account (equipment)

The documents for nonintegrated asset acquisition posting have a similar structure, with line items posted to the asset clearing account.

Next, the *acquisition from an internal activity* method includes capitalization of assets' costs collected in maintenance or production orders. You can either post the acquisition from internal activity manually or settle the orders to a fixed asset. (You'll need to add the asset as a settlement receiver in the settlement rule of the order.)

Asset Retirement

Like asset acquisition, you can post an asset retirement with or without integration with accounts receivable accounting. The asset accounting module provides retirement postings to support the following asset retirement types:

- **Asset retirement with a revenue (with or without customer)**
  You can sell an asset by posting an asset retirement with the customer. In this case, you can use Transaction F-92 to debit the customer account and credit the revenue account.

  Another approach is to use Transaction ABAON (Asset Sale Without Customer). In this case, the asset is sold, the revenue account is credited, and a clearing account is debited.

- **Asset retirement without a revenue**
  To remove an asset from your asset portfolio without generating any revenue (e.g., by scrapping), you can use Transaction ABAVN, which does not create any postings to revenue but posts a loss from asset retirement without a revenue posting in the amount of the netbook value being retired.

Asset Depreciation

Depreciation is the reduction in the recorded value (cost) of an asset due to wear and tear during the asset's useful life. Depending on the depreciation type, the system can automatically calculate (plan) depreciation values using the depreciation keys. Planned depreciation values are not posted to general ledger depreciation accounts automatically and are kept in the system (as planned values) until you post a periodic depreciation run. The values of some depreciation types are usually planned (calculated) manually. All planned depreciation values are reflected in the asset master record (asset account) and in general ledger accounts when you post depreciation from a depreciation posting run. You can see the planned depreciation values in the asset explorer (Transaction AW01N). The periodic depreciation posting run is a system transaction that companies use to calculate their assets' cumulative depreciation during the period-end closing. A periodic depreciation posting run posts general ledger depreciation accounts by the amount of accumulated depreciation, which means the company's cumulative depreciation is reflected in the financial statement after the periodic depreciation posting run.

Depreciation values can also be posted to cost centers, internal orders, and WBS elements assigned to the asset master record.

The asset accounting module supports the following asset depreciation types:

- **Ordinary depreciation**
  A planned deduction for the actual wear and tear due to an asset's regular use. The system calculates the value of this type of depreciation automatically based on depreciation keys.

- **Special depreciation**
  A planned deduction for wear and tear based on percentage depreciations usually determined by a tax authority. The value of this type of depreciation is calculated automatically based on depreciation keys and does not consider the actual wear and tear.

- **Unplanned depreciation**
  A deduction for wear and tear due to unusual influences, such as damage, that leads to a permanent decrease in the value of an asset. The value of this type of depreciation is planned manually.

- **Transfer of reserves/reduction of acquisition and production costs**
  A reduction of an asset's depreciation base by a given amount called acquisition and production costs (APC). This type of depreciation is posted manually (without using depreciation keys).

- **Imputed interest**
  In some cases, for cost accounting purposes, you may need to calculate imputed interest on the capital tied up in an asset. The system provides depreciation keys to support the automatic calculation of this interest in different depreciation areas.

Often, a company must calculate different depreciation values in parallel for each fixed asset to meet various external and internal reporting requirements. For instance, financial statements, cost accounting, and tax calculation processes may require different fixed asset values. SAP S/4HANA supports the parallel valuation of assets by providing several *depreciation areas*. In the system, depreciation areas are identified by two-digit numeric keys. In Customizing, you can define depreciation areas and activate them for asset classes, as shown in Figure 2.27. When you create an asset master record, you'll choose an asset class, resulting in the assignment of the asset's depreciation areas. During the asset master record creation, the system allows you to deactivate some depreciation areas assigned to the asset class. Depreciation areas in an asset master record include some essential control parameters, including the following:

- Depreciation key
- Useful (estimated) life
- Depreciation starting date
- Previous usage
- Index

Figure 2.27 Depreciation Areas for an Asset Class

By using *depreciation keys*, you can define all control data necessary to calculate annual planned depreciation for the following depreciation types:

- Ordinary depreciation
- Special depreciation
- Imputed interest

In Customizing, you can define the depreciation calculation methods and assign them to depreciation keys. You can define the following control data in depreciation keys, as shown in Figure 2.28:

- Depreciation type (and assigned calculation method)
- Scrap value key
- Changeover method, percentage
- Control indicators

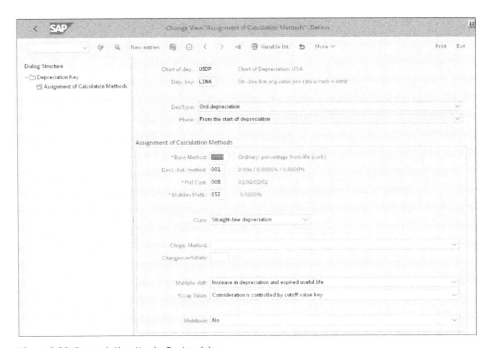

Figure 2.28 Depreciation Key in Customizing

Reporting and Monitoring

Now, let's turn to the reporting and monitoring tools available in the asset accounting module, in the asset accounting information systems, and through SAP Fiori. Some key tools include the following:

- **Asset history sheet**
  With this submodule of asset accounting information systems, you can use the asset history sheet (Transaction AR02) to create a comprehensive report for year-end closing. The structure of the asset history sheet is determined according to a country's legal reporting requirements. This sheet is a legal reporting requirement in some countries and includes all financial transactions/postings for a range of assets or asset classes.

- **Asset explorer**
  From a financial accounting perspective, an asset is an account. As shown in Figure 2.29, the asset explorer (Transaction AW01N), part of the asset accounting module, can help you see the financial transactions in this account.

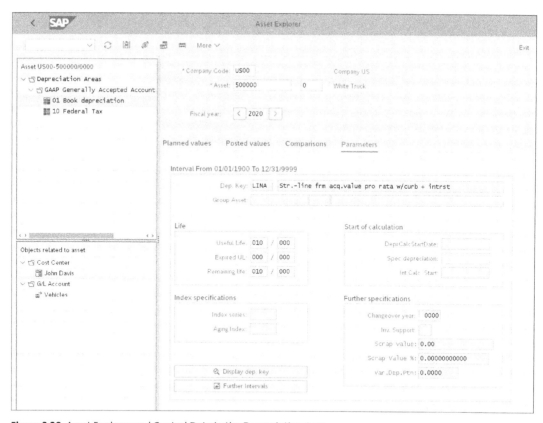

Figure 2.29 Asset Explorer and Control Data in the Depreciation Area

In particular, you can use asset explorer to perform the following actions:
- See the transactions posted to an asset (display financial accounting documents)

- See planned and posted depreciation by depreciation area, by period, for each fiscal year
- Drill down to the details of accounting transactions
- Branch master data and other cost objects (e.g., cost center) and perform simulations
- Check depreciation area control parameters

- **Managing fixed assets in SAP Fiori**
  Using the Display Asset Master Worklist app in SAP Fiori, you can collectively manage and monitor your fixed assets. This application displays all asset master data in a single list from which you can drill down into the asset master record details.

2.4 Integration with Other Modules

In this section, we'll explain several potential integration scenarios for financial accounting. We'll cover both cross-module data assignments and transactions.

2.4.1 Integration via Cross-Module Data Assignments

Cross-module data assignments in the system connect the business processes in SAP S/4HANA and enable data flows between the system's components. Some examples of cross-module data assignments include the following:

- **Management accounting (controlling)**
  Integration between controlling and financial accounting occurs via the following data assignments:
  - A cost center is master data in controlling. You can assign a cost center to fixed assets in the asset master record.
  - A controlling area is organizational data in controlling. To achieve cross-company code cost accounting, you must assign company codes to the controlling area. A prerequisite for this organizational data assignment is that all company codes assigned to a controlling area must be assigned the same operating chart of accounts and same fiscal year variant.
  - An internal order is master data in controlling. You can assign a general ledger account as a settlement receiver to an internal order.
  - Primary cost and revenue elements are master data in controlling. These elements are created in general ledger accounting as P&L accounts.
- **Logistics**
  Organizational and master data in financial accounting can be assigned several organizational and master data logistics processes, such as purchasing, sales and distribution, production, plant maintenance, and Project System:

- **Project System**
  You can assign project WBS elements to asset master records. A profit center is a master record in general ledger accounting. You can assign profit centers to project definitions, networks, network activities, or WBS elements. You can assign a general ledger account as a settlement receiver of projects.
- **Plant maintenance**
  Equipment and functional location master records can be assigned to business areas and assets in their master records.
- **Purchasing and sales and distribution**
  Purchasing organizations and sales organizations are organizational data in purchasing and sales and distribution, respectively. These organizations can be uniquely assigned to a company code. Business partner master records for customers and vendors are assigned to reconciliation accounts in the financial accounting vendor role and financial accounting customer role data, as shown in Figure 2.30.

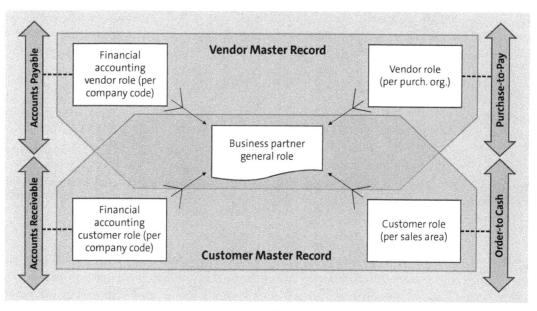

Figure 2.30 Business Partner Roles and Their Connection with Processes

- **Human experience management (HXM)**
  A personnel area is organizational data in HR. You must assign each personnel area to a company code.

2.4.2 Integration via Transactions

Other system components integrate with the financial accounting module during business transactions in business processes. Some examples of business transactions that affect financial accounting records include the following:

- **Depreciation posting runs**
  A depreciation posting run can post cost centers, WBS elements, and cost elements assigned to the asset, thus integrating asset accounting with other modules, such as controlling and Project System.
- **Asset acquisitions**
  You can use standard transactions (e.g., purchase requisitions, purchase orders, goods receipts) in materials management for external asset acquisition, which integrates materials management and financial accounting. When you create a purchase order line item for an asset, you must choose **A** as the account assignment category. The system allows you to trigger the creation of an asset master record for a new asset derived from a purchase order line item. You can also produce an asset with a production order or internal order, which integrates asset accounting with production or controlling, respectively.
- **Goods movements**
  Goods movements in various business processes usually impact financial accounting since they lead to a decrease or increase in inventory levels and the transfer of expenses to cost elements. The system creates accounting documents to record the financial accounting impact of goods movements. Some examples of goods movements in various business processes include the following:
  - **Goods receipts**
    Goods receipt postings in purchase-to-pay, plan-to-produce, plant maintenance, and project management (for nonstock materials assigned to operations and project activities) result in postings to several general ledger accounts such as GR/IR accounts; inventory accounts (e.g., finished goods); settlement accounts (e.g., manufacturing settlement account); and expense accounts, thus integrating financial accounting (general ledger accounting) with these business processes.
  - **Goods issues**
    Goods issue postings in order-to-cash, plant maintenance, and plan-to-produce (for material withdrawal) business processes result in postings to several general ledger accounts such as GR/IR accounts, inventory accounts, and expense accounts, thus integrating financial accounting (general ledger accounting) with these business processes.
  - **Transfer postings**
    If a transfer posting is relevant for valuation (e.g., material-to-material postings after processing a material), an accounting document is generated to update financial accounting records.
  - **Stock transfers**
    A stock transfer is evaluated at the valuation price of the material in the issuing (shipping) plant, and one accounting document is created to update financial accounting records. In a cross-company code stock transfer, two

accounting documents are created at the time of posting, one for each company code.

- **Settlements**
The settlement of internal orders, production orders (acquisitions from internal production), maintenance orders, and projects (and WBS elements) can result in updates in asset or general ledger accounts, thus integrating asset accounting or general ledger accounting with these business processes.

- **Master data maintenance**
In Customizing, you can set up the system to synchronously create/edit asset master records in asset accounting and equipment master records in plant maintenance, thus integrating asset accounting with plant maintenance.

- **Billing**
In the billing process of the order-to-cash business process, the system creates an accounting document including a debit for a customer account and a credit to revenue account (general ledger account).

- **Payments**
Making payments to vendors is a part of the purchase-to-pay business process. You can manually pay vendor invoices or use the payment program, which results in postings to vendor subledger accounts, accounts payable reconciliation accounts, and bank accounts. In the order-to-cash business process, you'll receive payments by posting to the vendor and several general ledger accounts, such as bank accounts.

- **Assessments and distributions**
Both assessments and distributions (in controlling) result in allocations of costs booked to primary cost elements linked to general ledger accounting, thus integrating financial accounting with controlling.

2.5 Important Terminology

In this chapter, the following terminology we use is important to know for the exam:

- **Account group**
An account group categorizes general ledger accounts into user-defined segments. When you create a general ledger account, you must choose an account group. The account group determines the number range and field status of general ledger accounts.

- **Accounts payable accounting**
A key process of financial accounting concerned with accounting records for vendors.

- **Accounts receivable accounting**
A key process of financial accounting concerned with accounting records for customers.

- **Asset accounting**
  A key process of financial accounting concerned with accounting records for fixed, tangible assets.

- **Asset class**
  To create an asset master record, you must choose a company code and an asset class. Each asset belongs to only one company code, and every asset in the system must be assigned to an asset class. An asset class provides account determination keys and determines the number ranges valid for general ledger accounts.

- **Asset explorer**
  The asset explorer is a reporting tool in the asset accounting module. You can display planned and posted depreciation by depreciation area and by fiscal year for each fixed asset. From the asset explorer, you can drill down into the details of an asset's financial transactions asset and branch the master data of an asset or cost object.

- **Asset history sheet**
  The asset history sheet is a reporting transaction in asset information systems. You can use the asset history sheet (Transaction AR02) to create a comprehensive report for year-end closing. The asset history sheet includes all transactions/posting for a range of assets or asset classes.

- **Balance sheet**
  A financial statement including a comparison of assets and liabilities.

- **Balance sheet accounts**
  General ledger accounts recording postings from business transactions.

- **Bank ledger accounting**
  A key process of financial accounting concerned with accounting records for bank transactions.

- **Business area**
  A business area is organizational data representing a separate operational and responsibility area in the organization. You can use business areas in external segment reporting based on significant operation areas (e.g., product lines, branches) across company codes.

- **Business partner category**
  You must choose a business partner category when creating a business partner master record in the system. Three business partner categories exist: organization, person, and group.

- **Business partner grouping**
  Determines the internal and external number ranges valid for various kinds of business partners, such as customers and vendors.

- **Chart of accounts**
  A chart of accounts is an ordered list of all general ledger accounts used by one or more company codes.

- **Document splitting**

  A function of general ledger accounting that supports the requirement to create complete financial statements for several dimensions, including segments, profit centers, business areas, and custom-defined segments. If document splitting is active, you'll see the splitting of accounting document line items into segments in a general ledger view.

- **Financial statement version**

  The structure of financial statements and the general ledger accounts reported in the financial statements are defined in the form of a financial statement version. You must define financial statement versions in Customizing to structure and print out financial statements.

- **General ledger**

  A general ledger is a central record-keeping ledger used to sort, store, and summarize accounting data that flows from subledgers and financial transactions. A company's financial statements are generated from the summary totals calculated in general ledgers.

- **General ledger accounting**

  A key process of financial accounting concerning legal reporting.

- **Parallel accounting**

  In the system, you can use multiple ledgers (general ledgers) to perform parallel accounting, which is vital for multinational companies to meet different accounting principles and reporting standards. One of these ledgers must be designated the leading ledger and will be based on the accounting principles (e.g., IFRS) for the consolidated financial statements.

- **Profit and loss (P&L) or income statement**

  A financial statement including a comparison of revenues and expenditures.

- **Profit and loss (P&L) or income statement accounts**

  General ledger accounts record expenses or revenues from operating and non-operating expenses.

- **Profit center**

  Master data in financial accounting. You can use profit centers as a dimension for internal reporting purposes in the system.

- **Reconciliation accounts**

  General ledger accounts that connect subledger accounts to the general ledger. Reconciliation accounts are closed for direct posting, which guarantees real-time reconciliation between the general ledger and subledgers.

- **Segment**

  A segment represents a company's division for which you can create financial statements for legal reporting. A segment is organizational data in financial accounting. You can use a segment as a dimension for reporting purposes in the system.

- **Subledger account**

  Concerned with the individual accounting records of customers, vendors, or fixed assets.

2.6 Practice Questions

These practice questions will help you evaluate your understanding of the topics covered in this chapter. The questions shown are similar to those found on the certification examination. Although none of these questions will be found on the exam itself, they will allow you to review your knowledge of the subject. Select the correct answers and then check the completeness of your answers in the next section. Remember that you must select all correct answers on the exam and select only correct answers to receive credit for the question.

1. Which of the following are the key processes in financial accounting? (There are two correct answers.)
   - ☐ A. Profit center accounting
   - ☒ B. Asset accounting
   - ☐ C. Cost element accounting
   - ☒ D. General ledger accounting

2. Which of the following receives most of its data from individual accounts for suppliers?
   - ☐ A. Accounts receivable
   - ☐ B. Supplier expense account
   - ☒ C. Accounts payable
   - ☐ D. Profit center accounting

3. Which of the following are correct about financial accounting? (There are two correct answers.)
   - ☐ A. Internally focused
   - ☒ B. Externally focused
   - ☒ C. Subject to a country's laws and other regulations
   - ☐ D. Defined by company's management needs

4. Which of the following is *not* organizational data in financial accounting? (There are two correct answers.)
   - ☒ A. Cost center
   - ☒ B. General ledger account
   - ☐ C. Business area
   - ☐ D. Segment

5. Which of the following represents a division of a company and a dimension in financial statements?

☐ A. Business area
☐ B. Segment
☐ C. Company code
☐ D. Organizational unit

6. Which of the following are master data in financial accounting? (There are two correct answers.)

☐ A. General ledger account
☐ B. Cost center master record
☐ C. Leading ledger
☐ D. Asset account

7. Which of the following are subledger accounts? (There are two correct answers.)

☐ A. Accounts receivable reconciliation account
☐ B. Vendor account
☐ C. Contract accounts receivable
☐ D. Inventory-finished goods

8. Which of the following is *not* correct about the reconciliation accounts?

☐ A. They are closed for direct posting
☐ B. They connect subledger accounts to the general ledger
☐ C. They are subledger accounts
☐ D. They are general ledger accounts

9. Which of the following must be first selected to create a business partner master record?

☐ A. Business partner grouping
☐ B. Partner function
☐ C. Business partner role
☐ D. Business partner category

10. Which of the following business partner roles includes a reconciliation account number for the business partner? (There are two correct answers.)

☐ A. Business partner general role
☐ B. Financial accounting vendor role
☐ C. Customer role
☐ D. Financial accounting customer role

11. Which of the following are correct about organizational and master data in financial accounting? (There are three correct answers.)

☐ A. Segments are created at the client code level
☐ B. A business area can be activated for multiple company codes
☐ C. Only one business partner can be assigned to each reconciliation account
☐ D. Each company code must be assigned to the operational chart of accounts
☐ E. A company code can be assigned to only one chart of accounts

12. Which of the following are correct about the scope of general ledger accounting? (There are two correct answers.)

☐ A. Represents internal accounting
☐ B. Represents external accounting
☐ C. Includes all details of the business transactions with individual business partners
☐ D. Concerned with legal reporting

13. Which of the following is *not* correct about parallel accounting?

☐ A. There can be multiple general ledgers, but only one of them can be the leading ledger
☐ B. All company codes must be assigned to the leading ledger
☐ C. A currency must be assigned to a company code and ledger
☐ D. All parallel ledgers are assigned the same international accounting principles

14. Which of the following information can be found in the chart of accounts? (There are two correct answers.)

☐ A. A list of general ledger account balances
☐ B. Postings to general ledger accounts
☐ C. General ledger account numbers
☐ D. Type of general ledger account (P&L or balance sheet)

15. Which of the following are correct about the account group? (There are three correct answers.)

☐ A. It must be maintained in company code segment data of general ledger account
☐ B. A general ledger account can belong to several account groups
☐ C. It determines the field status of data field categories for general ledger accounts
☐ D. It determines the number range for the general ledger accounts
☐ E. Account groups are defined per chart of accounts

16. Which of the following can be found in the company code segment data of the general ledger account master record? (There are two correct answers.)

☐ A. Account group
☐ B. Account currency
☐ C. General ledger account type
☐ D. Interest data

17. Which of the following header-level data can help you to identify an accounting document? (There are two correct answers.)

☐ A. Fiscal year
☐ B. Document date
☐ C. Company code
☐ D. General ledger account number

18. Which of the following are correct about the posting key? (There are two correct answers.)

☐ A. You must enter the posting key for each line item during the general ledger document posting
☐ B. The posting key is valid for the entire accounting document
☐ C. Determines the type of posting (debit or credit)
☐ D. Determines the field status for each line item in the accounting document

19. For which dimensions document splitting enables preparation of financial statements (There are three correct answers.)

☐ A. Segment
☐ B. Profit center
☐ C. Work center

☐ D. Plant
☐ E. Business area

20. Which of the following provides a comparison of assets and liabilities?

☐ A. Income statement
☐ B. P&L statement
☐ C. Balance sheet
☐ D. Asset history sheet

21. What do you have to enter first to create an asset master record? (There are two correct answers.)

☐ A. Asset class
☐ B. Asset category
☐ C. Company code
☐ D. Account determination key

22. Which of the following are correct about the assets? (There are three correct answers.)

☐ A. An asset can be owned by several company codes
☐ B. Each asset must be assigned to an asset class
☐ C. Assets can only be acquired externally
☐ D. An asset master record in asset accounting can be created synchronously with an equipment master record in plant maintenance
☐ E. Assets are linked to multiple general ledger accounts through account determination key

23. Which of the following must be entered during the asset posting for external acquisition? (There are two correct answers.)

☐ A. Transaction type
☐ B. Purchase order number
☐ C. Vendor number
☐ D. Posting key

24. Which of the following are correct about a fixed asset's depreciation? (There are two correct answers.)

☐ A. For each fixed asset, the system can calculate only one type of depreciation
☐ B. Asset depreciation is automatically calculated and reflected in the balance sheet in real time

☐ C. You must execute a periodic depreciation posting run to transfer all depreciation to the asset master record

☐ D. Depreciation keys are used in the system for the calculation of planned depreciation

25. Which of the following can be done in the asset explorer? (There are two correct answers.)

☐ A. You can see planned and posted depreciation per fiscal year and per depreciation area

☐ B. You can list all financial transactions for a group or class of assets

☐ C. You can branch master data of asset and other cost objects

☐ D. You can change depreciation keys for an asset

26. Which of the following can be assigned to an asset in the asset master record? (There are three correct answers.)

☐ A. Maintenance work center
☐ B. Profit center
☐ C. Cost center
☐ D. Maintenance planning group
☐ E. Business area

27. Which of the following results in a posting to asset accounts? (There are two correct answers.)

☐ A. Goods receipts
☐ B. Settlements for an internal order
☐ C. Purchase requisitions for an asset
☐ D. Depreciation posting runs

2.7 Practice Question Answers and Explanations

1. Correct answers: **B and D**
   Financial accounting's key processes are general ledger accounting, accounts receivable accounting, accounts payable accounting, asset accounting, and bank ledger accounting. Profit center accounting and cost element accounting are key processes in management accounting and are concerned with the profits and costs of areas of responsibility.

2. Correct answer: **C**

    Accounts payable is concerned with individual accounting records for vendors (suppliers). Accounts receivable receives most of its data from postings to customer accounts in the order-to-cash business process. Profit center accounting is concerned with the profitability of areas of responsibilities (profit centers) and receives data from the cost objects to which profit centers are assigned.

3. Correct answers: **B and C**

    Financial accounting is externally focused and concerned with financial reporting defined by a country's laws and regulations. Financial reports and statements in financial accounting can also be used internally for management purposes. Management accounting is internally focused, and the company's management requirements determine the content of management accounting.

4. Correct answers: **A and B**

    A cost center is master data in controlling. A general ledger account is master data (not organizational data) in financial accounting. Client, company code, business area, and segment are organizational data in financial accounting.

5. Correct answer: **B**

    A segment represents a division of a company for which you can create financial statements for legal reporting. A segment is organizational data that you can use as a dimension for reporting purposes. Segment reporting is used to meet reporting requirements determined by several accounting principles such as IFRS and GAAP.

6. Correct answers: **A and D**

    General ledger accounts and subledger accounts (customer, vendor, asset) are master data in financial accounting. A cost center is master data in controlling. All company codes must be assigned to the leading ledger, and all general ledger accounts are summarized in the leading ledger. However, the leading ledger is not master data in financial accounting.

7. Correct answers: **B and C**

    All reconciliation accounts are general ledger accounts. An accounts receivable reconciliation account is a part of accounts receivable but not a subledger account. Subledger accounts are not general ledger accounts. Inventory accounts are general ledger accounts. Customer, vendor, asset, and contract accounts receivable accounts are subledger accounts in the system.

8. Correct answer: **C**

    Reconciliation accounts are general ledger accounts connecting subledger accounts to the general ledger. They are closed for direct posting, which guarantees real-time reconciliation between the subsidiary ledger and the general ledger.

9. Correct answer: **D**

   You must first select a business partner category to create a business partner master record. Then, you can create business partner roles (customer or vendor) based on your interactions with the business partner. A business partner grouping controls the internal and external numbering of business partner master records.

10. Correct answers: **B and D**

    Business partner general data is created at the client level and valid for the business partner's roles. A reconciliation account is accounting-relevant data that must be maintained at the company code level in the financial accounting customer or financial accounting vendor roles. A customer role includes data relevant to sales and distribution.

11. Correct answers: **A, B, and D**

    In Customizing, segments are created at the client level. Several business areas can be activated for a company code, and a business area can be activated for several company codes. Each company code must have an operating chart of accounts and based on accounting requirements, a company code can be assigned to up to two more charts of accounts (country-specific and group chart of accounts). Several customers (or vendors) are assigned to the same reconciliation account for customers (or vendors) in their master records.

12. Correct answers: **B and D**

    General ledger accounting is responsible for a full representation of external accounting. The details for business transactions with individual business partners are recorded in subledger accounts for business partners and summarized in general ledger accounts. General ledger accounts do not include details of individual transactions. General ledger accounting is mainly concerned with legal reporting to stakeholders and tax authorities.

13. Correct answer: **D**

    You can use multiple general ledgers in parallel to meet different reporting standards determined by the country's accounting principles. However, one of these ledgers must be the leading ledger. This ledger must be assigned all company codes. Parallel ledgers can use different accounting principles. The leading ledger and all assigned company codes are subject to consolidated accounting principles valid for all countries. You must set a currency for the management of a ledger assigned to a company code.

14. Correct answers: **C and D**

    A chart of accounts is an ordered list of general ledger accounts and includes general ledger account numbers, type of general ledger account, and account description. A chart of accounts does not include any transactional details from general ledger accounts, such as postings or balances.

15. Correct answers: **C, D, and E**

    Account groups can be maintained in the chart of accounts segment data of general ledger accounts. A general ledger account can be assigned to only one account group. The account group defines the number range for accounts and the field status. In Customizing, you can define account groups for charts of accounts.

16. Correct answers: **B and D**

    Account group and general ledger account types are maintained at the chart of accounts segment data of general ledger account master data. You can find the currency, interest data, account control, and account management data in the company code segment of the general ledger account master data.

17. Correct answers: **A and C**

    All documents in the system have document data in the header-level data. However, you can differentiate an accounting document by the fiscal year and company code at the header level. General ledger account numbers can be seen in the item-level data.

18. Correct answers: **C and D**

    The document type key and the posting key are two essential keys used in general ledger account document postings. The posting key determines the account type (general ledger account or subledger account) to which you're posting, the type of posting, and the field status of additional details required for line items. Unlike SAP ERP 6.0, in SAP S/4HANA, you do not need to enter the posting key in item-level data during a general ledger account document posting. The system automatically generates the posting key from the debit/credit indicator and the general ledger account number you entered. The generated posting keys are displayed in the line items of the resulting accounting document.

19. Correct answers: **A, B, and E**

    Document splitting is a function of general ledger accounting and supports requirements for the creation of complete financial statements for segments, profit centers, business areas, and custom-defined segments.

20. Correct answer: **C**

    A balance sheet is a financial statement that provides a comparison of the company's assets and liabilities. An income statement and a P&L statement are the same; they compare expenditures and revenues. The asset history sheet provides a detailed report of all financial transactions for the company's fixed assets but does not report on a company's liabilities.

21. Correct answers: **A and C**

    Each asset can belong to only one company code and must be assigned to an asset class, so you must enter a company code and an asset class when you create an asset master record. The account determination key is defined by the asset class and assigned to an asset master record when you select the asset class.

22. Correct answers: **B, D, and E**

    Each asset can belong to only one company code and must be assigned to an asset class. The account determination key is defined by asset class and connects the asset to multiple general ledger accounts. For a fixed asset (say equipment), asset master records in asset accounting and equipment master records in plant maintenance are created separately but synchronously (requires setup in Customizing).

23. Correct answers: **A and D**

    An external acquisition can be made without reference to a vendor and purchase order (nonintegrated asset acquisition). However, in all asset postings, you must enter a transaction type and a posting key.

24. Correct answers: **C and D**

    SAP S/4HANA supports the parallel valuation of assets by providing several depreciation areas. For a fixed asset, several depreciation values can be planned according to several depreciation areas. Depreciation values can be planned manually or automatically (by using depreciation keys). Planned (or calculated) depreciation values are not reflected in the asset master record or the balance sheet until the execution of the depreciation posting run.

25. Correct answers: **A and C**

    The asset explorer can display planned and posted depreciation values for a fixed asset by depreciation area and fiscal year. You can also branch master data and drill down into the details of the postings for a selected asset. You can list transactions for selected assets. To see all transactional details for a group of assets, you must use the asset history sheet. Depreciation keys for an asset can be changed by editing the asset master record (not in the asset explorer).

26. Correct answers: **B, C, and E**

    You can assign a profit center, cost center, or a business area to an asset in its master record. The maintenance work center and maintenance planning group are data that you can maintain in the equipment master record (for a fixed asset).

27. Correct answers: **B and D**

    Depreciation posting runs and settlements for internal orders can post to asset accounts. A purchase requisition does not trigger any accounting posting. goods receipts can result in updates to several general ledger accounts (inventory and expense) and cost centers, but they do not lead to postings to subledger accounts (asset, vendor, and customer).

2.8 Test Takeaway

In this chapter, you learned the key processes of financial accounting and the system application components supporting those key processes. General ledger accounting supports the legal reporting requirements of a company. Accounts receivable accounting, accounts payable accounting, and asset accounting are concerned with administering the individual accounting records of customers, vendors, and assets, respectively. General ledger accounts, subledger accounts, and profit centers are master data that support transactions in financial accounting. A company's financial-organizational structure is mapped into the system with the following organizational data: client, company code, segment, and business area. Company codes are assigned to the client, and segments are created at the client level.

Business areas are activated for company codes. The system supports parallel accounting by enabling the use of parallel ledgers to meet different accounting principles. One of these ledgers must be designated the leading ledger. Customer, vendor, and asset accounts are subledger accounts that are connected to the general ledger through reconciliation accounts. Reconciliation accounts are general ledger accounts closed for direct posting and guarantee the automatic reconciliation between subledgers and the general ledger. Cross-module data assignments and business transactions in other business processes integrate financial accounting with other system modules. Goods movements, settlements, depreciation postings, billing, payments, assessments, and distributions are examples of business transactions that affect financial accounting records. For cross-company code cost accounting, you can assign company codes to a controlling area, which is organizational data in management accounting. Company codes assigned to the same controlling area must use the same fiscal year variant and the same operating chart of accounts.

We've now covered financial accounting in SAP S/4HANA. The next chapter covers the key processes in management accounting and controlling that support management accounting processes in SAP S/4HANA.

Chapter 3
Core Finance: Management Accounting

Techniques You'll Master

- Describe the key processes in management accounting and the scope of the key processes

- Explain the master and organizational data that support allocations and the analysis of costs and revenues that flow into the controlling module

- Understand the use of controlling objects and the requirements of controlling transactions

- Identify the touchpoints of integration between the controlling module in SAP S/4HANA and other system modules

This chapter of the book covers all certification-relevant topics related to management accounting in SAP S/4HANA. We'll describe the master data, organizational data, and controlling transactions supporting management accounting and explain several potential integration scenarios.

Management accounting is a particular branch of accounting that provides managers in an organization with several views of costs and revenues across controlling areas. A business organization must know the types and sums of costs and revenues to measure its overall profits and losses. Financial accounting already provides cost and revenue accounts to track and analyze costs and revenues. To maximize an enterprise's overall profitability across country boundaries and to plan core business operations efficiently, managers will need enhanced views of costs and revenues, such as the following:

- By location
- By area of responsibility
- By business process
- By product
- By cost object (manufacturing orders, process orders, objects)
- By external market segment

The controlling module in SAP S/4HANA provides controlling objects assigned or linked to all system elements where costs and revenues occur. The system enables the use of controlling objects in all financial accounting postings to cost and revenue accounts. Some controlling objects (e.g., cost centers, profit centers) are assigned to elements (e.g., assets, materials) of other application components to receive cost and revenue information. Controlling objects are also used for internal cost and activity allocations. The goal is to accurately plan and monitor the real costs and revenues of units, processes, products, and market segments. Unlike financial accounting, management accounting is mainly concerned with internal reporting.

> **Real-World Scenario**
>
> Management accounting is an integral part of planning, execution, and reporting in all business processes where costs and revenues occur. For instance, part of management accounting, product cost accounting enables you to provide answers to some critical questions in production planning, such as "What are the production, material, and overhead costs?," "Can we sell the produced item at a competitive price?", or "How can production efficiency be improved?"
>
> In SAP S/4HANA, the controlling module supports all key management accounting processes in a business organization. The controlling and financial accounting modules are directly connected, transmitting data to each

other. They update the same data table for reporting (table ACDOCA), which requires that organizational structures be compatibly configured in the system in both financial accounting and management accounting.

For effective use of the controlling module to support decision-making, planning, and internal reporting, an SAP consultant should clearly understand the structure of the data in controlling and understand how controlling objects are closely integrated with other system components.

3.1 Objectives of This Portion of the Test

This portion of the certification aims to test your knowledge of the key management accounting processes and how they are mapped into the system. In particular, the certification exam includes questions about the organizational data, master data, and standard transactions of controlling. SAP consultants are expected to understand all integrations between the controlling module and other system modules.

For the certification exam, business process integration consultants must have a good understanding of the following topics:

- Master data and organizational data assignments in controlling
- Scope of management accounting and its key processes
- True and statistical controlling objects and postings with controlling objects
- Potential integration scenarios between controlling and other system modules

Note
The topic of management accounting covers more than 12% of the questions in the certification exam.

3.2 Data Structures for Management Accounting

In this section, we explain the certification-relevant topics related to management accounting. We'll introduce you to the organizational and master data used in the key processes of management accounting.

SAP S/4HANA provides the controlling module to support the following key processes in management accounting:

- Cost and revenue element accounting
- Overhead cost controlling
- Product cost controlling
- Profitability analysis and sales controlling

We'll also cover the relationships between organizational and master data in controlling.

3.2.1 Organizational Data

The controlling module uses the following organizational data to map the management accounting-relevant organizational structure of your enterprise into the system:

- Client
- Operating concern
- Controlling area

In previous chapters, we described in detail the role of a *client* in the system. As the highest organizational level in the system, a client represents a self-contained enterprise and separates its master data, transactional data, and other clients' tables.

In the real world, the *operating concern* represents a view of external market segments with its own structure for sales (e.g., banking, airline route profitability, and textiles). In the system, the operating concern is the highest organizational level in controlling-specific organizational structure and the valuation level for profitability analysis. An operating concern is identified by a four-character alphanumeric key in the system.

Finally, the *controlling area* represents a subdivision of an enterprise from a cost accounting perspective. In Customizing, you can define controlling areas to create self-contained organizational structures in which costs and revenues are managed and allocated. Being self-contained means cost and revenue allocations cannot be made across controlling areas. A controlling area is identified by a four-character alphanumeric key in the system. In a business organization, costs and revenues are recorded in general ledger accounts managed in company codes. To integrate financial accounting and management accounting, you must assign company codes to controlling areas in Customizing. This relationship can be one-to-one if the external and internal accounting viewpoints are identical in the business organization, as shown in Figure 3.1. However, for enterprises with company codes subject to different countries' accounting principles, you may want to use decentralized external accounting and centralized internal accounting—in other words, cross-company code cost accounting, which can be set up in Customizing by assigning several company codes to the same controlling area. The assigned company codes may use different currencies and country-specific charts of accounts; however, they must share the same operating chart of accounts and the same fiscal year variant. The system records all transactions with a period designation, and the fiscal year variant defines this period.

Figure 3.1 Assigning a Company Code to a Controlling Area in Customizing

You can specify the currency of the controlling area in Customizing. The following currencies can be used in controlling:

- **Controlling area currency**
  The controlling area currency is the currency used in cost accounting.
- **Controlling object currency (company code currency)**
  This currency is defined in the master record of a controlling object, such as a cost center, a profit center, an internal order, or an activity type. Controlling objects are assigned to company codes. As a result, the company code currency is the default currency for objects assigned to a company code. However, the currency can be changed if the company code currency is the same as the controlling area currency.
- **Transaction currency**
  This currency is the currency used in documents posted in controlling. This currency can be different than the controlling area currency or the controlling object currency. The system converts this currency to other currencies using predetermined rates.

A controlling area plays a central role in overhead cost controlling. In Customizing, you can also manage the overhead controlling options within the controlling area, as shown in Figure 3.2. For instance, the following activities are possible:

- You can activate activity-based costing or commitment management.
- You can determine whether system orders are validated or are used as account assignment objects.

Usually, several controlling areas are assigned to an operating concern. Furthermore, the operating concern and the assigned controlling areas must have identical fiscal year variants.

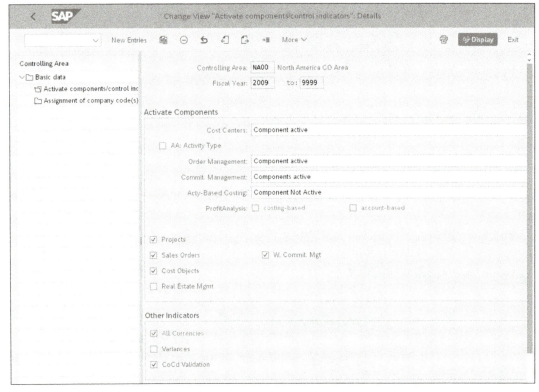

Figure 3.2 Overhead Cost Controlling Settings in Controlling Area

3.2.2 Master Data

The following master data creates a foundation for the transactions in controlling:

- Cost element
  - Primary cost or revenue element
  - Secondary cost element
- Cost center
- Activity type
- Statistical key figure
- Internal order
- Profit center
- Business process

In this section, we briefly describe the master data and explain their use cases in the real world. We'll cover master data in more detail in Section 3.3.

Note
We'll cover profit center master records and business process master records in Section 3.3.7 and Section 3.3.3, respectively.

Cost Element

In the real world, a *cost element* represents a type of cost that occurs in several cost centers or represents the expense of a resource consumed in various business activities. Business organizations systematically track the totals of certain types of costs (e.g., labor, material, utilities, supplies) resulting from their business operations. Thus, defining cost elements can help you understand what costs occur in your company's business operations.

In the system, cost elements are master data in cost element accounting and cost center accounting. Cost elements are also used in the general ledger accounting as they record the company's primary and secondary costs. Cost element master records (both primary and secondary) are created in the general ledger accounting application component or in Customizing; you do not need to create them separately in cost element accounting (or in the controlling module). Two types of cost and revenue elements exist:

- Primary cost or revenue elements
- Secondary cost elements

We'll define primary and secondary cost elements and explain their roles in Section 3.3.1.

Cost Center

In the real world, a *cost center* is an organizational unit within the controlling area representing an enclosed location (e.g., department or area of responsibility) where the costs occur. From a cost controlling standpoint, you can structure the organizational divisions (i.e., cost centers) according to several criteria, such as the following:

- Area of responsibility (e.g., management cost center)
- Spatial (e.g., cafeteria cost center)
- Functional requirements (e.g., technical services cost center)
- Activity related (e.g., production assembly cost center)
- Position or group related (e.g., chief executive officer [CEO] cost center)

In the system, a cost center is a master record in cost center accounting. A cost center is a cost bucket that collects various costs (e.g., supplies, utilities, maintenance hours) of a delimited location within the controlling area.

Activity Type

An *activity type* represents the productive output of cost centers, measured in time or unit increments, such as labor hours, machine hours, maintenance hours, or units produced. Activity types are necessary for the following activities:

- Cost calculation at the cost center providing the activity.
- Cost allocation between the cost center providing the activity and the receiver of the activity, which may be another cost center, project, order, or activity-based process.

Example
A maintenance cost center can serve as both an assembly and a machinery cost center. The cumulative costs of maintenance activities are calculated based on the planned price of activity and allocated to the receiver cost centers (via assessments) in proportion to their usage hours (debit to receiver's credit to provider cost center).

In the system, an activity type is master data in cost center accounting. The system uses activity types as a tracing factor in cost allocation.

Statistical Key Figures

A *statistical key figure* represents a basis for cost allocation in controlling postings such as distributions and assessments. In some cases, you may not be able to measure a cost center's accumulated cost in terms of activity type quantities. For instance, an administrative cost center can collect primary costs (e.g., supplies, salaries) during its operations. You may need to assess this accumulated cost to the individual cost centers receiving services from the administrative cost center. In this case, you can consider the number of employees as a criterion for cost allocation. The accumulated cost in the administrative cost center can then be distributed in proportion to the number of employees in the receiving cost centers. Another example of a statistical key figure is square footage, which can be a basis for allocating costs accumulated in a sanitation cost center.

In the system, statistical key figures are master data in cost center accounting. Statistical key figures are created in the controlling area and identified by four-digit numeric keys.

Internal Order

An *internal order* is a flexible management tool that you can use as an interim cost collector of time-restricted jobs or small projects in a controlling area. You can also use internal orders to monitor revenues from revenue-generating activities outside the scope of core business operations. Although you can use internal orders for simple maintenance/production of assets or revenue-generating activities, internal orders are not complicated planning tools like maintenance orders, production orders, sales orders, or projects in Project System. However, internal orders can collect costs or revenues during an accounting period (or event) and go through a periodic process called settlement when the job is completed.

In the system, an internal order is a master record in overhead cost controlling. Internal orders are created at the controlling area level. Four categories of internal orders exist:

- Overhead orders
- Investment orders
- Accrual orders
- Orders with revenue

3.2.3 Data Assignments

By assigning organizational data in controlling, you can map your management accounting-relevant organizational structure into the system. The following organizational data assignments are possible within controlling:

- You must assign each operating concern at least one controlling area.
- Several controlling areas can be assigned to an operating concern.

The following master data assignments are possible within controlling:

- Cost centers are created in the controlling area level and assigned to the standard hierarchy. In this standard hierarchy, supporting cost centers can be assigned to other cost centers.
- Activity types are created in the controlling area and assigned to cost centers in activity type planning.
- Internal orders are created in the controlling area and assigned to a responsible cost center.
- Statistical key figures are created in the controlling area.

3.3 Key Processes of Management Accounting

In this section, we'll explain the key processes of management accounting. The following key processes complement each other for efficient internal reporting and accurate cost allocations in management accounting:

- Cost (and revenue) element accounting
- Overhead cost controlling
  - Cost center accounting
  - Internal orders
  - Activity-based costing
- Profitability analysis and sales controlling
- Product cost controlling
- Profit center accounting

We'll discuss each key process in the following sections.

3.3.1 Cost Element Accounting

In your company, three types of costs and expenditures may exist:

- **Neutral expenditures**
  Neutral expenditures are nonoperational expenses reflected only in financial accounting but not in management accounting (e.g., gifts, donations). These costs are recorded in general ledger accounts as nonoperational expenses and income.

- **Operational expenditures or costs**
  Operational expenditures or costs are expenditures related to the core business operations of the company. These costs are reflected both in financial accounting and management accounting.

- **Imputed costs**
  These costs are reflected only in management accounting but not in financial accounting. Examples include opportunity costs (e.g., unrealized interest from money invested in your company); differences between legal depreciation and actual depreciation; and missing rent costs (you bought the building but would like to reflect missing rent costs in products).

Cost element accounting is concerned with recording and monitoring costs and revenues reflected in management accounting. Most of its values flow automatically from financial accounting.

Cost and revenue elements are master data in cost element accounting and cost center accounting. However, in general ledger accounting, these elements are expense and revenue accounts. You can create cost and revenue elements in general ledger accounting application components by maintaining data at the chart of accounts and company code segments. Unlike other general ledger accounts, when creating a cost element, you must also maintain settings in the controlling area under the **Control Data** view of the general ledger account master record, as shown in Figure 3.3. For instance, the cost element category determines how the cost element receives data, such as direct/indirect postings, settlements, and allocations. In Customizing, you can define account number ranges by configuring account groups for cost elements (e.g., profit and loss [P&L] or secondary cost).

Two types of cost elements exist:

- **Primary cost or revenue elements**
  These elements are general ledger accounts of type **Primary Cost or Revenue**. They record the company's expenses for core business operations, such as salaries, energy costs, material expenses, depreciation expenses, labor costs, consulting costs, and administration expenses. Primary cost or revenue elements are tightly integrated with general ledger accounting since they are income statement accounts. In other words, the total balances in these accounts (and nonoperating expense accounts) are reported in the company's income statement. Data flows to controlling as soon as primary cost or revenue elements are posted. These accounts can be posted directly (general ledger posting) by using a controlling object (e.g., a cost center).

Figure 3.3 Control Data for Costs Elements

- **Secondary cost elements**
  These elements are general ledger accounts of type **Secondary Costs**. They record the costs resulting from value flows within controlling, such as allocations (e.g., charging labor hours from a support cost center to an operational cost center) and management accounting adjustments. Internal activity allocation, overhead allocation, and order settlement are examples of secondary cost elements. These accounts are not posted directly but instead indirectly through the objects they are assigned to, such as activity types. Secondary cost elements receive data from internal activity allocations, assessments, and internal settlements. The balances in secondary cost elements are used only in controlling.

> **Note**
> The following postings are possible for primary cost elements:
> - Posting a primary cost element using a true controlling object
> - Posting a primary cost element using a true and statistical controlling object
>
> Secondary cost elements cannot be posted directly.

Figure 3.4 shows the connections between cost elements in management accounting, general ledger accounts, and financial statements in general ledger accounting.

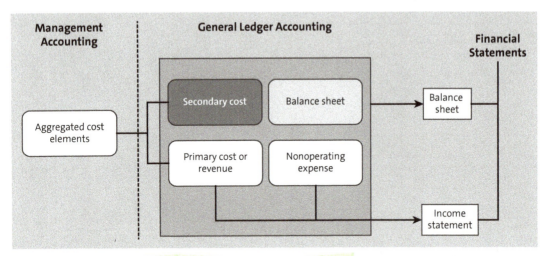

Figure 3.4 Cost Elements and General Ledger Accounting

3.3.2 Cost Center Accounting

Cost center accounting is part of overhead cost controlling. Overhead cost controlling is concerned with coordinating, monitoring, and optimizing a business organization's overhead costs. By structuring your business organization into cost centers, cost center accounting provides you with an overview of costs in delimited locations and areas of responsibility. Operational cost centers provide services in production and maintenance processes, and support cost centers provide services to assigned cost centers.

In this section, we'll walk you through the key processes of cost center accounting.

Working with Cost Centers

Cost centers are tightly integrated with all processes that incur costs. Cost centers may receive data in different ways, including the following:

- Direct postings
- Business processes
- Periodic postings
- Allocations
- Assessments and distributions
- Settlements

A prerequisite to creating a cost center master record is to define a standard hierarchy, a tree-like structure of all the cost centers in a controlling area. You can display or change a standard hierarchy by using Transaction OKENN in the controlling module, as shown in Figure 3.5. You can create a standard hierarchy of cost centers (or profit centers) at the controlling area level in Customizing.

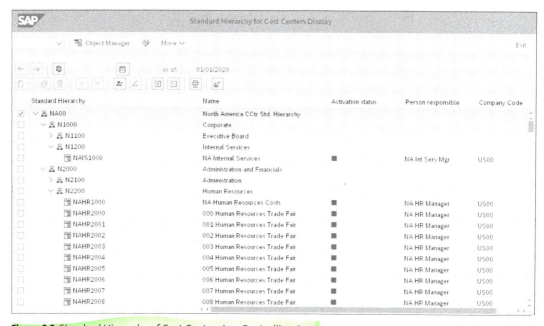

Figure 3.5 Standard Hierarchy of Cost Centers in a Controlling Area

In a standard hierarchy, you can create cost center groups according to specific criteria and assign cost centers to cost center groups. Cost center groups reflect the organizational structure from a cost standpoint and enable you to perform evaluations and allocations at the group level.

To create a cost center master record, you must choose a controlling area and a validity period. Then, you'll maintain data in several views, such as **Basic data**, **Control Data**, **Address**, and **Communication**, as shown in Figure 3.6. The **Control Data** view includes a record quantity indicator and lock indicator that locks the cost center against planning and posting activities. You must maintain the following mandatory data in the **Basic data** view of the cost center master record:

- Name
  Define the name for the cost center.
- Cost Center Category
  Choose one of the cost center categories defined in the system. Cost center categories are defined in Customizing. Some activity types are available only for specific cost center categories. Categories are also necessary for reporting and evaluations.

- **Hierarchy area**
  The classification of the cost center in the standard hierarchy.

- **Person Responsible**
  In this field, enter the name of the cost center manager.

- **Currency**
  In this field, specify the cost center currency. Note that the controlling area currency is the default value for this field.

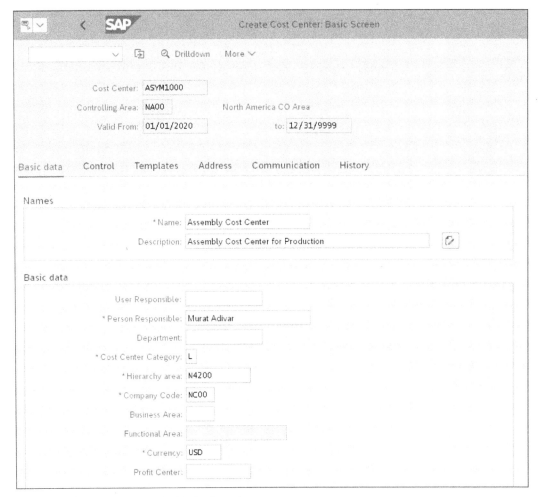

Figure 3.6 Cost Center Master Record

In cost center master data, a cost center can be assigned to the following objects:

- Company code
- Business area
- Profit center
- Functional area

The following system objects can also be assigned to a cost center in their master records:

- Asset
- Equipment and functional location
- Work center
- Work breakdown structure (WBS) element

> **Tip**
> The system will not display the company code field in the cost center master record if only one company code has been assigned to the controlling area. In this case, all cost centers within the controlling area are assigned to that unique company code. If several company codes exist in the controlling area, you must specify the company code assignment when maintaining the cost center master record.

Company code and profit center assignment links the cost center to financial accounting. Recall that segments in financial statements are derived from profit centers assigned to cost centers. Profit center assignment is optional. In Customizing, for cost center accounting, you must activate profit center accounting in the controlling area. The system will display a warning if you do not enter a profit center in the cost center master record.

The calculation of cost allocations between cost centers and other controlling objects is performed based on the following tracing factors:

- Activity types
- Statistical key figures

Working with Activity Types

An activity type is a master record in cost center accounting. To create an activity type master record, you must enter a controlling area and specify a validity period, as shown in Figure 3.7. Then, maintain data in the **Basic data**, **Indicators**, and **Output** views. You must maintain the following mandatory fields in the **Basic data** view of an activity type master record:

- **Activity Unit**
  This value is the quantity unit (e.g., hours, each, kilowatt-hours) the system should use when recording and posting consumed activity quantities.
- **CCtr Categories**   *Cost Center*
  By using this field, you can restrict the use of the activity type to certain cost center categories. If you choose *, the activity type will be unrestricted.
- **ATyp category**   *Activity Type*
  This indicator is necessary to determine the method of activity quantity calculation (manual or indirect) and activity allocation method (manual or indirect).

Furthermore, you can optionally maintain allocation default values using the following fields:

- **Allocation cost elem**
  In controlling postings, you must use cost elements. In particular, you must enter a secondary cost element for internal cost allocations. The system records the value of the activity type in a secondary cost element. In this field, you can define the default value for the secondary cost element that will be used in cost allocations for this activity type.

- **Price indicator**
  In this field, you can specify how the system calculates (e.g., manually or automatically) the activity type's price for a cost center.

Figure 3.7 Basic Data View in Activity Type Master Record

An activity type can be linked to a cost center or several cost centers using activity type planning (Transaction KP26). With this transaction, you can assign a planned price to a combination of cost center and activity type, which is how you assign an activity type to a cost center in the system. For instance, you can plan a maintenance cost center activity type for the price of maintenance hours, as shown in Figure 3.8. You can also assign several activity types (or no activity types) to a cost center. Activity type assignment is not a mandatory configuration in the system.

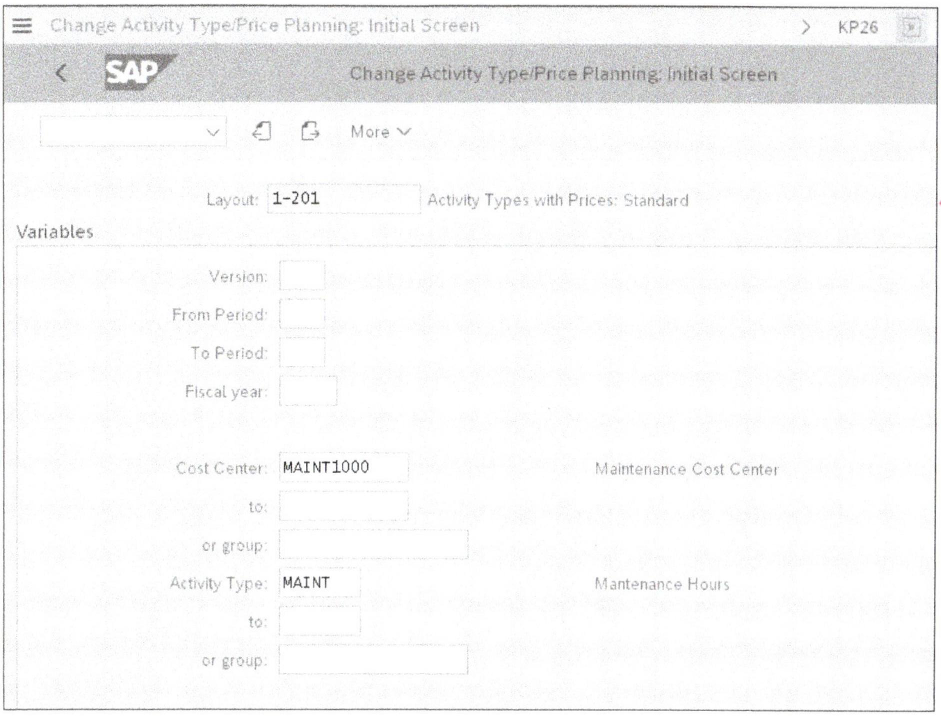

Figure 3.8 Activity Type Assignment to Cost Center via Activity Type Planning

Working with Statistical Key Figures

You must enter a controlling area to create a statistical key figure. To specify the validity period, you can use the key figure category indicator, with the following options:

- Total values: Valid only in the posting period in which the key figure is entered (**Tot. values**)
- Fixed values: Valid for all subsequent posting periods of the fiscal year (**Fxd val.**)

You must also determine the unit with which the statistical key figure is recorded in the system, as shown in Figure 3.9, where the **Stat. key fig. UnM** field value **EA** represents "each."

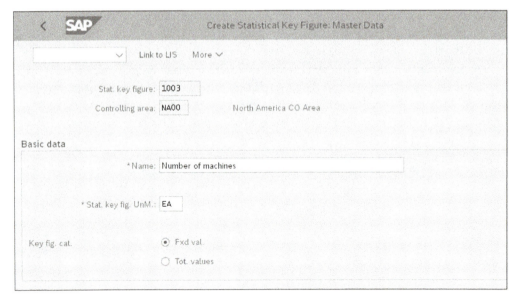

Figure 3.9 Statistical Key Figure Master Data Maintenance

You can use statistical key figures as a tracing factor in periodic cost and activity allocations, such as distributions and assessments.

Postings and Allocations with Controlling Objects

The controlling module provides true and statistical controlling objects to record and monitor a controlling area's costs and revenues. The system also supports postings and allocations between controlling objects.

Some true controlling objects to which you can make true postings include the following:

- Cost centers for account assignment of costs
- Projects (true projects, i.e., not marked as statistical)
- Networks
- Cost objects (manufacturing orders, sales order line items, projects, and WBS elements)
- Profitability segments
- Fixed assets
- Internal orders (true)
- Make-to-order (MTO) sales order (a sales order with cost collector)
- Business process (master data in activity-based costing)

Some statistical controlling objects to which you can make statistical postings include the following:

- Statistical projects (projects marked as statistical in the control view of the project definition)

- Statistical internal orders
- Profit centers
- Cost centers for account assignment of revenues

When you manually post primary costs from financial accounting to a cost element, you must enter a true controlling object (e.g., a cost center). Otherwise, the system will generate an error message, as shown in Figure 3.10. The cost element specifies what costs occur: Entering a true controlling object tells the system where the costs occurred. In this way, the controlling module reconciles with all relevant financial accounting elements. You can also post the same cost item to up to three statistical objects for informational purposes, which is called *statistical posting*. Statistical postings cannot be standalone; you must always enter a true controlling object for the cost item. You cannot assign the same item to more than one true controlling object.

Figure 3.10 General Ledger Posting to the Primary Cost Element

True controlling objects must be assigned to purchase order line items (via account assignment) if you buy a nonstock item or stock item for consumption. In this case, true controlling objects receive postings automatically during the goods receipt posting. True controlling objects can be settlement receivers, and they can send or receive allocations.

You can post true revenues to the following controlling objects:
- Profitability segments
- MTO sales orders
- Projects with revenues
- Order with revenues
- Real estate objects

In a true posting of revenues, you can also post revenues statistically to the statistical objects, such as profit centers and the cost centers for account assignment of revenues.

You can also manually transfer the recorded costs from one controlling object to another using internal controlling postings for adjustment purposes. In this case, you must enter sender and receiver controlling objects; the original cost element must be preserved. Figure 3.11 shows a manual primary cost reposting between cost centers. Other examples of manual adjustment postings or allocations are reposting revenues manually and reposting internal activity allocations.

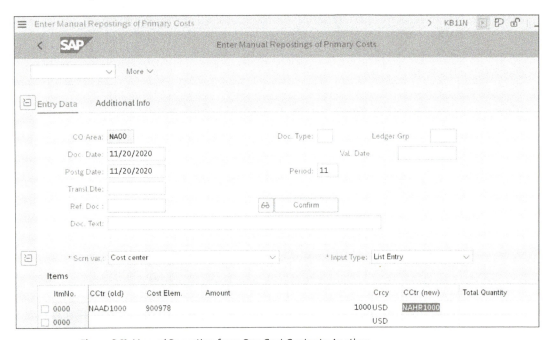

Figure 3.11 Manual Reposting from One Cost Center to Another

Period-End Closing

Period-end closing is the periodic cost allocation process companies carry out at period end. Period-end closing consists of several tasks you must perform in a certain sequence. Some examples of period-end closing tasks in controlling include the following:

- Periodic reposting of costs from allocation cost centers
- Distribution of primary costs
- Accrual cost calculations
- Indirect internal activity allocations
- Allocation of process costs
- Overhead calculations

- Settlement of overhead orders and projects
- Assessment of primary and secondary costs
- Template allocations

To prepare for the certification, we'll focus on cycle segment methods, which are periodic reposting, distribution, and assessment. To use these methods, you must create a cycle, which consists of a sequence of steps that define the following:

- Group of receivers
- Group of senders
- Group of costs (or quantities) to be allocated
- Tracing factor (e.g., statistical key figure)

Once you create the cycle, you can use the following methods for period-end closing:

- **Periodic reposting**
  This method posts only the primary cost elements between sender and receiver controlling objects (e.g., cost center, WBS element, order, cost object). In this method, the sender does not see the results of the allocation.

- **Distribution**
  This method periodically allocates primary cost elements from a sender cost center (or business process master record in activity-based costing) to the receiving controlling objects (e.g., cost center, WBS element, order, cost object, or business process master record). Primary cost elements keep their identities in both the sending and receiving controlling objects; thus, the sender can see the original cost element. The system documents the sender and receiver controlling objects in a unique controlling document.

- **Assessment**
  This method allocates both primary and secondary cost elements from a sender cost center (or business process master record in activity-based costing) to the receiving controlling objects (e.g., cost center, WBS element, order, cost object, real estate object, or business process master record). Primary and secondary cost elements are grouped and sent to receiver cost centers using a secondary cost element. The original costs and the allocation are visible to the sender, but only the summarized cost element is visible to the receiver. Therefore, you may prefer assessment if the cost drill down for the receiver is not essential. The system documents the sender and receiver controlling objects in a unique controlling document.

Figure 3.12 shows the distribution and assessment of costs based on the statistical key figures, i.e., the square footage and the number of employees in the receiver cost centers.

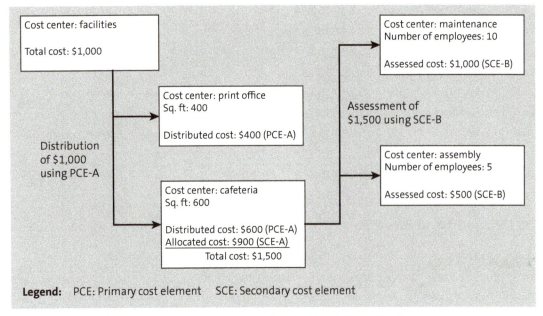

Figure 3.12 Distribution and Assessment of Costs Using Statistical Key Figures

3.3.3 Activity-Based Costing

Our next topic, activity-based costing, is another part of overhead cost controlling. Cost center accounting provides a location-based view of overhead costs. However, activity-based costing is concerned with providing a process-oriented, cross-functional perspective of overhead costs. By assigning the cost sources to their originating business process, activity-based costing provides an enhanced product costing view.

Activity-based costing provides a tree structure representing the standard hierarchy of business processes and business processes assigned to this hierarchy. A business process master record in activity-based costing represents and describes the cross-functional structure in your organization. Business process master records in activity-based costing can receive overhead costs via manual postings in controlling. They can be senders and receivers of overhead in period-end closing postings, such as template allocations, periodic repostings, distributions, and assessments. To create and use a business process master record, you must activate activity-based costing in Customizing and create a business process standard hierarchy in the controlling area. A business process must be assigned a company code and currency. Depending on its use case, a business process can be assigned to a business area, profit center, plant, sales area, and cost center in its master record, as shown in Figure 3.13.

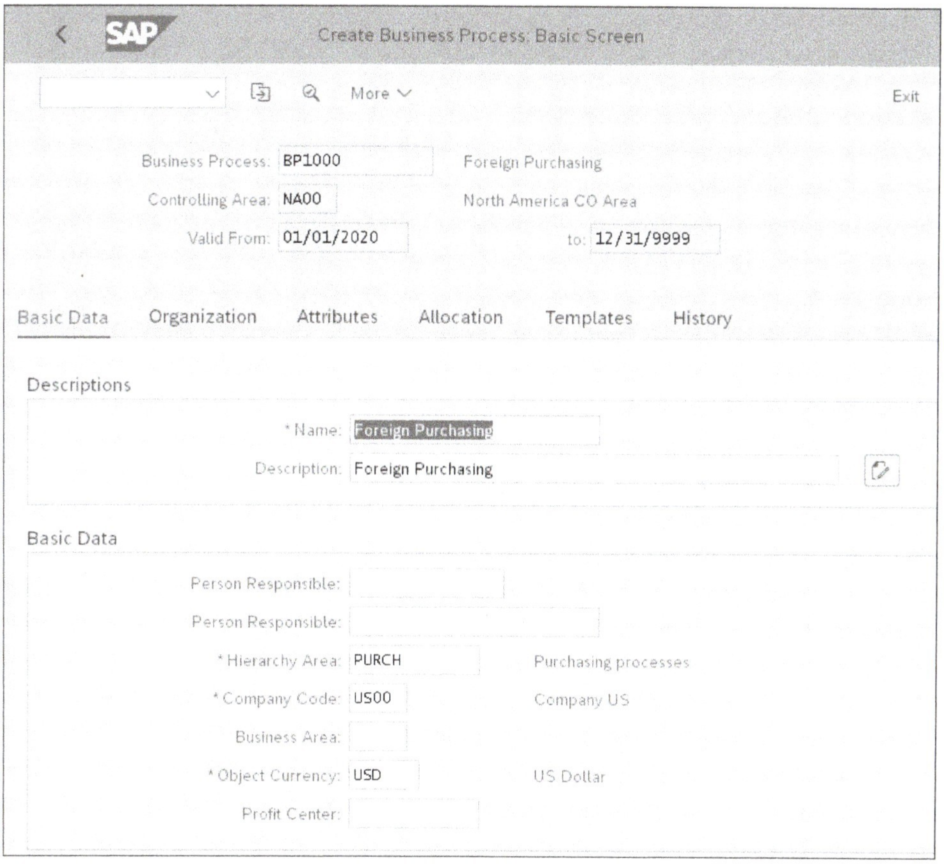

Figure 3.13 Business Process Master Record in Activity-Based Costing

3.3.4 Internal Orders

Internal orders are the next (and final) part of overhead cost controlling. You can use internal orders to plan, collect, and settle the collected costs of small jobs and tasks in the controlling area.

In terms of their usage and settlement, internal orders can be categorized in the following ways:

- **Overhead orders**
  You can use overhead orders to track the overhead costs of time-restricted jobs. These orders can be settled to other cost objects, such as profitability segments, cost centers, projects, or orders.
- **Investment orders**
  You can use investment orders to track the costs of simple jobs relevant to fixed assets (e.g., repair of pieces of equipment, the building of a storage room in a warehouse). These orders can be settled to assets, projects, cost centers, or general ledger accounts.

- **Accrual orders**
  You can use these orders to offset postings of costs calculated in controlling to cost centers. These orders can be settled to profitability segments and cost centers.

- **Orders with revenue**
  These orders can be used to monitor costs and revenues arising from activities with external partners or internal activities not belonging to core business operations. The costs collected in these orders can be settled to any receiver, and revenues can be transferred to general ledger accounts, sales orders, billing elements in a project, or other internal orders with revenue.

We'll take a closer look at managing internal orders and the settlement process in the following sections.

Working with Internal Orders

An internal order is a master record in overhead cost controlling. You must activate order management in Customizing to use internal orders in controlling (refer to the order management settings shown earlier in Figure 3.2).

You can use the order manager (Transaction KO04) to manage the internal orders. To create an internal order, you must first set a controlling area and choose an appropriate option in the **Order Type** field, as shown in Figure 3.14.

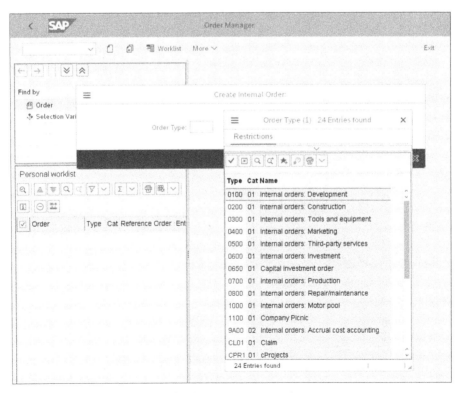

Figure 3.14 Order Manager: Internal Order Master Data Creation

The order type includes critical control functions that determine how the order is processed and the default values of the master data fields. When you choose an order type, these control functions are transferred to the internal order. Some examples of control functions included in an order type include the following:

- Number range interval: Controls an order's valid number range
- Settlement profile: Controls an order's settlement routine
- Commitment management: Enables commitment management for an order
- Revenue postings: Determines whether an order can collect revenues
- Release immediately: Controls whether an order is released upon saving

You can define order types and assign them to order categories in Customizing.

Depending on the order type, you can maintain data in several views (tabs), such as **Assignments**, **Control data**, **Prd-end closing**, and **General data**. In the **Assignments** view, you can make organizational assignments, such as company code and business area. You can set the responsible cost center carrying out the order and define the origin that requests the internal order (e.g., requesting company code, requesting order, and requesting cost center). An internal order can collect costs for a sales order. In this case, you must enter the sales order number in the **Assignments** view. In the **Control data** view, as shown in Figure 3.15, you can define the order currency (can be different from the controlling area currency), mark the order as a statistical order, and see if commitment management is active for the internal order.

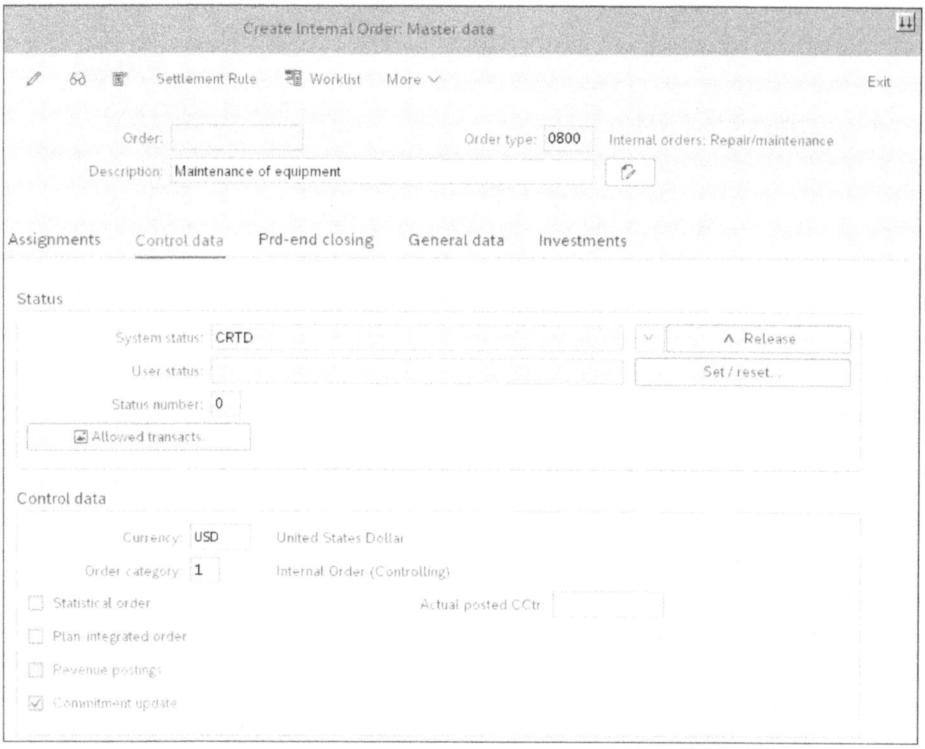

Figure 3.15 Control Data View in Internal Order Master Record

In the **Prd-end closing** view, you can define the parameters necessary for period-end closing and specify a receiver if you would like to fully settle the order to only one receiver (without specifying several receivers in the settlement rule). The **General data** view includes information about the person responsible and communication data (e.g., phone number, department).

Statistical orders can include costs only for information purposes, not for allocation. You cannot apply overhead to a statistical order or settle it. If the order is a real (not statistical) internal order, it can receive costs via postings, periodic allocations, or settlements of other orders or projects (debiting the order). In postings from financial accounting, controlling, or materials management, you can post simultaneously to a statistical order. You cannot post to statistical order only, as shown in Figure 3.16.

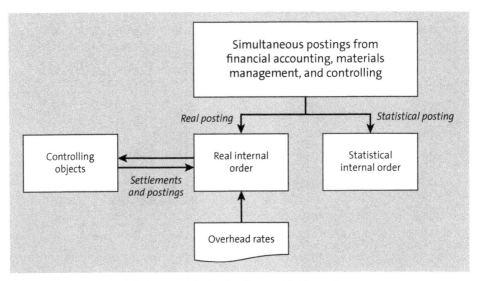

Figure 3.16 Real and Statistical Internal Orders: Postings and Settlements

Settlement

A *settlement* is the distribution of costs collected on an internal order. In the settlement process, the system transfers collected costs to one or more cost receivers by crediting the internal order and debiting the receivers. For instance, when you settle an investment order to an asset (say a piece of equipment), the internal order's actual costs are passed to the asset master record (subledger account). This step credits the order. Successful completion of the settlement results in a zero balance in the order. A prerequisite for settlement is to define a settlement rule in every sender. The order type determines the potential settlement receivers of the internal order. In general, internal orders can be settled to the following objects:

- Cost objects, including cost centers, orders, projects, profitability segments, and assets
- General ledger accounts
- Sales orders with cost collectors

By clicking the **Settlement Rule** button (shown earlier in Figure 3.15), you can define distribution rules for the settlement process. Each distribution rule determines the following, as shown in Figure 3.17:

- Account assignment category (classifying the settlement receivers)
- A settlement receiver
- The portion of the actual costs that should be settled to the receiver

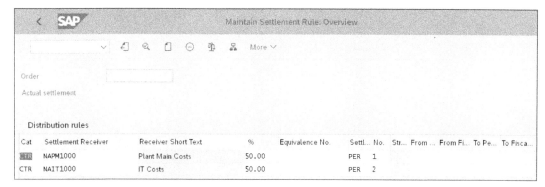

Figure 3.17 Settlement Rule for an Overhead Order

> **Note**
> An order type plays a critical role in determining settlement receivers. The settlement receivers that you can enter in a settlement rule are limited to the possible settlement receivers as defined by the order type. You can set up the system, in Customizing, to generate settlement rules automatically (via strategy sequence assignments).

3.3.5 Profitability Analysis and Sales Controlling

Profitability analysis is concerned with analyzing a company's external market segments in terms of revenue, sales, discounts, returns, and cost of goods sold (COGS). An operating concern is the valuation level for profitability analysis, and it structures the enterprise's external market segments. Profitability analysis extracts data from other application components to enable comprehensive analysis of individual market segments.

In this section, we'll walk through key processes for profitability analysis and sales controlling.

Working with Operating Concerns

Profitability analysis receives data from sales orders, cost centers, assessments, settlements, projects, and costs and revenues from direct postings (e.g., general ledger postings). During these data transfers, the system derives the operating concern from the controlling area. To ensure this integration, you must assign each operating concern at least one controlling area in Customizing, as shown in Figure 3.18.

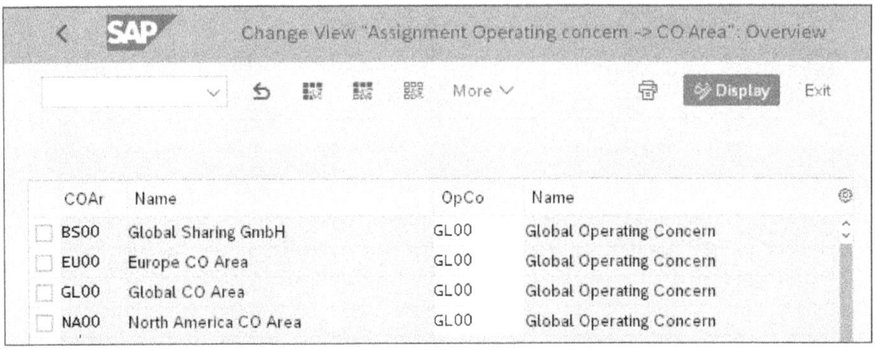
Change View "Assignment Operating concern -> CO Area": Overview
More
Display
Exit
COAr
Name
OpCo
Name
BS00
Global Sharing GmbH
GL00
Global Operating Concern
EU00
Europe CO Area
GL00
Global Operating Concern
GL00
Global CO Area
GL00
Global Operating Concern
NA00
North America CO Area
GL00
Global Operating Concern

Figure 3.18 Assigning Controlling Areas to Operating Concern in Customizing

To set up an operating concern for profitability analysis, you must include the following information:

- The operating concern's data structure, including the following:
  - Characteristics: Specify at which level you want to analyze the operating concern (e.g., sales organization, division, region, product, or customer).
  - Value fields: Specify which values or key figures you want to analyze in the operating concern (e.g., gross sales, surcharges, discounts, and cost of sales). Value fields are necessary only for costing-based profitability analysis.
- The operating concern's currency and fiscal year variant.

Characteristics and value fields are reporting elements in profitability analysis. The system supports reporting P&L statements by characteristics, including by customer, distribution channel, plant, and sales organization.

Profitability Segment

A profitability segment represents an external market segment of a company. A profitability segment is a combination of values of characteristics (i.e., a multidimensional segment for analyzing the profit). A profit center is always one of the characteristics (i.e., dimensions). A profitability segment does not have its own master data; it is created automatically in the system when it is addressed in transactions such as settlements or profitability analysis reports. A profitability segment is a true controlling object. You can transfer costs to profitability segments from cost centers, orders, and projects. Profitability segments can also be the receivers of costs and revenues in direct postings (e.g., general ledger account postings in financial accounting) or settlements or orders received in materials management. Using settlements or periodic overhead allocations, you can transfer overhead costs from other areas of management accounting (e.g., internal orders, cost centers, business processes) to profitability segments.

In general, profitability analysis receives costs and activity allocations through the following transactions from controlling:

- Direct and indirect activity allocations
- Order or project settlements
- Assessments
- Template allocations

Profitability Analysis Methods

Sales and distribution is an important data source for profitability analysis. In terms of their reporting structure and data collection points, two types of profitability analysis methods are available:

- **Account-based profitability analysis**
  With this method, you can create profitability analysis reports at the general ledger account (cost and revenue elements) level and slice and dice data by characteristics, such as by product, customer, and region. Account-based profitability analysis collects data from sales and distribution when a goods issue is posted and when an invoice is generated for the goods issue.

- **Costing-based profitability analysis**
  With this method, you can create profitability analysis reports at the value fields level. Costing-based profitability analysis collects data from sales and distribution when a sales order is created and when an invoice is generated for the order.

Table 3.1 shows a comparison between account-based reporting and costing-based reporting.

Account-Based		Costing-Based	
Cost Element		Value Field	
Revenues	600,000	Revenues	600,000
Sales deductions	100,000	Sales deductions	100,000
Net Revenues	**500,000**	**Net Revenues**	**500,000**
Cost of sales	190,000	Variable material costs	100,000
Price differences	10,000	Variable production costs	40,000
R&D	20,000	Production variances	350,000
Marketing	20,000	**Cont. Margin 1**	**350,000**

Table 3.1 Account-Based Profitability Analysis versus Costing-Based Profitability Analysis

Account-Based		Costing-Based	
Sales costs	20,000	Material overhead	15,000
		Production overhead	35,000
Result	240,000	Cont. Margin 2	300,000
		R&D	20,000
		Marketing costs	20,000
		Sales costs	20,000
		Cont. Margin 3	240,000

Table 3.1 Account-Based Profitability Analysis versus Costing-Based Profitability Analysis (Cont.)

You can use the new margin analysis functionality to ensure that cost and revenue information is always current and wholly reconciled with the income statement. Note that, in the new product, account-based profitability creates a technical basis for margin analysis. Account-based profitability analysis must be activated to enable margin analysis functionality.

In Customizing, you can define the company's operating concerns and specify which type of profitability analysis (account-based/costing-based) should be used, as shown in Figure 3.19.

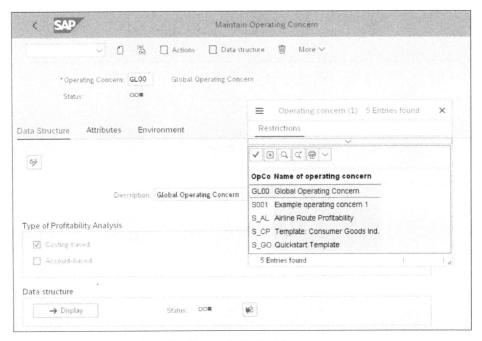

Figure 3.19 Maintaining an Operating Concern in Customizing

You can choose the type of profitability analysis and display the data structure in the **Data Structure** view. You can maintain the operating concern currency and fiscal year variant in the **Attributes** view.

3.3.6 Product Cost Accounting

Product cost accounting is concerned with the following activities:

- Planning the cost of products or services
- Collecting and tracking the actual cost of production orders
- Providing the actual costs of products or services

Product cost accounting is structured into three subareas to support these requirements, which we'll discuss in the following sections: product cost planning, cost object controlling, and actual costing with the Material Ledger.

Product Cost Planning

Product cost planning is concerned with creating a standard cost estimate for products/services and for price updates.

Creating a standard cost estimate for products and services requires data. Product cost planning uses the following data structures for this purpose:

- **Quantity structure**
  This structure includes the bill of materials (BOM) and routing. When you use this structure, you should specify the material, plant, lot size, and costing variant.
- **Value structure**
  A quantity structure may not be available for some products or services (e.g., consulting). In this case, you can use a value structure involving the following data: material prices, activity prices, process prices, and overhead costs.

You can display and save cost estimate results by cost component splits (e.g., material, labor, overhead, and process) or by the itemization of cost elements or cost components.

Cost estimate results (in a standard cost estimate) can serve as a basis for price updates and as an important source of information for the following use cases in other application components:

- **Cost object controlling**
  Calculation of material usage costs, valuation of inward stocks, calculation of work in process (WIP) at actual costs in product cost by period, variance calculation including scrap variances, and results analysis.
- **Materials management**
  Calculation of material and stock valuations.
- **Sales and distribution**
  Determination of sales pricing.
- **Profitability analysis**
  Determination of contribution margins.

Note
The sales price is not the same as the standard price of a material. The sales price is stored in the **Sales: Sales Org 1** view of the material master record, whereas the standard price is stored in the **Accounting 1** view of the material master record.

A price update is the process of marking and releasing a standard cost estimate to update the standard price of materials or services in their master records. Updating the standard price results in an inventory revaluation in the system. Companies typically create standard cost estimates and update the standard prices of materials at the beginning of the fiscal year or of a new season. The updated standard prices remain unchanged during the year or season.

Note
To mark and release a standard cost estimate, you must ensure that your standard cost estimate does not include any errors and that the system allows the marking and releasing of the standard cost estimate in the company code.

Three types of standard prices exist in material master records: the previous price, the current price, and the future price. Marking and releasing standard cost estimates lead to updates in these standard prices. In particular, when you mark a standard cost estimate, the estimated price becomes the material's future (standard) price. The future price turns into the current (standard) price when you release the standard cost estimate. If you release a new cost estimate, the current standard price becomes the previous standard price.

Figure 3.20 shows the process of creating a standard cost estimate and updating prices in product cost planning.

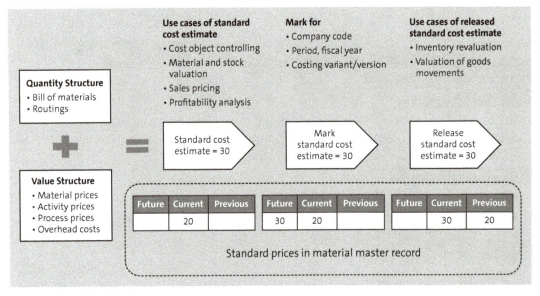

Figure 3.20 Product Cost Planning

Price control is a critical indicator in the material master record and is controlled through the **Prc. Ctrl** field, shown in Figure 3.21. If you choose **S**, the system uses the standard price in the following calculations:

- Inventory valuations
- Valuations of goods movements

If you choose **V**, the system uses the moving average price, which changes in response to goods movement and invoice entries.

The standard price is kept constant in the system and thus does not reflect the actual costs incurred. If the actual costing component is active, the **S** price is not an option for the current posting period's valuation price. You can combine the advantages of price control with the **S** price and the **V** price using a periodic unit price.

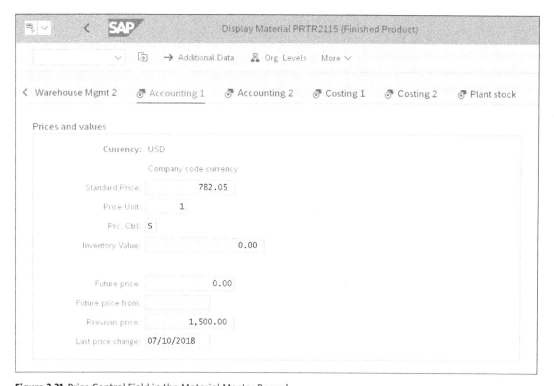

Figure 3.21 Price Control Field in the Material Master Record

Cost Object Controlling

Cost object controlling is concerned with preliminary, simultaneous, and final costing of objects such as production orders or sales orders for an MTO manufacturing strategy. Cost object controlling enables a manufacturing enterprise to perform the following activities:

- Calculate planned costs (budgeted costs)
- Record/collect actual costs for the cost objects

- Compare actual costs with both target and planned costs and analyze variances
- Calculate WIP values
- Settle variances to other components such as profitability analysis and financial accounting

Actual Costing and Material Ledger

This product cost accounting component is concerned with providing the actual costs of materials and services at the end of the production cycle. The system uses the standard price of materials to evaluate the consumption and movements of materials. Variances are calculated and used to determine the material's actual price during the invoice entry and settlements.

In SAP S/4HANA, the Material Ledger and actual costing are two separate application components. The new actual costing is a standalone component and is not technically linked to the Material Ledger. Actual costing periodically calculates an actual price (periodic unit price) for each material (and valuation type, if applicable) that includes all actual costs for the period in question. The Material Ledger, meanwhile, is a mandatory approach in SAP S/4HANA. This subledger for inventory is fully integrated into the general ledger. The Material Ledger enables the evaluation of inventories using the standard price and moving average price methods. With the new Material Ledger, you can flexibly manage your inventories in multiple currencies and multiple valuations in parallel.

3.3.7 Profit Center Accounting

Profit center accounting is concerned with the analysis of internal P&L for the profit centers. A profit center is master data in profit center accounting. You can assign a profit center to each object for which you want to analyze P&L. You can analyze selected balance sheets or income statement items by profit center. Profit centers can be structured according to the various criteria, such as the following:

- Region (branch offices, plants)
- Function (production, sales)
- Product (product ranges, divisions)

Profit centers are created in the controlling area. Like cost centers, profit centers must belong to a standard hierarchy of profit centers created in the controlling area. You must define a standard hierarchy of profit centers to create a profit center master record in the system. A profit center is assigned to a segment and company code in its master record, as shown in Figure 3.22.

Master data assignments integrate profit centers with other components of the system. Through the profit center assignments, the values in different system components flow into profit center accounting. The system sends data to profit centers in real time when an original object is posted.

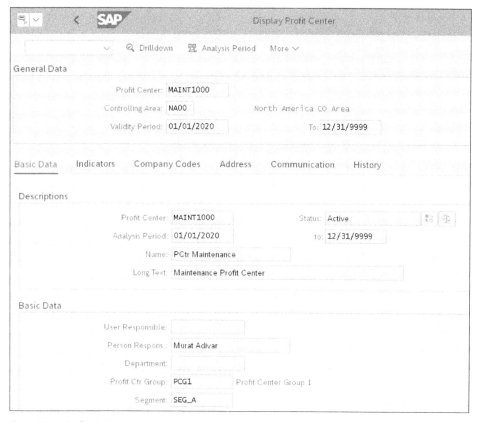

Figure 3.22 Profit Center Master Record

The following objects can be assigned a profit center in their master records:

- Cost centers
- Fixed assets (directly or through the cost center in the asset master record)
- Internal orders
- Materials

The following objects can be assigned a profit center, as shown in Figure 3.23:

- Sales orders (each sales order line item is assigned to a separate profit center)
- Projects (project definition or other project elements can be assigned to a profit center)
- Networks
- Network activities
- WBS elements
- Production orders (can be derived from the material master record or entered manually)
- Maintenance orders (cost and credits collected on the order sent to profit center)

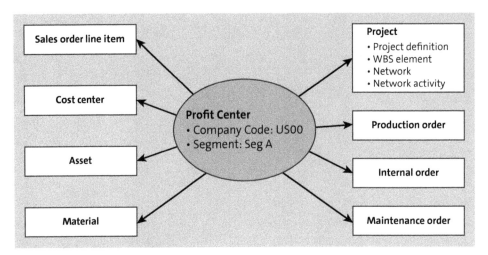

Figure 3.23 Profit Center Assignments

There is no profitability segment master record. A profitability segment is created as a combination of several characteristics when it is addressed in postings, allocations, settlements, or profitability analysis reports. For instance, Figure 3.24 displays the creation of a profitability analysis report in which you need to choose characteristics and key figures (Transaction KE91). One of those characteristics is always a profit center.

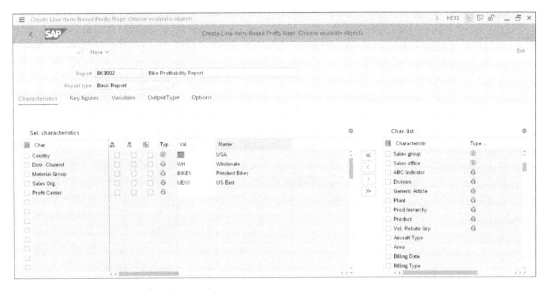

Figure 3.24 Profitability Analysis Report

When you post to a cost or revenue element in financial accounting, you must enter a true controlling object, such as a WBS element, internal order, or cost center. In this case, the profit center assigned to these objects receives data automatically. You can also use the profit center as a statistical object in postings.

Without entering a controlling object, you can also use a profit center in all postings in financial accounting.

Postings and allocations within management accounting also send data to profit centers through the cost objects assigned to the profit center. Another way that profit centers can receive data is by distributing or assessing balance sheet items between profit centers.

3.4 Integration with Other Modules

In this section, we explain the touchpoints of integration between controlling and other system modules. We can organize the cross-module integrations into two categories:

- Integrations via cross-module data assignments
- Integrations via transactions

3.4.1 Integration via Cross-Module Data Assignments

Cross-module data assignments in the system connect the business processes in SAP S/4HANA and lead to data flows between the system's components. Some examples of cross-module data assignments include the following:

- **Financial accounting**
  Some potential integrations between financial accounting and controlling via data assignment include the following:
  - An asset is a master record in financial accounting. You can assign cost centers or investment orders to fixed assets in the asset master record.
  - A profit center is a master record in profit center accounting and in general ledger accounting. You can assign a profit center to an asset in the asset master record (sometimes indirectly using the cost center stored in the asset master record). Cost centers can be assigned to company codes and profit centers in their master records. Segments in document splitting and financial statements are derived from profit centers.
  - A controlling area is organizational data in controlling. To achieve cross-company code cost accounting, you must assign company codes to the controlling area. A prerequisite for this organizational data assignment is that all company codes assigned to a controlling area must be assigned the same operative chart of accounts and same fiscal year variant.
  - A general ledger account is a master record in financial accounting. An internal order is master data in controlling. You can assign a general ledger account as a settlement receiver to an internal order. Internal orders can also be assigned business areas in the internal order master record.

- Primary cost and revenue elements are master data in controlling. They are created in general ledger accounting as P&L accounts and assigned to company codes.
- Company codes and business areas are organizational data in financial accounting. Cost centers, profit centers, business process master records, and internal orders can be assigned to company codes and business areas in their master records.
- In the system, controlling and financial accounting use the same line items of the data table ACDOCA, as shown in Figure 3.25. This data table, also called the Universal Journal, provides a simple but holistic data model and creates a single source of truth for all accounting applications, thus creating seamless integration and reconciliation between financial accounting and controlling.

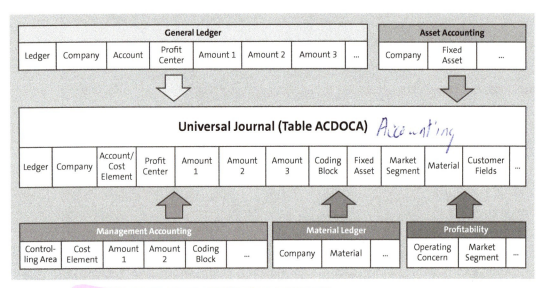

Figure 3.25 Universal Journal (Table ACDOCA)

- **Logistics**

  Controlling master data can be assigned to several organizational and master data in the following ways:

  - **Key logistics processes**

    A material is a master record in all key logistics processes including purchasing, sales and distribution, and production. You can assign a profit center to a material in the **Costing 1** view of the material master record.

  - **Production**

    A work center is master data in production. An activity type is assigned to a cost center in activity planning, and that cost center can be assigned a work center in its master record. You can see the cost enter and activity types in the costing view of a work center master record.

- Logistics processes
  A plant is an organizational data in all logistics processes except for Project System. An internal order is a master record in controlling. You can assign the internal order to a plant in its master record.
- Project System
  An internal order can be assigned to the WBS elements of projects. Profit centers can be assigned to several project elements, such as project definitions, WBS elements, networks, and network activities.
- Plant maintenance
  Equipment and functional location are master records in plant maintenance. You can assign a cost center to them in their master records.
- Human experience management (HXM)
  Cost centers can be assigned to positions, persons, and organizational units in the organizational structure of human resources (HR).

3.4.2 Integration via Transactions

The controlling module tightly integrates with other system modules via transactions involving controlling objects. The following transactions can lead to updates in the controlling module:

- Transactions in management accounting
  The following transactions are touchpoints of integration between controlling and other system components:
  - Manual actual postings
    Customer orders, network activities, WBS elements, and fixed assets can be receivers of manual actual postings in controlling, such as direct activity allocations, cost or revenue repostings, or manual cost allocations, thus integrating controlling with the relevant system components.
  - Assessments and distributions
    Both assessments and distributions (in controlling) result in allocations of costs booked to primary cost elements linked to general ledger accounting, thus integrating controlling with financial accounting. Real estate objects and WBS elements can be receivers of assessments.
  - Internal order settlements
    An internal order is a part of controlling; it serves as an interim cost collector during its lifecycle and settles to different objects, including general ledger accounts, assets, projects, and sales orders with the cost object, thus integrating controlling with other system components.
- Transactions in financial accounting
  All cost and revenue postings to financial accounting flow into cost element accounting. Also, transactions in financial accounting are tightly integrated

with controlling. Some examples of financial accounting transactions include the following:

- **Depreciation posting run**
  A depreciation posting run can post cost centers and cost elements assigned to the asset, thus integrating asset accounting with controlling.

- **Asset acquisitions**
  You can produce assets internally by using internal orders, thus integrating asset accounting with controlling.

- **Financial accounting postings**
  When you post to a cost or revenue element in financial accounting, you must enter a true controlling object, such as a WBS element, internal order, or cost center. In this case, the profit center assigned to these objects receives data automatically. You can also use the profit center as the statistical object.

- **Transactions in purchase-to-pay**
  Controlling objects can be used for account assignments in purchase orders. When you post a goods receipt for these orders, the system generates an accounting document to record the postings to controlling objects, such as cost centers. Some transactions in purchase-to-pay with a controlling impact include the following:

  - **Goods receipt**
    If you buy a stock item for stock, the goods receipt posting does not create a controlling document. Suppose you buy a stock item for consumption (or a nonstock item or a nonvaluated item). In that case, you need to select an account assignment category and maintain account assignment data (general ledger account and controlling object) in the purchase order line item. The goods receipt posting for this order creates an accounting document and a controlling document to record updates in the consumption accounts and the controlling objects, such as cost centers.

  - **Invoice verification**
    If the total invoice amount is different than the total invoice line item amount, the system creates a controlling document that includes updates to the previously defined cost center/object for procurement costs.

- **Transactions in plan-to-produce**
  A production order is a true controlling object and collects and transfers costs (debits and credits) during its lifecycle. The system records these debits and credits by creating a controlling document, thus integrating controlling with production. Some production transactions that impact controlling include the following:

  - **Goods receipt in production**
    In production, you post a goods receipt to deliver the finished good into inventory. In this case, the system creates a controlling document (recording

the credit posted to the production order) and an accounting document (recording the debit posted to the material's stock account).

- **Goods issue posting in production**
  In production, the goods issue is posted for material withdrawal. In this case, a controlling document is created to record actual costs posted to the production order.

- **Confirmation in production**
  Confirming a production order (for exact times and quantities) creates a further debit on the production order. In this case, a controlling document is created to record this debit in the order, thus integrating production with controlling.

- **Settlement in production**
  If a WIP balance exists on a production order, settlement leads to postings to controlling. The settlement also credits the order for the variance and posts the variances to profitability analysis. The credit is recorded in a controlling document.

- **Transactions in sales and distribution**
  Profitability analysis, part of controlling, receives data from sales orders, goods issues, and invoice postings. When you post a goods issue, the system generates a controlling document to update controlling objects (e.g., cost element, cost center) based on the cost of selling the material, thus integrating controlling with sales and distribution.

- **Transactions in plant maintenance**
  The following transactions in maintenance can create an integration between maintenance and controlling:

  - **Material processing**
    If you're using a nonstock item in maintenance, you'll need to purchase it. The system generates a purchase requisition to start the standard process with the maintenance order as an account assignment object. The system generates controlling documents during goods receipt by posting an invoice entry to update the data in the order and the cost center assigned to the equipment.

  - **Completion confirmation**
    A completion confirmation triggers an internal activity allocation between the cost centers assigned to work centers and the plant maintenance order, debiting the order with the costs, thus integrating plant maintenance with controlling.

  - **Settlement**
    Settlement credits the order for the actual costs and transfer debits to the cost elements, asset master records, and cost centers assigned to them, thus integrating plant maintenance with controlling.

- **Transactions in Project System**
  The following transactions in project management can create an integration between Project System and controlling:
  - **Confirmations**
    You can confirm actual activity times and reasons for time variances by using the cross-application time sheet (CATS) (Transaction CAT2), which can trigger an internal activity allocation activity in controlling.
  - **Material processing**
    Purchasing of nonstock materials assigned to project network activities creates an integration between controlling and Project System.
  - **Settlement**
    In settlement of a project, costs and revenues are transferred to fixed assets, orders, cost centers, or profitability segments.

3.5 Important Terminology

In this chapter, the following terminology related to controlling is important to know for the exam:

- **Activity allocation**
  Transfer of activity type quantities from a cost center to other controlling objects by using either a direct or an indirect activity allocation.
- **Activity-based costing**
  This key process in management accounting provides a process-oriented, cross-functional perspective of overhead costs.
- **Activity price**
  The price of an activity planned for a cost center. This rate is used to calculate the costs transferred in activity allocations.
- **Activity type**
  This master data in cost center accounting represents labor or services provided by a cost center to other objects.
- **Assessment**
  This controlling transaction is used to allocate primary and secondary costs from a sender cost center to receiver controlling objects (e.g., cost center, WBS element, order, cost object, real estate object, or business process master record) using a secondary assessment cost element.
- **Business process (master record)**
  A master record in activity-based costing.
- **Characteristic**
  This reporting element in profitability analysis defines the level at which you would like to analyze the operating concern.

- **Controlling area**
  A controlling area is organizational data that represents a subdivision of an enterprise from a cost accounting perspective. This self-contained organizational structure is where costs and revenues are managed and allocated.

- **Controlling object**
  An object to which you post quantities and values in controlling. Controlling objects are necessary for all controlling postings. There are true and statistical controlling objects.

- **Cost and revenue element accounting**
  This key process in management accounting provides a view of costs and revenues by cost and revenue elements; general ledger accounts provide details for reconciling financial accounting and controlling.

- **Cost center**
  A cost center is master data in cost center accounting that represents a delimited location or area of responsibility where costs are incurred.

- **Cost center accounting**
  This key process in management accounting provides a view of overhead costs and revenues by cost centers representing locations, responsibility areas, and allocation areas.

- **Cost center category**
  This attribute defines how a cost center is used.

- **Cost element category**
  This category classifies cost elements in terms of their usage and origin.

- **Cost object**
  These controlling objects collect the results of costs or revenue from value-add processes. Examples include manufacturing orders, sales order line items, projects, and WBS elements. Cost centers and internal orders are not cost objects.

- **Direct activity allocation**
  This process manually allocates activity quantities from a cost center to other cost objects.

- **Distribution**
  This controlling transaction is used to allocate primary costs from cost centers to particular controlling objects (e.g., cost center, WBS element, order, cost object, or business process). The original cost element is retained in the receiver cost center.

- **Internal order**
  An internal order is master data in overhead cost controlling and an interim cost collector for short-period projects or events. Internal orders are settled at the end of the period of their lifecycle.

- **Operating concern**
  This organizational data in controlling and valuation level in profitability analysis represents a view of the external market structure in sales. An operating concern has its own fiscal year variant and currency. Controlling areas are assigned to operating concerns.

- **Order type**
  The order type includes critical control functions that determine number ranges, settlement profile, commitment management, and the default values of master data fields.

- **Periodic reposting**
  This allocation method in controlling is based on defined rules to allocate primary costs from a sender to other receivers. In this method, you don't need to use a cost center for the sender.

- **Primary cost and revenue element**
  This element is a P&L account reported in the income statement. The primary cost and revenue element is a master record in cost element accounting.

- **Product cost controlling**
  This key process in management accounting is concerned with the planning and valuation of products and services as well as the ability to monitor production costs. Product cost controlling consists of product cost planning, product cost controlling, and the Material Ledger/actual costing.

- **Profitability analysis**
  This key process of management accounting is concerned with analyzing a company's external market segments in terms of revenue, sales, discounts, returns, and cost of goods sold (COGS).

- **Profitability segment**
  A combination of characteristics in profitability analysis. A profitability segment is not a master record and is only created in the system when it is addressed.

- **Profit center**
  This master data in general ledger accounting and profit center accounting is used to analyze the P&L of an internal operational unit.

- **Profit center accounting**
  Profit center accounting is concerned with the analysis of internal P&L for profit centers representing regions, functions, or products of the company.

- **Repost**
  This posting method in controlling is used to correct primary costs from the original receiving object under the original cost element.

- **Secondary cost element**
  These general ledger accounts (of type **Secondary Costs**) are used within controlling for internal allocations. These accounts are not posted to directly; they receive data from internal activity allocations, assessments, and internal settlements.
- **Settlement**
  A period-end process that transfers all collected costs on some particular controlling objects to other receivers.
- **Settlement rule**
  This set of distribution rules define account assignments and the portions of actual costs to be settled to receivers.
- **Standard cost estimate**
  This group of cost items is generated in product cost planning to value materials and services. This value can be based on quantity structures or value structures.
- **Standard hierarchy**
  A standard hierarchy is a tree-like structure used to organize one of the following controlling objects in the system: cost centers, profit centers, and business processes.
- **Statistical key figure**
  This master data in cost center accounting can be used as a basis for allocations.
- **Statistical object**
  This controlling object is used for information purposes only. A statistical cost object must always be accompanied by an additional entity that carries the actual value.
- **Tracing factor**
  A user-defined rule defines a basis for transferring values from the sender to the receiver. In particular, a tracing factor is a specific statistical key figure or activity type that is posted to the receiver cost object.
- **True (real) object**
  This is an account assignment (controlling) object which can carry individual postings without the support of other cost objects.

3.6 Practice Questions

These practice questions will help you evaluate your understanding of the topics covered in this chapter. The questions shown are similar to those found on the certification examination. Although none of these questions will be found on the exam itself, they will allow you to review your knowledge of the subject. Select the correct answers and then check the completeness of your answers in the next section. Remember that you must select all correct answers on the exam and select only correct answers to receive credit for the question.

1. Which of the following are organizational data in controlling? (There are two correct answers.)

   ☐ A. Operating concern
   ☐ B. Work center
   ☐ C. Cost center
   ☐ D. Controlling area

2. Which of the following is *not* master data in controlling?

   ☐ A. Profitability segment
   ☐ B. Activity type
   ☐ C. Statistical key figure
   ☐ D. Internal order

3. Which currencies can be used in controlling? (There are two correct answers.)

   ☐ A. Purchasing organization currency
   ☐ B. Sales area currency
   ☐ C. Object currency
   ☐ D. Transaction currency

4. Which of the following must be identical for the company codes assigned to the same controlling area? (There are two correct answers.)

   ☐ A. Currency
   ☐ B. Operative chart of accounts
   ☐ C. Fiscal year variant
   ☐ D. Country-specific chart of accounts

5. Which of the following controlling master data is created in general ledger accounting? (There are two correct answers.)

   ☐ A. Cost center
   ☐ B. Primary cost element
   ☐ C. Activity type
   ☐ D. Secondary cost element

6. Which of the following statements are correct about management accounting? (There are two correct answers.)

   ☐ A. Internally focused
   ☐ B. Determined by laws and regulations

☐ C. Concerned with external reporting
☐ D. Provides controlling objects for different views of costs and revenues

7. Which of the following is master data that represents a delimited location where costs occur?

☐ A. Work center
☐ B. Profit center
☐ C. Cost center
☐ D. Activity center

8. Which of the following can be used in costing the productive output of a cost center?

☐ A. Activity type
☐ B. Statistical key figure
☐ C. Value field
☐ D. Standard hierarchy

9. Which of the following is a tracing factor in cost allocation?

☐ A. Settlement rule
☐ B. Statistical key figure
☐ C. Distribution rule
☐ D. Cost center number

10. Which of the following assignments are correct? (There are two correct answers.)

☐ A. Several operating concerns can be assigned to a controlling area
☐ B. Several controlling areas can be assigned to an operating concern
☐ C. Only one controlling area can be assigned to an operating concern
☐ D. Several company codes can be assigned to a controlling area

11. At which organizational level can controlling master data be created?

☐ A. Controlling area
☐ B. Company code
☐ C. Standard hierarchy
☐ D. Operating concern

12. Which of the following is *not* correct about activity types?

    ☐ A. Activity types are assigned to work centers
    ☐ B. Activity types can be restricted for the use of particular cost center categories
    ☐ C. You must specify a secondary cost element in the activity master record
    ☐ D. You can define an object currency in the activity type master record

13. Which of the following assignments in the cost center master record connects the cost center to financial accounting? (There are two correct answers.)

    ☐ A. Company code
    ☐ B. Standard hierarchy
    ☐ C. Profit center
    ☐ D. General ledger account

14. What data do you have to maintain in the cost center master data? (There are three correct answers.)

    ☐ A. Person responsible
    ☐ B. User responsible
    ☐ C. Description
    ☐ D. Hierarchy area
    ☐ E. Currency

15. Which of the following determines the list of potential receivers of settlement for internal orders?

    ☐ A. Order type
    ☐ B. Settlement rule
    ☐ C. Settlement master data
    ☐ D. Order number

16. Which of the following are correct about primary cost and revenue elements? (There are three correct answers.)

    ☐ A. They are general ledger accounts of type P&L
    ☐ B. They are linked to the balance sheet
    ☐ C. They are linked to the income statement
    ☐ D. They are concerned with internal cost allocations
    ☐ E. You must maintain a cost element category in controlling area settings

17. Which of the following are correct about secondary cost elements? (There are two correct answers.)

    ☐ A. They are used in controlling for internal cost allocation purposes
    ☐ B. They are used in distributions
    ☐ C. They cannot be posted directly
    ☐ D. They are not created in general ledger accounting

18. Which of the following are true controlling objects? (There are two correct answers.)

    ☐ A. Project (statistical)
    ☐ B. Profit center
    ☐ C. Profitability segment
    ☐ D. Real estate objects

19. Which of the following allocates primary and secondary costs using a secondary cost element?

    ☐ A. Distribution
    ☐ B. Assessment
    ☐ C. Periodic reposting
    ☐ D. Manual primary cost reposting

20. Which of the following provides a process-oriented and cross-functional view of overhead costs?

    ☐ A. Cost center accounting
    ☐ B. Profitability analysis
    ☐ C. General ledger accounting
    ☐ D. Activity-based costing

21. Which of the following can be the cost receiver of an internal order settlement? (There are two correct answers.)

    ☐ A. Profit center
    ☐ B. Profitability segment
    ☐ C. General ledger account
    ☐ D. Statistical order

22. Which of the following is the profitability analysis method collecting data when you create a sales order?

    ☐ A. Activity-based profitability analysis
    ☐ B. Costing based profitability analysis
    ☐ C. Sales-based profitability analysis
    ☐ D. Account-based profitability analysis

23. Which of the following is always one of the characteristics of a profitability segment?

    ☐ A. Cost center
    ☐ B. Cost element
    ☐ C. Profit center
    ☐ D. Sales order

24. Which of the following is the product cost controlling component concerned with the cost estimate and price update for products?

    ☐ A. Cost object controlling
    ☐ B. Actual costing and Material Ledger
    ☐ C. Activity-based costing
    ☐ D. Product cost planning

25. Where can you use the standard cost estimate? (There are two correct answers.)

    ☐ A. Material and stock valuation
    ☐ B. Valuation of goods movements
    ☐ C. Inventory revaluation
    ☐ D. Sales pricing

26. When does the future price of material become the current price?

    ☐ A. As soon as you create the standard cost estimate
    ☐ B. When you mark the standard cost estimate
    ☐ C. When you mark and release the standard cost estimate
    ☐ D. When you edit the material master record after the price update

27. Which of the following is concerned with inventory valuation?

    ☐ A. Price control
    ☐ B. Sales price

☐ C. Previous price
☐ D. Standard cost estimate

28. Which of the following can be assigned a profit center in their master records? (There are two correct answers.)

☐ A. Profitability segment
☐ B. Asset
☐ C. General ledger account
☐ D. Material

29. How can profit centers receive data? (There are two correct answers.)

☐ A. Direct postings to profit centers
☐ B. Distributions and assessments
☐ C. Cost or revenue postings in financial accounting by using profit center as a statistical object
☐ D. From general ledger accounts automatically

30. Which of the following can be assigned a cost center? (There are two correct answers.)

☐ A. Profitability segment
☐ B. Persons and positions
☐ C. General ledger account
☐ D. WBS element

31. Which of the following are touchpoints of integration for controlling? (There are three correct answers.)

☐ A. Postings to nonoperating expense accounts
☐ B. Postings to balance sheet accounts
☐ C. Goods receipts for nonstock items
☐ D. Confirmations
☐ E. Settlement

3.7 Practice Question Answers and Explanations

1. Correct answers: **A and D**
   The controlling module uses operating concerns and controlling areas as organizational data. Cost centers are master data in controlling. A work center is master data in production.

2. **Correct answer: A**

   Activity types, statistical key figures, and internal orders are master data in overhead cost controlling. A profitability segment is a multidimensional reporting structure in profitability analysis. However, a profitability segment does not have master data and is created in the system only when they are addressed.

3. **Correct answers: C and D**

   SAP S/4HANA is a multilingual and multicurrency system. You can use the following currencies in controlling: controlling area currency, object currency, and transaction currency.

4. **Correct answers: B and C**

   Company codes assigned to the same controlling area may use different currencies and country-specific charts of accounts. However, they must have the identical operative chart of accounts and fiscal year variant.

5. **Correct answers: B and D**

   Cost center and activity type are master data in overhead cost controlling. You must create them in the cost center accounting application component. Primary and secondary cost elements are master data in cost element accounting and general ledger accounts in general ledger accounting. You can create them in general ledger accounting.

6. **Correct answers: A and D**

   This question is to remind you of the differences between financial accounting and management accounting. Management accounting is internally focused, while financial accounting is externally focused and intended for external reporting. The law determines the principles and content of financial accounting, while management requirements determine the principles and content of management accounting. Management accounting provides cost elements and controlling objects for different views of costs and revenues, while financial accounting provides accounts and ledgers to record, manage, and report financial activities in the company.

7. **Correct answer: C**

   The cost center represents an enclosed location, area of responsibility, or organizational unit where the costs are incurred and is master data in cost center accounting. A profit center is master data in general ledger accounting and profit center accounting. Profit centers are used to analyze the P&L of an internal operational unit. A work center is master data in production and represents a location (or a group of persons) where core business operations are carried out. Cost centers are assigned to work centers to collect the costs of work center activities.

8. **Correct answer: A**

   The word "costing" in this context refers to the calculation of costs in a cost center. Activity types are mostly used to calculate the cost of the productive output of an operational cost center. A statistical key figure is a basis for cost allocation between cost centers. A value field is a reporting dimension in profitability analysis. A standard hierarchy is a tree-like structure of cost centers and profit centers.

9. Correct answer: **B**

   Statistical key figures and activity types can be used as a tracing factor in cost allocations. A settlement rule includes distribution rules that determine which receivers receive what portion of costs.

10. Correct answers: **B and D**

    Controlling areas are assigned to an operating concern. Company codes can be assigned to a controlling area under certain circumstances. These relationships are one-to-many relationships.

11. Correct answer: **A**

    A controlling area is a self-contained structure in which the company manages and allocates costs and revenues. Controlling master data is created at the controlling area level.

12. Correct answer: **A**

    Within the framework of creating an activity type master record, you can maintain an object currency and a secondary cost element for the internal cost allocations originating from the activity type. The cost center category is a data field through which you can restrict the use of an activity type to specific cost centers (e.g., production, service, maintenance). However, an activity type is not directly assigned to a work center but a cost center in the activity price planning.

13. Correct answers: **A and C**

    A company code is the highest organizational data in external reporting (financial accounting). A profit center is master data in financial accounting. Cost centers can be assigned to company codes and profit centers in their master records.

14. Correct answers: **A, D, and E**

    You must maintain the following mandatory data fields in the cost center master record: the person responsible, hierarchy area, and object currency. The other fields are optional.

15. Correct answer: **A**

    Some orders can be settled to certain types of receivers. An order type has control functions determining the potential list of receivers that you can use in the settlement rule. An order type also determines the number range that you can use for several order categories.

16. Correct answers: **A, C, and E**

    Primary cost and revenue elements are general ledger accounts of type P&L. Depending on the financial statement version, they are summarized in the income statements. Secondary cost elements are used in controlling for internal cost allocations. Since cost elements are master data in cost element accounting, you must maintain the cost element category in the controlling area settings.

17. Correct answers: **A and C**
Secondary cost elements are created in the general ledger accounting application component. They can be used in assessments for internal cost allocations but cannot be posted directly. A distribution is the act of allocating primary (not secondary) cost elements between cost centers and other receivers.

18. Correct answers: **C and D**
Profit centers are statistical controlling objects. They receive information about costs for statistical purposes only; they cannot be the real receivers of actual costs and revenues. Internal orders and projects can be marked as statistical in their master records. In this case, they should accompany a true object in true postings. Profitability segments, real estate objects, real projects, real orders, and cost centers are other examples of true (real) objects.

19. Correct answer: **B**
Assessment is a controlling transaction that allocates primary and secondary costs from a sender cost center to receiver controlling objects (e.g., cost center, WBS element, order, cost object, real estate object, or business process master record) using a secondary assessment cost element. Distributions and other activities are used to allocate primary cost elements.

20. Correct answer: **D**
Upon its activation in the Customizing, activity-based costing provides a process-oriented and cross-functional view of overhead costs by using business process master records.

21. Correct answers: **B and C**
A real internal order must be settled at the end of its lifecycle or period. You must create a settlement rule to determine the settlement receivers of real internal order. During settlement, the receivers are debited, and the order is credited, leading to a zero balance on the order. True controlling objects or general ledger accounts can be the receivers of actual costs in the settlement. Profit centers and statistical orders are statistical objects; they cannot be settled nor can they serve as settlement receivers.

22. Correct answer: **B**
Two profitability analysis reporting methods exist: account-based profitability analysis and costing-based profitability analysis. Account-based profitability analysis collects data from sales and distribution when a goods issue is posted and when an invoice is generated for the goods issue. Costing-based profitability analysis collects data from sales and distribution when a sales order is created and when an invoice is generated for the order.

23. Correct answer: **C**

A profitability segment is a multidimensional reporting structure in profitability analysis. It represents an external market segment and is a combination of values of characteristics (reporting dimensions). One of these characteristics is always a profit center.

24. Correct answer: **D**

Product cost controlling has three components: product cost planning, cost object controlling, and actual costing/the Material Ledger. The product cost planning component is concerned with creating standard cost estimates for products and for price updates in material master records. Cost object controlling is concerned with preliminary, simultaneous, and final costing of controlling objects, such as production orders. Actual costing and the Material Ledger are concerned with the analysis of actual costs of products and services. Activity-based costing is not a part of product cost controlling.

25. Correct answers: **A and D**

A standard cost estimate is a group of cost items generated in product cost planning to value materials and services. It can be based on a quantity structure or a value structure. A standard cost estimate can be used in sales pricing or material and stock valuation. The released cost estimate is used in the valuation of goods movements and inventory revaluation.

26. Correct answer: **C**

Three standard prices of a material in the master record exist: the previous price, the current price, and the future price. When you mark the standard cost estimate for a product, it becomes the material's future price. When you release the marked cost estimate, it becomes the material's current price.

27. Correct answer: **A**

The price control indicator is an important data field in the material master record. It determines whether the standard price or moving average price is used in the inventory valuation.

28. Correct answers: **B and D**

Profit centers can be assigned to materials and assets in their master record. The profitability segment does not have a master record. You can address a profit center when you post to a general ledger account in financial accounting, but you do not assign a profit center to general ledger accounts directly in their master records.

29. Correct answers: **B and D**

You can use the profit center as a statistical object in cost and revenue postings in financial accounting. Postings and allocations within management accounting indirectly send data to profit centers through the cost objects assigned to the profit center. Another way that profit centers can receive data is by distributing or assessing balance sheet items between profit centers.

30. Correct answers: **B and D**

    Persons and positions in human capital management (HCM) can be assigned a cost center. The following system objects can also be assigned cost center in their master records: assets, equipment, functional locations, work centers, and WBS elements.

31. Correct answers: **C, D, and E**

    Nonoperating expense accounts record the costs that are not linked to management accounting (and the company's core business activities). Balance sheet accounts are for recording the results of business transactions and thus usually do not require input for a controlling object during the postings in financial accounting. However, postings to primary cost and revenue accounts and goods receipts for nonstock items include controlling objects as account assignment objects and are linked to controlling. Confirmations in production, maintenance, and project management debit the object for actual times and quantities and can trigger internal activity or cost allocations in controlling.

3.8 Test Takeaway

In this chapter, you learned the key processes of management accounting and the system application components supporting these key processes. SAP S/4HANA provides the controlling module and controlling objects to support management accounting processes. Cost element accounting is a key process that provides a view of costs and revenues by types. Using cost and revenue elements created in general ledger accounting, cost element accounting provides a real-time reconciliation between financial accounting and management accounting. Overhead cost controlling (consisting of cost center accounting, internal orders, and activity-based costing) provides a location, task, and process-based view of overhead costs in the business organization. Cost centers, internal orders, and business processes are master data in overhead cost controlling. They are assigned to several objects (e.g., assets, orders, project elements) to seamlessly collect overhead costs. Profitability analysis and profit center accounting provide a comprehensive view of P&L by external market segments and internal organizational units. A profit center is a master record in profit center accounting. It can be assigned to cost centers, assets, sales order line items, financial accounting postings, project elements, materials to fetch the information of costs and revenues. The profitability segment is a multidimensional reporting structure in profitability analysis and is a combination of several characteristics, one of them always a profit center. Product cost accounting is concerned with preliminary, simultaneous, and final costing of products and orders. The cost estimates generated in product cost planning are used in sales pricing, material and stock valuation, and standard price updates in the material master record. The system then uses the (marked and) released cost estimates in inventory revaluations and in the valuation of goods movements.

Your company's organizational structure in management accounting can be mapped into the system creating operating concerns and controlling areas. The operating concern represents a view of external market segments and is the valuation level in profitability analysis. The controlling area is a self-contained structure in which the company manages and allocates costs and revenues. Several controlling areas can be assigned to an operating concern. To establish a connection between cost accounting and external accounting in multiple company codes, you can assign several company codes to a controlling area. These assignments are possible if all company codes use the same operative chart of accounts and fiscal year variant.

We've now covered all certification-relevant topics for management accounting and its key processes. The next chapter covers source-to-pay processing in SAP S/4HANA.

Chapter 4
Source-to-Pay Processing

Techniques You'll Master

- Describe the key topics of the source-to-pay business process and SAP S/4HANA's purchasing module supporting the source-to-pay business process

- Understand the system transactions and cloud solutions supporting the key tasks of the source-to-pay business process

- Explain and maintain master and organizational data in purchasing

- Perform purchasing transactions in source-to-pay

- Identify the touchpoints of integration between purchasing and other system modules

This chapter of the book covers all certification-relevant topics of the source-to-pay business process in the intelligent enterprise suite and core purchasing process in SAP S/4HANA. We'll describe the master data, organizational data, and system transactions supporting source-to-pay in SAP S/4HANA and explains the potential integration scenarios.

Source-to-pay (formerly procure-to-pay) describes the end-to-end business process on SAP's intelligent enterprise suite enhanced with strategic sourcing enabled by SAP Ariba and intelligent procurement planning empowered by SAP Integrated Business Planning for Supply Chain (SAP IBP). Source-to-pay is a part of SAP's Intelligent Spend Management strategy, consisting of three end-to-end processes:

- Source-to-pay
- External workforce management
- Travel-to-reimbursement

These processes are supported by SAP S/4HANA, SAP Analytics Cloud, SAP Concur, SAP Fieldglass, and SAP Ariba. This chapter focuses on source-to-pay, which spans from strategic supplier selection (strategic sourcing) to invoice verification and payment.

> **Real-World Scenario**
>
> Every business must procure (and sell) goods or services to keep their business running to generate revenue. A well-designed procurement process is essential for the profitability of products (or services) and protecting the company and its suppliers from unexpected expenses, delays, and legal issues. As a business process integration consultant, you'll need to understand the key components of procurement and how you can seamlessly integrate the system components relevant to purchasing.
>
> Source-to-pay describes an end-to-end business process starting with the determination of requirements and ordering the merchandise, continuing with receipts of goods, and ending with payments. Buying goods or services for business operations or assets includes several complexities. Several vendors may supply the same material under various conditions. You can also source materials internally from another plant. Thus, choosing between internal and external procurement and determining the source of supply is of critical importance. A purchaser may want to utilize outline agreements, such as scheduling agreements, to expedite the procurement process or may wish to proceed with a purchase order. A purchase order is a binding contract between the purchaser and a supplier that includes all terms and conditions regulating further procurement steps.
>
> Therefore, purchase order handling and monitoring are vital for successfully managing the subsequent steps, such as receiving goods, invoice processing,

and payment. During the receipt of products or services, a quality inspection process or a warehouse workflow may be initialized, or you may want to transfer the material to a maintenance work center directly. Choosing an appropriate stock type (quality inspection, unrestricted-use, or blocked stock) is critical for materials management. Processing vendor invoices includes comparing them to documents for the receipt of goods and purchase orders and passing the process to the accounting department for payment. The bottom line is that a seamless source-to-pay process requires the complete orchestration of materials management, warehouse management, and financial accounting.

Knowing the building blocks of the source-to-pay process, understanding data- and procurement-relevant transactions in SAP S/4HANA, and mastering integration points of the purchasing module are crucial skills for a business process integration consultant.

4.1 Objectives of This Portion of the Test

This portion of the certification aims to test your knowledge of master data, organizational data, key processes of procurement, and integration points of the source-to-pay business process. The integration occurs in two ways: cross-module data assignments (organizational data/master data) and cross-module transactions.

For the certification exam, business process integration consultants must have a good understanding of the following topics:

- Scope and sequence of the key tasks of the source-to-pay process
- Definitions and assignments of purchasing organizational data
- Definitions and assignments of purchasing master data
- The scope, sequence, data, and impacts of purchasing transactions
- Integration points between procurement and other business processes

Note
The source-to-pay business process covers 8%–12% of the questions in the certification exam.

4.2 Data Structures for Source-To-Pay

The source-to-pay business process can be mapped into your system by creating (organizational and master) data and performing appropriate data assignments in Customizing (SAP Implementation Guide [IMG]). In this section, we explain the master data, organizational data, and transactional data used in purchasing. We also explain the relationships and assignments between the organizational and master data in the source-to-pay business process.

4.2.1 Organizational Data (units) w/in source to pay

In procurement, the organizational structure of your enterprise and responsible organizational units must be known to answer simple questions, such as the following:

- Which legal entity is financially responsible for procurement?
- Where should purchased merchandise be delivered?
- Where should materials be stored?
- Who is responsible for purchasing and negotiating terms and conditions?
- Who will plan and conduct day-to-day purchasing activities?

Organizational data in purchasing represents the real-world enterprise structure in the source-to-pay business process. You can create and assign organizational data to each other to translate areas of responsibility for the entire source-to-pay business process into SAP S/4HANA.

Note

You'll need to use the IMG to create/edit organizational data in SAP. Organizational data cannot be created or edited by using standard user-level transactions available through an SAP Easy Access screen or through SAP Fiori.

Organizational data in purchasing includes the client, company code, plant, storage location, purchasing organization, and purchasing group. Let's explain their roles in the enterprise structure:

- **Client**
  The highest-level unit of all organizational elements in the SAP system, a client represents the enterprise or headquarters group in the real business. In SAP S/4HANA, organizational data, master data, and transactional data are all maintained at the client level. The technical role of the client in SAP S/4HANA is to keep this data separate from other clients.

Tip

People use the words *client* and *customer* interchangeably in daily life. We use those words to refer to different data in the system. The client in the SAP system defines the highest hierarchical organizational data. The transactions performed and data stored at the client level are valid and applicable to all company codes in the enterprise structure. However, a customer is master data in the sales and distribution module. Customer master data is maintained at different organizational levels, such as client, company code, and sales organization (see Chapter 5).

- **Company code**

  A company code is an independent legal entity that enables the modeling of a business organization based on financial reporting requirements, such as balance sheets and profit and loss (P&L)/income statements. The company code is the highest organizational unit in financial accounting and is usually created based on geographic considerations. Every business process relevant to financial accounting (e.g., sales, procurement, production, maintenance) uses company codes as organizational data. An enterprise must have at least one company code. A client may have multiple company codes.

- **Plant**

  In purchasing, a plant represents the receiving plant for purchased materials and services. In particular, a plant defines the delivery address on purchasing documents and the physical location where materials are stored. A plant is also necessary for material requirements planning (MRP) and to differentiate forecast data for materials. In an SAP system, a plant must be assigned to a company code uniquely. A company code may have multiple plants, which enables different valuation methods for materials. A plant can have different roles in other business processes, such as a facility for production, a regional sales office, or a maintenance location.

- **Storage location**

  A storage location represents a physical location in the plant where your stock of materials is being kept. A storage location is an organizational unit that enables the differentiation between material inventories in a plant (e.g., finished goods, trading materials, raw materials). Inventory management is implemented in the plant at the storage location level. A business must have at least one storage location per plant, even if no inventory is held at any storage location.

> **Note**
> Storage locations are uniquely identified within a plant by a four-character alphanumeric key. For instance, the key FG00 can be used to identify a storage location for finished goods in a plant. An alphanumeric key for a storage location must be unique within the plant. However, the same key can be used for a similar storage location in a different plant.

- **Purchasing organization**

  A purchasing organization represents the purchasing department that negotiates with vendors and is responsible for purchasing activities. By creating different purchasing organizations, you can subdivide purchasing activities according to various purchasing requirements. Every purchase order or stock transport order must include purchasing organization information. Based on the purchasing needs of the organization, the system offers three types of purchasing organizations:

- **Central (cross-company code) purchasing organization**: Responsible for the purchasing needs of all plants under all the company codes
- **Cross-plant (company code level) purchasing organization**: Responsible for the purchasing needs of all plants under the company code to which the purchasing organization assigned
- **Plant-specific**: Responsible for the purchasing needs of a single plant

- **Purchasing group**

A purchasing group represents a buyer, or a group of buyers, that is responsible for the day-to-day planning of purchasing requirements and ordering of merchandise. These tasks include creating purchasing documents (i.e., purchase requisitions or purchase orders) for a purchasing organization and sending vendors requests for quotations (RFQs). A purchasing group is not assigned to a purchasing organization or any other organizational unit. Internally, the purchasing group is responsible for the procurement of a material or a class of materials (i.e., it can be assigned to a material or material categories). Externally, as the medium through which the organization contacts the vendor, purchasing documents must include purchasing group data.

4.2.2 Master Data

[handwritten: Tells the system what to do]

Users need to address some simple questions in purchasing documents:

- What to procure?
- From whom to procure?
- Who sells what?
- What conditions will apply?

Master data in purchasing represents the objects, subjects, object-subject relations, and conditions used in the tasks of the source-to-pay business process. Master data in purchasing can be created and edited by using user-level transactions in the SAP Easy Access screen or SAP Fiori. Do not confuse master data with transactional data (e.g., quantities, dates, notes) maintained in purchasing transactions such as requisitions or orders. You do not create master data within purchasing transactions, but you call previously created master data by entering the corresponding key/number for the master data.

Master data in purchasing includes the following records, which we'll explore in subsequent sections:

- Material master record
- Vendor master record *[handwritten: = business partner =]*
- Purchasing info record

Material Master

Materials can be objects that different business processes have in common. For example, a raw material is purchased, processed in production, stored in the warehouse, valuated in accounting. Further, its cost is determined in product cost accounting, and its consumption or movements are tracked in inventory management. Then, the same type of material can be handled, valuated, and planned differently at different organizational levels, such as plants and storage locations. Thus, the data for materials in your system should be subdivided according to each specific user department or view. In the system, you can create a material master record centrally to support all material management requirements of integrated business processes.

To create a material master record, you must first choose a *material type* on the initial screen, shown in Figure 4.1. The material type is essential for the valuation of the material and for the determination of the fields that must be maintained in the material master views. The material type also determines the number range from which the material number is taken and which screens appear and in what sequence during material master record maintenance. Another important key you must choose during master data creation is the *industry sector.* The industry sector key determines the selection of data fields on screens or the screen sequence. Subdividing materials into different industry sectors is essential since the basic characteristics of master data are different for the materials in different industries.

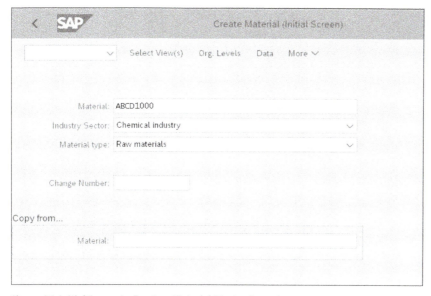

Figure 4.1 Initial Screen to Create a Material Master Record

The material master record consists of views. The material master views connect the material to different business processes and departments. The data in material master views is maintained at the organizational level, such as plant, storage location, warehouse number, sales organization, and distribution channel. To create material master views, you'll choose them after the initial screen, shown in Figure 4.2. Based on your selection of views, you'll be asked for the organizational levels at which you want to maintain data. For instance, if you choose sales views, you'll be asked for the sales organization and distribution channel. For purchasing-relevant items, you'll be asked only for inventory management-relevant organizational levels, plants, and storage locations.

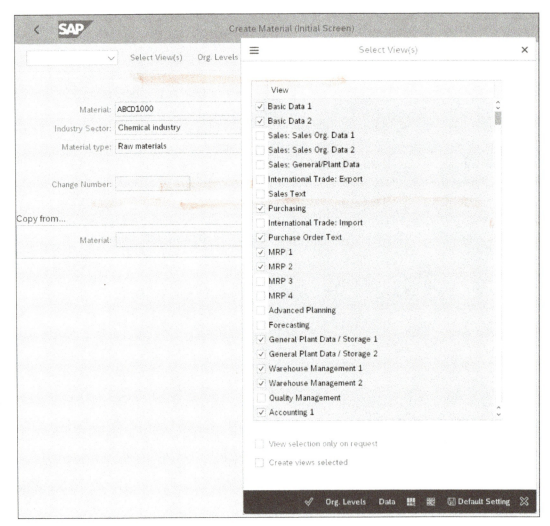

Figure 4.2 Select the Views to Maintain

After the initial screen, following a two-step procedure will create a material master record in the system:

1. **Select views**

   To create a material in the system, you must first select the views you want to maintain, as shown in Figure 4.2.

   The data in the material master record is grouped into several tabs, called *views*. This view structure is necessary to connect the material to different business processes, such as procurement, sales, and production. For instance, a material master record for a finished good may not have a purchasing view but has a sales view. In contrast, material master data for raw material may not have a sales view. Material master views and their connection to several business processes are summarized in Table 4.1.

View	Org Levels	Business Process
Basic Data	Client	General data
Sales	Sales organization and distribution channel	Lead-to-cash
MRP	Plant and storage location	MRP (for procurement and production)
Purchasing	Plant	Source-to-pay
General Plant Data/Storage	Plant and storage location	Inventory management
Warehouse Management	Warehouse number and storage type	Warehouse management
Accounting	Plant	Financial accounting and inventory management (valuation class)
Costing	Plant	Design-to-produce and product cost controlling
Quality Management	Plant	Quality management

   Table 4.1 Material Master Record Views and the Organizational Levels of the Data in Views

   > **Note**
   > To change or display an existing material master record, you'll also need to choose the views you would like to change or display. In the **Select View(s)** menu, you'll only see the existing views for the material.

2. **Select plant**

   A material will be kept at a storage location in the plant. To create a material master record in the system, you must specify the plant in which you want to create the material, as shown in Figure 4.3. Storage location- and warehouse-relevant data can be created during the maintenance of views such as **General Plant Data/Storage 1-2** and **Warehouse Management 1-2**.

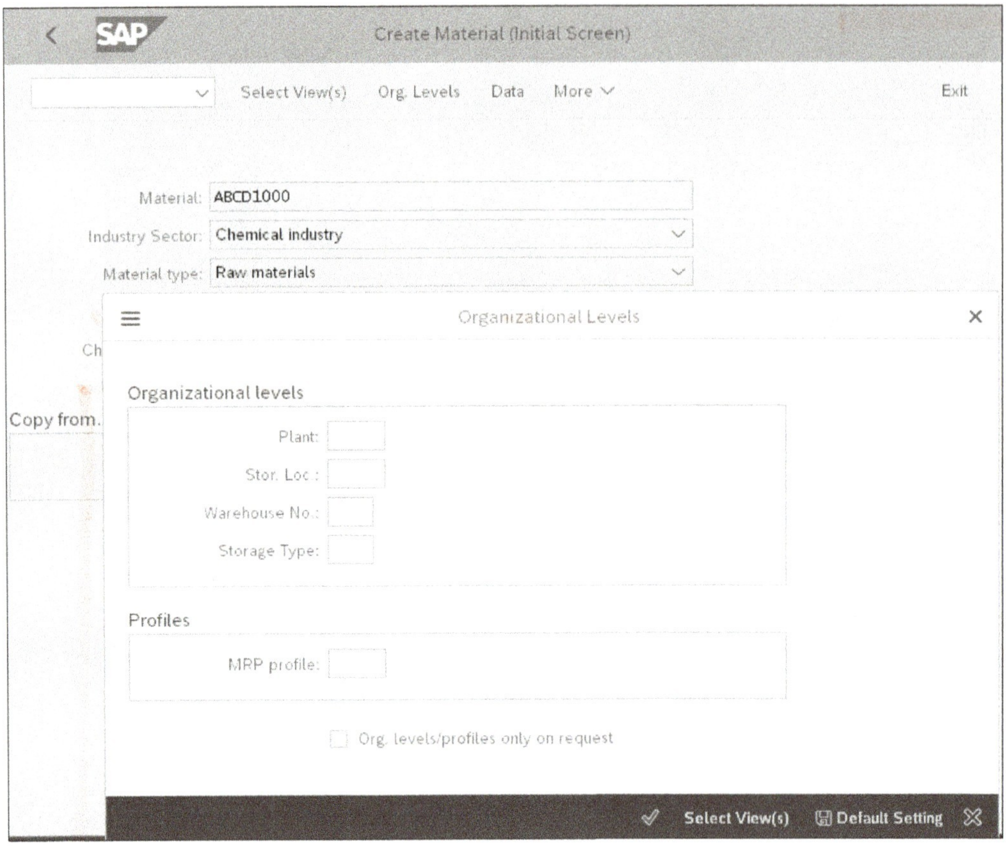

Figure 4.3 After Selecting Views, Choosing the Org Levels Where a Material Is Created

The data in material master views is valid for the different organizational levels. In particular, the data in the views of a purchasing-relevant material master can be grouped into the following three categories:

- The data valid for the whole enterprise
- The data valid within the plant (selected in step 2)
- The data valid for the storage location (selected in step 2)

For instance, the material number, material short text, and the other data in the **Basic data 1** view are valid for the whole enterprise (i.e., for the client), as shown in Figure 4.4. The data in the **Basic data 1** view must be maintained for all materials in the system. The data in the **Purchasing** view of the material master record is valid for the plant you have selected, as shown in Figure 4.5. Navigating through the views listed earlier in Table 4.1, you can also see the organizational levels of material master data of sales-relevant or warehouse management-relevant materials.

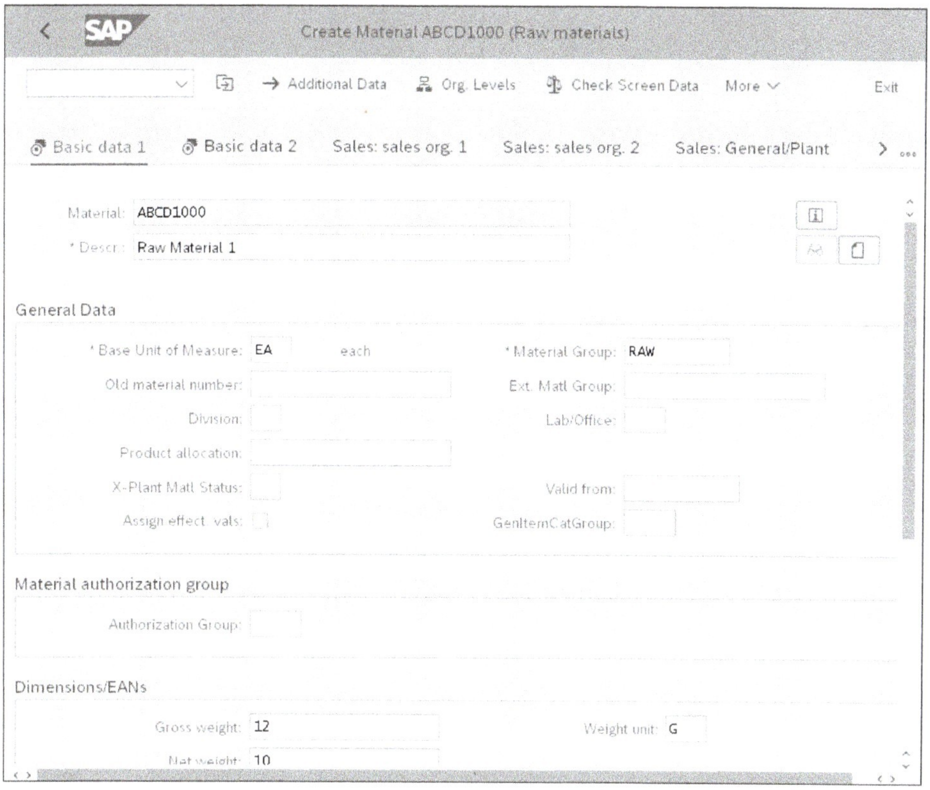

Figure 4.4 Basic Data 1 View of a Material Master Record

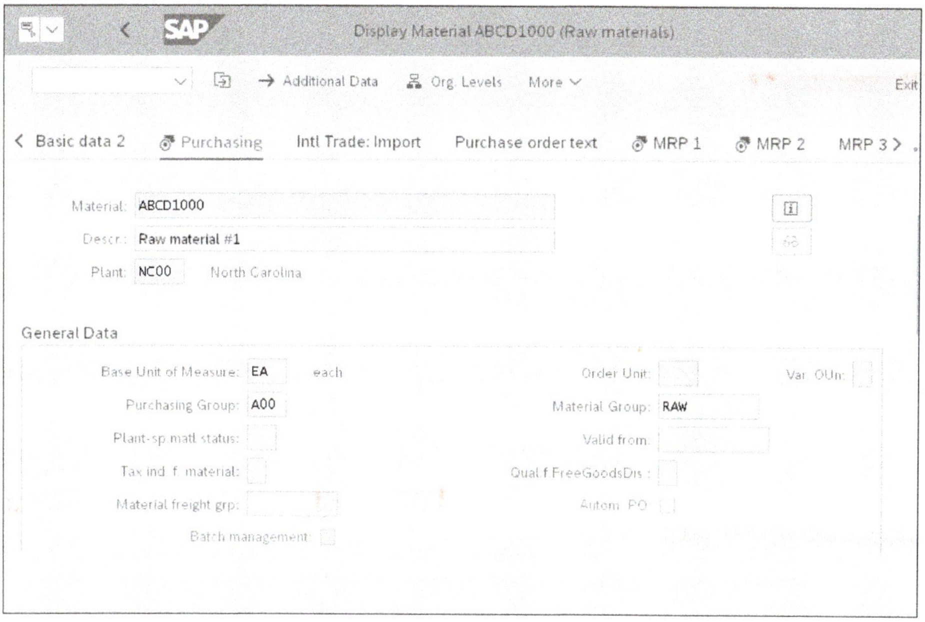

Figure 4.5 Data in the Purchasing View Valid for the Selected Plant

An example of data that is valid for storage location is the data in the **Plant data/ stor. 1-2** views where you can choose the storage location first (by clicking the **Org. Levels** button located at the top) and define storage location-specific data, such as storage bin, picking area, and storage conditions, as shown in Figure 4.6.

Figure 4.6 Selecting the Storage Location Where You Want to Maintain Data

> **Note**
> In SAP S/4HANA, materials are planned and managed at the plant. Thus, the material master record is plant specific. To extend a material to another plant, you must copy the material master record from one plant to another plant.

Vendor Master

Vendor master data represents a supplier in the source-to-pay business process. Vendors may interact with the company in different business processes and various areas of responsibility. A vendor for your company may also be your customer. To avoid redundant data for the same entities interacting with a company in different roles, SAP S/4HANA has a new data structure called the *business partner approach*. The new business partner approach unifies the master data of business partners with different roles and fosters a seamless customer/vendor integration. In the system, you don't create vendor master data directly. Instead, you create a business partner and assign the roles (vendor/customer), depending on the usage of the business partner.

To create a vendor in the system, you must first choose one of the following business partner categories, as shown in Figure 4.7:

- **Person**: Represents an individual supplier
- **Organization**: Represents units such as a company or parts of a legal entity such as a department
- **Group**: Represents a shared living arrangement, a married couple, or an executive board

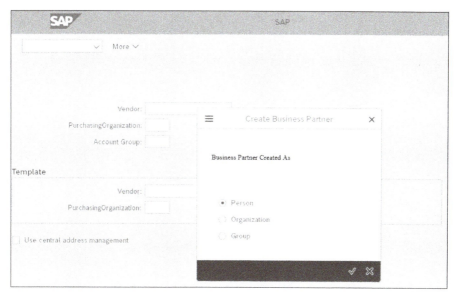

Figure 4.7 Business Partner Categories

The second step is to maintain the business partner data for the vendor. The business partner data for the vendor can be maintained in three different roles:

- Business partner general role (**Business Partner (Gen.)**)
- Vendor role (**Vendor**)
- Financial accounting vendor role (**FI Vendor**)

By using the dropdown menu, you can choose the role in which you want to maintain data. The business partner general role data includes address data, personal data, bank information, and control data. Business partner role data can be maintained in any role. Once created, this role data is copied to all roles (vendor or financial accounting vendor roles) of the business partner and will be valid for all roles and their layers.

Vendor role data includes vendor general data (containing vendor number, account group, vendor tax data) and vendor texts. Vendor role data also includes purchasing data that should be maintained for each purchasing organization with which the vendor interacts. You can proceed to the purchasing data layer by clicking the **Purchasing** button at the top of the screen, as shown in Figure 4.8.

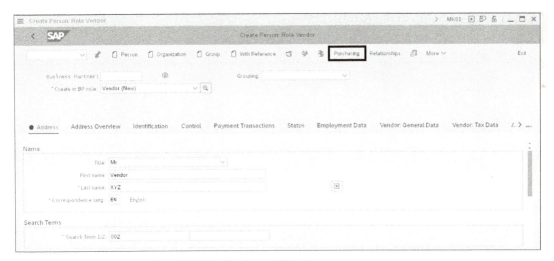

Figure 4.8 Vendor Role Data in the General Data Layer

In the **Purchasing Data** view, you'll maintain purchasing-relevant data, including order currency, payment terms, incoterms, and partner functions. A vendor can be the supplier of multiple purchasing organizations in the company. In this case, you'll need to create purchasing data for each purchasing organization, as shown in Figure 4.9.

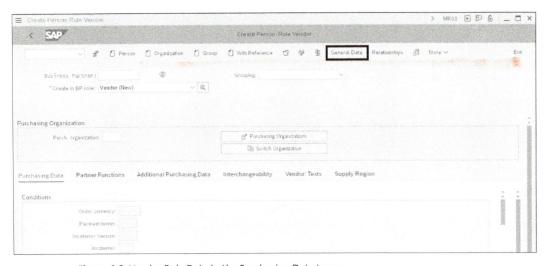

Figure 4.9 Vendor Role Data in the Purchasing Data Layer

Financial accounting vendor role data includes general data and accounting-relevant data defined in the **Company Code** layer, as shown in Figure 4.10.

Data Structures for Source-To-Pay Section 4.2 197

Figure 4.10 Accessing the Company Code Layer in the Financial Accounting Vendor Role Data

To maintain data in the **Company Code** layer, you must first enter the company code.

From an accounting perspective, vendor master data is an account (i.e., a subledger account). A subledger account must be connected to the general ledger through a reconciliation account. The **Reconciliation acct.** field must be maintained in the **Company Code layer.** Recall that the general ledger is maintained at the company code level. If the vendor works with multiple company codes in the enterprise, then you need to create company code layer data for each company code.

The **Company Code** layer, shown in Figure 4.11, includes account management data (reconciliation account number, interest calculation, withholding tax); payment transaction data; and correspondence data for dunning procedures. You can also see the vendor (account) number in this layer. The vendor account number can be different than the business partner number.

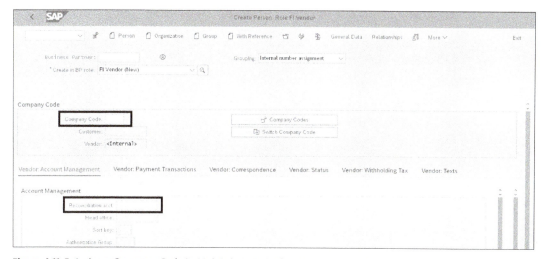

Figure 4.11 Entering a Company Code to Maintain Data in the Company Code Layer

Table 4.2 summarizes the business partner roles, the data in those roles, and the organizational levels for which the data is valid.

Business Partner Role	Data	Org Level
Business partner general role	Address, communication, control data, and bank information	Client
Vendor role	Purchasing data, including order currency, payment terms, incoterms, and partner functions	Purchasing organization
Financial accounting vendor role	Accounting data, including account management data (reconciliation account number, interest calculation, withholding tax), payment data, and correspondence	Company code

Table 4.2 Business Partner Roles and the Data in the Roles

Purchasing Info Record

The purchasing info record (or info record) represents the relationship between a supplier and the material that the supplier provides. The relationship between a material and a vendor is essential information for the source determination functionality in the source-to-pay business process. In layman's terms, the purchasing info record provides information about who sells what under which conditions.

You can use info records to compare prices of a material by different vendors or to compare the prices of all materials supplied by one vendor (Transactions ME1M and ME1L). Another critical use case for info records is the creation of purchasing documents. When you create a purchase order, the system transfers some data from the info record to the document as default values.

An info record is created for a combination of material number and vendor number. The purchasing info record master data includes the following information:

- Vendor number
- Material number
- Conditions (for example, price, freight, and discounts)
- The last purchase order number
- Control/delivery data (for example, planned delivery time, the standard quantity)
- Internal comments and text from the purchase order

The data in an info record is grouped into the following views:

- **General Data**: For example, supplier data, origin data
- **Purch. Organization Data 1**: For example, control data, responsible purchasing group, net price, and the effective price calculated from conditions data in the **Conditions** view
- **Purch. Organization Data 2**: For example, the last quotation number, the last purchase order number

- **Conditions:** The conditions used for calculating the net price, for example, gross price, discount, and freight
- **Texts:** For example, info record notes and purchase order texts

You can access the views of an info record by clicking the relevant buttons at the top of the screen, as shown in Figure 4.12.

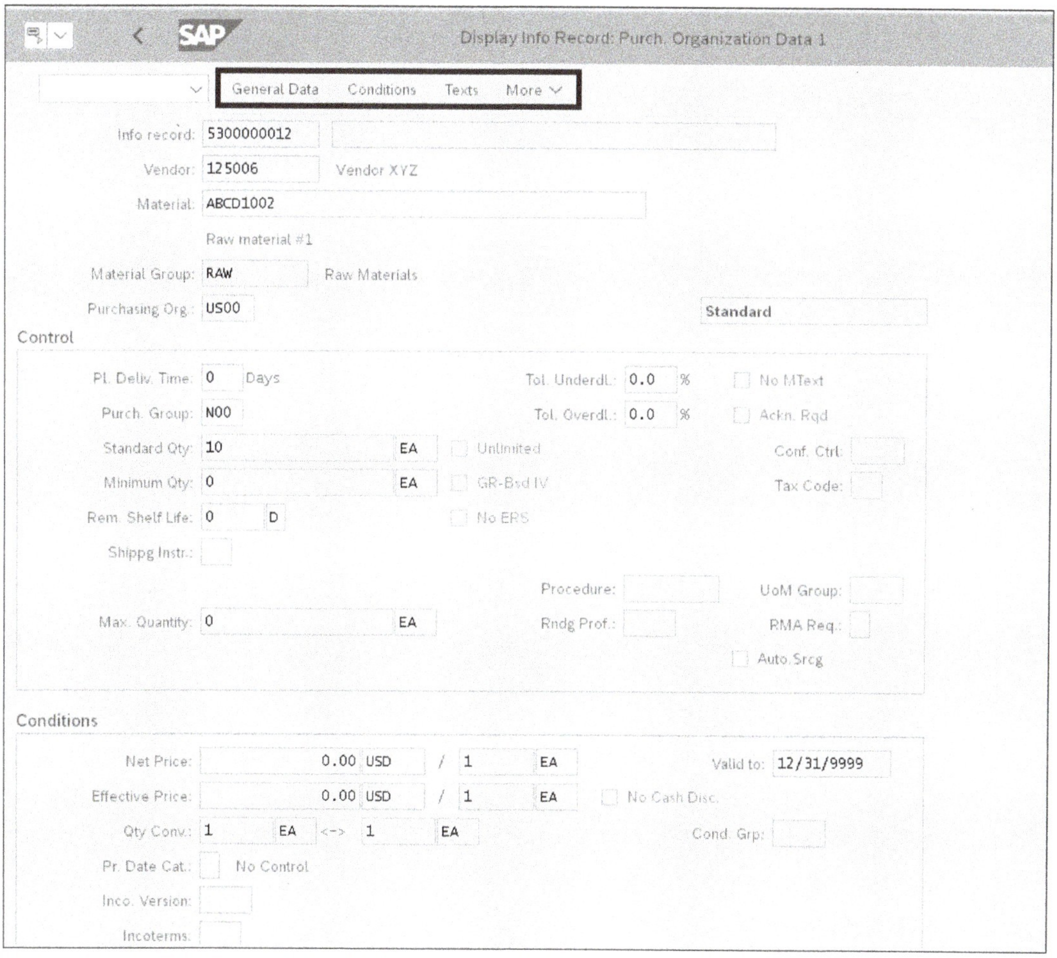

Figure 4.12 Data in Purch. Organization Data 1 View

To create an info record, you must first choose the material and the vendor you want to link to each other on the initial screen shown in Figure 4.13.

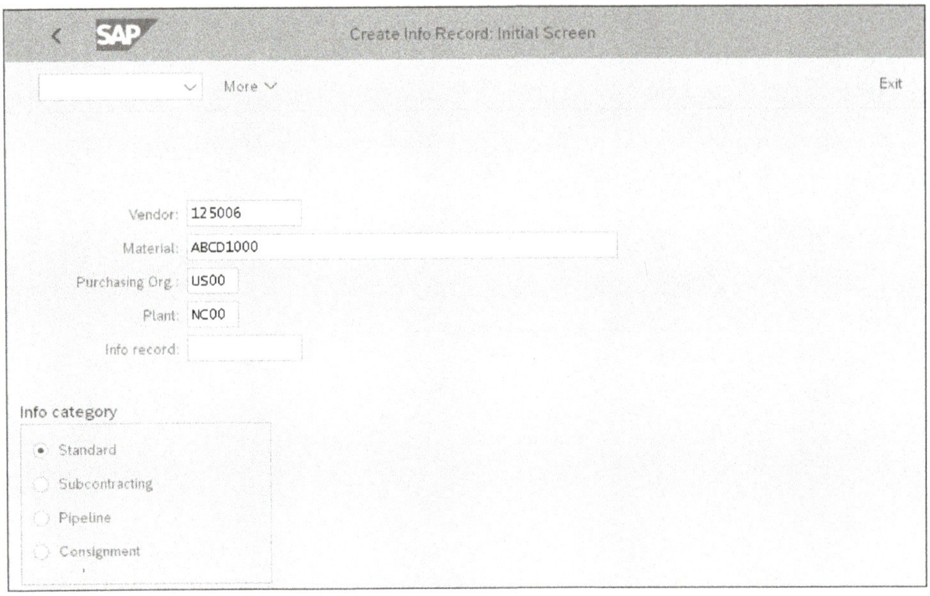

Figure 4.13 Create Info Record: Initial Screen

In the initial screen to create an info record, you can also choose the organizational levels for which you want the info record's prices and conditions to be valid. You can enter one of the following:

- No org level
- A purchasing organization
- A combination of purchasing organization and plant

You can also create info records for different procurement types by choosing one of the info categories (standard, subcontracting, pipeline, and consignment).

Based on your selection of organizational levels on the initial screen, three categories of data can be created in the system:

- Generally applicable data valid for the client, for example, the data in the **General** view
- Purchasing organization-specific data, for example, the data in the **Purch. Organization Data**, **Conditions**, and **Texts** views
- Data that is specific for the combination of purchasing organization and plant, for example, the data in the **Purch. Organization Data**, **Conditions**, and **Texts** views

You can create/change info records in two ways:

- Manually: Create/change info record manually
- Automatically: When creating or changing quotations, scheduling agreements, contracts, and purchase orders, you can use the **InfoUpdate** field to specify that a new info record should be created or an existing info record updated

Conditions

Conditions represent time-dependent/independent elements, such as the following:

- Gross price
- Discounts on a vendor's price
- Freight

A condition record can be seen as second-level master data that can be defined in other master data in purchasing. In particular, you can create conditions in an info record, as shown in Figure 4.14. The conditions maintained in an info record will apply to all purchase order line items containing the material and vendor. Alternatively, you can maintain conditions on a purchase order. However, the conditions maintained in the order will only apply to that order.

Conditions can also be maintained in quotations or outline agreements, including scheduling agreements and contracts.

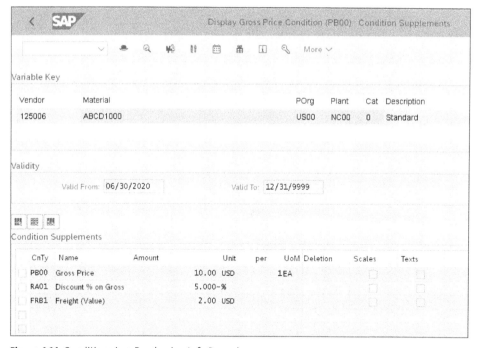

Figure 4.14 Conditions in a Purchasing Info Record

4.2.3 Data Assignments

In this section, we discuss organizational and master data assignments used in the purchasing module. We begin with organizational data assignments.

Organizational Data Assignments

By assigning purchasing organizational data to each other, you can map your enterprise's organizational structure into SAP S/4HANA. You use the IMG to make organizational data assignments.

Figure 4.15 shows the organizational data assignments in purchasing, with the split arrows representing one-to-many relationships between the organizational levels.

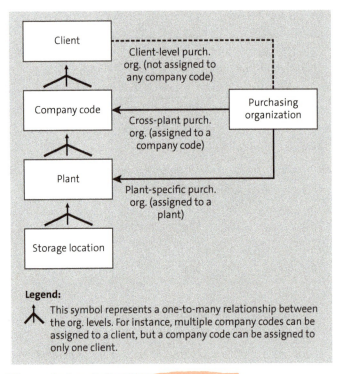

Figure 4.15 Organizational Structure in Purchasing

The following organizational data relationships are possible in purchasing:

- Multiple company codes can be assigned to a client. A company code can be assigned to only one client.
- Multiple plants can be assigned to a company code. A plant can be assigned to only one company code.
- Multiple storage locations can be created within a plant. A storage location can belong to only one plant.
- A purchasing organization can be made a client-level (or cross-company code) purchasing organization by not assigning it to any company code (or client). In other words, when a purchasing organization is not assigned to a company code, the system assumes that it is at the client level.

- A purchasing organization can be assigned to a company code via the IMG. This type of purchasing organization is called a company code-specific purchasing organization or a cross-plant purchasing organization.
- A purchasing organization can be assigned to a plant via the IMG. This type of purchasing organization is called a plant-specific purchasing organization.

> **Note**
>
> You must specify a purchasing organization when you create a purchase order. Depending on the hierarchical level of the purchasing organization, you may need to enter additional data, such as the following:
>
> - When you create a purchase order for a client-level purchasing organization, the system asks you to enter the company code for which you want to procure the material.
> - When you enter a company code-specific purchasing organization in a purchase order, the system automatically brings the assigned company code to the company code field.
> - Let's say you use a plant-specific purchasing organization in a purchase order. In this case, the system automatically pulls the company code information as soon as you maintain the plant in the line item.

Master Data Assignments

You can create master data in purchasing by maintaining data in different layers assigned to specific organizational data. For instance, to create material master data, you must maintain data in several views, including information valid for different organizational levels (listed earlier in Table 4.1).

Vendor master data is indirectly created by maintaining data in different business partners' roles (i.e., business partner general role, the vendor role, and the financial accounting vendor role). The vendor role includes purchasing data that is specific for a purchasing organization. If the vendor interacts with multiple purchasing organizations, you must create different sets of purchasing data for each of those purchasing organizations. Similarly, the financial accounting vendor role includes accounting-relevant data that is specific for a company code, as shown in Figure 4.16. Therefore, the following assignments are possible:

- A vendor can be assigned to multiple purchasing organizations in its master data.
- A vendor can be assigned to multiple company codes in its master data.

A purchasing info record connects the material to a vendor and includes the following information:

- General data, which is valid for the client
- Purchasing, conditions, and text data, which are valid for a purchasing organization or a combination of purchasing organization and plant

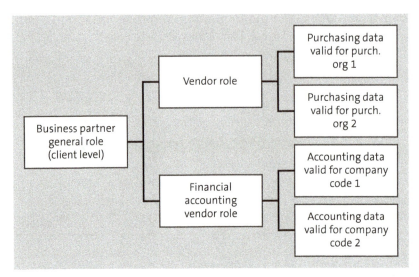

Figure 4.16 Business Partner Roles for Vendor

In the purchasing data layer, you can assign a purchasing info record to a purchasing group (shown earlier in Figure 4.12).

You can assign a material to a purchasing group in the **Purchasing** view of the material master (shown earlier in Figure 4.5). Moreover, for a specific plant, a single material group or a range of material groups can be mapped to the purchasing group, as shown in Figure 4.17. You can set up this restrictive assignment in Customizing if you want to prevent all purchasing groups from procuring from all material groups. Recall that the **Material Group** field is a mandatory field in the **Basic data 1** view of the material master record (shown earlier in Figure 4.4).

Figure 4.17 Mapping Material Group to the Purchasing Group

4.3 Key Processes of Source-to-Pay

The source-to-pay business process is an enhanced procurement process in SAP's intelligent enterprise suite and includes strategic sourcing. This process consists of a series of key tasks supported by SAP S/4HANA's transactions in purchasing, inventory management, and financial accounting.

As shown in Figure 4.18, the key tasks of source-to-pay business process include the following:

1. Determine requirements
2. Determine the source of supply
3. Select the vendor
4. Handle and monitor purchase orders
5. Receive goods
6. Verify the invoice (three-way match)
7. Payment

The system supports these seven key task requirements in source-to-pay through several transactions in purchasing, inventory management, and accounting. Those transactions include purchase requisitions, RFQs, quotation maintenance, purchase orders, goods receipts, logistics invoice verification, and automatic payment runs, as shown in Figure 4.18.

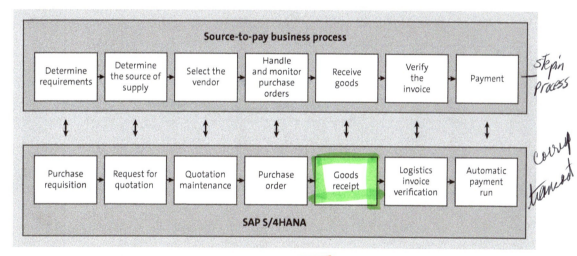

Figure 4.18 Key Tasks of Source-to-Pay and System Transactions

In the following sections, we'll describe the key tasks in source-to-pay in more detail.

4.3.1 Determination of Requirements

An authorized business user or department with purchasing needs can request goods or services by creating purchase requisitions in the system. A purchase requisition is an internal document determining the purchasing requirements for a quantity of a particular material or a service for a particular date.

A purchase requisition can be created manually or automatically via other system components, such as MRP, sales orders, maintenance orders, network activities, or production orders. You can create purchase requisitions in SAP Fiori or SAP Ariba Sourcing and SAP Ariba Procurement.

A purchase requisition includes line items consisting of data fields, such as the following:

- Material number
- Quantity
- Delivery date
- Receiving plant and storage location
- Material group

Depending on the material or service you want to procure, you would maintain data in some of these fields. For instance, if you're buying a stock item, you must enter the material number, plant, and quantity. However, if you're buying a service, you do not need to enter a material number; instead, the material/service group, quantity, and unit of measure need to be entered.

The following data fields in the line items are critical in structuring the entire data entry procedure during the purchase requisition creation and shape subsequent steps of the source-to-pay process:

- **Item category (I)**
  As shown in Figure 4.19, an item category is a single letter key that determines which line item data fields will be selectively displayed and maintained. The item category also determines the subsequent steps (or path) of procurement. For instance, if you leave the item category field blank (standard), the system assumes that you are initiating a procurement process that requires goods receipts and invoice receipts. In this case, you must enter a material number or account assignment category. In contrast, if the item category key is **K (Consignment)**, then the material number and goods receipt are mandatory, an account assignment and invoice receipt are not required, and the material is stock managed.

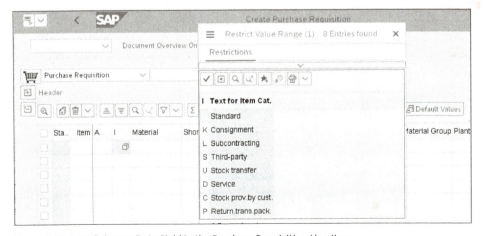

Figure 4.19 Item Category Data Field in the Purchase Requisition Line Item

- **Account assignment category (A)**
  For items that require account assignments, you must enter an account assignment category. An account assignment category is a single letter key that determines the mandatory account assignment data you'll need to enter in the **Account Assignment** view, as shown in Figure 4.20.

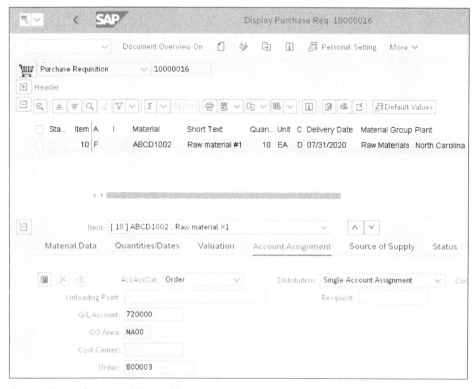

Figure 4.20 Purchase Requisition with Account Assignment

> **Example**
> If your account assignment category is **K** (**Cost Center**), then you must specify a cost center and a general ledger (expense) account in the **Account Assignment** view of the line item, as shown in Figure 4.20.
>
> If you choose account assignment category **A** (**Asset**), you'll only have to enter an asset number in the **Account Assignment** view. The system automatically pulls the general ledger account to charge from the asset master record.

The account assignment category must be left blank if you're buying a stock item for stock. In this case, the system automatically pulls a general ledger account to charge from the material master record. How does this step happen? When you create a material master record, you must define the material type (e.g., raw materials, finished goods) at the initial screen and a valuation class in the material master record's **Accounting** view. In Customizing, certain "material types" are marked as subject to inventory updates on a valuation basis, as shown in Figure 4.21. Then, those material types are linked to valuation classes, and general ledger accounts are assigned to valuation classes.

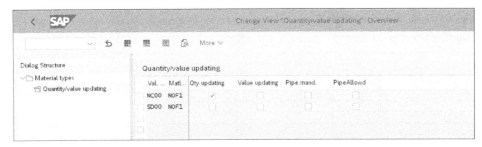

Figure 4.21 Material Types and Inventory Update (on Quantity/Value Basis)

You must choose an account assignment category and define account assignment data if you request one of the following items:

- A consumable that does not have a material master record
- A consumable/material with a master record that is either:
  - Subject to inventory update on a quantity but not a value basis (e.g., nonvaluated materials)
  - Not subject to inventory updates either on a quantity or a value basis (nonstock materials)
- A service
- Stock material for consumption

> **Note**
> If you know the source of supply, you can assign a source of supply to a line item in a purchase requisition, as shown in Figure 4.22.

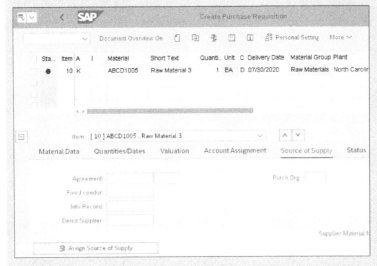

Figure 4.22 Source of Supply View: Assigning a Source of Supply to a Purchase Requisition Line Item

Note that you can create a purchase requisition without a source of supply. Through the **Source Determination** indicator at the header level of the purchase requisition, if only one source of supply exists for an entered material, the system suggests this source. If several potential sources of supply exist, you can select the desired source from the existing sources in the **Source of Supply** view, in the item details section. You can convert a purchase requisition to a purchase order by creating a purchase order with reference to purchase requisition, or the system can convert it automatically. Note that a company can define some additional approval or release procedures to convert a purchase requisition to an order.

4.3.2 Source of Supply Determination

The next step after creating a purchase requisition is the source of supply determination (which can be automated). In procurement, source determination is vital since this capability allows a buyer to find the most suitable source of supply to meet specific purchasing needs. To determine the best source of supply, you can use the source lists as well as purchasing info records, outline agreements, and RFQs. We discussed purchasing info records in Section 4.2.2, so we'll cover outline agreements and RFQs next.

Outline Agreements

If the source of supply (vendor) is known, you can directly convert your purchase requisition to a purchase order and initiate the procurement process with the vendor. If not, you can use outline agreements (i.e., contracts and scheduling agreements) for source of supply determination, as shown in Figure 4.23.

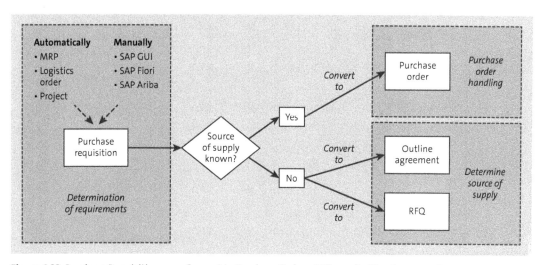

Figure 4.23 Purchase Requisitions can Convert to Purchase Orders, RFQs, or Outline Agreements (Contracts and Scheduling Agreements)

In the system, you can create outline agreements by converting a purchase requisition to a contract or scheduling agreement, as shown in Figure 4.24.

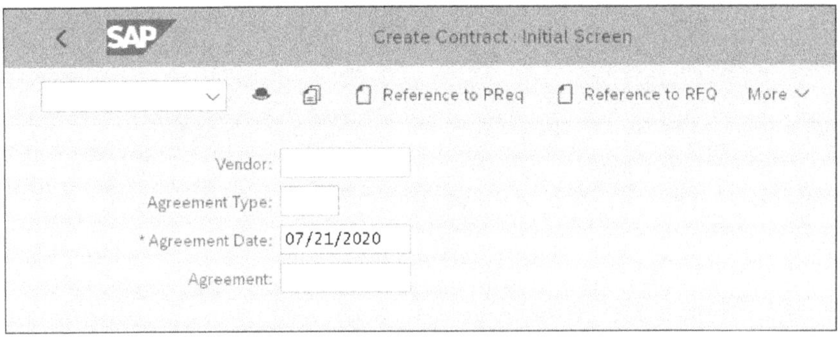

Figure 4.24 Create a Contract with Reference to Purchase Requisition

A *contract* is a long-term agreement between a buyer and a supplier that commits to the purchase of the agreed-upon quantities (or value) of materials from a vendor over a specified period. You can refer to a contract number for source determination when you create a purchase requisition or a purchase order. You still must issue orders (with reference to contracts) to initiate the procurement process.

Alternatively, a *scheduling agreement*, shown in Figure 4.25, is a particular type of outline agreement that you can use when you want to procure materials based on a schedule repetitively. Scheduling agreements include items and schedule lines through which delivery of the total quantity of material specified in a scheduling agreement is spread over a certain period in a delivery schedule. Based on the scheduling agreement type (e.g., **LP** or **LPA**), schedule lines may require a release or be transmitted to the vendor immediately when you save them (without release).

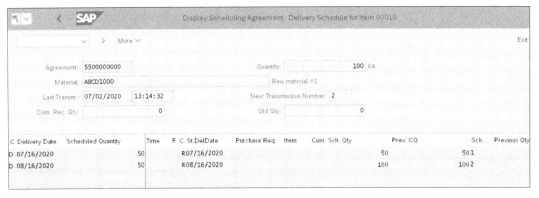

Figure 4.25 Schedule Lines for the Item in a Scheduling Agreement

Requests for Quotations

If the source of supply cannot be identified for a purchase requisition, you can send an RFQ to a list of vendors. Simply create an RFQ with reference to the purchase requisition and send it to vendors. Thus, the RFQ is an external document.

The vendors who receive the RFQ then create quotations to send back to the buying organization.

4.3.3 Vendor Selection

Once all quotations are received, the purchasing department enters all quotations in the system and compares them by using the price comparison capability (Transaction ME49), as shown in Figure 4.26. The next step is to choose the best quotation and reject others. The system can send rejection letters automatically. The best quotation is converted to a purchase order in the planning phase.

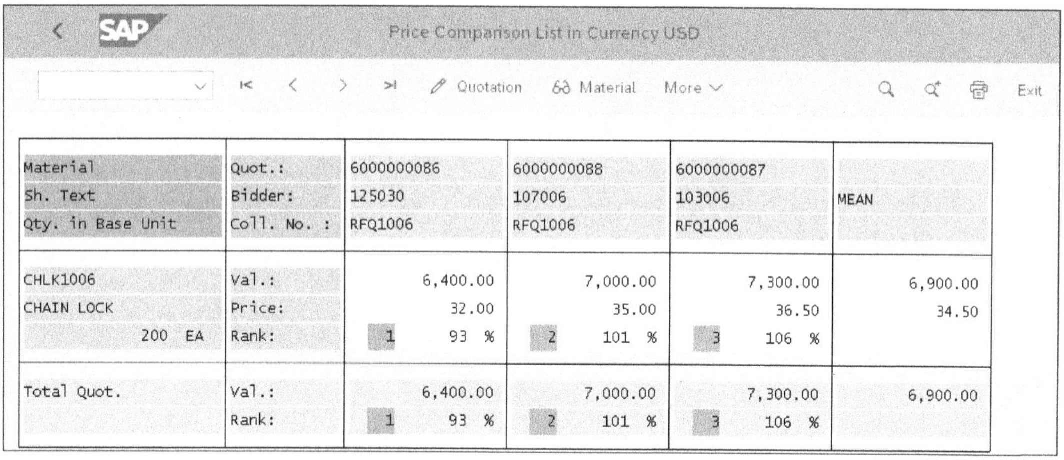

Price Comparison List in Currency USD
Quotation
Material
More
Exit
Material
Sh. Text
Qty. in Base Unit
Quot.:
Bidder:
Coll. No. :
6000000086
125030
RFQ1006
6000000088
107006
RFQ1006
6000000087
103006
RFQ1006
MEAN
CHLK1006
CHAIN LOCK
200 EA
Val.:
Price:
Rank:
6,400.00
32.00
1 93 %
7,000.00
35.00
2 101 %
7,300.00
36.50
3 106 %
6,900.00
34.50
Total Quot.
Val.:
Rank:
6,400.00
1 93 %
7,000.00
2 101 %
7,300.00
3 106 %
6,900.00

Figure 4.26 Price Comparison for Three Quotes

4.3.4 Purchase Order Handling

A purchase order is an external document sent to the vendor. Depending on the agreed-upon purchase order's general terms and conditions, a purchase order can be considered a legally binding agreement between the purchasing organization and supplier. Based on the preferred procurement type, you can choose one of several types of purchase orders, such as the following:

- Standard order (for external procurement)
- Stock transport order (for internal procurement)

Multiple purchase requisitions can be combined into one purchase order by dragging the purchase requisition items to the shopping cart icon next to the standard purchase order type. You may need to click the **Document Overview On** button to see a list of purchase requisitions on the same screen.

You can create a purchase order directly without reference to any document. Alternatively, you can create a purchase order with reference to some prior purchasing documents, such as the following:

- A purchase requisition
- A quotation
- A contract
- Another purchase order

A purchase order consists of header-level data and item-level data. At the header level, a purchase order has a purchase order number, vendor, document date, and document currency as well as organizational data (purchasing organization, purchasing group, and company code). At the item-level of a purchase order, you have a material number, material description, account assignment category, delivery data, plant, storage location, account assignment data, quantities, conditions, and prices, as shown in Figure 4.27.

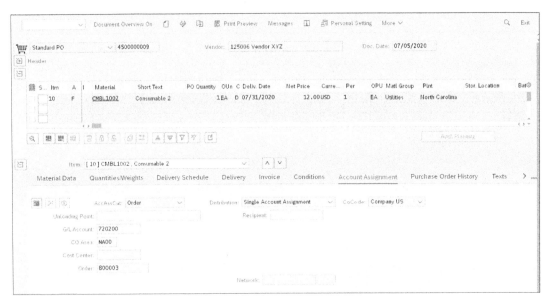

Figure 4.27 Standard Purchase Order with Account Assignment

Purchase requisitions and purchase orders can create financial commitments to reserve the funds for costs that will be incurred in the future. You can manage commitments by using account assignments (to orders, cost centers, or projects) in purchase requisitions and purchase orders. Using commitment management, you can enter and analyze commitments at an early stage and account for them in controlling. This capability enables you to control the financial impacts of commitments on cost objects (orders or projects) before they become actual costs. Commitment management is useful for effective budget management in projects. In Customizing, you must activate commitment management for the controlling area and the orders, as shown in Figure 4.28. When commitment management is activated, data from controlling and materials management is processed in an integrated way.

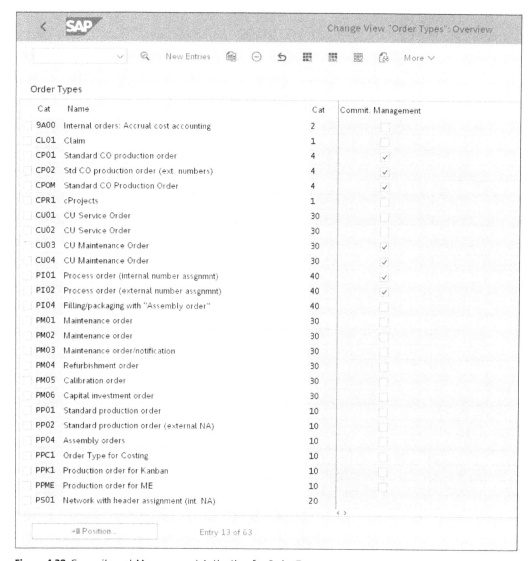

Figure 4.28 Commitment Management Activation for Order Types

How does the data flow occur between controlling and materials management through commitments? First, commitments are assigned to initial commitment objects, such as the following:

- Orders, such as internal orders, sales orders, maintenance orders, and production orders
- Cost centers
- Projects, such as networks, network activities, and work breakdown structure (WBS) elements

Then, commitments are recorded on a purchase requisition or purchase order when you enter the initial commitment objects in these purchasing documents' account assignment data.

Initial commitment objects can also create purchase requisitions automatically. In this case, commitments are transmitted to a purchase requisition. For instance, you can create externally processed activities in a project network. The system automatically generates a purchase requisition commitment associated with the network activity. When a purchase requisition is converted to a purchase order, as shown in Figure 4.29, the purchase requisition commitments are reduced ❶ and transferred to the purchase order ❷. Purchase order commitments are created for the delivery date, not for the document date ❸.

As shown in Figure 4.29, commitments on the purchase order are reduced either when goods are received or when invoices are received ❹. The goods receipt indicator (i.e., goods receipt **non-valuated** checkbox) in the **Delivery** view of purchase order line items determines when the commitments are reduced (valuated or nonvaluated goods receipt). If the goods receipt indicator is selected, the system uses the invoice data to reduce the commitments. Otherwise, the system uses goods receipt data to reduce the commitments. When commitments are reduced on the purchase order, the initial commitment object (e.g., internal order, WBS element) is posted for actual costs, and the associated general ledger account (e.g., determined in the account assignment) is debited, as shown in Figure 4.30. The actual costs on the initial commitment object (e.g., internal order, WBS element) are transferred to settlement receivers during settlement.

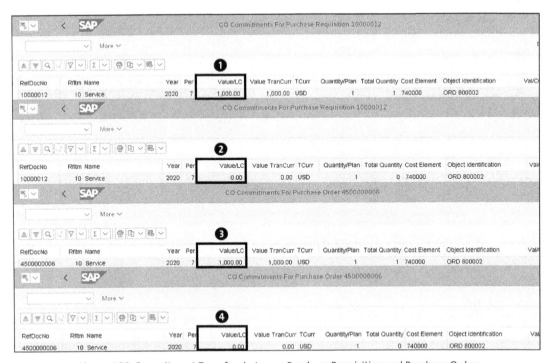

Figure 4.29 Commitment Transfers between Purchase Requisition and Purchase Order

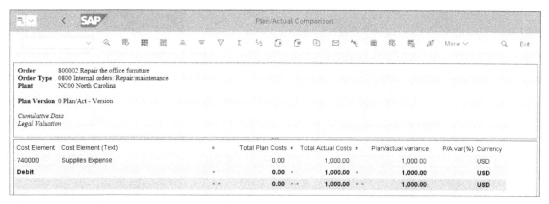

Figure 4.30 Commitment Management: Actual Costs on Internal Order after Goods Receipt Posting

Note
Commitment management is an optional tool and must be activated in controlling. Commitment management is not a prerequisite to use account assignment in purchase requisitions or purchase orders. Without commitment management activation, you can still assign purchasing costs to several cost objects.

4.3.5 Goods Receipt

A goods receipt is a goods movement that shows the formal approval for the receipt of goods from a supplying source or production. The system has the following main categories of goods receipts:

- Goods receipts with reference to a reservation
- Goods receipts with reference to an order
- Other goods receipts

In this section, we'll focus only on goods receipts for purchase orders. We'll introduce you to the other types of goods movements in Chapter 8 in the context of warehouse management.

Note
You can use the Transactions MIGO or MIGO_GR to post the receipt of goods for the materials (not services) in purchase order line items. To enter and accept that services in the purchase order are received, you need to create a service entry sheet.

When you record a goods receipt against a purchase order, you must check the following details:

- The correct material has been delivered.
- The correct quantity of material has been delivered (not an over- or underdelivery).
- Perishable goods meet the minimum shelf criteria. (The shelf-life expiration date check must be active in this case.)

Now, let's dive into the specific data, impact, and documents related to goods receipts.

Data in Goods Receipt

Like other purchasing transactions, you must maintain goods receipt data at the header and item levels. To post a goods receipt against a purchase order, enter the purchase order number at the header, and then the system shows the line items for which a goods receipt can be posted. In the line item-specific views, you'll need to enter the following information:

- Movement type
- Stock type
- Quantity
- Storage location

A *movement type* is a three-character key used for performing all kinds of goods movements in the system, including goods receipts, goods issues, and transfer postings. For instance, movement type 101 is used for goods receipts of all types of purchase orders. Movement type 102 is used to reverse a goods receipt (you need to cancel the material document for goods receipt). Movement type 122 is used for a return delivery to the vendor. The movement type determines which accounts will be updated during the goods movement. For instance, movement type 101 is usually linked to a GR/IR clearing account and a stock account.

You can post a goods receipt for the following stock types:

- Unrestricted-use stock
- Quality inspection stock
- Blocked stock

When you create a purchase order, you can assign a default stock type to the line items. You can change this default value unless quality management is active. If quality management is active, a goods receipt posting for a quality management-relevant item triggers the opening of an inspection lot.

Note

The stock type is essential for materials planning and material withdrawals. The following characteristics are important to keep in mind:

- You can post withdrawals for consumption only from unrestricted-use stock.
- The materials in quality inspection stock or blocked stock cannot be withdrawn for consumption or issued out.
- The materials in quality inspection stock are available from an MRP perspective.
- Stock transfers from a storage location to another storage location in the same plant are possible for all stock types.

Impacts of Goods Receipt

A goods receipt posting leads to several updates in other system components and triggers various system documents. In this section, we discuss the potential impacts of a goods receipt posting.

Let's start with quantity and value updates in the material master record. If the goods receipt is relevant to inventory management, then a goods receipt posting leads to quantity and value updates in the material master record. You can see the new quantities and values in the plant/stock view of material master data or stock overview. The relevant stock (e.g., unrestricted-use stock) levels are also updated. Recall that consumables without a master record and nonstock items are not subject to inventory management, so a goods receipt posting for these materials is optional and does not lead to any quantity or value updates. In the system, the goods movement and quantity updates are recorded in material documents, and the value updates are recorded in documents in accounting (i.e., accounting documents and Material Ledger documents). Note that material documents are created for all successful goods receipt postings, regardless of the need for quantity updates.

Stock items (e.g., raw materials) are subject to inventory management on a value basis (and hence on a quantity basis). Stock items must have a material master record. You can buy stock items either for stock (for later use) or for direct consumption. If you buy a stock item for stock (to use later), then the goods receipt posting leads to a change in the stock quantity and thus a change in the stock value. Recall that the stock value is calculated by using the following formula:

Stock value = Stock quantity × Material price

If you buy a stock item for consumption, then the goods receipt posting does not lead to any change in the stock quantity or the stock value (even the purchase order price is different). When you buy a stock item for consumption, you must enter account assignment data in the purchase order line item.

Nonvaluated items are subject to inventory management on a quantity basis but not on a value basis. Nonvaluated materials must have a material master record in the system and are the items for which you want to track consumption. For nonvaluated materials, you must maintain the account assignment data in the purchase order line item. You cannot post goods receipts of nonvaluated materials directly to consumption or usage. Instead, you must post the goods receipt to warehouse stock first and then post a goods issue for consumption or usage. If you buy a nonvaluated item, then the goods receipt posting leads to a change in the warehouse stock quantity but not in the stock value (even if the purchase order price is different).

Next, let's consider accounting updates. If the goods receipt is relevant to financial accounting, the goods receipt posting leads to updates in inventory or consumption accounts. Accounting updates are recorded in documents in accounting.

Depending on the material type, item category, and account assignment category specified in the purchase order line item, one or more documents can be created in accounting, as shown in Figure 4.31.

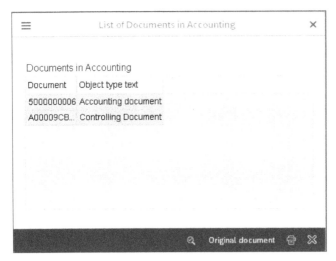

Figure 4.31 Goods Receipt Posting: Documents in Accounting

If the purchase order price is different from the material price, the item's material price is also updated, as is its stock value. Stock value updates are also recorded in Material Ledger documents, which we'll discuss in the next section. Inventory or consumption account updates are recorded in accounting documents. Updates in controlling (e.g., commitments, cost center updates, actual cost transfers to cost objects) are recorded in controlling documents. Let's consider a few examples for the accounting updates led by goods receipt posting:

- If you buy a stock item for the stock, the goods receipt posting creates an accounting document that includes a debit to an inventory account and credit to the GR/IR clearing account. The system also creates a Material Ledger document to record the value changes in stock and update the moving average price.

- Let's say you buy a stock item for consumption (or a nonstock item or a nonvaluated item). In this case, you must select an account assignment category and maintain account assignment data (general ledger account and controlling object) in the purchase order line item, as shown in Figure 4.32. In this case, the goods receipt is not relevant to inventory valuation, so a Material Ledger document is not created. This goods receipt posting creates an accounting document and a controlling document to record updates in the consumption accounts and the controlling objects, such as cost centers.

In some exceptional cases, a goods receipt posting may not generate accounting documents. For instance, if you buy a consignment material, you must choose an item category (**K**, for consignment). In this case, goods receipt is not relevant to accounting, and no document in accounting is created since the consignment stock belongs to the vendor. (The material document is created only to record the quantity updates in consignment stock.)

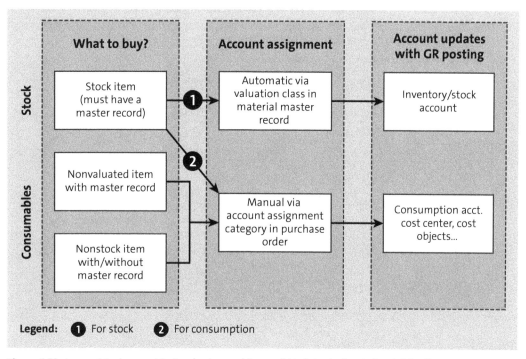

Figure 4.32 Account Assignment in Purchasing and Account Updates in Goods Receipt Posting

In addition to the major impacts we've discussed, several additional effects of the goods receipt process should be kept in mind, such as the following:

- **Updates in purchase order history**
  In the line item details of the purchase order, the purchase order data in the **History** view is updated, the goods receipt is recorded, and the material document is added. The goods receipt accounting documents can be viewed by clicking the **FI Documents** button in the material document's **Doc. Info** view.

- **Commitments on purchase order**
  If commitment management is active for the account assignment object (e.g., internal order, project), commitments on the purchase order are reduced, and the actual costs are posted to the account assignment object.

- **Impacts on quality management**
  Let's say the quality management component is active for procurement in the material master record's **Quality Management** view. In this case, you can define whether a certificate is required for the material so you can confirm the receipt of the certificate during the goods receipt posting. In the material master record, you also can maintain data for quality inspection. In the goods receipt posting, the system automatically creates an inspection lot.

- **Impacts on warehouse management**
  If warehouse management is active and the material is managed in a warehouse, a transfer requirement is created. A transfer requirement is a request to warehouse management for putaway. The details of physical movements in the warehouse are covered in Chapter 8.
- **Outputs for goods receipt**
  When you enter a goods receipt, you can print out a goods receipt slip or a pallet note at the same time. If you set the goods receipt **Message** indicator in purchase order's header, the buyer automatically receives a message informing him/her of the delivery.

Documents for Goods Receipt

When you post a goods receipt, the system creates a material document as proof of the goods movement. Depending on procurement type, the system can also generate accounting, controlling, and Material Ledger documents, as shown in Figure 4.33.

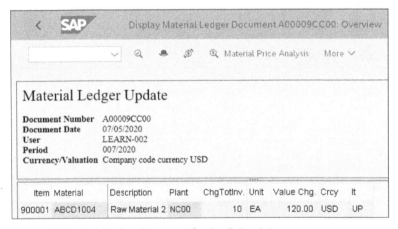

Figure 4.33 Material Ledger Document for Goods Receipt

Table 4.3 summarizes the data common in documents for goods receipt.

Document Type	Header-Level Data	Item-Level Data
Material document	Document number, date, delivery note number	Material, quantity, plant, movement type
Accounting document	Document number, date, company code, fiscal year, reference, currency	Account number, description, posting amount, posting key

Table 4.3 Data in Documents for Goods Receipt

Document Type	Header-Level Data	Item-Level Data
Controlling document	Document number, controlling area currency	Object type, object, cost element, amount, quantity, offset account
Material Ledger document	Document number, date, period, fiscal year, currency, delivery note number, bill of lading number	Material, plant, quantity, value change

Table 4.3 Data in Documents for Goods Receipt (Cont.)

4.3.6 Invoice Verification

Invoice verification is the process that completes the purchasing process in materials management and passes related information to financial accounting for payment. When you receive an invoice from a supplier, you must enter it into the system for verification. You can use Transaction MIRO (Document Entry) to enter a vendor's invoice, which initiates the verification process. The system allows you to use two different invoice verification scenarios:

- **Goods receipt-based invoice verification (three-way match)**
  In this scenario, a goods receipt posting is a prerequisite for invoice posting. The system matches invoice quantities with the delivered quantities specified on the purchase order. In other words, the invoice quantities and values are compared to the delivered quantities in the goods receipt's material document and the quantities and values on the purchase order.
- **Purchase order-based invoice verification**
  In this scenario, you can post an invoice for purchase order items, even though they have not been delivered yet. Purchase order-based invoice verification can be useful for procurement processes in which you need to pay the vendor before the items are delivered.

You can use the **Gr-Bsd IV** indicator in the **Invoice** view of purchase order line items to choose between a goods receipt-based invoice verification or purchase order-based invoice verification.

In the invoice, you must maintain some data at the header and line item levels. You can enter dates, total invoice amounts, currencies, payment data (payment terms and dates), and tax data at the header level. Then, you can refer to a relevant document (e.g., a purchase order or delivery note) to transfer data to invoice document line items. At the line item level, you'll enter material-specific data such as invoice prices, quantities, tax codes, and jurisdiction codes, as shown in Figure 4.34. Data will transfer to the invoice from relevant documents when you enter any of the following information:

- Purchase order number or scheduling agreement number
- Delivery note number
- Bill of lading number
- Service entry sheet number

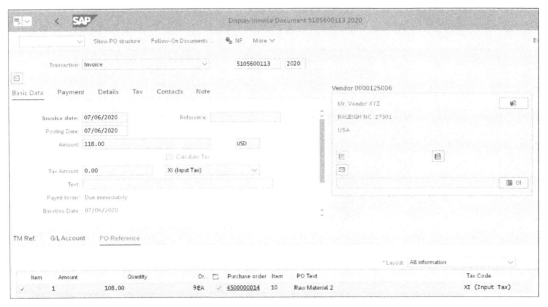

Figure 4.34 Invoice Document with Price Differences

When you post the invoice, the following activities occur:

- The invoice document is added to the purchase order history.
- The system creates an accounting document, shown in Figure 4.35, that includes the following updates to the GR/IR clearing account and the vendor account:
  - A credit to the vendor account (an open item is created)
  - A debit to the accounts payable reconciliation account (automatically)
  - A debit to the GR/IR clearing account (provisions are reversed)
- If the total invoice line item price is different than the total purchase order line item price, the following occurs:
  - The stock value and the current moving average price are updated in the material master record (if you're buying for stock). The system creates a Material Ledger document that records the resulting stock value updates. All value updates can be viewed by using the material price analysis in the **Accounting 1** view of the material master record.
  - The accounting document includes a posting to an inventory account (if you're buying for stock) for the line item price differences. If you're not buying for stock, the accounting document includes a posting to a consumption account determined in the account assignment data.

- If the total invoice amount is different than the total invoice line item amount, the following occurs:
  - The accounting document includes a posting to a previously defined purchase difference account, as shown in Figure 4.35 (item **4**).
  - The system creates a controlling document that includes updates to the previously defined cost center/object for the procurement costs, as shown in Figure 4.36.

Figure 4.35 Accounting Document for Invoice

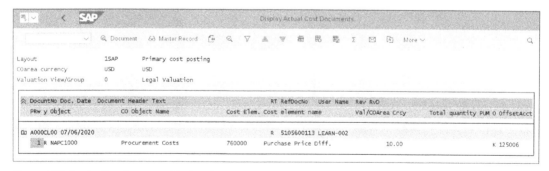

Figure 4.36 Controlling Document for Invoice

4.3.7 Payment

The payment process usually includes the following elements:

- Selecting a payment method and a bank
- Selecting items for payment

- Calculating the payment amount (considering cash discount periods)
- Posting the payment document
- Create the payment medium

After posting an invoice, you must ensure that the invoice is not blocked for payment. If blocked, you must release the invoice. You can pay vendors manually or by using an automatic payment program. The automatic payment program is part of financial accounting. To execute an automatic payment run, you must follow this procedure:

1. Maintain parameters
2. Start proposal run
3. Edit proposal
4. Start payment run
5. Create payment media

When you start the payment run, the system posts the payment documents, clears open items, and prepares the data for creating the payment media, such as checks, Electronic Data Interchange (EDI), or Data Medium Exchange (DME). The system uses the Payment Medium Workbench (PMW) to create payment media. As a result of payment, a debit to the vendor account is posted, as well as a credit to the bank account. A debit to the accounts payable reconciliation account also occurs automatically.

4.4 Integration with Other Modules

In this section, we discuss the potential integration points of the source-to-pay business process. We'll touch on data assignments, transactions, and SAP Ariba.

4.4.1 Integration via Cross-Module Data Assignments

Data assignments can link other processes to procurement, such as in the following examples:

- Vendors are master data in procurement. In the financial accounting vendor business partner role, you must assign a reconciliation account to the vendor. Through this reconciliation account, vendors are linked to the general ledger.
- Bills of materials (BOMs) are master data in production, and they can include nonstock items linked to procurement.
- Material types are assigned to the valuation classes. The valuation class is entered in the material master record and determines general ledger accounts updated during the receipt of materials.

4.4.2 Integration via Transactions

Integration between procurement and other business processes occurs during some transactions of purchasing at the following touchpoints:

- **Management accounting (controlling)**
  In a purchase requisition or a purchase order, the user must specify the account assignment for consumed items. The account assignment connects the purchase requisition line item to a cost center. Recall that a cost center is master data in controlling. A goods receipt posting transfers the cost of consumable items to cost centers.

  An internal order is master data in controlling. If commitment management is active for an internal order type, commitments are created on purchase requisitions when defining that internal order as the account assignment object. Converting the purchase requisition to a purchase order transfers the commitments to purchase order. A goods receipt posting reduces the commitments on a purchase order and transfers the actual costs to the internal order.

- **Financial accounting**
  General ledger accounts are master data in financial accounting. Depending on the item category and account assignment on the purchase order, a goods receipt posting (and invoice posting) will update several general ledger accounts, such as the GR/IR account, the general ledger expense account, and the inventory account. Invoice posting also updates the vendor accounts, which are part of accounts payable.

- **Inventory management**
  Goods receipt is part of inventory management and is posted against the purchase order. When you post a goods receipt, quantities and values are updated in inventory management.

- **Warehouse management**
  If warehouse management is active, a warehouse transfer request will be created when you post the goods receipt for a warehouse-managed item.

- **Quality management**
  If quality management is active and quality management data is maintained in the material master record, quality management integration occurs during the goods receipt posting.

- **MRP, production, sales and distribution, plant maintenance, asset accounting, and Project System**
  You can manually create purchase requisitions, and purchase orders, by using account assignments to cost objects such as a production order, project, maintenance order, sales order, or asset. Conversely, other system components can generate purchase requisitions automatically. For instance, the release of the operations in production/maintenance orders and of network activities in projects can generate purchase requisitions automatically when they are assigned a

nonstock material. External processing activities in a project can also trigger an automatic purchase requisition. During the goods receipt posting, relevant cost objects are posted for actual costs.

Figure 4.37 shows the touchpoints of integration in procurement.

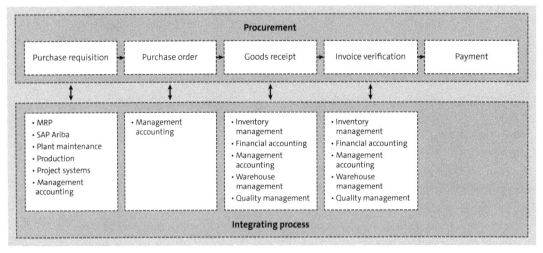

Figure 4.37 Processes Integrating with Procurement

4.4.3 SAP Ariba Integration

SAP S/4HANA supports the operational transactions of procurement such as materials management, purchase order, and operational contract. Strategic collaboration is supported by cloud LoB solutions such as SAP Ariba, SAP Concur, and SAP Fieldglass. SAP Ariba is not a single product; it consists of several solutions including Ariba Network, SAP Ariba Sourcing, and SAP Ariba Procurement. Ariba Network is a cloud-based platform that connects purchasers with suppliers. By integrating SAP Ariba with SAP S/4HANA, companies can manage their procurement processes within SAP S/4HANA and benefit from procurement content and collaboration capabilities that Ariba Network provides.

SAP Ariba and SAP S/4HANA integration include the following capabilities:

- Document acceptance automation for purchase orders and invoices
- Identifying and avoiding potential errors in purchasing documents
- Conversion services for paper-based documents

In a typical integration scenario, the process works in the following way:

- Contract terms and pricing are determined in the SAP Ariba Catalog.
- Authorized buying users use the SAP Ariba Catalog to search for purchasing items and to create purchase orders in SAP S/4HANA, which are sent to the suppliers on Ariba Network for processing.

- On Ariba Network, vendors confirm orders, let their customers know items have shipped, and send purchase order invoices for payment.
- Users receive invoices in SAP S/4HANA and prepare the system for payment.

4.5 Important Terminology

In this chapter, the following terminology we use is important to know for the exam:

- **Account assignment category**
  A single-character key you must specify for purchase order line items you are buying for consumption. This key connects a material to expense accounts in financial accounting and cost objects in controlling.
- **Automatic payment run**
  A financial accounting transaction used to create payment proposals and to make payments for the open items.
- **Client**
  The highest hierarchical organizational data that represents the enterprise in the system.
- **Company code**
  Organizational data that represents the legal entity of an enterprise.
- **Conditions**
  Represent provisions (e.g., prices, discounts, freight) in procurement. You can maintain conditions in purchase orders, outline agreements, RFQ, and info records.
- **Goods receipt**
  A transaction used to confirm the receipt of goods. This transaction updates inventory and accounting records.
- **Intelligent Spend Management**
  SAP's new spend management strategy for the intelligent enterprise. It consists of source-to-pay external workforce management and travel-to-reimbursement.
- **Invoice**
  Vendor's request for payment. A vendor's invoice must be entered, verified, and posted in the system.
- **Material master record**
  Master data that represents the merchandise in purchasing. This master data consists of views at different organizational levels. These views connect the material to several business processes.
- **Outline agreement**
  A long-term vendor-customer agreement in the form of a contract or scheduling agreement.

- **Plant**
  Organizational data that represents the physical location where the materials are managed and delivered.
- **Purchase order**
  An external document that you send to a vendor. A purchase order is a binding contract between the purchaser and a supplier and includes all terms and conditions regulating further steps of the procurement.
- **Purchase requisition**
  An internal request that determines the requirements for purchasing.
- **Purchasing info record**
  Also called an info record, master data providing information about which vendor sells what and the purchasing conditions.
- **Quotation**
  A vendor's response to RFQ. This document is legally binding for the seller.
- **Request for quotations (RFQ)**
  An external document that invites vendors to bid for purchasing requirements.
- **Source-to-pay**
  A new and enhanced end-to-end procurement process for the intelligent enterprise. It is enhanced by strategic sourcing, embedded intelligence, and insights across the business process.
- **Storage location**
  Organizational data that represents a physical location within a plant where you keep stock.
- **Three-way match**
  A goods receipt-based invoice verification procedure that the system uses to compare quantities and values on the purchase order, material document (for goods receipt), and the vendor's invoice.
- **Vendor master record**
  Master data that represents the supplier in the system.

4.6 Practice Questions

These practice questions will help you evaluate your understanding of the topics covered in this chapter. The questions shown are similar to those found on the certification examination. Although none of these questions will be found on the exam itself, they will allow you to review your knowledge of the subject. Select the correct answers and then check the completeness of your answers in the next section. Remember that you must select all correct answers on the exam and select only correct answers to receive credit for the question.

1. Which of the following are master data in source-to-pay? (There are two correct answers.)

   - ☒ A. Purchasing organization
   - ☐ B. Plant
   - ☒ C. Vendor
   - ☒ D. Info record

2. Which of the following are organizational data in source-to-pay? (There are three correct answers.)

   - ☐ A. Sales organization
   - ☒ B. Plant
   - ☒ C. Storage location
   - ☐ D. Info record
   - ☒ E. Purchasing organization

3. Which of the following represents the correct sequence of tasks in the source-to-pay business process?

   - ☐ A. Handle and monitor purchase orders → determine the source of supply → vendor selection → receive goods → payment → invoice verification
   - ☐ B. Vendor selection → determine requirements → purchase order handling → receive goods → invoice verification → payment
   - ☐ C. Purchase order handling → vendor selection → invoice verification → receive goods → payment
   - ☒ D. Determine requirements → vendor selection → purchase order handling → receive goods → invoice verification → payment

4. Which of the following purchasing organizations is *not* assigned to a company code or plant?

   - ☐ A. Cross-plant purchasing organization
   - ☒ B. Cross-company code purchasing organization
   - ☐ C. Plant-specific purchasing organization
   - ☐ D. Company code-level purchasing organization

5. Which of the following can be directly assigned to a company code in its master data?

- ☒ A. Vendor
- ☐ B. Storage location
- ☐ C. Material
- ☐ D. Purchasing group

6. The conditions in a purchasing info record can be which of the following? (There are two correct answers.)

- ☐ A. Plant specific
- ☐ B. Company code specific
- ☒ C. Purchasing organization and plant specific
- ☒ D. Purchasing organization specific

7. What conditions can be used in purchasing? (There are two correct answers.)

- ☒ A. Conditions in a purchase requisition
- ☒ B. Conditions in a contract
- ☒ C. Conditions in a purchasing record
- ☐ D. Conditions in a billing document

8. Which of the following data in the material master record connects a material to the general ledger?

- ☒ A. Reconciliation account
- ☒ B. Valuation class
- ☐ C. Account determination key
- ☐ D. General ledger account number

9. Which of the following can be assigned to a plant in its master record? (There are two correct answers.)

- ☒ A. Material
- ☒ B. Info record
- ☐ C. Vendor
- ☐ D. General ledger account

10. You can convert a purchase requisition to which of the following? (There are two correct answers.)

- ☒ A. Quotation
- ☒ B. RFQ

☒ C. Outline agreement
☐ D. Goods receipt

11. You can create a purchase order with reference to which of the following? (There are two correct answers.)

☒ A. Purchase requisition
☒ B. Quotation
☐ C. Internal order
☐ D. Project

12. In which of the following cases do you have to enter an account assignment in a purchase order? (There are two correct answers.)

☐ A. When you buy a stock item for stock
☒ B. When you buy an item without a master record
☒ C. When you buy a service
☐ D. When you procure a consignment material (item category K)

13. Which of the following procurement transactions update the stock value when you buy a consumable?

☐ A. Goods receipt
☐ B. Invoice posting
☐ C. Purchase order creation
☒ D. None of the above

14. Which of the following documents can be created when you post an invoice for a consumable item? (There are two correct answers.)

☒ A. Material document
☒ B. Material Ledger document
☐ C. Controlling document
☐ D. Accounting document

15. Which of the following are touchpoints for the integration between procurement and financial accounting? (There are two correct answers.)

☐ A. Goods receipt for consignment
☐ B. Goods receipt for consumables
☒ C. Invoice posting
☒ D. Purchase order creation

16. Which of the following are the touchpoints of the integration between a purchase order and an internal order? (There are two correct answers.)

    ☐ A. Item category
    ☒ B. Account assignment
    ☒ C. Settlement rule
    ☐ D. Commitment management

17. Which of the following is a touchpoint for the integration between procurement and accounts payable?

    ☒ A. Invoice posting
    ☐ B. Goods receipt posting
    ☐ C. Quotation
    ☐ D. Creating a scheduling agreement

18. Commitments on a purchase requisition are reduced at what time?

    ☒ A. When you convert purchase requisition to purchase order
    ☐ B. When you post a goods receipt
    ☐ C. When you post the invoice
    ☐ D. When the payment is complete

19. Which documents are compared during the invoice verification (three-way match) process? (There are three correct answers.)

    ☐ A. Material Ledger document
    ☒ B. Material document for goods receipt
    ☒ C. Vendor's invoice
    ☒ D. Purchase order
    ☐ E. Billing document

20. Which of the following items are subject to inventory management only on a quantity basis?

    ☐ A. Stock items
    ☐ B. Nonstock items
    ☒ C. Nonvaluated items
    ☐ D. Consumable materials without master records

21. Which of the following is not a financial accounting impact of payment?

    ☐ A. Debit to the vendor account
    ☐ B. Credit to the bank account

- ☐ C. Debit to accounts payable reconciliation account (automatically)
- ☒ D. Credit to inventory account

4.7 Practice Question Answers and Explanations

1. Correct answers: **C and D**

   Material master records, vendor master records, and purchasing info records are master data in source-to-pay. Plant and purchasing organization in other options are the organizational data in source-to-pay.

2. Correct answers: **B, C, and E**

   Client, company code, plant, storage location, purchasing organization, and purchasing group are organizational data in source-to-pay. The sales organization is organizational data in sales and distribution. An info record is master data in source-to-pay.

3. Correct answer: **D**

   The correct sequence of key tasks in source-to-pay is determine requirements → source of supply determination → vendor selection → purchase order handling → receive goods → invoice verification → payment.

4. Correct answer: **B**

   A central purchasing organization (cross-company code) is not assigned to any company code or plant in Customizing. A plant-specific purchasing organization is assigned to a plant. Cross-plant purchasing organizations and company code-level purchasing organizations are the same and must be assigned to a company code.

5. Correct answer: **A**

   The keyword here is master data. Only vendors and materials are master data in purchasing. Storage locations and purchasing groups are organizational data. A vendor is assigned to a company code in its master record. A material is assigned to a plant.

6. Correct answers: **C and D**

   When you create purchasing info record, you can specify the organizational level at which you want to create the master record. The selection of the organizational level at this step makes a purchasing info record either purchasing organization-specific or purchasing organization- and plant-specific.

7. Correct answers: **B and C**

   Conditions represent the time-dependent/independent elements, such as gross price, discounts on a vendor's price, and freight. A condition record is second-level master data that can be defined in other master data or documents, such as in info records, contracts, or purchase orders.

8. **Correct answer: B**

   You can maintain the valuation class in the **Accounting 1** view of the material master record. The valuation class connects the material to general ledger accounts. An account determination key is used in the asset master record. A reconciliation account is used to connect a subledger account to the general ledger. A general ledger account number is not maintained in a material master record.

9. **Correct answers: A and B**

   Materials and info records are assigned to a plant in their master records. A purchasing organization can be assigned to a plant in Customizing. Vendor master records and general ledger accounts are not assigned to a plant, but to a company code.

10. **Correct answers: B and C**

    A purchase requisition can be converted into RFQ, an outline agreement, and a purchase order, which makes the data entry process easier and more accurate in subsequent transactions. A goods receipt is posted against a purchase order, not a purchase requisition.

11. **Correct answers: A and B**

    A purchase order can be created with reference to a purchase requisition, a quotation, or a contract, which makes the data entry process easier and more accurate when creating the purchase order. The reference also connects preceding documents to the purchase order. Internal orders or projects can be defined as account assignments in the purchase order, but they cannot serve as reference documents for purchase order creation.

12. **Correct answers: B and C**

    Consignment material is not relevant to financial accounting, so you do not need to enter an account assignment for this material category. Account assignment is not necessary when you buy a stock item for stock. The system pulls the necessary account assignment from the material master record of the stock item. In the latter cases, you must enter an account assignment.

13. **Correct answer: D**

    Consumables are not subject to inventory management on a value basis. So, none of the transactions in options A through C can lead to a value update in stock.

14. **Correct answers: C and D**

    When posting an invoice for consumable material purchase, an accounting document is created, recording the updates in the vendor's subledger account and GR/IR clearing account. If a price difference exists, a controlling document is created to update cost centers for the differences.

15. **Correct answers: B and C**

    Goods receipts for consumable purchases and invoice postings are relevant to financial accounting. An accounting document is created to document this impact. However, goods receipts for consignment material are not relevant to financial accounting, and thus, purchase order creation has no impact on financial accounting.

16. Correct answers: **B and D**

    You can enter an internal order number as an account assignment when you create a purchase order line item relevant to the internal order. Commitment management is also a connection between a purchase order and internal an order. Commitments on the purchase order are reduced either when goods are received or when invoices are received. When commitments are reduced on the purchase order, the initial commitment object (e.g., internal order, WBS element) is posted for actual costs.

17. Correct answer: **A**

    A vendor account is a subledger account, and it is a part of accounts payable accounting. Invoice posting leads to a credit posting to the relevant vendor account. The same account is debited when you pay the vendor. Purchase order or scheduling agreement creation has no impact on the vendor account. The goods receipt posting can lead to postings to general ledger accounts but not to the vendor account.

18. Correct answer: **A**

    Commitments on the purchase requisition are reduced on the purchase requisition and transferred to the purchase order when the purchase requisition is converted to a purchase order. Commitments on the purchase order are reduced either when goods are received or when invoices are received.

19. Correct answers: **B, C, and D**

    In the goods receipt-based invoice verification (three-way match), the invoice quantities and values are compared to the delivered quantities in the goods receipt's material document and to the quantities and values on the purchase order.

20. Correct answer: **C**

    A nonvaluated item is subject to inventory management only on a quantity basis but not on a value basis. Stock items are subject to inventory on a value and quantity basis. Nonstock items are not subject to inventory management. Three types of consumables exist: consumables without master records, consumables with master records and without inventory management, and consumables with master records and inventory management on a quantity basis. Consumables without master records are not inventory managed.

21. Correct answer: **D**

    Invoice verification ends the procurement process in materials management and passes the process over to financial accounting. After this step, inventory accounts are not posted. However, payment leads to debit posting to the vendor account (and an automatic debit posting to accounts payable reconciliation account) and credit posting to the bank account.

4.8 Test Takeaway

In this chapter, you learned about key topics in the source-to-pay business process and about SAP solutions supporting the key tasks in source-to-pay processing.

The determination of requirements, specifying sources of supply, vendor selection, purchase order handling, goods receipt, invoice verification, and payment are key tasks of the source-to-pay business process in SAP S/4HANA. Using the relevant transactions in purchasing, inventory management, and financial accounting, you can carry out these tasks. The purchasing-relevant enterprise organization can be mapped into the system by creating organizational data, including client, company code, plant, storage location, purchasing organization, and purchasing group. Purchasing organizations can be structured centrally (cross-company code) in a client. They can also be cross-plant (company code level) or plant specific. Material master data, vendor master data, and purchasing info records form the foundation of source-to-pay transactions in SAP S/4HANA.

A purchase requisition is a request to a purchase order and can be triggered by other system applications, such as production orders, projects, maintenance orders, and MRP. SAP Ariba is a cloud-based solution enabling self-requisitioning and strategic sourcing.

A purchase order is a detailed document that includes all the data necessary for subsequent steps of procurement. A purchase order can be created with reference to a purchase requisition, an RFQ, a quotation, a contract, or another purchase order.

To receive delivered items, you post a goods receipt in inventory management. Depending on the received material, the goods receipt posting leads to updates in inventory management and financial accounting records. A goods receipt may also impact warehouse management, quality management, and management accounting. The system creates accounting, controlling, material, and material documents to record these impacts.

A vendor's invoice must be entered into the system and verified. Invoice verification based on goods receipt compares invoice quantities to the quantities on the associated purchase order and quantities on the goods receipt's material document. Invoice verification triggers postings to the vendor's subledger account in accounts payable and the GR/IR clearing account in general ledger accounting.

Payments can be carried out manually or automatically by using an automatic payment run. This activity results in a debit posting to the vendor's account and a credit posting to the company's bank account.

We've now completed our overview of the source-to-pay business process and its handling in SAP S/4HANA. The next chapter covers lead-to-cash processing in SAP S/4HANA and its connections with other business processes in SAP S/4HANA.

Chapter 5
Lead-to-Cash Processing

Techniques You'll Master

- Describe the subprocesses and tasks of the lead-to-cash business process
- Identify the master and organizational data that supports the lead-to-cash business process
- Perform system transactions enabling order-to-cash processing in SAP S/4HANA
- Identify the touchpoints of integration between the sales and distribution module in SAP S/4HANA and other system modules

Chapter 5 Lead-to-Cash Processing

This chapter of the book covers all certification-relevant topics of the lead-to-cash business process. We'll describe the master data, organizational data, and system transactions supporting the lead-to-cash business process and explain the potential integration scenarios.

Lead-to-cash describes an end-to-end process consisting of five subprocesses:

- Contact-to-lead
- Lead-to-opportunity
- Opportunity-to-quote
- Quote-to-order
- Order-to-cash

Tip
Out of these five subprocesses, the exam focuses on order-to-cash. See Section 5.3 for more information.

Lead-to-cash is a customer experience-oriented, end-to-end business process supported by several components of the SAP intelligent suite, including SAP Customer Experience, SAP S/4HANA, SAP Business Technology Platform (SAP BTP) for analytical and machine learning scenarios, and SAP Analytics Cloud for reporting purposes. Every company is different, but in a typical lead-to-cash business scenario, including industry, business-to-business (B2B), or business-to-customer (B2C) customer scenarios and direct sales or e-commerce, eight tasks are performed:

- Unidentified contact to identified contacts
- Lead management
- Opportunity management
- Quote management
- Customer order management
- Contract/order management
- Fulfillment
- Invoicing (and payment)

The tasks and subprocesses of the lead-to-cash business process are shown in Figure 5.1.

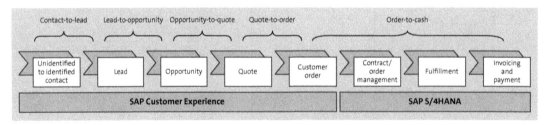

Figure 5.1 Subprocesses and Tasks of Lead-to-Cash Processing

> **Real-World Scenario**
>
> Every business sells products or services to generate revenue. An efficient sales process must be a seamless end-to-end process that puts the customer at the center of everything. The development of intelligent technologies enables the orchestration of operational data (O-Data) and customer experience data (X-Data) in intelligent enterprise systems.
>
> A typical lead-to-cash process consists of presales activities as well as the core sales tasks triggered by sales order generation. In presales, a marketing expert interacts with a customer with the intention of generating leads for sales. *Leads* are business transactions that describe, store, and manage a customer's potential interest to buy in a specific time frame. Using predictive analytics along with O-Data and X-Data, experts can generate scores for customers, such as purchasing propensity for a particular product or service. A company may use a lead to analyze the potential chance to conduct business and to convert the lead into an opportunity. An *opportunity* is a transaction that describes the estimated sales possibility, the potential sales volume, and the sales prospect's budget for specific products or services. A sales rep can work on opportunities and create quotes to win the deal. If the customer accepts the terms and conditions in the quote, they place a (purchase) order. After this step, the process moves along to order-to-cash, which starts with creating a sales order for fulfillment and provisioning. At this point, the seller should check the availability of the merchandise in real time and confirm the requested delivery time and quantities. This process continues by issuing the goods from the warehouse, billing, and invoicing the customer. As fulfillment goes along, the buyer should be able to see the process's status and receive notifications.
>
> A consultant should be able to explain how the system supports these tasks in lead-to-cash via organizational data and master data management. Lead-to-cash aims to create a seamless demand and supply chain that connects customers' interest in purchasing, which is a company's realization of revenue. Thus, a consultant must clearly understand how system components are integrated to achieve this seamless connection between elements of demand and supply chains.

5.1 Objectives of This Portion of the Test

This portion of the certification aims to test your knowledge of the tasks and subprocesses of the lead-to-cash business process and SAP's intelligent suite solutions. In particular, the certification exam includes questions about the organizational data, master data, and core transactions of the order-to-cash business process.

Consultants are expected to explain the workflow in order-to-cash and all touchpoints of integration between the sales and distributions module and other system modules.

For the certification exam, business process integration consultants must have a good understanding of the following topics:

- Master data and organizational data in lead-to-cash processing
- Sales order and outbound delivery handling and billing processes
- Touchpoints of integration

Note
The lead-to-cash business process covers 8%–12% of the questions in the certification exam.

5.2 Data Structures for Lead-to-Cash

SAP S/4HANA includes the sales and distribution module to support the order-to-cash subprocess in lead-to-cash processing. This section defines the organizational data and the master data that supports the lead-to-cash business process.

5.2.1 Organizational Data

The sales and distribution module's organizational data represents a company's enterprise structure in the lead-to-cash business process. The organizational data must be known to answer sales and distribution-relevant questions, such as the following:

- Which entity is financially responsible for sales?
- Which organizational unit is responsible for product liability and the right of recourse?
- Which unit is responsible for distributing goods and services?
- How should products be supplied to customers?
- Which product lines are used in sales?
- Where should sales-relevant materials be stored?
- Where are the products shipped from?

Tip
Lead-to-cash is the customer-oriented, end-to-end business process in SAP's intelligent suite. Order-to-cash is the core end-to-end business process in the digital core, the SAP S/4HANA suite. Sales and distribution is the application component (module) in SAP S/4HANA that supports the order-to-cash business process.

In the system, tasks in order-to-cash processing are enabled by the sales and distribution module transactions. The organizational data that supports those transactions include the following:

- Client
- Company code
- Sales area, including the following:
  - Sales organization
  - Distribution channel
  - Division
- Plant
- Storage location
- Shipping point

Client, company code, plant, and storage location are standard organizational levels of logistics, which were described in detail in Chapter 4, Section 4.2. For the purposes of this chapter, we'll explain the organizational data that is specific to the lead-to-cash business process, such as the following:

- **Plant**
  A plant in the lead-to-cash business process represents a physical location where products or services are delivered (i.e., the delivering plant). A plant can be a distribution center, a regional sales office, or a production facility. In Customizing, the delivering plant is assigned to a combination of sales organization and distribution channel.

- **Sales organization**
  A sales organization represents the highest level of a selling entity in the enterprise structure. Sales organizations are created based on regional, national, or international subdivisions of the market. For instance, US East and US West can be two sales organizations in a company in the US. The sales organization prepares and executes all sales transactions and is responsible for distributing goods and services, negotiating sales conditions, and handling product liability and rights of recourse. The business success of a sales area is the responsibility of the sales organization. Thus, the sales organization is the highest level of aggregation in sales-related reporting. Every organization using order-to-cash business processes needs at least one sales organization. In the system, you can use a four-character alphanumeric key to identify a sales organization. Sales document line items and master data in sales and distribution are created at the sales organization level. In Customizing, a sales organization can be assigned to a single company code. You can assign several sales organizations to a company code, as shown in Figure 5.2.

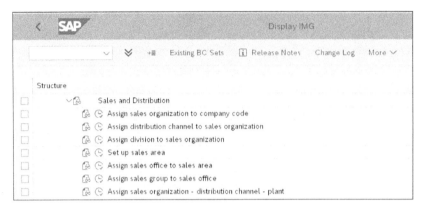

Figure 5.2 Organizational Data Assignment in Customizing

- **Distribution channel**
  In the system, a distribution channel represents the way in which sales-relevant materials or services reach the customer. Wholesale trade, retail trade, direct sales, and e-commerce are some examples of distribution channels. In other words, a distribution is a grouping of various distribution methods through which a company distributes goods and services to its customers. Within a sales organization, a customer can be supplied through several distribution channels. A sales-relevant item must have master data with the sales view, including sales-specific data (e.g., prices, minimum order quantity, minimum quantity delivered, and delivering plant) that might be different for each sales organization and distribution channel. Every organization using the order-to-cash business process needs at least one distribution channel assigned to a sales organization. In the system, you can use a two-character key to identify a distribution channel. In Customizing, you can assign a distribution channel to one or more sales organizations. By assigning different distribution channels to a sales organization, you can create a small structure to define responsibilities, achieve flexible pricing, and differentiate sales statistics.

- **Division**
  A division represents a group of similar products (or services) or product lines in an organization. A division can be spare parts, services, bikes, accessories, etc. In the system, a division can be defined by using a two-digit numeric or alphanumeric key. Every sales and distribution module must have at least one division assigned to a sales organization. In Customizing, you can assign several divisions to a sales organization. By assigning a division to a sales organization, you can determine which product or service divisions can be sold from the sales organization.

- **Sales area**
  A sales area is a combination of sales organization, distribution channel, and division. A sales organization is the highest organizational unit in a sales area. To set up a sales area, you must first assign a distribution channel and a division to a sales organization in Customizing. Then, you can create a sales area by

using the previously assigned distribution channel and division, as shown in Figure 5.3.

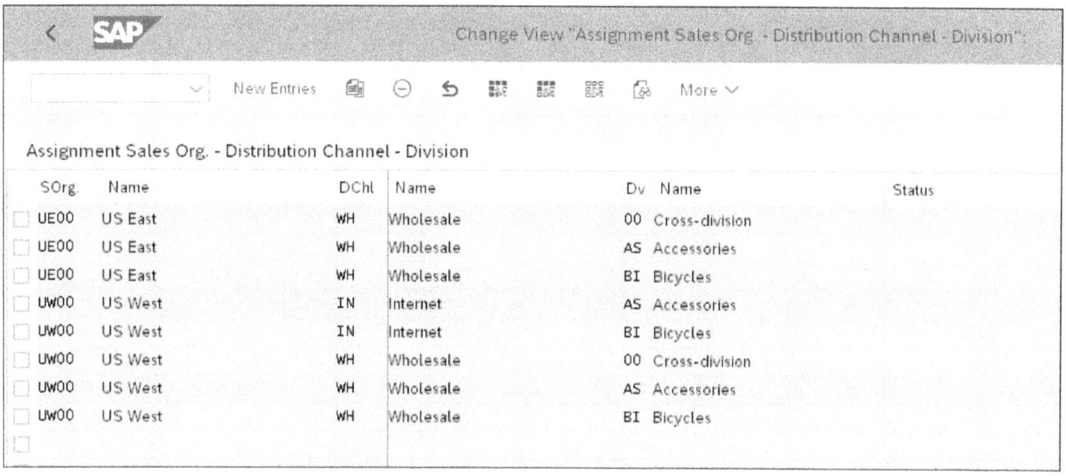

SOrg.	Name	DChl	Name	Dv	Name	Status
UE00	US East	WH	Wholesale	00	Cross-division	
UE00	US East	WH	Wholesale	AS	Accessories	
UE00	US East	WH	Wholesale	BI	Bicycles	
UW00	US West	IN	Internet	AS	Accessories	
UW00	US West	IN	Internet	BI	Bicycles	
UW00	US West	WH	Wholesale	00	Cross-division	
UW00	US West	WH	Wholesale	AS	Accessories	
UW00	US West	WH	Wholesale	BI	Bicycles	

Figure 5.3 Setting Up a Sales Area in Customizing: Each Row Representing a Sales Area

When you create a sales document, such as a customer inquiry, quotation, outline agreement, complaints, or sales order, you must choose a sales area. Thus, every sales document must be assigned to a sales area. You cannot change this assignment after the sales document is created. The master data (e.g., customer, material) that can be used in sales documents is limited to master data associated with the sales area chosen in the sales document. A sales area can belong to only one company code. This relationship between company code and sales area is established in the system when you assign the sales organization within the sales area to a company code.

- **Shipping point**
  A shipping point represents a part of a company where the deliveries are processed. A shipping point can be a mail depot, a loading ramp, a rail depot, or a group of employees responsible for expedited shipping in the real world. In the system, the shipping point is the highest level of organizational data for shipping (i.e., the header-level data in outbound delivery). Each plant must have at least one shipping point to process deliveries. In the system, you cannot create deliveries without a shipping point. Thus, outbound deliveries are created at the shipping point level. You also must use the shipping point as a selection criterion for some activities when processing deliveries like picking or goods issues. A plant may have multiple shipping points.

5.2.2 Master Data

In this section, we'll introduce you to the master data that supports the order-to-cash business process in SAP S/4HANA. Master data is a foundation for transactions executed in the system. For instance, when you create a sales order to sell a product or service to a specific customer, you must enter a customer number and material number. The system determines the price, discounts, and other sales-specific conditions for this selected customer based on these entries. The master data in the order-to-cash business process includes the following records:

- Material master record
- Customer master record
- Conditions master record
- Output master record

We begin by discussing the material master record for sales-relevant items.

Material Master Record

In the sales and distribution application component, you can create and process different types of sales-relevant materials, such as the following:

- **Trading goods**
  These movable goods are intended for commercial exchange, including goods bought and resold by the company (e.g., goods for consumption and durable goods). SAP uses the key **HAWA** for trading goods.

- **Nonstock material**
  Materials not managed on an inventory basis (e.g., small parts such as screws) although physically in stock. SAP uses the key **NLAG** for nonstock materials.

- **Services**
  In SAP, services are managed as materials (immaterial goods that differ from other goods). Services are managed in the SAP system with the key **DIEN**.

- **Packaging material**
  Materials needed for packaging (e.g., boxes or crates). In the system, packaging materials are managed with the key **VERP**.

- **Other material**
  Materials that cannot be associated with any of the standard material types or services.

A material master record can also be created centrally in the materials management module. The material type must be selected when you create a material master record.

Depending on material type, some vital control functions are activated in the subsequent screens for material master record maintenance, such as field selection, screen sequence, and material number range. The material type also determines which data screens (called views) should be maintained.

The material master record consists of views. We discussed the view structure of the material master record in Chapter 4, Section 4.2.2. Creating views in the material master record makes the material accessible from different business processes and departments. **Sales: sales org. 1-2** and **Sales: General/Plant Data** are the sales views of the material master record, and they connect a material to sales and distribution. In **Sales: sales org. 1-2** views, you can maintain sales data, such as tax data, price conditions, minimum order quantity, minimum delivery quantity, general item category group, material price group, as shown in Figure 5.4. In the **Sales: General/Plant** view, you can maintain data used in shipping, such as the loading group, transportation group, and packaging material data.

In practice, a material may have different sales and shipping conditions in different sales areas. The system supports this requirement by enabling data maintenance in sales views at the sales organization and distribution level. For instance, to determine the price conditions in the **Sales: sales org. 1** view, you must enter a sales organization and a distribution channel through which the material is sold.

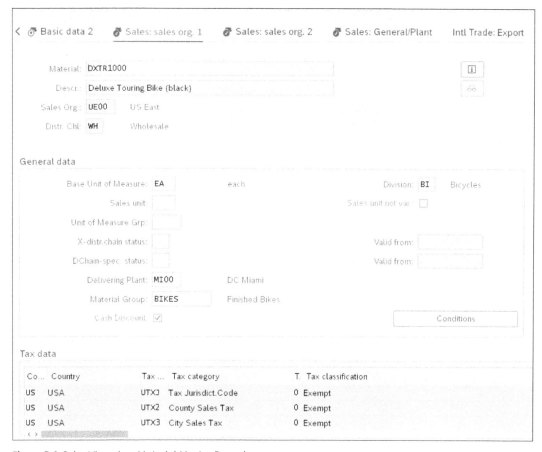

Figure 5.4 Sales Views in a Material Master Record

Customer Master Record

A customer represents the business partner to whom the company provides goods or services. You do not create the customer master record directly in the system. Instead, you create a business partner and assign (customer) roles to the business partner. If the customer (business partner) is also providing the company with goods or services, you can also assign vendor roles (i.e., financial accounting vendor and vendor) to this business partner, as shown in Figure 5.5. We discussed business partner creation and business partner general data in Chapter 4, Section 4.2.2.

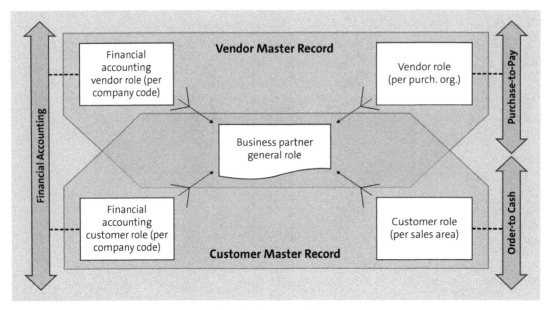

Figure 5.5 Business Partner Roles and Relevant Business Processes

A customer master record is structured into three parts maintained at different organization levels:

- **Business partner general role (Business Partner (Gen.))**
  Includes client-level data, such as an address, communication data, control data, and bank information.

- **Financial accounting customer role (FI Customer)**
  Includes accounting data maintained at the company code level, such as reconciliation account (in account management data), payment data, correspondence, insurance data, and withholding tax. This role is created for each company code that interacts with the business partner. The financial accounting customer role data connects the business partner to financial accounting, as shown in Figure 5.5. Defining a reconciliation account in the financial accounting customer role connects the customer's account to the general ledger.

- **Customer role (Customer)**
  Includes sales data maintained at the sales area level, such as shipping data, billing data, and partner functions. The customer role is created for each sales area that interacts with the business partner. Customer role data connects the business partner to sales and distribution.

In real-life scenarios, the customer-affiliated organization may deploy different persons or entities for different purchasing tasks. For instance, a customer-affiliated company (or a subsidiary office) can place the order, but its headquarters must pay the invoice. The system supports this requirement by using *partner functions* data in the customer role layer of customer master data. When you create a sales order, partner functions defined in the customer master record are transferred to the sales order as default values. You can still customize the default partner functions copied to the sales order during the sales order creation. Mandatory partner functions in sales order processing include the following functions:

- Sold-to party: Who places the order for your goods or services
- Ship-to party: Who receives the goods or services provided by your company or a third-party supplier
- Bill-to party: Who receives the invoice for the goods or services provided by your company
- Payer: Who sends the payment for your invoice

You can optionally define other partner functions such as contact person, forwarding agent, and responsible employee.

Conditions Master Record

Conditions are used when pricing materials and services in the order-to-cash business process. In the system, the conditions master record is the pricing data that includes the following condition types:

- Prices
- Discounts/surcharges
- Freight
- Taxes

To create a condition master record, you must first choose the condition type. The condition type allows you to control the properties of condition master records, such as the following:

- Condition class (e.g., price and discount)
- Scales (e.g., enable value or quantity scales)
- Level (e.g., header-level or item-level condition)
- Validity period (default validity period for the condition record)

Condition master records are usually managed and maintained at the sales organization and distribution channel level. You can define a validity period and dependencies (e.g., customers, materials) for a condition master record to restrict its usage to sales processes that include the parameters on which the condition depends. For instance, prices in condition records can be material-specific or customer-specific; discount/surcharges can be specified for a material group or a combination of customer and material group, as shown in Figure 5.6. The condition master record is retrieved for price calculation during the sales order processing. You can still maintain these conditions on the sales order.

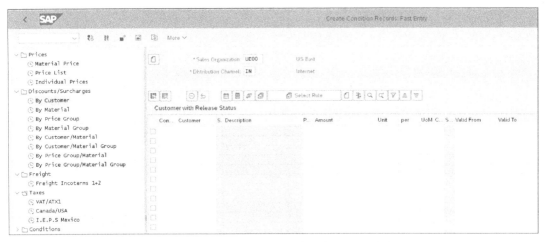

Figure 5.6 Creating Customer-Specific Discounts/Surcharges Conditions

Output Master Record

The output represents the messages, confirmations, and notifications sent to customers or other users upon completing some business transactions. Some examples of outputs include the following:

- **Order confirmations**
  The confirmation that the customer receives when you enter and confirm the sales order.
- **Credit processing**
  The message that the credit representative receives when a credit block is generated for a sales order.
- **Advanced shipping notifications**
  The message that the customer receives when you ship the product.
- **Invoices**
  The official document that the customer receives when you complete the billing process. The invoice shows all the pricing elements, including the total amount the customer owes.

In the output master record, you can define output generation time, output recipient, and the way and format in which the output is generated. In the system, you must first choose an output type and a sales organization to create an output master record. Then, you should specify the condition records for the output.

> **Note**
> A condition record for output is a combination of several keys listed next but is not the same as the condition master records we discussed earlier.

In a condition record for an output master record, you can maintain the following parameters, as shown in Figure 5.7:

- **Transmission medium (M)**
  The means through which you send the output (e.g., print output, mail, fax, electronic data interchange [EDI]).

- **Time (Date...)**
  The time you send the output (e.g., send periodically, send immediately, send with the job, with additional time specification).

- **Partner function (Funct)**
  The recipient of the output (also defined in customer master record but can be specified in output master record).

- **Language (Langu...)**
  The language in which the system displays and prints the message.

You can define the layout of output by a form in SAP script, Smartform, or Adobe.

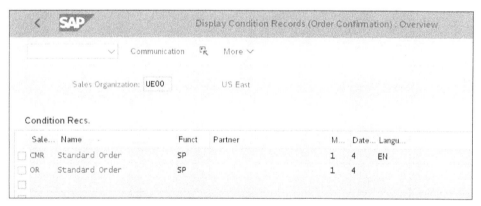

Figure 5.7 Condition Records in Output Master Record for Order Confirmation (Output Type ba00)

5.2.3 Data Assignments

In this section, we discuss organizational and master data assignments in the sales and distribution module. We begin with organizational data assignments.

Organizational Data Assignments

In Chapter 4, Section 4.2, we discussed the assignments among standard organizational data in logistics, such as client, company code, plant, and storage location. In Customizing, you can create and assign organizational data to represent your enterprise organizational structure in the system.

For sales-specific organizational data, the following assignments are possible in sales and distribution, as shown in Figure 5.8:

- A combination of sales organization, distribution channel, and division defines a sales organization.
- Multiple sales organizations can be assigned to a company code, but a sales organization can be assigned to only one company code.
- Multiple distribution channels can be assigned to a sales organization, and a distribution channel can be assigned to multiple sales organizations.
- Multiple divisions can be assigned to a sales organization, and a division can be assigned to multiple sales organizations.
- Multiple plants can be assigned to a sales organization, and a plant can be assigned to multiple sales organizations.
- Multiple shipping points can be assigned to a plant, and a shipping point can be assigned to multiple plants (requires physical proximity).

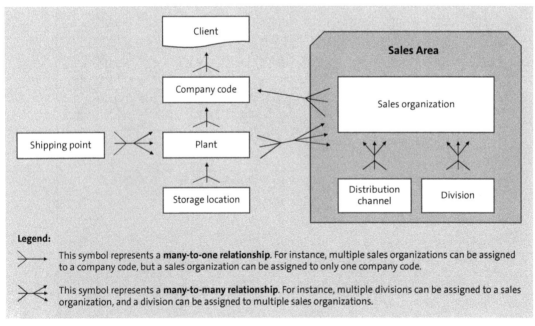

Figure 5.8 Organizational Data Assignments in Sales and Distribution

Master Data Assignments

In the system, materials are managed at the plant level, and plants are assigned to sales organizations. In its master record, a saleable material must have sales views maintained at the sales organization and distribution channel level. This assignment defines the sales organization and the medium through which the material can be sold.

The customer master record is structured into three roles maintained at different organization levels. The business partner general role includes general data maintained at the client level, the financial accounting customer role (**FI Customer Role**) includes accounting data maintained at the company code level, and the customer role includes sales data maintained at the sales area level. Assigning the customer master record's roles to a sales area and company code, you can define how your company deals with the customer in sales and in finance.

Condition master records can be material-specific, customer-specific, or specific for a combination of material and customer. A condition record is created at the sales organization and distribution channel level. Assigning condition records to materials or customers, you can use consistently and flexibly priced materials or services for the customers in a sales organization.

In the condition records for an output master record, you can specify the partner (shown earlier in Figure 5.7) who receives the output message. The specified partner must be previously defined in the customer master record. By linking the output master record to a customer master record, you enable the system to determine the recipient (and the medium) of the output from the master record for the specified partner function.

5.3 Key Processes of Lead-to-Cash

At the beginning of this chapter, we described and outlined a typical lead-to-cash business process. This section aims to cover more details of the subprocesses in lead-to-cash processing.

Various variants of the lead-to-cash business process exist in discrete industries. The naming convention for the subprocesses in lead-to-cash are based on the preceding and following steps (tasks). Thus, these subprocesses can be categorized in the following way:

- **Contact-to-lead**
  In this phase, the marketing expert creates a new campaign on a new offer either by targeting existing customers via email (or via phone calls) or by targeting new contacts on a website. The goal is to have customers give consent, share information, and interact with the offer. If the customer gives consent for further processing, all interactions are captured and scored. When customer interactions reach a certain score threshold, the contact qualifies to be converted into a lead for the sales team.

- **Lead-to-opportunity**
  In this phase, the marketing expert creates and assesses leads. A sales representative can use the available analytics tools to assess the potential of different leads. If a lead is worth pursuing, the lead qualifies to be converted into an opportunity.

- **Opportunity-to-quote**
  In this phase, a sales representative creates and assesses the potential of opportunities. The goal is to determine whether the opportunities are ready for quotes. The customer can directly create a quote in the webshop.
- **Quote-to-order**
  The quote is created and presented to the customer for review. If the customer confirms the quote, the customer order is generated, and the process is passed to the order-to-cash business process.
- **Order-to-cash**
  In this phase, the contract and/or sales order is created. Products or services are issued and delivered to the customer. The process ends with invoicing the customer and customer payment.

In general, SAP Customer Experience solutions support the first four subprocesses of lead-to-cash (up to the customer order). The SAP Customer Experience suite includes the following products:

- **SAP Marketing Cloud**
  Supports campaign automation, segmentation, and other marketing-related activities.
- **SAP Commerce Cloud**
  An e-commerce application providing a webshop for customers and supporting content management and experience management.
- **SAP Customer Data Cloud**
  Enables customers to use and control their personal data. Supports profile management and consent management.
- **SAP Sales Cloud**
  A mobile-first enablement tool that supports sales automation and configure, price, and quote (CPQ). This solution uses predictive analytics to support lead management.
- **SAP Service Cloud**
  A mobile-first platform supporting customer service processes (e.g., ticket management, interaction management, and field service management).

Depending on the industry, products, and services, several of these solutions may play a role in order-to-cash. However, the SAP S/4HANA core plays a primary role in the order-to-cash business process. The C_TS410 certification is mainly focused on integrated business processes in SAP S/4HANA Enterprise Management. Thus, our focus in the following sections will be on the order-to-cash business process.

5.3.1 Order-to-Cash Overview

Order-to-cash describes an end-to-end process that starts with the generation of a sales order or scheduling agreement and ends with a customer payment. You may prefer scheduling agreements to sales orders if you're continuously providing customers with prenegotiated quantities of goods at predetermined intervals. The certification covers the typical process that starts with the order. The order-to-cash process has five phases with several key tasks that can mostly be handled by the sales and distribution and financial accounting modules of SAP S/4HANA, as shown in Figure 5.9. The phases of the order-to-cash process and their tasks can be described in the following way:

1. **Sales order handling**
   Create sales order (transaction), availability check (functionality of sales order), save sales order (order document is created), and order confirmation (output) sent to the customer.

2. **Outbound delivery handling**
   Create outbound delivery (a delivery document is created), picking, packing, and goods issue (material and accounting documents are created).

3. **Billing**
   Create billing document (an accounting document is created), invoice (an output) is created, and sent to the customer.

4. **Payment**
   Post customer accounts and bank accounts (an accounting document is created).

Figure 5.9 shows the transactions of the sales and distribution module supporting the order-to-cash business process. At the end of every successful transaction, the system generates a document. Depending on the system configuration, outputs can also be generated.

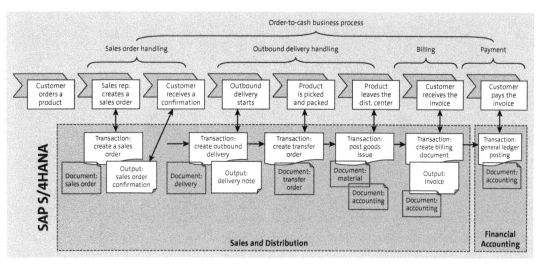

Figure 5.9 Order-to-Cash Business Process Phases and Sales and Distribution Transactions in SAP S/4HANA

5.3.2 Sales Order Handling

In this phase of the order-to-cash business process, the sales order is created and saved. A sales order is an agreement between a seller and customer for the sale and delivery of goods and services. Transaction VA01 (Create Sales Order) is a transaction in the sales and distribution module. Successful completion of this transaction generates a sales order document. A sales order document contains data describing the customer's firmed request for your products or services and other data that will be used in later phases in the order-to-cash business process. Depending on the output master data, the customer receives a confirmation (via email, fax, or EDI) when the sales order is confirmed.

Let's explore the key data, functions, and processes that fall within sales order handling.

Data in the Sales Order

A sales order is created at the sales area level. The data in a sales order is structured into header-level data and item-level data. A sales document can have one header and several line items, as shown in Figure 5.10. Header-level data is valid for the entire document (i.e., for all line items). Item-level data is valid for the specified line item.

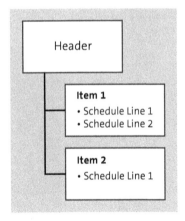

Figure 5.10 Structural Breakdown of Data in a Sales Order

To create a sales order, you must enter a customer number (sold-to party) and choose a sales area (a combination of sales organization, distribution channel, and division) at the header level, as shown in Figure 5.11. If only one sales area is defined for the customer, that sales area information is directly copied from the customer master data. A ship-to party can be entered at the header level if all sales order items will be shipped to the same address. Otherwise, you can define item-specific ship-to parties at the item level.

A sales order may include multiple items ordered by the customer. At the item level, you can enter a material or service number, quantities ordered, pricing conditions for materials and services, required delivery dates, delivering plant, shipping data (e.g., incoterms), and billing data for payment. Incoterms are internationally recognized terms of delivery, reflecting the standards set by the International Chamber of Commerce (ICC). Each item in the sales order includes its own data, including schedule lines in which you define delivery dates and quantities. Schedule lines are item-specific, and you can define multiple schedule lines for a sales order item if you would like to deliver different quantities at different times.

> **Note**
> Header-level data is valid for all line items in the sales document. Schedule line items are line item specific.

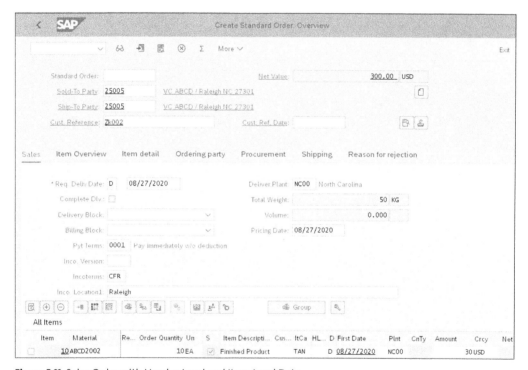

Figure 5.11 Sales Order with Header-Level and Item-Level Data

The header-level data and item-level data in a sales order are outlined in Table 5.1.

Header-Level Data (Valid for All Items in the Order)	- Customer number (sold-to party) - Ship-to party (optional) - Incoterms - Payment terms - Required delivery date
Item-Level Data	- Material number - Order quantity - Item category - Customer material number (optional) - Amount - Net price - Delivering plant - Schedule lines: delivery date, order quantity, confirmed quantity, delivery quantity, schedule line category, etc. - Shipping data: shipping point, delivery plant, route, item weight, and volume, etc. - Conditions - Partner functions

Table 5.1 Data in Sales Order

Note
Entering a ship-to party at the header level is optional. Enter a ship-to party at the header level if all items are delivered to the same address. Otherwise, you can maintain ship-to party data for each line item.

Master records in the system are the foundation for sales order handling. As soon as you enter a customer number and a material number, the majority of the information required for a sales order (e.g., delivery plant, prices, conditions, shipping data, billing data, partner functions) will be derived from the following records:

- Material master record
- Customer master record
- Conditions master record

You can also create a sales order with reference to a quotation created in the quote-to-order process. In this case, the reference quotation will be the origin of the data populated into the sales order. The customer number, sales area information, material or services ordered, quantities, prices, conditions, required delivery dates, shipping data, and billing data for payment will be transferred from the quotation to the sales order.

> **Tip**
> If a document in the system is used as a reference document (origin of data) for another document, you cannot change the reference document without canceling the subordinate document.

Functions of the Sales Order

When creating a sales order, the system performs several functions to assist in sales order processing. Some of these sales order functions are shown in Figure 5.12, which we'll discuss further throughout this section.

The *availability check* is one of the most critical functions of a sales order. This function helps you avoid making overcommitments. When you enter a material, quantity, and requested delivery date in a sales order line item, the system automatically performs an availability check. This function uses a backward scheduling strategy based on the requested quantities and the desired delivery date. If the requested materials can be delivered on the desired date, the system confirms the sales order. Confirmed quantities can be seen in the line item details. Otherwise, the system uses a forward scheduling strategy to propose a new delivery date with confirmed quantities. The available quantity will be displayed in the confirmed quantity field of schedule lines.

You can also initiate an availability check manually. In the **Sales: General/Plant** view of the material master record, you can determine what type of availability check must be carried out for a sales-relevant item, as shown in Figure 5.13.

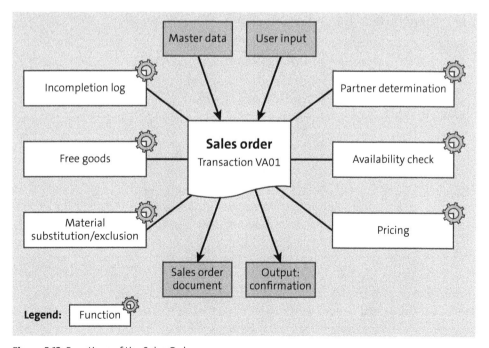

Figure 5.12 Functions of the Sales Order

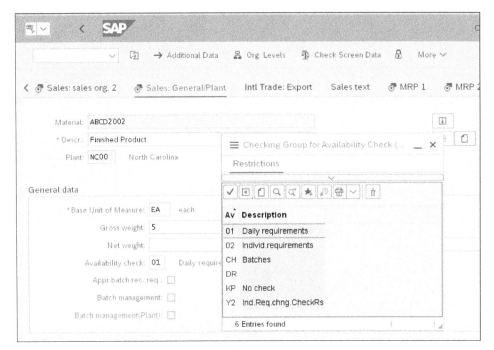

Figure 5.13 Availability Check Determination in the Master Record

In the schedule lines, you can use the schedule line category to specify whether an availability check and transfer of requirements should be carried out in the sales documents. The schedule line category's possible entries depend on the requirements class, which is determined by the requirements type of the material.

Three types of availability checks are available in the system:

- **Check against available-to-promise (ATP) quantities**
  Considers the current stock; the planned inward movements of stock (production orders, purchase orders, planned orders); and the planned outward movements of stock (sales orders, deliveries, reservations) in the future. Planned independent requirements (PIRs) are not considered.
- **Check against product allocation**
  Considers the previously determined maximum limit for the material quantity that a customer can order. For instance, the order quantity is 50, but the product allocation for the customer is 30 at that time of order entry. Then, an alternative delivery date is proposed in the availability control screen.
- **Check against planning**
  Considers the PIRs generated from demand planning.

In Customizing, you can define whether an availability check is to be carried out against the ATP quantity or planning. The check against product allocations is controlled in the material master (product allocation determination procedure must be entered in the **Basic data** screen for general data).

If the goods are not available on the requested date, then the system branches to the **Availability Control** screen, as shown in Figure 5.14, in which you can choose between different delivery proposals.

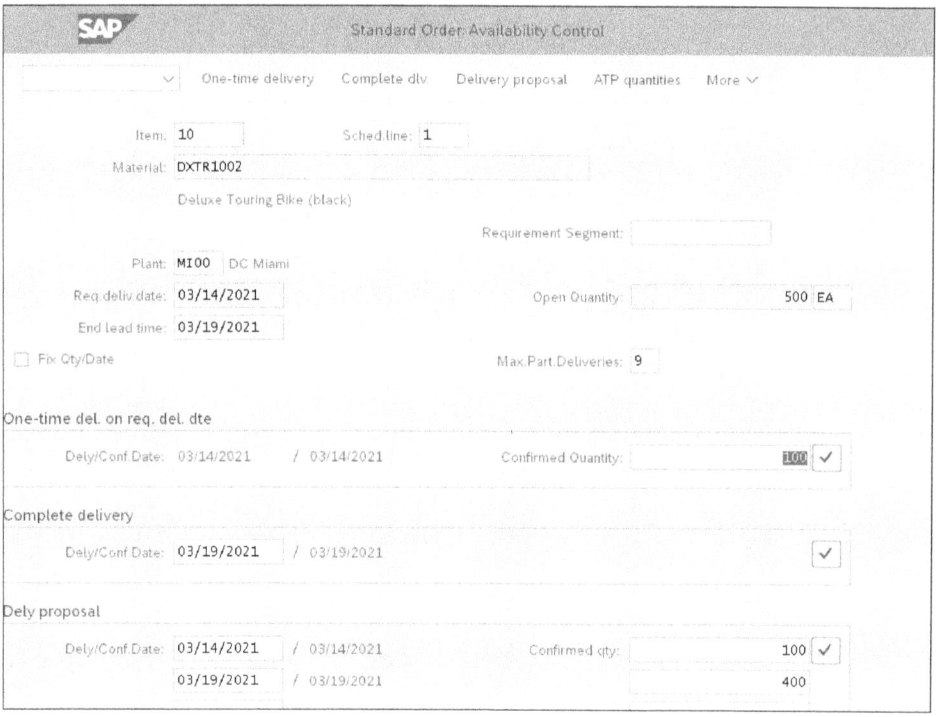

Figure 5.14 Availability Control Screen for Sales Order

In the **Availability Control** screen, you can perform the following activities:

- See ATP quantities
- Access the scope of check for determining available quantities
- Check if other plants have the material

When you create a sales order, the automatic *pricing* function transfers the conditions (e.g., prices, surcharges, discounts, freight, and taxes) from the material master record and conditions master record to the sales order. However, you can manually alter the conditions on the sales order, as shown in Figure 5.15.

When the sales order is created, partner functions are copied from the customer master record to the sales order. You can also manually determine the partner functions (if permitted in Customizing) at the line item level, as shown in Figure 5.16.

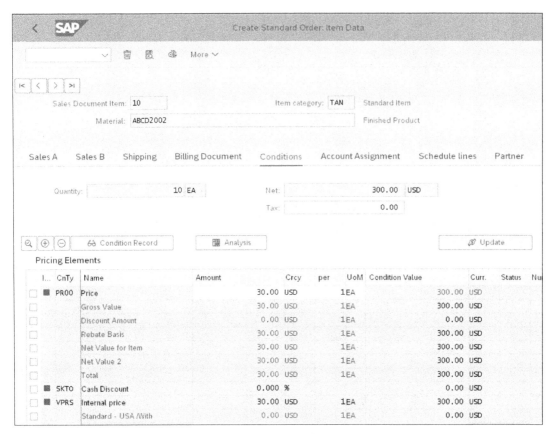

Figure 5.15 Conditions for a Line Item in a Sales Order

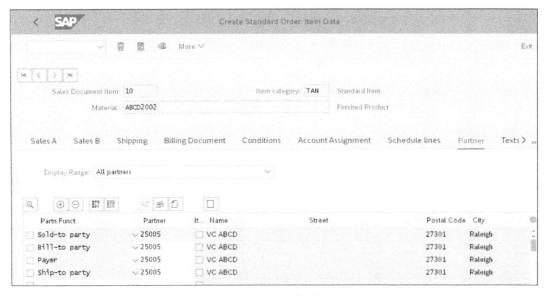

Figure 5.16 Mandatory Partner Functions in a Sales Order Line Item

> **Note**
> Sales order-specific alterations in conditions and partner functions do not change the relevant master records in the system.

A sales order is a data source for all subsequent steps (e.g., outbound delivery, billing) of the order-to-cash business process. Thus, the completeness of the data on the sales order is of vital importance. The *incompletion log* is a function of the sales order that logs data missing from the sales order. When you save a sales order, the system displays the incompletion log. For instance, as shown in Figure 5.17, the incompletion log lists the missing data in the schedule lines of **Item 10**.

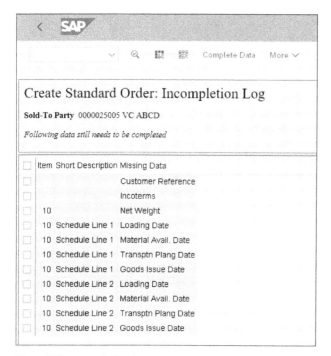

Figure 5.17 Incompletion Log

You can also call the incompletion log manually by navigating to **Edit • Incompletion Log**. You can complete the missing data by clicking the **Complete Data** button. The system may allow you to save a sales order without completing the missing data. However, the system will block sales orders with missing data from further transactions in order-to-cash. For instance, if the sales order's payment terms are missing, you can deliver the order, but you cannot invoice the customer.

To encourage customers to make bulk purchases, you may want to use *free goods* in sales and distribution. The system supports this requirement with free goods master data (a condition record) and the sales order's free goods function. During sales order processing, the system can automatically create free goods items based on the (free goods) condition records for a customer. The free goods items are free of charge. Two categories of free goods exist:

- Inclusive free goods: For instance, the sales order quantity is 10, and the customer pays for 8 items and gets 2 items for free.
- Exclusive free goods: For instance, the sales order quantity is 10, and the customer receives an additional 2 pieces of material (total quantity is 12).

To use free goods in sales, you must customize the system for free goods and create free goods condition records (free goods master data) for combinations of customer and material.

For instance, with the condition record for free goods, as shown in Figure 5.18, the customer will pay for 95 items for every 100 items purchased (5 pieces of inclusive free goods). This condition is automatically applied to any sales order if the sales order quantity reaches the minimum quantity threshold (i.e., **150** units of **ABCD2002**).

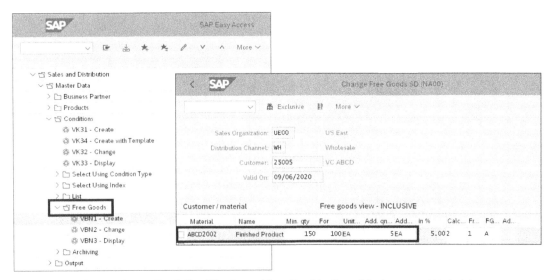

Figure 5.18 Free Goods Condition Record for a Combination of Customer and Material

An organization may want to restrict the sale of certain materials to specific customers. The *material exclusion* function of the sales order supports this requirement. After activating material listing/exclusion in Customizing, you can create exclusion lists for a combination of material and customer in sales and distribution, as shown in Figure 5.19. The condition record in the exclusion list will prevent the customer from purchasing the item determined in the exclusion list. When you enter the restricted item in the sales order, the system will generate an error, and you'll need to remove the material from the item list.

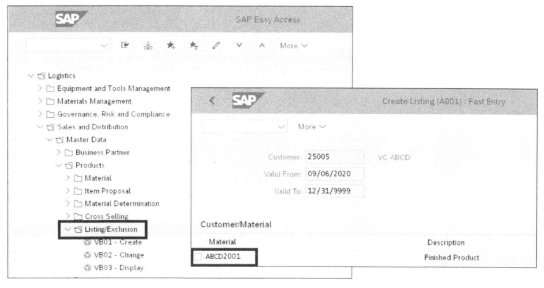

Figure 5.19 Example of a Material Exclusion List for a Customer

Similar to the material exclusion list, you can create a *material determination* list to control material substitutions in sales and distribution. This capability might be useful if you want to substitute one product for another product during a specific period. For instance, as shown in Figure 5.20, we're substituting one product with the same type of product (with special promotional packaging or with additional features) due to an advertising campaign.

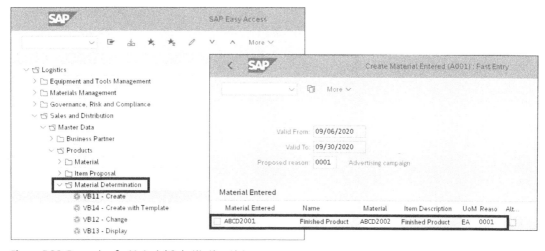

Figure 5.20 Example of a Material Substitution List

When you save the sales order, the output (sales order confirmation) can be sent based on the combination of partner functions in the customer master record and the condition records in the output master record. Outputs can also be sent through a standard program that runs periodically. Note that, in addition to the existing output types, you can use customization to create new output types and specify how these outputs should be accessed by the system.

Backorder Processing

Sometimes a sales order availability check may not completely confirm the required quantity for an order item within the requested delivery date. In this case, the sales order is called a backorder. You can use the backorder processing (BOP) as an option to change confirmed quantities on the sales orders.

> **Example**
> For instance, a high-priority customer might increase the requested quantity for a particular material, but your current stock isn't sufficient to confirm that change. In this case, you could consume the quantity of stock currently confirmed in another sales order.

You can run BOP manually or automatically. To set up automated backorder processing, you must first configure the BOP segment, BOP variant, and BOP run in the system. In the BOP variant, you can assign the following confirmation strategies to BOP segments:

- **Win**
  With this strategy, assigned requirements will be entirely confirmed on the requested date. If they are not confirmed, the BOP run stops immediately.

- **Gain**
  With this strategy, assigned requirements will be retained. If they are not retained, the BOP run stops immediately. All requirements for the same material/plant combinations are excluded from the BOP run.

- **Redistribute**
  With this strategy, assigned requirements will be able to get a better, equal, or worse confirmation. BOP may release quantities of requirements so that they can be utilized to fulfill higher priority requirements.

- **Fill**
  With this strategy, assigned requirements will not gain additional quantity or get an earlier confirmation date. They can get an equal or worse confirmation.

- **Lose**
  With this strategy, assigned requirements will lose their current confirmation and not be confirmed. The released quantity of the lose requirements can be used to confirm high priority requirements or kept as quantity available to confirm future requirements.

Note that you can use BOP only for materials with the availability check setting **Individual Requirements** in their material master records (in the **Sales: General/Plant Data** view).

5.3.3 Outbound Delivery Handling

In this phase of the order-to-cash business process, the outbound delivery document is created at the shipping point. A prerequisite for outbound delivery is that schedule lines must have a confirmed quantity and the order is due. Next, the delivery items are picked, packed, staged, and loaded if these functions are used in your business process. The outbound delivery handling process is shown in Figure 5.21.

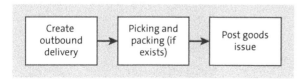

Figure 5.21 Outbound Delivery Handling

If the goods are managed at the warehouse, outbound delivery creation triggers a picking process in the warehouse. The picking process in the warehouse is initiated and controlled by transfer orders. The confirmation of a transfer order completes the picking process. If you're using SAP Transportation Management (SAP TM) embedded in SAP S/4HANA, you can determine a route for the outbound delivery document, start collaborating with freight service providers, initiate a tendering process, and create a shipment cost document. The goods issue posting completes the process and results in changes in inventory records and financial accounting.

We'll walk through these key processes in the following sections.

Outbound Delivery Document

An outbound delivery for a sales order can be directly created within the sales order screen (**Sales Document • Deliver**) or by selecting the **Logistics Execution** menu item on the SAP Easy Access screen. If the sales transaction volume is very high, you can also create outbound deliveries collectively by using the delivery due list (e.g., Transactions VL10A and VL10C), as shown in Figure 5.22.

When you create an outbound delivery, the system performs several activities, including:

- Checks the sales order and materials to make sure the outbound delivery is possible
- Copies shipping-relevant data from the sales order to a delivery document (the sales order is the origin of data for the delivery document)
- Determines the delivery quantity for sales order line items and checks the availability of material
- Calculates the weight and volume of the delivery

- Assigns a picking location
- Updates the sales order and changes the sales order status (status overview)

Figure 5.22 Transactions to Create Outbound Delivery

Once you complete and save the outbound delivery, an outbound delivery document is created and added to the sales order's document flow. Depending on your output settings, a delivery note can be created as an output and sent to the customer.

Based on the customer's delivery preferences (as determined on sales agreements) and on material availability, you can deliver on the sales orders by using different delivery strategies, including the following:

- Complete delivery: The order is delivered in a single delivery at the same time.
- Partial delivery: The order is delivered through multiple outbound deliveries at different times.
- Order combination: Multiple orders are combined into one outbound delivery. This delivery strategy is possible only if the sales orders have some certain characteristics in common.

Data in Outbound Delivery Document

Like other sales documents, the outbound delivery document's data is structured into header-level data and item-level data. Header-level data is valid for all items in the outbound delivery document. The shipping point is the highest organizational level in the outbound delivery process and a header-level data in the outbound delivery document, as shown in Figure 5.23.

In the sales order, you can specify shipping points at the line item level. When you create an outbound delivery with reference to a sales order, the system automatically copies the shipping point data from the order line item to the **Shipment** view in the outbound delivery document's header level. As a result, the same shipping point must deliver all line items in the outbound delivery document. You cannot change this shipping point information in the outbound delivery document. Different sales order line items may have different shipping point assignments. In this case, order items with different shipping point assignments are copied to different outbound delivery documents.

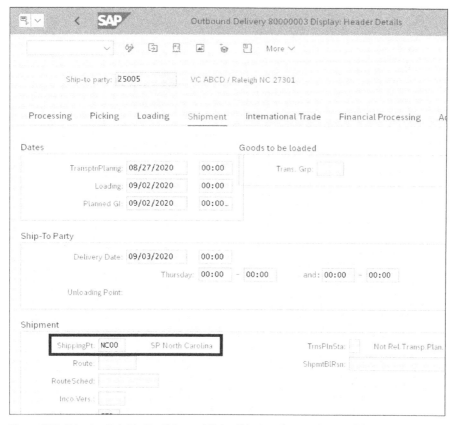

Figure 5.23 Shipping Point in the Shipment Tab of the Header-Level Data of the Outbound Delivery Document

Another critical header-level data in the outbound delivery document is the ship-to party. Ship-to party information is copied from the sales order line item to the header of the outbound delivery document when you create a delivery with reference to an order. As a result, sales order line items with different ship-to party assignments must be delivered through different outbound delivery documents. The schedule lines for sales order line items are converted into the outbound delivery document line items when you create an outbound delivery for a sales order. No schedule lines exist in the outbound delivery document. Figure 5.24 shows the relationship between the header-level and item-level data in the sales order and the outbound delivery document.

Note
If the customer permits order combinations, multiple sales orders (for the same sold-to party) can be combined into a single outbound delivery if the orders have the same characteristics, such as the following:
- Ship-to party
- Shipping point
- Delivery date
- Incoterms
- Sales organization

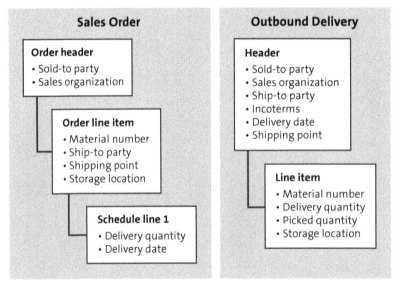

Figure 5.24 Data in Sales Order and Outbound Delivery Document

The header-level and the item-level data in the outbound delivery document are grouped into tabs. Some important data in the outbound delivery document are outlined in Table 5.2.

Note
The outbound delivery document does not include schedule lines but line items. When you create an outbound delivery document for a sales order, the data in the schedule lines (in the sales order) are copied into line items in the outbound delivery document.

Header-Level Data (Valid for All Items in the Document)	■ Document number ■ Ship-to party ■ Delivering plant ■ Shipping point ■ Incoterms ■ Sales organization ■ Route ■ Picking, packing, and loading data (for all items): status, total weight, total volume, picking deadline, loading date, delivery date, etc. ■ Partner functions ■ Data for international trade means of transport, destination country, etc.
Item-Level Data	■ Material number ■ Item category ■ Item quantities: picked quantity, delivery quantity, etc. ■ Item loading data ■ Storage location ■ Item weight and volume ■ Item status: status for picking, packing, goods issue, billing, etc.

Table 5.2 Data in Outbound Delivery

Picking

The creation of an outbound delivery document triggers the picking process. Once you complete the picking process, you can execute the packing activities and post the goods issue. In the picking process, all items requested by the outbound delivery document are taken from a storage location and staged in a picking area where the goods will be prepared for shipping. You can pick multiple deliveries collectively by using a picking list. The picking status and pick quantities are recorded in the relevant outbound delivery document. This step is necessary for monitoring the picking process. You can check the picking status of the outbound delivery and the delivery item in the **Status Overview** view of the outbound delivery document, as shown in Figure 5.25.

You can see the picked quantity and delivery quantity in the **Picking** view of the outbound delivery document, as shown in Figure 5.26. You cannot post a goods issue for the outbound delivery if not all delivery items have been picked. Thus, to process the goods issue, the delivery quantity and the picked quantity must be the same on the delivery order.

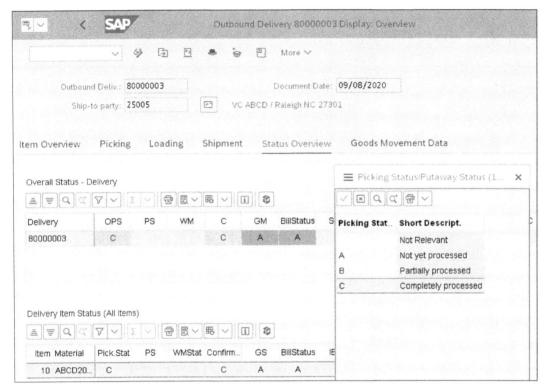

Figure 5.25 Status Overview in the Outbound Delivery Document

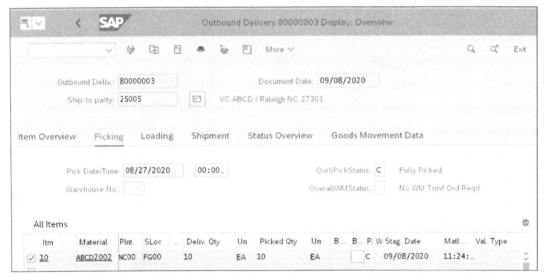

Figure 5.26 Picking View of the Outbound Delivery Document

The **Picked Qty** column on the delivery document is updated when the delivery document is confirmed. Depending on warehouse data in the material master record and on system configuration, picking activities (including confirmation of pick quantities) can be carried out in different ways:

- **Not warehouse-managed**
  If the material is not warehouse managed, then you only need to confirm the **Picked Qty** field in the outbound delivery document. This step updates the status of the outbound delivery document and completes the picking process.

- **Lean warehouse management system**
  If the material is stored in a fixed bin managed by a lean warehouse management system (WMS), you must create a transfer order to pick the items from fixed bins in the warehouse. Confirmation of this transfer order is not required. The picked quantity must be updated by changing the **Picked Qty** field in the outbound delivery document. This step updates the status of the outbound delivery document and completes the picking process.

- **Regular warehouse management system**
  Suppose the material is managed in a regular WMS. In that case, the picking process is initiated and controlled by a transfer order. The transfer order in WMS includes the storage bin's specific coordinates where the material is stored in the warehouse. To complete the WMS picking process, you must record the stock differences between the required quantity and the picked quantity and confirm the transfer order. This confirmation completes the picking process and automatically updates the status of outbound delivery and updates the **Picked Qty** field in the outbound delivery, as shown in Figure 5.27.

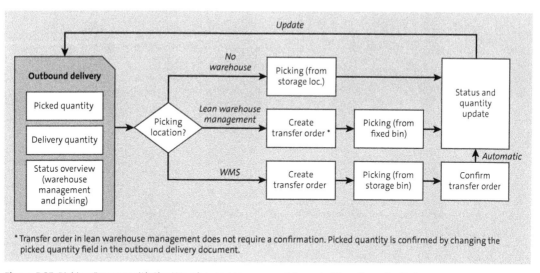

*Transfer order in lean warehouse management does not require a confirmation. Picked quantity is confirmed by changing the picked quantity field in the outbound delivery document.

Figure 5.27 Picking Process with the Warehouse Management Executed by a Transfer Order

- **Decentralized SAP Extended Warehouse Management (SAP EWM)**
  If the material is managed in decentralized SAP EWM, the material is picked by the outbound delivery order, as shown in Figure 5.28.

  By using the outbound delivery order, you can execute picking delivery, including canceling delivery picking, loading the delivery, and automatic packing of delivery in SAP EWM. The outbound delivery order document includes all data necessary for the whole outbound delivery process in SAP EWM. The outbound delivery order is a warehouse request for the execution of picking activities. Note that all physical movements in a warehouse are done by using warehouse tasks. The outbound delivery order is also a basis for goods issue posting. Once the items are picked and taken to the goods issue zone, you can post the goods issue. For the goods issue posting in SAP EWM, a final outbound delivery document is created to trigger the creation of the goods issue in the inventory management. The final outbound delivery document sends information about the goods issue posting back to SAP S/4HANA.

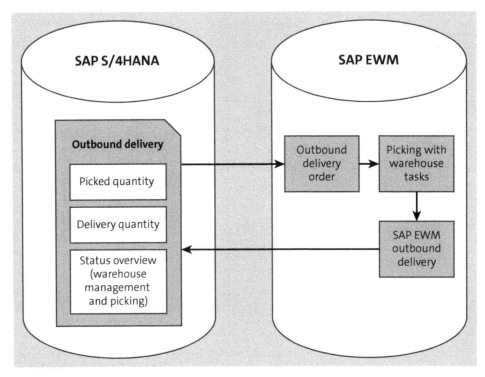

Figure 5.28 Picking Process with SAP EWM

Note
For more information about warehouse management and the differences between a lean WMS, a regular WMS, and SAP EWM, refer to Chapter 8, Section 8.3.

Note
Picking activities for a material in a warehouse are executed by using transfer orders. The outbound delivery order executes picking activities if the material is managed in an SAP EWM system.

Once you complete the picking process, the system updates the document flow of the sales order. The document flow shows you the progress in the order-to-cash business process and the list of tasks completed. As the tasks are completed in sales and distribution, the relevant documents are added to the document flow. For instance, as shown in Figure 5.29, the document flow shows that the outbound delivery document was created, and the requested delivery items were picked. You can select a document in document flow and display it by clicking the **Display Document** button. To display a document's status in the document flow, click the **Status Overview** button. Note that all sales and distribution documents (i.e., sales order documents, outbound delivery documents, billing documents) in sales and distribution have the **Status Overview** button to call the document flow.

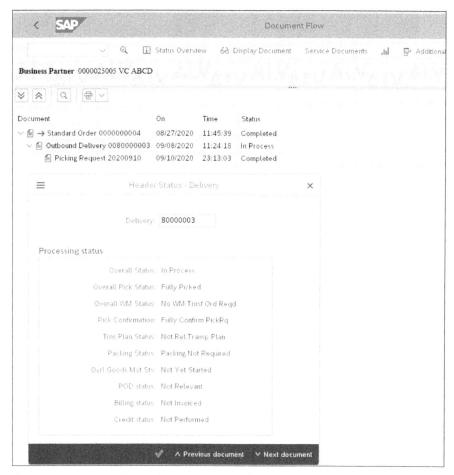

Figure 5.29 Document Flow and Status Overview of Outbound Delivery

Tip
In sales and distribution, all documents are linked to each other via the document flow, which shows you the completed tasks (and documents) in the order-to-cash business process.

Goods Issue

Once you complete all preceding tasks of outbound delivery (e.g., picking, packing, loading), you'll post the goods issue right before the material physically leaves the company. To post the goods issue for delivery, the delivery quantity and picked quantity must be the same in the outbound delivery document. Posting goods issues for an outbound delivery means the outbound delivery document's items are no longer part of the company's assets. The goods issue posting completes the outbound delivery handling process and precedes another important activity: billing. You cannot execute order-related billing until the goods issue is posted.

The system supports several options for posting goods issues, such as the following:

- Goods issue posting for individual outbound delivery
- Posting goods issue for multiple outbound deliveries (collective processing via the outbound delivery monitor)
- Posting goods issue in a decentralized SAP EWM system

Once you complete the goods issue posting, significant changes occur in several modules of the system, such as the following changes:

- The stock of the material is reduced by the delivery quantity. A material document is created documenting the goods movement and the change in the inventory quantity, as shown in Figure 5.30. You can click the **FI Documents** button in the material document to display other documents related to the goods issue.

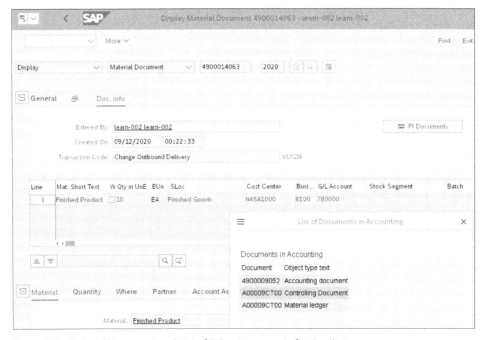

Figure 5.30 Material Document and List of Other Documents for Goods Issue

- The value of the delivery reduces the value of the inventory. An accounting document is created with journal entries for the inventory account and the cost of goods sold (COGS) account, as shown in Figure 5.31.
- A controlling document is created to update controlling objects (e.g., cost object, cost center) based on the cost of selling the material.
- Profitability analysis records can be updated along with the COGS (account-based profitability analysis).
- The stock requirements list is updated due to the loss of inventory.
- The goods issue is recorded in the document flow, and the statuses of the preceding documents (e.g., sales order, outbound delivery) are updated.
- The billing due list is updated.
- A Material Ledger document is created to record the change in the value of the stock.

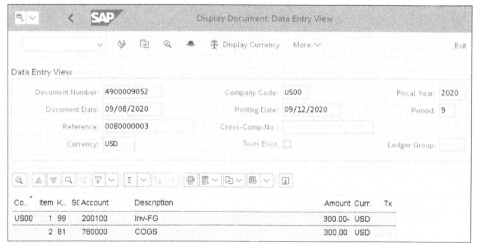

Figure 5.31 Accounting Document for Goods Issue

Tip
You can easily differentiate an accounting document from a material document by looking at the accounting-relevant header-level data: Accounting documents always have a fiscal year, company code, period, and currency.

5.3.4 Billing

Once all sales order tasks and the outbound delivery are complete, you can initiate the billing process to prepare the system for receiving customer payments. Billing is the final step of an order-to-cash business process. In this process, you'll create a billing document, and the system generates a customer invoice, the output sent to the customer for the goods or services provided. Accounting posting (debit) is carried out in accounts receivable. The billing document is a basis for customer payment processing in financial accounting. A general ledger posting is carried out when the customer payment is received.

The system allows you to create billing documents in three ways:

- **With reference**
  You can create an individual billing document with reference to a sales order (order-related billing) or an outbound delivery document (delivery-related billing). You can use Transactions VF01 or VF04 for this activity. Sales order-related billing may be necessary if you want to invoice a customer for services or items that do not require delivery.

- **Manual processing**
  You can collectively process the documents due for billing manually. You can use Transaction VF04 (Process Billing Due List) to collectively process documents due for billing, as shown in Figure 5.32.

- **Automatic processing**
  You can collectively process the documents as a background job using automatic billing due list. You can use Transaction VF06 to set up a background job for billing.

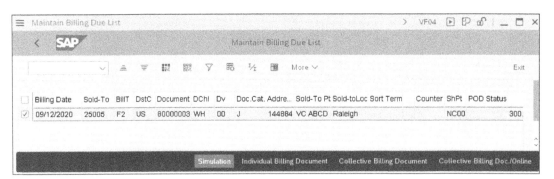

Figure 5.32 Billing Due List Maintenance

You can use different forms of settlement in billing processing, including the following, as shown in Figure 5.33:

- **Collective billing document**
  Combining several sales documents into a collective billing document, when header data such as payer, billing date, destination country, and payment terms are the same for all the sales documents.

- **Invoice splitting**
  Splitting a single sales document into several invoices: As a rule, the system combines into one billing document all transactions for the same customer, default billing date, and sales organization. If data from the related reference

documents differs in the header fields of the billing document, the system automatically splits the invoice (e.g., sales document item's partner functions are different than header partners of billing document).

- **Individual billing document**
  Creating an individual billing document for each sales document in the billing due list (i.e., one invoice per delivery), as shown in Figure 5.34.

Like other sales documents, the data in the billing document is structured into header-level data and item-level data. The header-level data includes information like payer, billing date, payment terms, document, currency, company code, header partners, and pricing conditions. The item-level data includes information like material number, billed quantity, pricing date, and the net value.

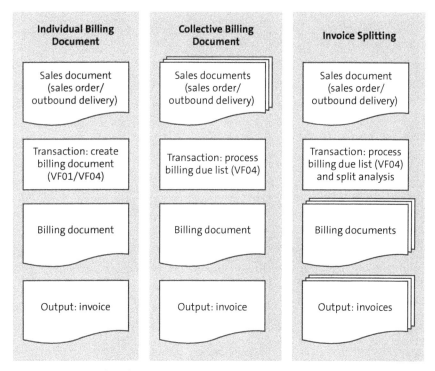

Figure 5.33 Forms of Settlement in the Billing Process

Figure 5.34 Individual Billing Document for Outbound Delivery

Saving the billing document impacts the system in the following significant ways:

- The system generates an accounting document to update (debit) the customer receivables account and (credit) the sales revenue account.
- The sales statistics in the sales information system (SIS) are updated.
- The invoice and the accounting document for the billing document are recorded in the document flow.
- The customer credit account is updated.
- The status overview for the sales order document and outbound delivery document is updated, as shown in Figure 5.35.
- Profitability analysis records can be updated along with revenue generated from invoice document.

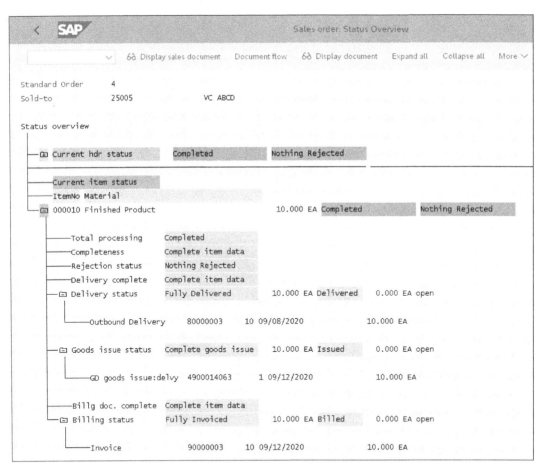

Figure 5.35 Sales Order Status Overview after Creating a Billing Document

Note
Multiple sales documents can be combined into a single billing document if they have the same characteristics, such as payer, billing date, destination country, and payment terms.

5.4 Integration with Other Modules

In this section, we discuss the potential integration points of the order-to-cash business process. We'll begin with data assignments before discussing transactions.

5.4.1 Integration via Cross-Module Data Assignments

Cross-module data assignments in the system connect the business processes in SAP S/4HANA. Some examples of cross-module data assignments include the following:

- A customer is a master record in sales and distribution. With the financial accounting customer role, in the business partner data for the customer, you must specify a reconciliation account, which is master data in general ledger accounting. This assignment thus connects the customer to financial accounting (i.e., accounts receivable).

- A warehouse number is organizational data in warehouse management. In the system, a warehouse number must be assigned to a combination of storage location and plant. A plant is organizational data in sales and distribution and is assigned to a sales organization. These assignments connect a warehouse to sales and distribution.

- In the material master record's sales views, you'll maintain sales and distribution-relevant data at the sales organization and distribution channel level. This data connects the material to sales and distribution.

5.4.2 Integration via Transactions

During sales and distribution transactions, other system components integrate with sales and distribution. Some examples of touchpoints of integration between sales and distribution and other system modules include the following, as shown in Figure 5.36:

- **Management accounting (controlling)**
  When you post a goods issue, the system creates a controlling document for the costs of sales and a Material Ledger document to record the value loss in the inventory. Profitability analysis also receives updates from the goods issue posting and billing, thus integrating controlling with sales and distribution.

- **Inventory management**
  When you create a sales order line item, the system performs an availability check and calculates an ATP quantity based on both the current stock and on future goods movements. The availability check creates an integration between inventory management and sales and distribution. A goods issue posting generates a material document that updates inventory quantities. Thus, this material document integrates inventory management with sales and distribution.

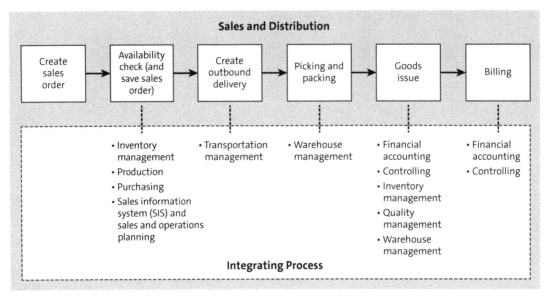

Figure 5.36 Sales and Distribution Integration Points

- **Financial accounting**

  When you post a goods issue or save a billing document, the system updates financial accounting data. These updates are recorded by creating an accounting document. This accounting document integrates financial accounting with sales and distribution. Another type of integration between financial accounting and sales and distribution occurs when you create a sales order in which the system performs a credit check for the customer and determines the taxes.

- **Production**

  During the availability check (in sales order creation), the system checks the planned orders and production orders, thus integrating sales with distribution and production. When you create a sales order, the SIS is updated. This SIS data can be used for forecasting the future demand in production planning, known as *sales and operations planning (S&OP)*. Another type of integration between sales and distribution and production can happen when you create a sales order for an item that needs to be produced, that is, in a make-to-order (MTO) strategy. In this case, the production order can be created with reference to the sales order. Once all production activities are complete, the produced quantity will be sent to the sales order stock. You cannot use this stock for another sales order.

- **Purchasing**

  When you create a sales order with a third-party item (i.e., item category TAS and schedule line category CS), the system automatically creates a purchase requisition. This third-party sales order creates an integration between SIS and purchasing. Note that your sales organization receives the customer order in a third-party process, and an external vendor delivers the products to the customer. Another integration can happen when you create a sales order for trading goods (stock item) that you do not produce but sell. During the availability check (of the sales order), the system creates a purchase requisition for inventory replenishment.

- **Quality management**
  Based on system settings and material master data, creating an outbound delivery may open a quality inspection lot automatically. After the goods issue posting, you can process customer complaints by creating quality notifications.

- **Transportation management**
  If you're using SAP TM, you can create a route in sales orders or outbound deliveries. Outbound delivery documents or sales orders may serve as transportation requests and trigger transportation planning and execution activities.

- **Warehouse management**
  After creating an outbound delivery, picking processing can be carried out in the warehouse. All physical movements (picking/putaway) in the warehouse are initiated and controlled by the transfer order. If a material is managed in an extended warehouse, picking and putaway are executed via an outbound delivery order. Once the picking process is complete, the goods issue can be posted within SAP EWM.

- **Project System**
  You can use tools from the sales and distribution module to manage sales, shipping, and billing processes in a project lifecycle for a customer project. For instance, quotations and sales orders can be assigned to a project (a billing element) for planning revenue and for creating billing plans.

5.5 Important Terminology

In this chapter, the following terminology we use is important to know for the exam:

- **Availability check**
  An important function that assists in sales order creation. When you enter the quantity and requested delivery date for a specific material in the sales order line item, the system carries out an availability check based on all inward and outward movements of stock.

- **Billing document**
  The transaction in sales and distribution that triggers the generation of customer invoices. The billing document passes the sales process to financial accounting and prepares the system for customer payment.

- **Customer**
  Represent the business partner to whom you sell goods or services. Master data that supports the transactions in the sales and distribution module.

- **Customer invoice**
  A document in sales and distribution that is used to charge a customer for the

delivery of goods or services. A customer invoice is created as an output of the transaction to create a billing document.

- **Distribution channel**
  A means by which sales-relevant goods and services reach your customers. Organizational data in sales and distribution. Internet sales and wholesale are examples of distribution channels.

- **Division**
  Organizational data in sales and distribution. Represents a group of similar products (or services) or product lines in an organization.

- **Document flow**
  Document flow logs all completed transactions and their documents in sales and distribution. You can display the documents in the document flow and check their status overviews.

- **Goods issue**
  The final step of the shipping that completes the outbound delivery handling process in the warehouse/distribution center.

- **Inquiry**
  An internal presales document that includes information about the inquiries received from the customer.

- **Lead**
  Leads are business transactions that describe, store, and manage the customer's potential interest to buy in a certain time frame.

- **Opportunity**
  An opportunity is a transaction that describes the estimated sales possibility, the potential sales volume, and the sales prospect's budget for certain products or services.

- **Outbound delivery document**
  A document that starts the outbound delivery process. This document is a basis and origin of data for all subsequent transactions in shipping.

- **Outbound delivery order**
  An order in extended warehouse management (EWM) that is used to execute warehouse tasks such as picking and putaway.

- **Quotation**
  A presales document that includes a companies' response to a customer's request. A quotation is a legally binding external document sent to the customer's purchasing organization. This document includes the material, the total quantity, the delivery date, and conditions.

- **Sales area**
  Organizational data in sales and distribution. A combination of sales organization, distribution channel, and division defines a sales area.

- **Sales document**
  A document that records business transactions in the sales department. Inquiries, quotations, scheduling agreements, contracts, sales orders, and complaints are examples of sales documents.
- **Sales item**
  The data in the sales order is structured into header-level data (valid for the entire document) and the item-level data. A sales item represents a line item in a sales order. A sales order may have many sales items.
- **Sales order**
  An internal document that includes all agreed-upon terms and conditions for a specific sales process between seller and buyer. A sales order officially starts the order-to-cash business process. This document is an origin of data and a basis for all subsequent transactions in the order-to-cash business process.
- **Sales organization**
  Organizational data in sales and distribution. Represents an organizational unit responsible for selling goods and services.
- **Schedule line**
  A sales order line item can be delivered in different outbound deliveries on different dates.
- **Scheduling agreement**
  A form of a sales agreement for the fulfillment of materials on predetermined dates within a specific time frame.
- **Transfer order**
  A warehouse order used to execute and record warehouse tasks for outbound delivery. In a warehouse, picking and putaway are carried out via transfer orders.
- **Worklist**
  Worklists are used in lead-to-cash processing to collectively process certain tasks such as shipping, picking, goods issue, and billing.

5.6 Practice Questions

These practice questions will help you evaluate your understanding of the topics covered in this chapter. The questions shown are similar to those found on the certification examination. Although none of these questions will be found on the exam itself, they will allow you to review your knowledge of the subject. Select the correct answers and then check the completeness of your answers in the next section. Remember that you must select all correct answers on the exam and select only correct answers to receive credit for the question.

1. Which of the following are master data in sales and distribution? (There are two correct answers.)

   ☐ A. Sales documents
   ☐ B. Conditions
   ☐ C. Vendor master records
   ☐ D. Customer master records

2. Which of the following are organizational data in sales and distribution? (There are three correct answers.)

   ☐ A. Distribution channels
   ☐ B. Distribution centers
   ☐ C. Divisions
   ☐ D. Shipping points
   ☐ E. Warehouse numbers

3. Which of the following is the correct hierarchy of an organizational structure in sales and distribution (top to bottom)?

   ☐ A. Company code → sales organization → plant → shipping point
   ☐ B. Sales organization → client → plant → storage location
   ☐ C. Company code → plant → storage location → division
   ☐ D. Client → company code → plant → distribution channel

4. Which of the following represents a correct sequence of tasks in sales and distribution? (There are two correct answers.)

   ☐ A. Create a sales order → outbound delivery → availability check → picking → goods issue → billing
   ☐ B. Create a sales order → availability check → outbound delivery → goods issue → billing
   ☐ C. Save a sales order → availability check → outbound delivery → goods issue → billing
   ☐ D. Create a sales order → outbound delivery → picking → goods issue → billing

5. Which of the following are the components of a sales area? (There are three correct answers.)

   ☐ A. Shipping point
   ☐ B. Sales manager

☐ C. Sales organization
☐ D. Division
☐ E. Distribution channel

6. Which of the following organizational units is responsible for distributing goods and services, negotiating sales conditions, and product liability and rights of recourse?

☐ A. Sales area
☐ B. Distribution channel
☐ C. Sales organization
☐ D. Sales management

7. Which of the following are uniquely assigned to a company code? (There are two correct answers.)

☐ A. Sales area
☐ B. Sales organization
☐ C. Plant
☐ D. Shipping point

8. Which of the following can be assigned to a sales organization? (There are three correct answers.)

☐ A. Plant
☐ B. Shipping point
☐ C. Storage location
☐ D. Division
☐ E. Distribution channel

9. Which of the following roles of the business partner master data for a customer includes partner functions?

☐ A. Business partner general role
☐ B. Vendor role
☐ C. Financial accounting customer role
☐ D. Customer role

10. Which of the following partner functions must be defined to create a sales order for a customer? (There are three correct answers.)

☐ A. Contact person
☐ B. Sold-to party

- ☐ C. Ship-to party
- ☐ D. Payer
- ☐ E. Employee responsible

11. Which of the following activities can connect a customer to the general ledger?

- ☐ A. Defining a reconciliation account in the financial accounting customer role
- ☐ B. Defining partner functions in the customer role
- ☐ C. Assigning the customer to a plant associated with a company code
- ☐ D. Assigning the customer to a company code

12. Which of the following statements are correct about the conditions master record in sales and distribution? (There are two correct answers.)

- ☐ A. Condition master records are usually managed and maintained at the plant level and storage location level
- ☐ B. Condition master records are usually managed and maintained at the sales organization and distribution channel level
- ☐ C. Prices in condition master records can be material specific or customer specific
- ☐ D. Once they are copied to the sales order, conditions cannot be altered

13. Which of the following are examples of outputs in sales and distribution? (There are two correct answers.)

- ☐ A. Sales documents
- ☐ B. Invoices
- ☐ C. Delivery notes
- ☐ D. Transfer orders

14. Which of the following data are valid for the entire sales order document? (There are two correct answers.)

- ☐ A. Schedule line
- ☐ B. Sold-to party
- ☐ C. Sales organization
- ☐ D. Ship-to party

15. Which of the following characteristics must be the same to combine multiple sales orders into one delivery? (There are three correct answers.)

☐ A. Ship-to party
☐ B. Shipping point
☐ C. Storage location
☐ D. Delivery due date
☐ E. Storage bin

16. Which of the following are data in the outbound delivery document? (There are two correct answers.)

☐ A. Schedule line
☐ B. Picked quantity
☐ C. Shipping point
☐ D. Fiscal year

17. Which of the following are correct about the picking process in sales and distribution? (There are three correct answers.)

☐ A. All delivery items must be picked before a goods issue posted for an outbound delivery
☐ B. A transfer order must be used to execute and record the picking process with SAP EWM
☐ C. A WMS is a prerequisite for picking
☐ D. The picked quantity field and the status overview in the outbound delivery document are updated when the picking process is complete
☐ E. Multiple deliveries can be collectively picked by using picking lists

18. Which of the following is not one of the impacts of posting goods issue?

☐ A. An accounting document is created to update the COGS account and the stock account
☐ B. Customer's account is debited by the value of the outbound delivery
☐ C. The material document is created to reduce the stock quantity by the quantity of the outbound delivery
☐ D. Billing due list is updated

19. Which of the following characteristics may not be the same in the sales documents that can be combined into a single billing document?

☐ A. Payer
☐ B. Pricing conditions

☐ C. Billing date
☐ D. Destination country

20. Which of the following is *not* an impact of creating a billing document?

   ☐ A. A customer invoice is generated
   ☐ B. The customer account is debited
   ☐ C. The revenue account is credited
   ☐ D. The billing document is sent to the customer

21. Which of the following are touchpoints for the integration between sales and distribution and financial accounting? (There are two correct answers.)

   ☐ A. Goods issue posting
   ☐ B. Create outbound delivery
   ☐ C. Billing
   ☐ D. Picking

22. Which of the following are touchpoints for the integration between sales and distribution and management accounting? (There are two correct answers.)

   ☐ A. Goods issue posting
   ☐ B. Outbound delivery
   ☐ C. Availability check
   ☐ D. Billing

23. Which of the following is a touchpoint for the integration between sales and distribution and warehouse management?

   ☐ A. Saving a sales order
   ☐ B. Payment
   ☐ C. Picking
   ☐ D. Billing

5.7 Practice Question Answers and Explanations

1. Correct answers: **B and D**

   Every successful transaction in the system results in a document. Sales documents (orders, quotations, outline agreements, inquiries) are created when the relevant transactions are completed. However, sales documents are not master data. A vendor master record is master data in purchasing but not in sales and distribution. Master data in sales and distribution include the master records for materials, customers, conditions, and outputs.

2. Correct answers: **A, C, and D**
   The sales and distribution module has specific organizational data that the other modules do not. For instance, sales areas, sales organizations, distribution channels, divisions, and shipping points are sales-specific organizational data. A warehouse number is organizational data in warehouse management. Warehouse management integrates with sales and distribution during outbound delivery handling. However, warehouse management is not part of the sales and distribution module. Option B, distribution centers, is tricky in this question. Remember that a plant is organizational data in the system and can represent a sales office or a distribution channel in the real world. However, no organizational data exists called a "distribution center."

3. Correct answer: **A**
   To answer this question, you must recall the assignments between organizational data. The client is the highest level of organizational data in the SAP system, and thus, option B is not correct. Multiple company codes can be assigned to a client, and multiple plants can be assigned to a company code. Distribution channels and divisions are assigned only to sales organizations. So, options C and D are also not correct. We know that multiple shipping points can be assigned to a plant, and plants are assigned to a sales organization. A sales organization can be assigned to only one company code.

4. Correct answers: **B and D**
   Availability checks are carried out during sales order creation, before saving the sales order. Thus, options A and C are not correct. Options B and D represent correct sequences of tasks in sales and distribution.

5. Correct answers: **C, D, and E**
   A sales area is a combination of sales organization, distribution channel, and division. A shipping area is organizational data in sales and distribution. However, a shipping point is not a part of a sales area. A sales manager can be a position in human capital management (HCM) but is not organizational data in sales and distribution.

6. Correct answer: **C**
   Every sales area includes a sales organization. A sales organization is responsible for distributing goods and services, negotiating sales conditions, and product liability and rights of recourse. A distribution channel can be used to create a small structure in which you can achieve flexible pricing and differentiate the sales statistics.

7. Correct answers: **B and C**
   The sales organization and the plant are uniquely assigned to a company code. As a result, multiple sales organizations and plants can be assigned to a company code. However, a sales organization (or plant) cannot be assigned to more

than one company code. Sales areas are not directly assigned to a company code. The relationship between a sales area and a company code is established when you assign the sales organization to a company code.

8. Correct answers: **A, D, and E**

    Divisions and distribution channels are assigned to sales organizations to set up sales areas. A sales organization can deliver products and services from many plants. On the other hand, many sales organizations can deliver products from a single plant (or a distribution center). To support this requirement, you can assign many plants to a sales organization, and a plant can be assigned to many sales organizations. Shipping points are assigned to plants but not to sales organizations.

9. Correct answer: **D**

    First, business partner master data for a customer includes the business partner general role, the financial accounting customer role, and the customer role. The vendor role is a part of business partner master data for a vendor. The business partner general role includes general data (e.g., address, communication) valid for the client level. The financial accounting customer role includes accounting-relevant data, such as reconciliation account, payment data, and withholding tax information. Customer role data is part of business partner master data and includes sales-relevant data. Partner functions are defined in the customer role of business partner master data.

10. Correct answers: **B, C, and D**

    To create a sales order, you must maintain the mandatory partner functions either on business partner master data for the customer or in the sales order. The mandatory partner functions are sold-to party, ship-to party, bill-to party, and payer. You can optionally define other partner functions such as the contact person and employee responsible.

11. Correct answer: **A**

    The customer account is a subledger account. This account is part of accounts receivables, not part of the general ledger. You can connect a customer account to the general ledger by defining a reconciliation account in the financial accounting customer role of business partner master data for a customer. Recall that reconciliation accounts connect subledger accounts (customer, vendor, asset) to general ledgers and are closed for direct posting.

12. Correct answers: **B and C**

    Condition master records in sales and distribution are usually managed and maintained at the sales organization and distribution channel level, not at the plant level. You can alter pricing conditions on the sales order. The condition changes on the sales order are specific to that transaction and will not change the master record in the system.

13. Correct answers: **B and C**

    An output in sales and distribution is the information sent to the customer by mail, EDI, or fax. Quotations, order confirmations, delivery notes, and invoices are examples of outputs in sales and distribution. Sales orders, transfer orders, and outbound deliveries are transactions that generate documents (and outputs) upon completion.

14. Correct answers: **B and C**

    This question tests your knowledge about the header-level and item-level data in a sales order. Recall that the header-level data is valid for the entire sales document. The sold-to party and the sales organization are header-level data in the sales order, while scheduling lines and ship-to party can be maintained at the item level.

15. Correct answers: **A, B, and D**

    To answer this question, you need to remember the header-level data in the outbound delivery document. The ship-to party, shipping point, delivery data, sales organization, and incoterms are examples of header-level data in the outbound delivery document. Sales orders combined into a single delivery must have these same characteristics. The material number, quantity, storage location, and storage bin are examples of data that can be maintained at the item level of the outbound delivery document.

16. Correct answers: **B and C**

    The outbound delivery document does not contain schedule lines but instead contains line items. When you create an outbound delivery for a sales order, the data in the sales order's schedule lines are copied to line items of the outbound delivery document. The outbound delivery document is not an accounting document and thus does not include the fiscal year data.

17. Correct answers: **A, D, and E**

    If the material is managed in the SAP EWM system, you must use outbound delivery orders to control physical movements (picking) in the warehouse. Transfer orders are used in a lean or regular WMS. A WMS is not a prerequisite for picking. You may have some materials that are not managed in a warehouse but require picking at a storage location.

18. Correct answer: **B**

    A customer account is part of accounts receivable. The goods issue posting has no impact on accounts receivable. The first update to the customer account in a sales and distribution cycle occurs when you create the billing document. That update is a debit memo. The second update occurs when the accounting department receives the payment and creates a general ledger posting to credit the customer account.

19. Correct answer: **B**

    To combine multiple sales documents into a single billing document, they must have the same characteristics, such as payer, destination country, and billing date. Sales documents may have several line items with different pricing conditions. They can still be combined into a single billing document as long as they share the same required characteristics.

20. Correct answer: **D**

    When you create a billing document, an invoice is generated as an output and sent to the customer. An accounting document is also created to debit the customer account and credit the revenue account. The billing document is not sent to the customer. Its role is to pass the process to the accounting department, which will handle the steps for receiving the customer's payment.

21. Correct answers: **A and C**

    To answer this question, consider the transactions that trigger the creation of an accounting document. The role of an accounting document is to update financial accounting records. When you post a goods issue or create a billing document, an accounting document is created. However, the creation of an outbound delivery document or picking process has no impact on financial accounting.

22. Correct answers: **A and D**

    Recall that a controlling document is created when you post a goods issue, which creates an integration between sales and distribution and management accounting. Another integration occurs through the data transfer to profitability analysis during the goods issue and billing.

23. Correct answer: **C**

    If the material is managed in a warehouse, you must initiate a picking process by using a warehouse order (e.g., a transfer order). Thus, the picking process leads to integration between sales and distribution and warehouse management.

5.8 Test Takeaway

In this chapter, you learned the key tasks of the lead-to-cash business process and SAP's intelligent enterprise solutions that support those key tasks. The lead-to-cash business process can be split into two end-to-end processes that can be handled in SAP Customer Experience and SAP S/4HANA, respectively: lead-to-order and order-to-cash.

The order-to-cash business process consists of four phases: sales order handling, outbound delivery, billing, and customer payment. A sales order is created at the sales area level and includes all data necessary for outbound delivery and billing, and customer payment. When you save a sales order, an incompletion log is displayed to show data missing from the sales order. An outbound delivery document is the key document created at the shipping point level and initiates the delivery process. The delivery process ends with a goods issue posting. This transaction reduces the inventory and updates accounts in financial accounting. Material and accounting documents are created to document the impacts of the goods issue posting. However, a goods issue posting has no impact on the customer's account. The customer account is updated when you create the billing document. A billing document passes the sales process to financial accounting. The output of this transaction is the customer invoice. The order-to-cash business process ends with posting the customer payment in financial accounting.

Completing this chapter, you should be able to explain in detail the following concepts:

- The sales and distribution module uses some organizational data (i.e., client, company code, plant, and storage location) in common with other logistics processes. However, the shipping point and the sales area are organizational data specific only to sales and distribution.
- Master data in sales and distribution includes the master records for materials, customers, conditions, and outputs.
- Cross-module data assignments and some transactions in sales and distribution create integrations between the system modules. For instance, the goods issue posting and billing process result in some credit and debit postings in general ledger accounting.

We've now covered the lead-to-cash business process enabled by SAP's intelligent enterprise framework. In the next chapter, we'll cover design-to-produce business processing and the production module in SAP S/4HANA.

Chapter 6
Design-to-Operate Processing

Techniques You'll Master

- Describe the key processes in design-to-operate and outline the phases of production planning and execution
- Explain the master and organizational data used in design-to-operate processing
- Understand strategic and detailed planning in manufacturing
- Execute routine transactions in production
- Identify the touchpoints of integration between the production module in SAP S/4HANA and other system modules

Chapter 6 Design-to-Operate Processing

This chapter of the book covers all certification-relevant topics of design-to-operate processing. We'll describe the master data, organizational data, and system transactions supporting production planning and execution in SAP S/4HANA and explain potential integration scenarios.

Design-to-operate represents a seamlessly integrated and intelligent end-to-end process on the SAP intelligent enterprise suite using the following technologies:

- SAP Intelligent Product Design
- SAP S/4HANA
- SAP 3D Visual Enterprise
- SAP Engineering Control Center
- SAP Asset Intelligence Network
- SAP Integrated Business Planning (SAP IBP)
- SAP Logistics Business Network, global track and trace option
- SAP Digital Manufacturing Cloud
- SAP Predictive Asset Insights
- SAP Asset Manager

The design-to-operate process consists of the following phases: design, plan-to-produce, plan-to-deliver, and operate. We'll focus on the plan-to-produce process in this chapter for the purposes of this exam.

Real-World Scenario

Manufacturing is the most critical component of a value chain since it directly affects the on-time delivery of products in sales and distribution. The standard procedures of manufacturing planning and execution are still the same. Manufacturers continuously responding to the digital transformation age has resulted in more complex and intelligent manufacturing processes, including the Internet of Things (IoT), artificial intelligence (AI), and advanced analytics. Customer feedback now plays a crucial role in designing and improving products, thus becoming an integral part of customer-oriented end-to-end manufacturing processes. The development of multicore processors, massive in-memory databases, and big data analysis enable demand sensing and the ability to quickly respond to instant supply and demand changes.

A company's profitability and customer satisfaction require careful planning of demand and an accurate forecast of future sales. Planning directly impacts material and capacity requirements in production. To cover material requirements in production operations and sales, a company must successfully plan in-house production and external procurement. For cost efficiency and productivity in manufacturing, strategic and detailed planning of manufacturing is vital. Material staging and delivery of finished products require seamless integration with inventory and warehouse management. Manufacturing execution is the central process in which most production-relevant costs occur. Tracking these costs and recording variances between planned and actual costs is important for determining real product costs and competitive sale prices.

As an SAP consultant, you must be able to explain how SAP's intelligent enterprise suite tightly integrates design, manufacturing, delivery, and management of assets used in production. For a successful system implementation, you need to know how to use the planning and manufacturing execution applications in the production module. To provide consulting for a seamlessly integrated manufacturing process, you need to understand the touchpoints of integration between production and other logistics processes (e.g., purchasing, sales and distribution) as well as with controlling, financial accounting, Project System, and human resources (HR).

6.1 Objectives of This Portion of the Test

This portion of the certification aims to test your knowledge of the key processes in design-to-operate processing and how these processes are handled in the SAP intelligent enterprise suite. The certification exam includes questions about the organizational data, master data, and the system transactions for production planning and manufacturing execution. SAP consultants are expected to understand all integrations between the production module and other system modules.

For the certification exam, business process integration consultants must have a good understanding of the following topics:

- Strategic and detailed planning in manufacturing
- Key tasks of manufacturing execution
- Master and organizational data in design-to-operate processing
- Touchpoints of integration between production and other processes

Note
The design-to-operate business process covers 8%–12% of the questions in the certification exam.

6.2 Data Structures for Design-to-Operate

In this section, we explain the certification-relevant concepts of design-to-operate processing. In particular, we introduce the organizational data and master data used in the design-to-operate business process. We also discuss database relationships between organizational and master data.

6.2.1 Organizational Data

The following organizational data is used to map the company's manufacturing-relevant organizational structure into the system:

- Client
- Company code
- Plant
- Storage location

In previous chapters, we described this organizational data in detail. In this chapter, a plant refers to a manufacturing plant. A storage location refers to a physical location where the materials in production (e.g., raw materials, semifinished goods, and finished products) are stored.

6.2.2 Master Data

The following master data is a foundation for the transactions in the design-to-operate business process:

- Material master records
- Material bills of material (BOMs)
- Routings
- Production versions
- Production resources and tools (PRTs)
- Work centers

We'll discuss each in the following sections.

Material Master Record

A material master record is structured into views, each of which contains data for the use of particular departments and integrated business processes. In this section, we'll provide a detailed explanation of the material master record for the source-to-pay business process.

Production-relevant materials must include general data in the **Basic Data** view, valid for the entire organization (client). Depending on the material, you can maintain data in sales, purchasing, accounting, warehouse, advanced planning, and plant views at different organization levels. For instance, a material master record for a raw material may have a purchasing view, maintained at the purchasing organization level, but not a sales view. To enable a material for several manufacturing stages, you must maintain data in the material requirements planning (MRP) views. **MRP 1-4** views in the material master record, as shown in Figure 6.1, include some important settings concerned with the procurement, production planning, and manufacturing execution processes for a material, such as the following settings, which we'll walk through next:

Data Structures for Design-to-Operate — Section 6.2

- MRP type
- MRP area
- Advanced planning
- Lot-sizing procedure
- Procurement type
- Safety stock
- Strategy group
- Forecasting requirements
- Production version

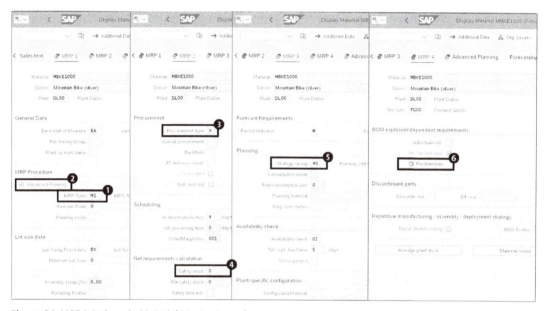

Figure 6.1 MRP 1-4 Views in Material Master Record

MRP 1 View — *Material Requirement Planning = MRP*

The **MRP 1** view, shown in Figure 6.1, contains two major MRP settings: the MRP type and MRP area.

The *MRP type* ❶ is a key you must maintain in the **MRP Procedure** section of the **MRP 1** view of the material master record. This value determines whether and how a material is planned in the MRP area. For each material, you can choose one of the following MRP types:

- **Consumption-based planning**
  This method uses past consumption data in the system to calculate future requirements for the material. In consumption-based planning, net requirements calculation (for material shortage) is triggered when the stock falls below a reorder point or forecast requirement but not by any independent requirements.

  The following MRP procedures are supported in consumption-based planning:

  - **Reorder point planning**
    The system continuously monitors material withdrawals from stock. If the available stock level meets the reorder point, the system creates an entry in the planning file for the next planning run. Net requirements calculation

considers the current stock, safety stock, firmed receipts, average consumption, and replenishment lead time to identify material requirements.

- **Time-phased planning**
  Material requirements are calculated based on the planning cycle determined in the material master record.

- **Forecast-based planning**
  This method uses historical and forecasted consumption values to calculate material requirements.

- **Material requirements planning**
  This method uses the current and forecasted sales as inputs to calculate the material requirements. MRP performs a net requirements calculation based on supply and demand requirements.

- **Master production scheduling**
  To plan the (bottleneck) items that use critical resources or significantly impact profitability, master production scheduling (MPS) uses the same principles as MRP for the calculation of requirements. If you set the MRP type to MPS, then the material is flagged as a master schedule item and planned in a separate planning run.

- **No planning**
  If you choose MRP type as no planning (ND), then the system will not carry out any planning runs for this material. You can use this setting for materials that, for instance, are not produced continuously.

- **Demand-driven replenishment**
  This new functionality in SAP S/4HANA enables MRP that considers disruptions in the supply chain or fluctuations in customer demand. You need to choose the MRP type with the MRP procedure **C** to enable a material for demand-driven material requirements planning (DDMRP).

The *MRP area* represents the organizational unit in which you plan material requirements independently using different lot-sizing and MRP procedures. MRP areas are defined in Customizing and assigned to materials in the **MRP 1** view of their master records. Several MRP areas can be assigned to a material by creating MRP area segments, which enables you to plan the same material differently (and flexibly) in different MRP areas. MRP can be carried out at the plant level or MRP area level independently. Three types of MRP areas exist in the system:

- **Plant MRP areas**
  The material requirements for a plant, including its storage locations and subcontractors, are planned.

- **MRP areas for storage locations**
  You can assign a particular storage location to an MRP area, and then, material requirements for the materials in the assigned storage location can be planned independently.

- **MRP areas for subcontractors (suppliers)**
  Some finished goods are produced by vendors (or subcontractors). In this case, you are providing the vendor with components or materials. To plan material requirements for these materials, you can assign a subcontractor to an MRP area, and material requirements for the assigned subcontractor can be planned separately in that MRP area.

As shown in Figure 6.1, the **Advanced Planning** indicator ❷ can be selected in the **MRP 1** or **Advanced Planning** views of the material master record. This checkbox determines whether the material is planned using advanced planning. In the **Advanced Planning** view of a material master record, you can control more settings necessary for advanced planning. The **Advanced Planning** view includes settings relevant to advanced planning supported by production planning and detailed scheduling (PP-DS).

MRP 2 View

As shown in Figure 6.1, the **Procurement type** key ❸ is defined in the **MRP 2** view of the material master record. This key determines how a material is procured, with the following options:

- In-house production only
- External procurement only
- Both in-house production and external procurement

In the **MRP 2** view of the material master record, shown in Figure 6.1, you can also specify the safety stock level used in consumption-based planning or net requirements calculation ❹. If you enter zero, no safety stock will be planned for the material.

MRP 3 View

In the **MRP 3** view of the material master record, you can define the periods in which consumption values and forecast values of the material should be managed. You can control more forecasting-relevant settings in the **Forecasting** view. Note that consumption values and forecast values are stored and continuously updated in the **Forecasting** view of the material master record

In the **MRP 3** view, shown in Figure 6.1, a strategy group is a two-character numeric key that controls the material's planning strategies ❺. Some examples of planning strategies that you can choose include the following:

- Make-to-stock (MTS)
- Make-to-order (MTO)
- Assembly or service orders
- Preplanning with or without assembly

MRP 4 View

In the **MRP 4** view of the material master record, shown in Figure 6.1, you can assign one or more production versions to a material ❻. A production version is master data in production that represents a manufacturing technique according to which you can produce the material using an alternative BOM and task lists under different lot-size restrictions.

Material Bills of Material

A material BOM master record, shown in Figure 6.2, includes a structured list of components necessary for manufacturing the material. Several system components can use material BOMs for planning, such as the following:

- MRP
- Product cost planning
- Plant maintenance
- Purchasing

In addition to a material BOM, you can also define BOMs for equipment, functional locations, work breakdown structure (WBS) elements, and sales orders in the system. We'll focus on the material BOM in this chapter.

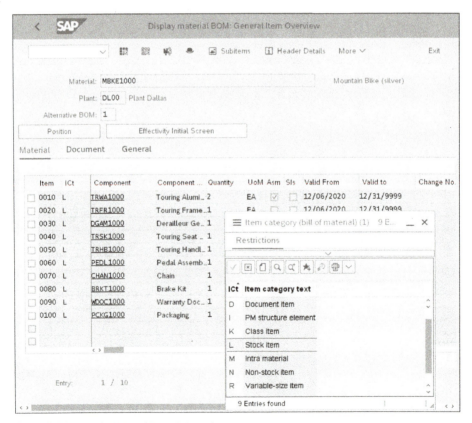

Figure 6.2 Material BOM and Item Categories

Some important characteristics of material BOM master records include the following:

- **Structured into header-level and item-level data**
  A material BOM consists of header-level data and item-level data. Header-level data includes the material number; base quantity (the quantity of the finished product); plant (in which the BOM is valid); and the BOM usage key that determines the specific area in which the BOM is used (e.g., production, design, engineering, or costing). You can display BOMs for specific usage.

  Each item-level data represents a specific component or assembly used to produce the material described in the BOM header. Item-level data includes the material number for the component (if the component has a material master record), component description, quantity, unit of measure, validity period, and item category. The item category determines the type of BOM item.

  Some examples of item categories that you can use in a material BOM include the following:
    - **Stock item**
      These items are kept in stock and include raw material, packaging material, and semifinished material. You must enter a material master number for this item category.
    - **Nonstock item**
      These items are not kept in your inventory. Nonstock items are procured for production orders.
    - **Variable-size item**
      You can use the variable-size item category if you want different-sized sections of a material to be used in a BOM (e.g., sheet metal).
    - **Document item**
      A material BOM can include supplementary documents describing the production process via photographs, drawings, and texts. The document item category is used for these documents.

- **Material BOMs are single level**
  All material BOMs for finished products or assemblies (a group of semifinished products or parts) are single level. A BOM item can be a raw material or an assembly with a single-level BOM. You can describe a multilevel production by using semifinished products or assemblies in BOM items.

Routing

A routing master record describes the path and steps (operations) used to produce a material. Along with a material BOM, a routing describes the production of a material and creates a basis for product costing.

A routing master record includes the following information:

- Header-level data
- Sequences
- Operations

Header-level data includes information valid for the entire routing sequences and operations, such as the following information:

- The usage key, which describes the areas you can use the routing (e.g., production plant maintenance)
- Lot-size ranges for which the routing can be used in production
- A validity period

A routing master record is identified by group and group counter numbers stored at the header-level data. A sequence is a series of sorted operations you must carry out in a routing. Similar to project networks, you can create structures in the routing by using standard, alternative, and parallel sequences. Figure 6.3 shows a standard sequence of operations in a routing.

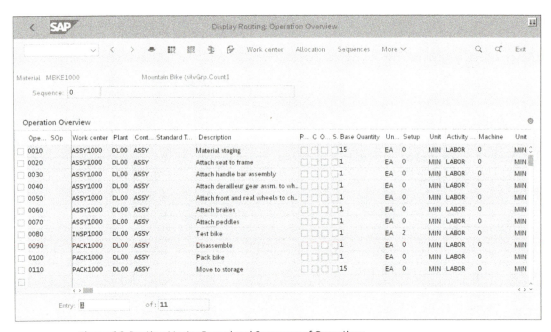

Figure 6.3 Routing Master Record and Sequence of Operations

An operation is an individual procedure performed at a work center during production. Each operation includes information valid only for that operation, such as the following information:

- Work center number
- Plant
- Description

- Activity type
- Duration
- Base quantity
- Unit of measure

A material BOM is assigned to routing in its master record. A routing along with a material BOM describes the production of a material. BOM components (items) can also be assigned to specific routing operations, as shown in Figure 6.4. If you don't assign BOM components to operations, the system explicitly assigns all BOM components to the sequence's first operation. For an overview of BOM component allocations, click the **Allocation** button on the screen to display the routing master record (shown earlier in Figure 6.3).

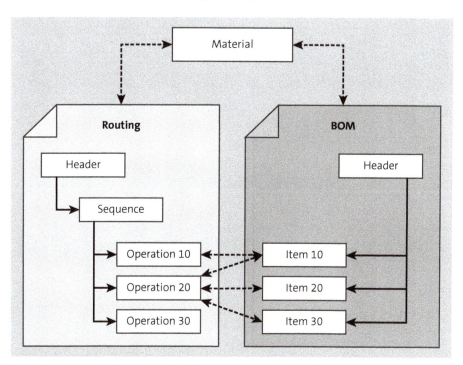

Figure 6.4 Assignments between BOM Components and Routing Operations

Note
Within the framework of creating a routing master record, you may not assign a material to a routing. However, a material master record must be assigned to a routing before planning a production order with that routing.

Production Version

A production version master record determines the manufacturing techniques you can use to produce a material. To minimize costs and increase productivity, you may prefer to use different tasks and alternative BOMs to produce small quantities. The system supports this requirement by enabling the assignment of several production versions to a material. A production version master record includes the following information, as shown in Figure 6.5:

- An alternative BOM
- Task list
- Lost-size restrictions
- Validity period

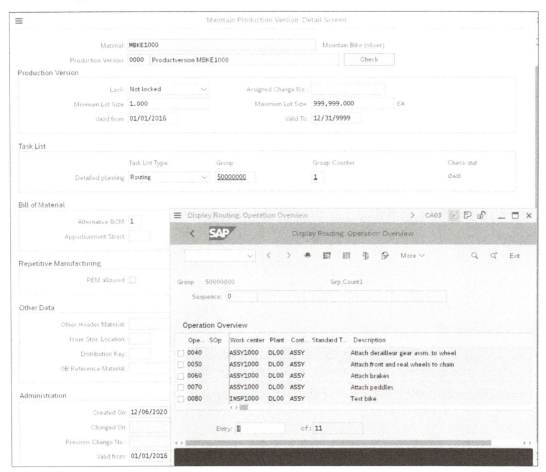

Figure 6.5 Production Version Master Record and Its Task List as a Routing Group

Production Resources and Tools

PRTs can represent movable or nonstationary operating resources (e.g., driller, hydraulic punch) required to carry out production activities. In production, PRTs are master data. Depending on their usage, you can create PRTs in the following ways, as shown in Figure 6.6:

- **Material PRT (material master data)**
  Material PRTs are PRTs managed in materials management and require materials management functions such as MRP and procurement. You can use Transaction MM01 to create PRT material master records, where you'll need to maintain the **Basic Data**, **Work Scheduling**, and **Production Resources and Tools** views.

- **Equipment PRT (equipment master data)**
  These PRTs require preventive maintenance planning in plant maintenance. You can use Transaction IE01 to create an equipment PRT master record, where you need to maintain the **Production Resources and Tools** data view.

- **Document PRT (document master data)**
  These PRTs, in the form of drawings or programs, require functions for document management. You can use Transaction CV01N to create a document PRT master record by choosing the document type **DRF** (**PRT Eng/Des. Drawing**).

- **Miscellaneous PRT (PRT master data)**
  These other PRTs require little or no maintenance. You can use Transaction CF01 to create this type of PRT.

You can assign PRTs to operations (in routings), activities, or phases in task lists, production orders, maintenance orders, and project networks.

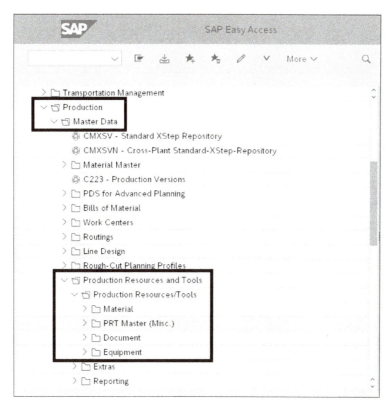

Figure 6.6 PRT Master Data Options in the Production Module

Work Center

A work center represents a machine group, a production line, a group of employees, or a physical location (e.g., assembly work center) in a plant where production operations or activities are carried out. A work center is master data in production and created at the plant level. To plan a work centers' cumulative capacities, you can create a work center hierarchy and assign work centers to that hierarchy in their master records. Work centers are assigned to operations in routings and to cost centers in cost center accounting. They can also be assigned to business processes in activity-based costing or organizational units in human capital management (HCM).

Work center master data is structured into views, controlling basic data, assignments, scheduling, hierarchy, and default values. In terms of their usage, data is organized into the following views of the work center master record:

- **Basic Data**
  The **Basic Data** view, shown in Figure 6.7, includes a description, the location of the work center, the person responsible, and a *standard value key*.

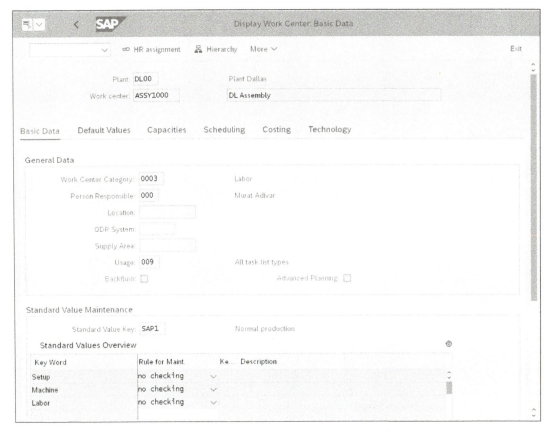

Figure 6.7 Basic Data in a Work Center

You can create standard value keys in Customizing, and they can be linked to up to six standard values. For instance, as shown in Figure 6.8, the standard value key **SAP1** defines three standard values: **Setup**, **Machine**, and **Labor**. Entering a standard value key in this view enables the work center to use standard values in capacity planning, costing, and scheduling. A *standard value* is a parameter used in formulas to calculate execution times (in scheduling), capacity requirements, and costs. You can define the values of a standard value in a routing task list when you assign a work center to operation. If you want to enable the work center for planning and scheduling in PP-DS, select the **Advanced Planning** checkbox in the **Basic Data** view.

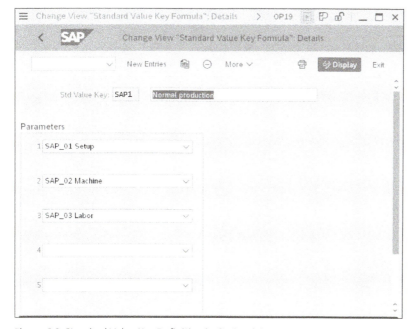

Figure 6.8 Standard Value Key Definition in Customizing

- **Default Values**
  In this view, you can maintain the default values for operations in the work center, such as wage type, control key, setup type key, activity type, and units of measurements for standard values.
- **Costing**
  A work center can use the resources of a cost center (which is master data in cost center accounting) or a business process (which is master data in activity-based costing). Depending on the resources used, a work center can be assigned to a cost center, as shown in Figure 6.9, or to a business process to collect the costs of operations carried out in the work center.

For instance, in costing with cost centers, the following costing mechanism would be set up:

- You'll plan activity prices for cost centers in activity type planning, which enables the calculation of activity costs collected by the cost center.
- You'll assign work centers to cost centers in their master records, which enables you to link (permissible) activity types with standard values in the work center.
- You'll assign a formula to each standard value, which enables the calculation of activity times, which is a basis for cost calculation.

Figure 6.9 Costing Data in a Work Center

Formulas (identified by formula keys) include the standard values as variables for calculating costs, execution times, and capacity requirements. For instance, Figure 6.9 shows a formula column, including a formula key **SAP003**, which calculates the labor time in production. Labor is a standard value listed in the first column, and it is linked to activity type **LABOR**. Figure 6.10 shows the rule of the formula **SAP003**. In this formula, labor time is a function of the labor (standard value) given in the first column. This labor time is the basis for the cost calculation. The system multiplies the unit price of the activity type **LABOR** by labor time to calculate an operation's labor cost at this work center.

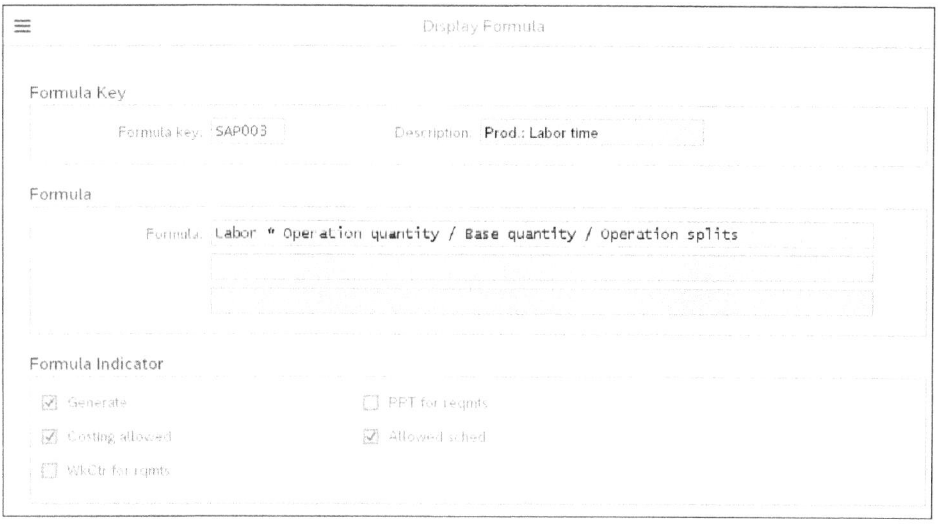

Figure 6.10 Work Center Formula Used in Costing and Scheduling

- **Scheduling**
  In the **Scheduling** view, you can define a scheduling basis, formulas to calculate execution times of operations using standard values, and interoperation times, as shown in Figure 6.11. Notice that the formula shown in Figure 6.10 is also used in scheduling.

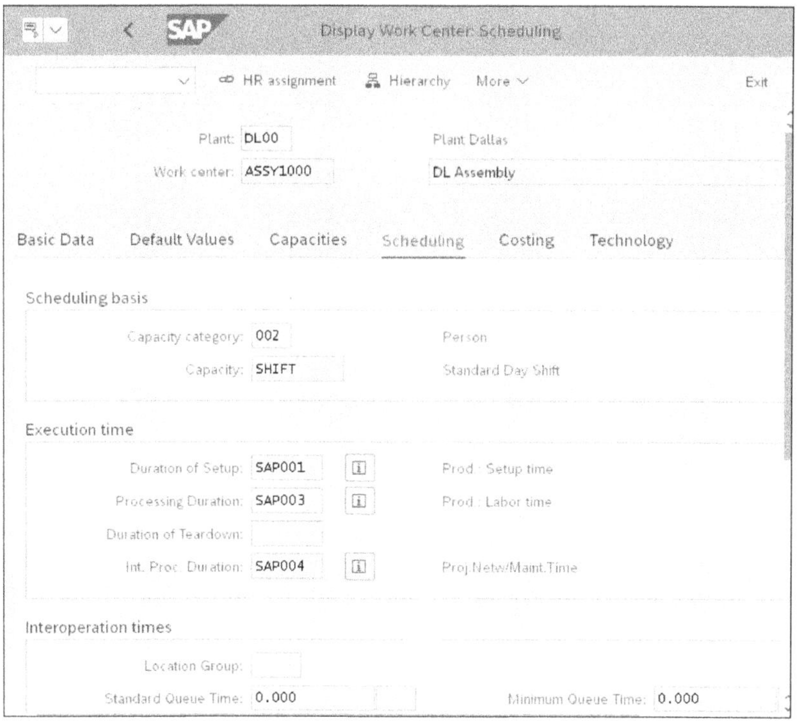

Figure 6.11 Scheduling Data in a Work Center

- **Capacities**
  In the **Capacities** view, you can define operating times, available capacity, and formulas for calculating capacity requirements. The data in this view is used in capacity requirements PP-DS.

6.2.3 Data Assignments

In Chapter 4, Section 4.2, we described organizational data assignments between client, company code, plant, and storage locations. Thus, in this section, we'll focus on the relationships between master data in design-to-operate processing. The following master data assignments are possible in the system, as shown in Figure 6.12:

- Materials are managed at the plant level. BOMs and routings are assigned to materials, and they are plant specific.
- Work centers are created in the plant. A plant may have multiple work centers, and a work center can belong to only one plant.
- A material BOM is assigned to a routing. A BOM component can be assigned to an operation in the routing. An operation in a routing can be assigned several components. If no BOM component is assigned to any operation, the system explicitly assigns all components in the material BOM to the first operation in the routing.

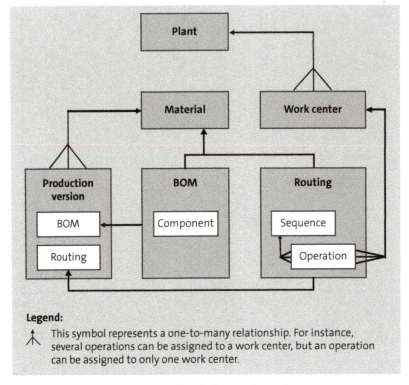

Figure 6.12 Data Assignments in Design-to-Operate Processing

- An operation in a routing can be assigned to only one work center. Several routing operations can be assigned to a work center.
- You can assign several PRTs to an operation in a routing.
- A production version is assigned a pair consisting of a material BOM and a routing to describe a variant of production. Several production versions can be assigned to a material in its master record.

6.3 Key Processes of Design-to-Operate

Design-to-operate represents a seamlessly integrated and intelligent end-to-end process on SAP's intelligent enterprise suite consisting of the following phases:

- **Design**
  In the design phase, you redesign a product or create a new product design based on customer feedback. The new design is passed to the manufacturing department for BOM and routing creation.
- **Plan-to-produce**
  The plan-to-produce process starts with demand planning based on historical demand and current market data. The process also covers capacity planning and production scheduling, which become the basis for manufacturing execution. The plan-to-produce process ends with receiving the finished product at the warehouse.
- **Plan-to-deliver**
  The plan-to-deliver process is concerned with the delivery of the finished product to the customer. The process starts with planning the delivery of the finished product, continues with performing (and tracking) outbound transportation, and ends with receiving proof of delivery.
- **Operate**
  In the operate phase, you monitor the assets (e.g., pieces of equipment or IoT devices) used in the production, predict asset failure, plan preventive maintenance or repair, and request an asset improvement (from the original equipment manufacturer) if necessary.

To prepare for the certification exam, we'll focus on the plan-to-produce business process, which consists of the following phases, as shown in Figure 6.13:

- Strategic planning
- Demand management
- Detailed planning
- Manufacturing control and execution

SAP S/4HANA's production module supports the tasks in all these phases of the plan-to-produce business process. We'll walk through each task in the following sections and also introduce you to SAP IBP, which supports strategic planning and demand management.

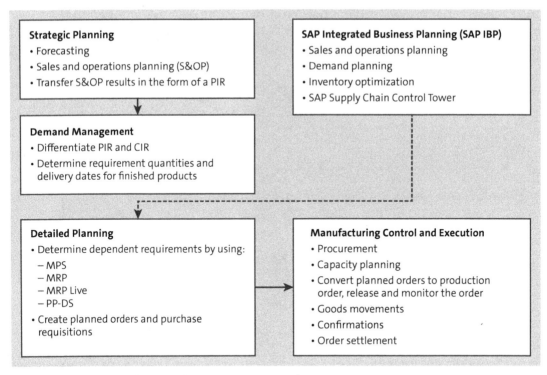

Figure 6.13 Plan-to-Produce Processing in SAP S/4HANA

6.3.1 Strategic Planning

In strategic planning, you forecast the future demand at the aggregated level for a product group or material. Based on the forecasted demand, the initial stock, and available capacities (at the aggregated level), you can plan the future quantities you can sell and produce for a medium- and long-term planning period.

SAP S/4HANA provides a flexible forecasting and planning tool, called *sales and operations planning (S&OP)*, to support strategic planning tasks. S&OP generates sales and production plans at the aggregate level using the system's historical data and forecasting tools. SAP provides two planning options for S&OP:

- Standard planning (fixed planning procedures and standardized plans)
- Flexible planning (customizable planning procedures and plans)

Figure 6.14 shows a rough-cut plan for sales and production at the product group level.

The product group in the rough-cut plan shown in Figure 6.14 includes three types of products with different proportions, as shown in Figure 6.15. The quantities in this plan are aggregated quantities for the product group. When you transfer the plan to demand management, these quantities are disaggregated and broken down to product-level quantities according to proportions defined in the product group.

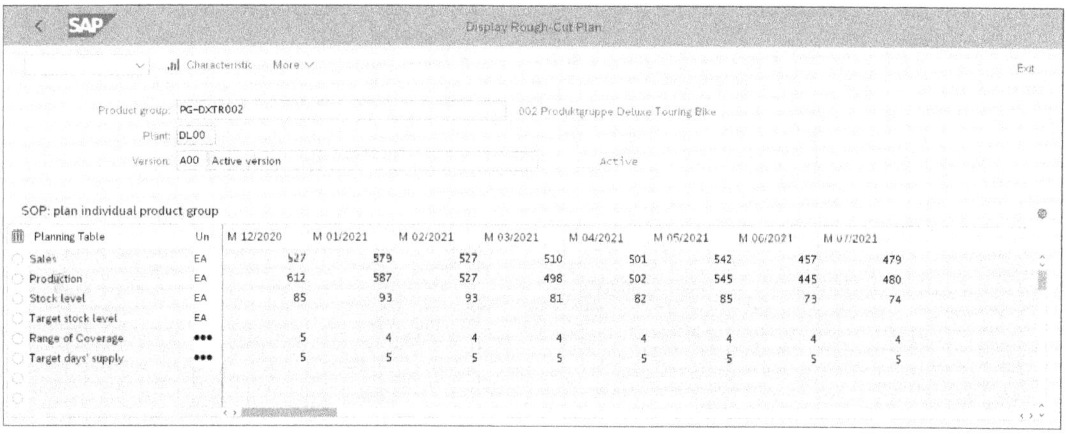

Figure 6.14 Rough-Cut Plan for a Product Group

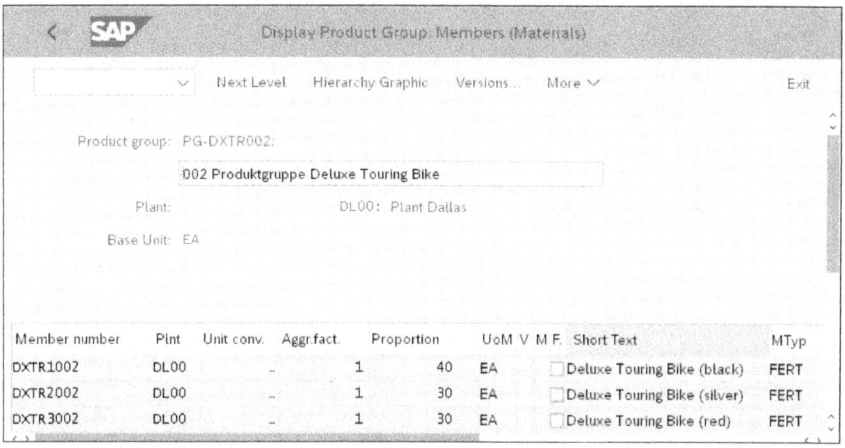

Planning Table	Un	M 12/2020	M 01/2021	M 02/2021	M 03/2021	M 04/2021	M 05/2021	M 06/2021	M 07/2021
Sales	EA	527	579	527	510	501	542	457	479
Production	EA	612	587	527	498	502	545	445	480
Stock level	EA	85	93	93	81	82	85	73	74
Target stock level	EA								
Range of Coverage	•••	5	4	4	4	4	4	4	4
Target days' supply	•••	5	5	5	5	5	5	5	5

Figure 6.15 Product Group Consisting of Three Products with Different Proportions

Member number	Plnt	Unit conv.	Aggr.fact.	Proportion	UoM	V	M	F.	Short Text	MTyp
DXTR1002	DL00	..	1	40	EA				Deluxe Touring Bike (black)	FERT
DXTR2002	DL00	..	1	30	EA				Deluxe Touring Bike (silver)	FERT
DXTR3002	DL00	..	1	30	EA				Deluxe Touring Bike (red)	FERT

Planned independent requirements (PIRs) are forecasted stock requirements (quantities) derived from future demand and available capacities. S&OP considers historical sales data but not current sales orders for the determination of independent requirements.

S&OP results are transferred to demand management after disaggregation in the form of PIRs, as shown in Figure 6.16. Demand management aligns these requirements with the current demand (sales orders) in the system.

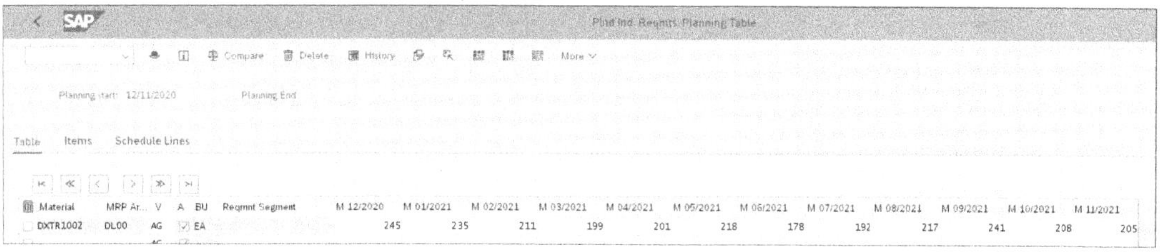

Material	MRP Ar...	V	A	BU	Reqmnt Segment	M 12/2020	M 01/2021	M 02/2021	M 03/2021	M 04/2021	M 05/2021	M 06/2021	M 07/2021	M 08/2021	M 09/2021	M 10/2021	M 11/2021
DXTR1002	DL00	AG	✓	EA		245	235	211	199	201	218	178	192	217	241	208	205

Figure 6.16 PIRs from S&OP

> **Note**
> S&OP is still being offered as an interim solution in SAP S/4HANA. SAP's new product SAP IBP will replace S&OP in future releases. SAP IBP enables S&OP on SAP HANA by providing new features, such as advanced statistical forecasting, multilevel supply planning, Microsoft Excel-based and web-based user interfaces (UIs), and collaboration tools.

6.3.2 Demand Management

Demand management aims to determine requirements (quantities) and delivery dates for finished products and assemblies in a specific plant. Demand management is an interface between strategic planning and detailed planning. Demand management provides a demand program. The demand program differentiates PIRs from customer independent requirements (CIRs) according to the planning strategy (e.g., MTO, MTS) defined in the material master record. CIRs are current sales orders in the system. Demand management aligns the requirements transferred from S&OP by differentiating CIR from PIR if the customer requirements are already forecasted in PIR.

PIRs are input into detailed planning process and form a basis for MPS in detailed planning and procurement.

6.3.3 SAP Integrated Business Planning

SAP IBP is a cloud-based solution and part of SAP's intelligent enterprise suite. Using SAP HANA's massive computation power, SAP IBP combines S&OP, demand management, inventory planning, supply planning, and supply chain monitoring. The idea is to combine sales, inventory, supply, and financial plans into a single and consistent plan that is optimal and applicable for the whole enterprise. SAP IBP consists of the following solutions:

- SAP Supply Chain Control Tower
- SAP IBP for sales and operations
- SAP IBP for demand
- SAP IBP for inventory
- SAP IBP for response and supply

SAP Jam is a separate collaboration tool supporting users, managers, and business partners in SAP IBP processes. With robust predictive analytics and flexible integration capabilities, SAP IBP offers the following business values:

- End-to-end supply chain visibility
- Faster planning cycles with more profitable responses
- More accurate forecasts that improve on-time delivery
- Instant reactions to changes and demand

- Effective balancing of supply and demand
- Synchronized planning processes
- Improved decision-making throughout the complete supply chain
- Cross-functional process orchestration
- Planning for distribution, production, and procurement

Note

The C_TS410_1909 and C_TS410_2020 exam versions only refer to SAP IBP for strategic planning and demand management.

6.3.4 Detailed Planning

Detailed planning is concerned with securing a material's availability for planned production and assembly processes. Detailed planning is a planning process that determines dependent requirements based on independent requirements (i.e., quantities for the finished product) provided by S&OP and demand management. Dependent requirements are the quantities of components required to produce the finished product or the assembly. They stem from the BOM explosion of independent requirements. In the BOM explosion, the system checks the material's multilevel component hierarchy (i.e., BOM) to determine what is needed to produce the PIR quantities.

Two major detailed planning processes are available in SAP S/4HANA, which we'll discuss in the following sections:

- MRP using classic MRP, MPS, or MRP Live
- Advanced planning using PP-DS

Material Requirements Planning

The purpose of MRP is to secure material availability for production and sales and distribution. SAP S/4HANA provides an MRP application component to determine dependent requirements and generate the procurement proposals for in-house production or external procurement of requirements. MRP uses the data in the MRP views of the material master record, BOM master record for the material, planned and current supply-demand quantities to generate procurement proposals. SAP S/4HANA provides the following MRP options:

- MRP (classic MRP or MRP Live on SAP HANA)
- MPS
- Demand-driven MRP (DDMRP)
- Predictive material and resource planning (pMRP)

You must use classic MRP if you need to determine capacity requirements with MRP. You can use Transaction MD_MRP_FORCE_CLASSIC to force the system to use classic MRP for specific materials or plants. SAP is planning to incorporate capacity requirements planning into MRP Live in the future. MRP Live is less manually intensive and faster than classic MRP. MRP Live explodes the massive computation potential of SAP HANA to provide more up-to-date supply and demand information in the system and react to the changes in demand more quickly than with traditional MRP. MRP Live reduces the risk of stock shortages and reduces the safety stock level (and costs). MRP Live also allows you to perform material planning across several plants.

If you choose the MRP type as MPS in the material master record, that material is determined as the master schedule item and planned using MPS. You can use this planning method for bottlenecks or critical items for which changes in the master production plan dramatically influence the entire production cycle. MPS uses the same planning principles (e.g., the same controlling parameters, the same planning modes) as traditional MRP. Unlike the traditional MRP, however, MPS plans only the master schedule at the item level. The system determines dependent requirements from the BOM, but lower BOM levels are not planned. Thus, you require the MRP application component as a prerequisite to using MPS.

DDMRP (also called demand-driven replenishment) helps you ensure high customer service levels at the lowest possible inventory. DDMRP functionality in SAP S/4HANA relies upon the demand forecast based on actual customer requirements or customer demand. In DDMRP, relevant material is detached from all the BOM dependencies from the supply chain and planned separately, a process called *decoupling*. Material classification enables the identification of materials that need to be decoupled from BOM dependencies. DDMRP proposes an optimal quantity of buffer inventory (also called decoupling inventory) for all identified materials.

pMRP allows production planners to identify capacity and material gaps in a plant before they occur. By performing simulations, production planners can evaluate potential solutions based on changed conditions such as demand planning, resource plans, preproduction, or make-or-buy decisions.

Net Requirements Calculation

In MRP, the system carries out a net requirements calculation in the planning run to determine the available stock. In the net requirements calculation, the system uses the following formula:

Available stock = Supply requirements – Demand requirements

Table 6.1 summarizes the supply and demand elements used in the net requirements calculation.

Supply Elements	Demand Elements
Plant stock	Safety stock
Firmed procurement proposals: planned orders, purchase requisitions	Material reservations, stock transfers
Production orders	PIRs (forecasted future sales)
Purchase orders	Sales orders (current sales)
Goods receipts	Dependent requirements

Table 6.1 Supply and Demand Elements in a Net Requirements Calculation

A negative available stock from the net requirements calculation represents a material shortage and triggers a procurement proposal (a planned order for in-house production or a purchase requisition for external procurement). The type of procurement proposal triggered depends on the **Procurement type** field in the **MRP 2** view of the material master record.

MRP can suggest the following solutions by generating planned orders or purchase requisitions:

- In-house production
- External procurement (from suppliers)

After the planning run, planned orders can be converted into production orders (or process orders), and purchase requisitions can be converted into purchase orders (or stock transport orders) by the authorized departments, as shown in Figure 6.17. In repetitive manufacturing, you can produce based on planned orders directly. Note that MRP does not directly generate purchase orders or production orders.

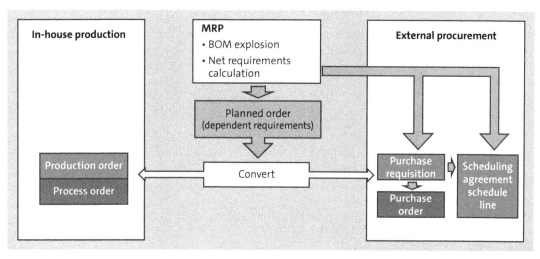

Figure 6.17 MRP Solutions: In-House Production and External Procurement

Planning Modes

Three planning modes for MRP are available in the system, as shown in Figure 6.18:

- MRP Live (planning several plants interactively)
- Total planning at the plant level (planning of all materials in a plant or all plants)
  - Online planning
  - Planning as a background job
- Single item planning (planning an individual material)
  - Single item single-level
  - Single item multilevel
  - Single item interactive

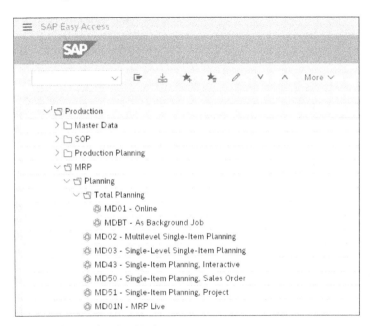

Figure 6.18 MRP Planning Modes

Control Parameters

To execute an MRP planning run, you must maintain the following MRP control parameters, as shown in Figure 6.19:

- **Processing Key**
  Specify the type of MRP or MPS run by entering one of two processing keys:
  - **NEUPL**: For regenerative planning of all MRP-relevant materials in the plant.
  - **NETCH**: For net change planning in the total horizon. This key is used for planning all materials to which an MRP-relevant change has been made.
- **Create Purchase Req.**
  You must maintain this field for items purchased externally. Based on the settings in this field, the MRP run can generate purchase requisitions or planned orders that will be manually converted into purchase requisitions later.

- **SA Deliv. Sched. Lines**
You must maintain this field for items purchased externally. This field determines whether the MRP run will generate scheduling agreement schedule lines.
- **Create MRP List**
This indicator provides three options: MRP list, no MRP list, or have the system create an MRP list depending on exception messages.
- **Planning mode**
Defines how the system handles procurement proposals from the last planning run.
- **Scheduling**
Using this indicator, you can specify whether the system determines only the basic dates for planned orders or whether lead time scheduling is also carried out.

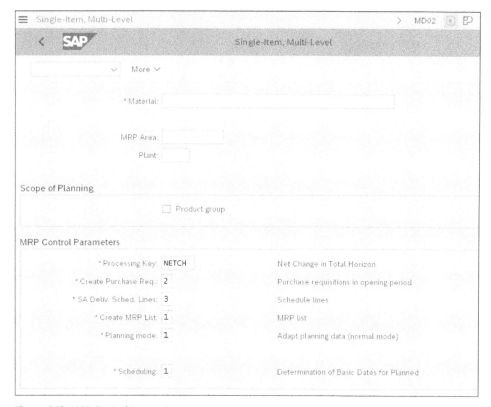

Figure 6.19 MRP Control Parameters

Note
SAP S/4HANA no longer provides the MRP processing key NETPL for net change planning in the planning horizon. MRP Live always identifies material shortages and requirements.

MRP List and Stock Requirements List

The outputs of an MRP run are dependent requirements documented in procurement proposals, as shown in Figure 6.20. Based on the procurement type specified in the material master record and the MRP control parameters, the MRP run can generate the following procurement proposals:

- Planned orders
- Purchase requisitions
- Scheduling agreement schedule lines

In the manufacturing control and execution phase, planned orders can be converted into production orders, purchase requisitions, or scheduling agreement lines.

As an example, Figure 6.20 shows the dependent requirements to produce 186 bikes.

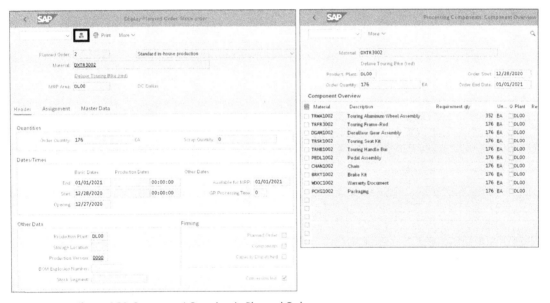

Figure 6.20 Component Overview in Planned Order

You can view independent requirements and procurement proposals in the stock requirements list and the MRP list (if created). The stock requirements list is a dynamic list showing all stock requirements in the system as soon as they occur. In contrast, the MRP list is static, and requirements on the MRP list remain the same until the next MRP run. The screen layout of the MRP list and stock requirements list is the same, as shown in Figure 6.21 and Figure 6.22.

Figure 6.21 Stock Requirements List after an MRP Run

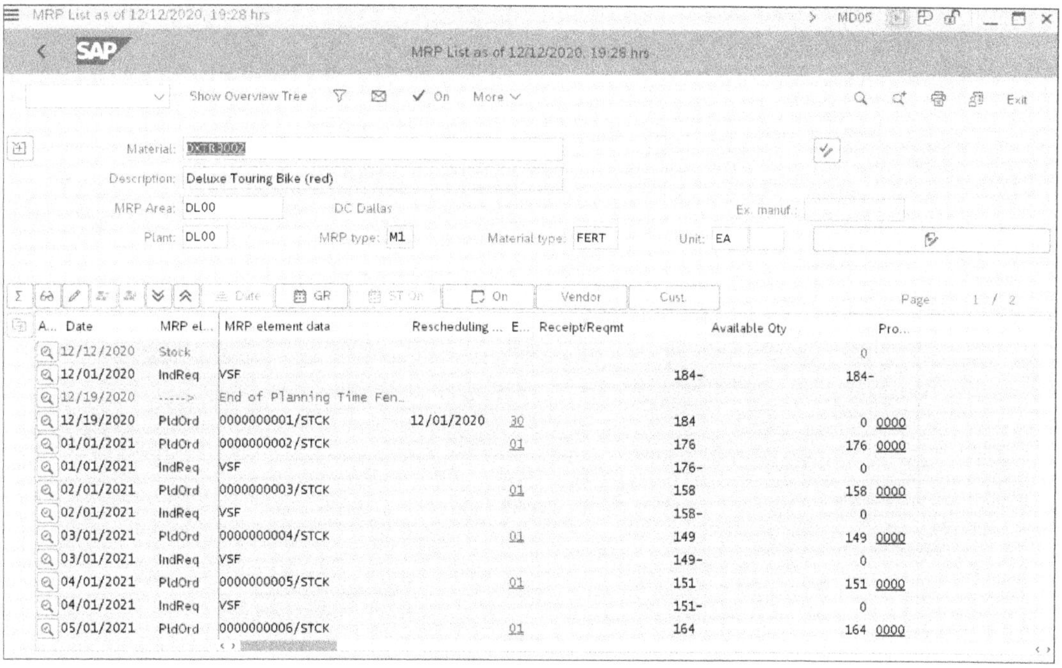

Figure 6.22 MRP List after an MRP Run

Advanced Planning

An alternative to the detailed planning of MRP is advanced planning using SAP S/4HANA's recently embedded tool, PP-DS.

Like MRP, advanced planning aims to cover material requirements in production and sales and distribution by creating procurement proposals for in-house production or external procurement. Unlike MRP, however, advanced planning generates proposals and orders with exact times and dates.

PP-DS was formerly a planning and optimization tool of SAP Advanced Planning and Optimization (SAP APO). SAP has recently added the functionality to SAP S/4HANA. You can use PP-DS to plan the critical products for which you need to optimize plans and resource schedules with exact dates and times in detail. For example, you can use PP-DS for products with long replenishment lead times or products using bottleneck resources. Planning critical products with PP-DS enables you to reduce lead times and stock costs and increase on-time delivery performance.

Some other advantages of using PP-DS in detailed planning include the following:

- Exact times (hours and minutes) in planning for independent and dependent requirements
- Multilevel view of material availability and capacity planning
- Enhanced options for capacity planning
- Optimization procedures for planning and scheduling

To prepare your system for planning material requirements with PP-DS, you must meet the following prerequisites:

- **Advanced planning settings in the material master record**
  To enable a specific product to be planned in PP-DS, select the **Advanced Planning** checkbox in the material master record, as shown in Figure 6.23.

Figure 6.23 Marking Material for Advanced Planning in the Material Master Record

You can also directly create an advanced planning-relevant material by maintaining data in the **Advanced Planning** view of the material master record. You can completely exclude some materials from MRP planning by changing the MRP type to **X** in the **MRP Type** field. For PP-DS, you should also define a production version, including BOM and routing.

- **Master data integration between SAP S/4HANA and PP-DS**
  PP-DS uses its own master data. To employ PP-DS in planning, you must integrate the master data in SAP S/4HANA with the master data in PP-DS. Table 6.2 shows the relationships between master data objects in SAP S/4HANA and PP-DS.

SAP S/4HANA Master Data	PP-DS Master Data
Plants (storage locations, distribution centers)	
Vendors	Locations
Customers	
Material master records	Products
Production versions (with BOMs and routings)	Production data structures
Work centers and their capacities	Resources

Table 6.2 Integration between SAP S/4HANA Master Data and PP-DS Master Data

Now, let's walk through the PP-DS process. Note that advanced planning is not a replacement for MRP Live, but MRP Live is a prerequisite to advanced planning. PP-DS does not plan all products or their BOM components in the system. Only products or BOM components for which the **Advanced Planning** checkbox has been selected are transferred to PP-DS. Other materials are planned in MRP Live.

Advanced planning provides two production planning options:

- Automated production planning and optimization
- Interactive production planning

PP-DS can create planning file entries for components that must be planned in the MRP planning run. PP-DS generates its own procurement proposals. You can transfer these procurement proposals to SAP S/4HANA. Manufacturing execution tasks (e.g., order release, confirmation, goods movements) are carried out in the production module of SAP S/4HANA, as shown in Figure 6.24.

You can transfer PP-DS planned orders to SAP S/4HANA and convert transferred planned orders to manufacturing orders in the production module of SAP S/4HANA. In this case, the SAP S/4HANA planned order copies only the start and end dates from PP-DS planned order, and operation dates are lost. However, SAP recommends converting PP-DS planned orders to manufacturing orders within the PP-DS component. In this way, you can trigger the conversion in PP-DS by using the conversion indicator. When you convert a PP-DS planned order into a manufacturing order within PP-DS, the generated manufacturing order contains the production dates generated in PP-DS.

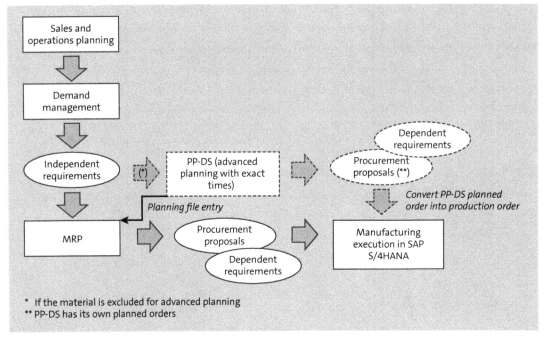

Figure 6.24 MRP and Advanced Planning in Plan-To-Produce Processing

PP-DS supports the following main processes in production:

- **Make-to-stock production**
  In MTS production, production is planned and executed based on requirements from forecasted demand and existing sales orders. Production orders are generated from planned orders, and finished products are kept in stock. PP-DS supports MTS production with various planning strategies, enhanced capacity planning options, different optimization procedures, and a capable-to-promise (CTP) check in the PP-DS horizon.

- **Make-to-order production**
  In MTO production, the product is not produced in advance. (The product may be expensive or highly customized.) A sales order for an MTO material triggers the generation of a production order. You must maintain the **Item Category Group** field with the value **0001** (MTO) in the **Sales org. 2** view of the material master record. The PP-DS horizon plays no role in MTO production; only planning for individual sales orders is possible. PP-DS supports MTO production with production planning optimization (or PP Optimizer) and CTP check (without time restrictions).

- **External procurement**
  In PP-DS, you can plan critical, externally procured products with planning tools and functions such as finite product scheduling and purchase order quantity optimization. PP-DS also supports source determination, scheduling agreement processing, and subcontracting.

You can use the alert monitor component of PP-DS to monitor the application centrally. If any problem arises, you can navigate to the application function to resolve the problem. You can use several standard alert types, or you can create your own prioritized alert types based on threshold values, such as the following alert types:

- Information
- Warning
- Errors

6.3.5 Manufacturing Control and Execution

The SAP S/4HANA production module supports the following manufacturing types:

- **Discrete manufacturing**
  This production type is on the basis of production orders. Discrete manufacturing is suitable for industries in which production is workshop-oriented, and the type of manufactured items changes frequently. This manufacturing type is the most common type of production.

- **Process manufacturing**
  This production type is on the basis of process orders. Process manufacturing is used for batch and recipe-oriented production of products or co-products. This manufacturing type is suitable for process industries, for instance, pharmaceutical, chemical, food, and process-based manufacturers.

- **Repetitive manufacturing**
  This manufacturing type is a period- and quantity-oriented production type. Instead of single-lot and order-based processing, repetitive manufacturing creates and processes production plans with the target of producing a certain number of products in a specific time interval. In this type of manufacturing, you can produce based on the planned orders directly. Repetitive manufacturing is preferable for industries using production lines to maximize productivity for the same type of products, such as the electronics and semiconductor industry.

- **Kanban**
  Kanban processing is a production strategy for controlling material production and flows based on actual stock quantities. Kanban provides control cycles for in-house production and external procurement. Material replenishment and production are triggered and controlled by control cycles. The idea is to produce or procure the material whenever needed. SAP S/4HANA's production module provides a special type of production order for Kanban processing. Kanban is suitable for industries in which inventory costs are too high (e.g., automotive) or where just-in-time (JIT) production is important.

To prepare for the certification exam, we'll limit ourselves to discrete manufacturing, which is based on production order management.

The cycle of production order management can be outlined in the following way:

1. Create a production order
   - Scheduling
   - Availability check (*)
   - Capacity requirements planning
2. Release the production order (*)
   - Printing order and shop papers (*)
   - Material staging
   - Material consumption posting (*)
3. Order confirmation (*)
4. Goods receipt (for finished products) (*)
5. Period-end closing
   - Overhead calculation
   - Work in process (WIP) calculation
   - Variance calculation
   - Settlement

The items marked by asterisks (*) can be automated in Customizing. Other activities can be executed through background processing.

We'll walk through these steps in the following sections, starting with production order maintenance and order release.

Production Order Maintenance and Release

A production order is a system order that officially initiates the manufacturing execution process. This detailed plan of production contains all the necessary information for subsequent steps of production. Basically, a production order includes all operational details and answers the following questions:

- What product in what quantities should be produced?
- When and where should production take place?
- Which tasks should be carried out and when and where?
- Which capacities, methods, and resources should be used in production?
- What are the expected and actual costs of production?
- Which settlement receivers should bear the costs of production?

You can create a production order in several ways:

- Manually with or without material
- With reference to a previous order (copying from a reference order)
- By converting a planned order
- With a sales order

A planned order for material with in-house production as the procurement type is a request for production. Thus, this planned order can be converted into a production order. Planned order conversion copies the data from the planned order (i.e., order quantities, order dates, BOM components, routing groups) into a production order. Planned orders can be converted in their entirety or partially.

When you create a production order, the system carries out the following actions:

- A production version is selected for the header material, and routing sequences, routing operations, and BOM components are transferred to the order.
- Depending on settings, reservations are generated for stock items, and purchase requisitions are created for nonstock items and externally processed operations.
- Capacity requirements are generated for the work centers assigned to operations.
- The planned costs for the order are generated.

A production order is structured into the data categories, as shown in Figure 6.25, such as header data, operation data, sequence data, component data, and documents. By clicking the buttons in the application toolbar ❽–❿, you can navigate to these data categories and change the data if necessary. The application toolbar also includes buttons for scheduling the order, costing, availability check, and capacity planning ❹–❼.

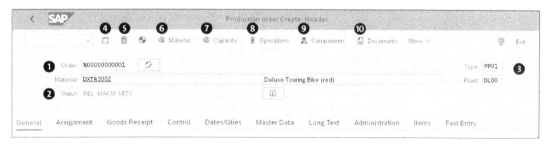

Figure 6.25 Application Toolbar in Production Order

Let's discuss the data categories found in the production order:

- **Header data**
  Header-level data includes information and control parameters for the header material (finished product) and the order as a whole. The data at this level is valid for the entire order. As shown in Figure 6.25, the header includes an order number ❶, an order type ❷, an order status ❸, and a production plant. You can also maintain the order's settlement rule at the header level. Header details are grouped into several views, as shown in Figure 6.26, such as the following:
  - **General**
    Includes total quantity, basic dates, and scheduling type.

- **Assignment**
  MRP controller, MRP area, and account assignment objects assignments (e.g., WBS element or sales order). Profit center assignment can be derived from the material master record or maintained manually in this view.

- **Goods Receipt**
  Data defining how finished product is received and moved.

- **Control**
  Control parameters for the order, such as costing parameters defining when and how planned costs are calculated, scheduling parameters controlling scheduling the order, and specifying whether capacity requirements are calculated when you save the order.

- **Master Data**
  This view includes the master data copied from the production version, material BOM, and routing of the product header when the order is created.

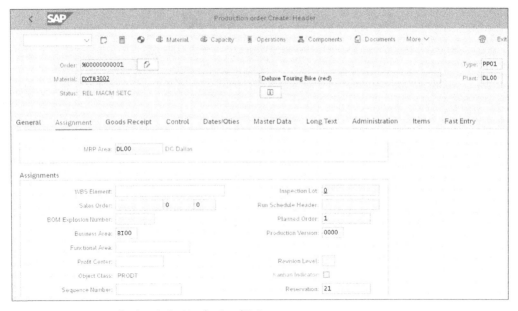

Figure 6.26 Production Order Header-Level Data

- **Operation data**
  Operation data is copied from the routing master record of the header material when the order is created. Operation data includes the task list, work centers, operation dates, execution times, quantities, standard values, and capacity splits for the operations' total requirements. On the operation data screen, shown in Figure 6.27, you can also display and edit operation trigger points, components, and PRTs assigned to operations.

- **Sequence data**
  Like operation data, this data is copied from the routing master record of the header material and includes operational steps.

Key Processes of Design-to-Operate   Section 6.3   331

Figure 6.27 Operation Data in Production Order

- **Component data**

   Component data is copied from the material BOM or the planned order. This data includes a list of components, item categories, operation assignments, committed quantities, requirement dates, and times. As shown in Figure 6.28, an indicator that determines whether reservations or purchase requisitions are generated for the components and when they are generated for each component. Nonstock items are relevant to external procurement.

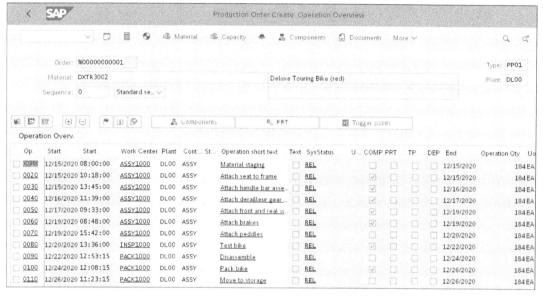

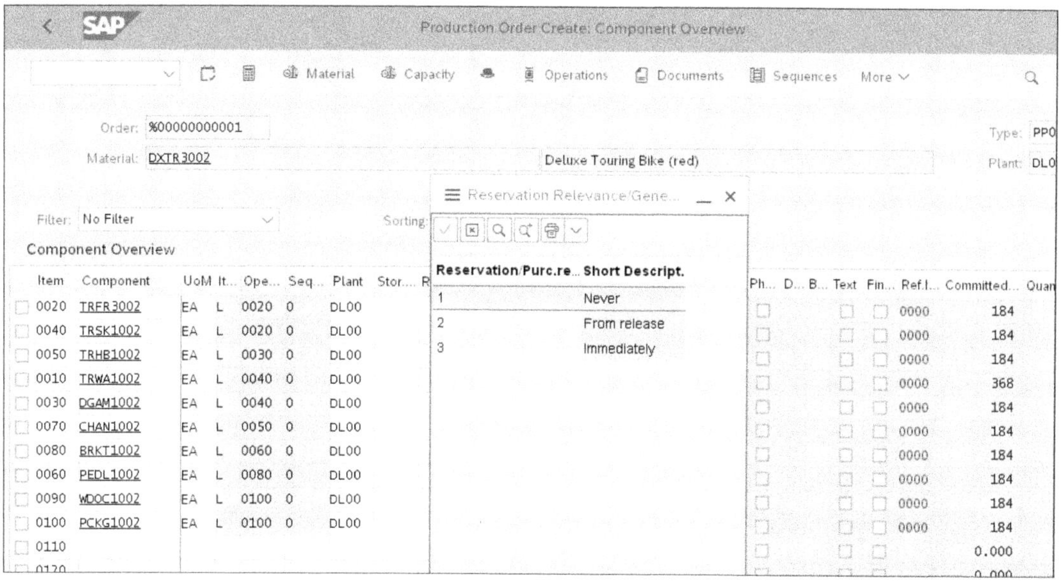

Figure 6.28 Component Data in Production Order

- **Documents**
  In this category, you can review documents, which are stored in the document management system. When you create a production order, for instance, the system checks the material BOM and automatically transfers all production-relevant documents/items to the document view of the production order.

Before saving the order, you can perform several control tasks, such as the following:

- **Scheduling**
  The schedule function enables the calculation of production dates and capacity requirements for all operations in a production order.
- **Availability check**
  Using this function, you can check the availability of the materials, PRTs, and capacities required for production operations.
- **Preliminary costing**
  You can calculate the order's planned costs by using the costing function, as shown in Figure 6.29. Planned costs can be automatically calculated when you save the order.

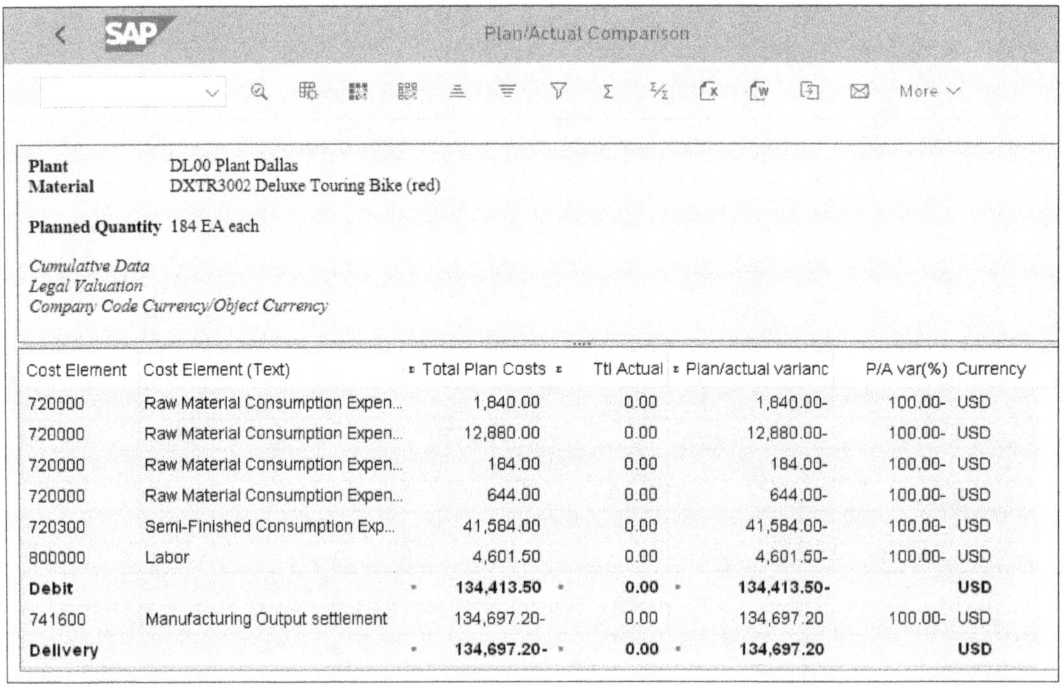
Plan/Actual Comparison

More

Plant DL00 Plant Dallas
Material DXTR3002 Deluxe Touring Bike (red)

Planned Quantity 184 EA each

Cumulative Data
Legal Valuation
Company Code Currency/Object Currency

Cost Element	Cost Element (Text)	Total Plan Costs	Ttl Actual	Plan/actual varianc	P/A var(%)	Currency
720000	Raw Material Consumption Expen...	1,840.00	0.00	1,840.00-	100.00-	USD
720000	Raw Material Consumption Expen...	12,880.00	0.00	12,880.00-	100.00-	USD
720000	Raw Material Consumption Expen...	184.00	0.00	184.00-	100.00-	USD
720000	Raw Material Consumption Expen...	644.00	0.00	644.00-	100.00-	USD
720300	Semi-Finished Consumption Exp...	41,584.00	0.00	41,584.00-	100.00-	USD
800000	Labor	4,601.50	0.00	4,601.50-	100.00-	USD
Debit		**134,413.50**	**0.00**	**134,413.50-**		**USD**
741600	Manufacturing Output settlement	134,697.20-	0.00	134,697.20	100.00-	USD
Delivery		**134,697.20-**	**0.00**	**134,697.20**		**USD**

Figure 6.29 Planned Costs in the Production Order

After saving the production order, it is assigned a created (**CRTD**) status, and the leading planned order is deleted from the stock requirements list. Depending on the settings, reservations and purchase requisitions are created. However, you cannot print the order out before releasing it. For further processing of the order, you must release the order, which consists of the following tasks:

- Material withdrawal
- Printing order and shop floor papers (e.g., operations-based lists, component-based lists, PRT lists)
- Confirmation
- Goods receipt
- Settlement

You can release the order in the following ways:

- **Header level release of an order**
  All operations in an order are released.
- **Release of an operation**
  Only selected operations in an order are released.
- **Release of multiple orders**
  Collective release of selected orders in a number range or a plant.

When you release the order, it is assigned the released status (**REL**). Note that the release of order and order printing can be automated in Customizing.

Material Withdrawal for a Production Order

The system supports two types of material withdrawal for production orders:

- **Planned withdrawal**
  For the stock items in the material component list, the system generates reservations (and reservation numbers) when creating a production order. You can withdraw these reserved materials from the warehouse after releasing the order. In this case, a goods issue is posted with reference to reservation numbers, which documents the reduction of inventory.
- **Unplanned withdrawal**
  You can also withdraw stock materials that are not planned in the production order's component list. You can execute an unplanned withdrawal by posting a goods issue with reference to the production order.

Depending on how you manage the stock items in the component list, you can control material staging with warehouse or extended warehouse activities. In this case, production integrates with warehouse management or EWM (see Chapter 8).

You can see all goods movements posted for a production order in the goods movement overview of the production order. The system carries out the following actions when a goods issue is posted for material components in a production order:

- Reservations for planned material are reduced.
- Actual costs for unplanned materials are updated in the order.
- A material document is created to document goods movements.
- Accounting documents (financial accounting documents and controlling documents) are created to document updates in the inventory and expense accounts (e.g., in financial accounting) and controlling (e.g., actual material and cost center costs recorded in the order by cost elements).
- Material consumption is recorded and evaluated. A Material Ledger document is created to document changes in the value and quantities of stock.
- The goods issue can be printed out.

Note that material consumption postings can be automated. Figure 6.30 shows a list of documents created by posting a goods issue for a production order.

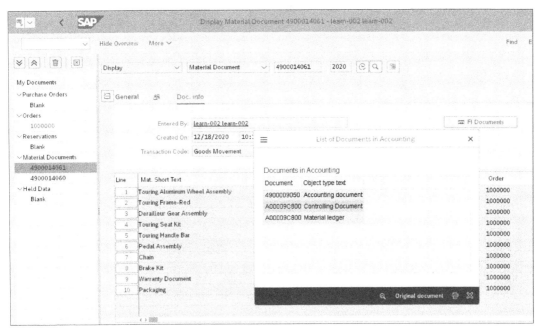

Figure 6.30 Documents for Goods Issue Posting for a Production Order

After posting a goods issue for the order, you can analyze the costs recorded on the order by itemization, as shown in Figure 6.31. Alternatively, you can display the total actual and target costs by the cost origin (material or labor).

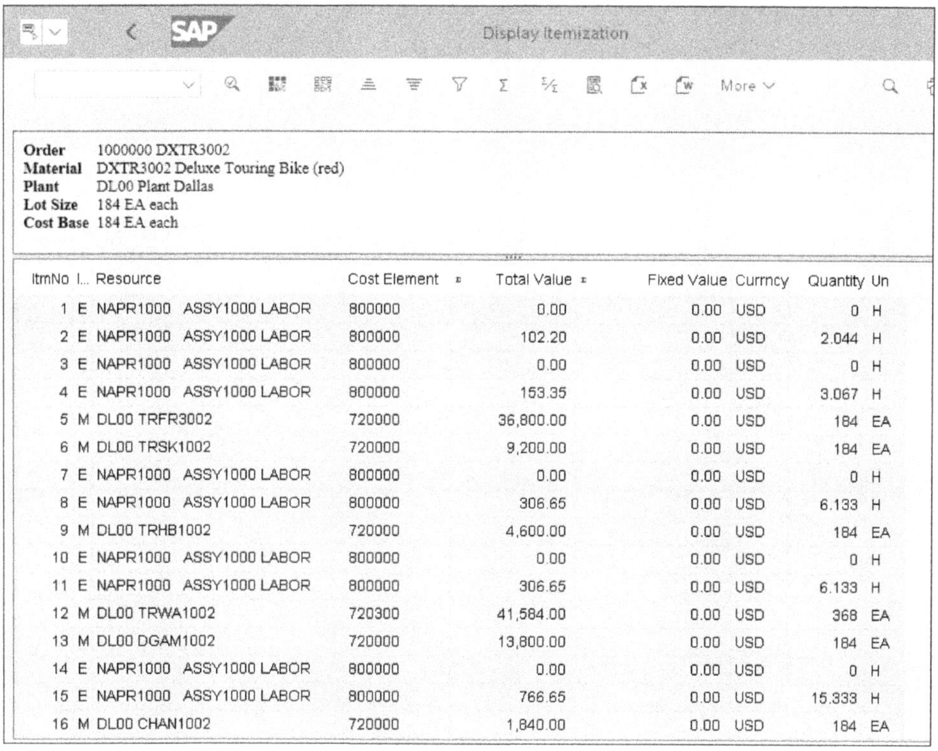

```
Order         1000000 DXTR3002
Material      DXTR3002 Deluxe Touring Bike (red)
Plant         DL00 Plant Dallas
Lot Size      184 EA each
Cost Base     184 EA each
```

ItmNo	I...	Resource	Cost Element	Total Value	Fixed Value	Currncy	Quantity	Un
1	E	NAPR1000 ASSY1000 LABOR	800000	0.00	0.00	USD	0	H
2	E	NAPR1000 ASSY1000 LABOR	800000	102.20	0.00	USD	2.044	H
3	E	NAPR1000 ASSY1000 LABOR	800000	0.00	0.00	USD	0	H
4	E	NAPR1000 ASSY1000 LABOR	800000	153.35	0.00	USD	3.067	H
5	M	DL00 TRFR3002	720000	36,800.00	0.00	USD	184	EA
6	M	DL00 TRSK1002	720000	9,200.00	0.00	USD	184	EA
7	E	NAPR1000 ASSY1000 LABOR	800000	0.00	0.00	USD	0	H
8	E	NAPR1000 ASSY1000 LABOR	800000	306.65	0.00	USD	6.133	H
9	M	DL00 TRHB1002	720000	4,600.00	0.00	USD	184	EA
10	E	NAPR1000 ASSY1000 LABOR	800000	0.00	0.00	USD	0	H
11	E	NAPR1000 ASSY1000 LABOR	800000	306.65	0.00	USD	6.133	H
12	M	DL00 TRWA1002	720300	41,584.00	0.00	USD	368	EA
13	M	DL00 DGAM1002	720000	13,800.00	0.00	USD	184	EA
14	E	NAPR1000 ASSY1000 LABOR	800000	0.00	0.00	USD	0	H
15	E	NAPR1000 ASSY1000 LABOR	800000	766.65	0.00	USD	15.333	H
16	M	DL00 CHAN1002	720000	1,840.00	0.00	USD	184	EA

Figure 6.31 Itemized Costs in Order after Goods Issue Posting

External Procurement and Processing

Depending on control settings in the order, the system generates purchase requisitions for the following items when you save or release an order:

- Nonstock items (or items not subject to inventory management) in material components list of order
- Externally processed operations in the task list of order

Purchase requisitions can be converted to purchase orders, thus triggering a standard procurement process. The goods receipt posting and invoice verification for purchased items/services debit actual costs from the order, and the consumption accounts are posted in financial accounting. However, this goods receipt posting does not cause any update to the quantity or value of the stock.

Order Confirmation

When creating a production order, you'll define the planned values for production. However, the actual values might be different for several reasons. Thus, order confirmation is a critical step in production. In this step, you'll specify how much work was actually done, who actually did the job, and/or how many items were actually produced or scrapped. Note that order confirmation can be automated in Customizing.

You can enter confirmations for the order, shown in Figure 6.32, operations, or individual capacity for an operation. At the confirmation step, you can confirm the following information:

- **Quantities**
  Goods quantity produced (yield), the quantity of scrap incurred, and a rework quantity.
- **Activities**
  You can confirm the actual production activities carried out, such as machine time, setup time, and processing time.
- **Dates**
  Actual dates for setup, processing, or teardown.

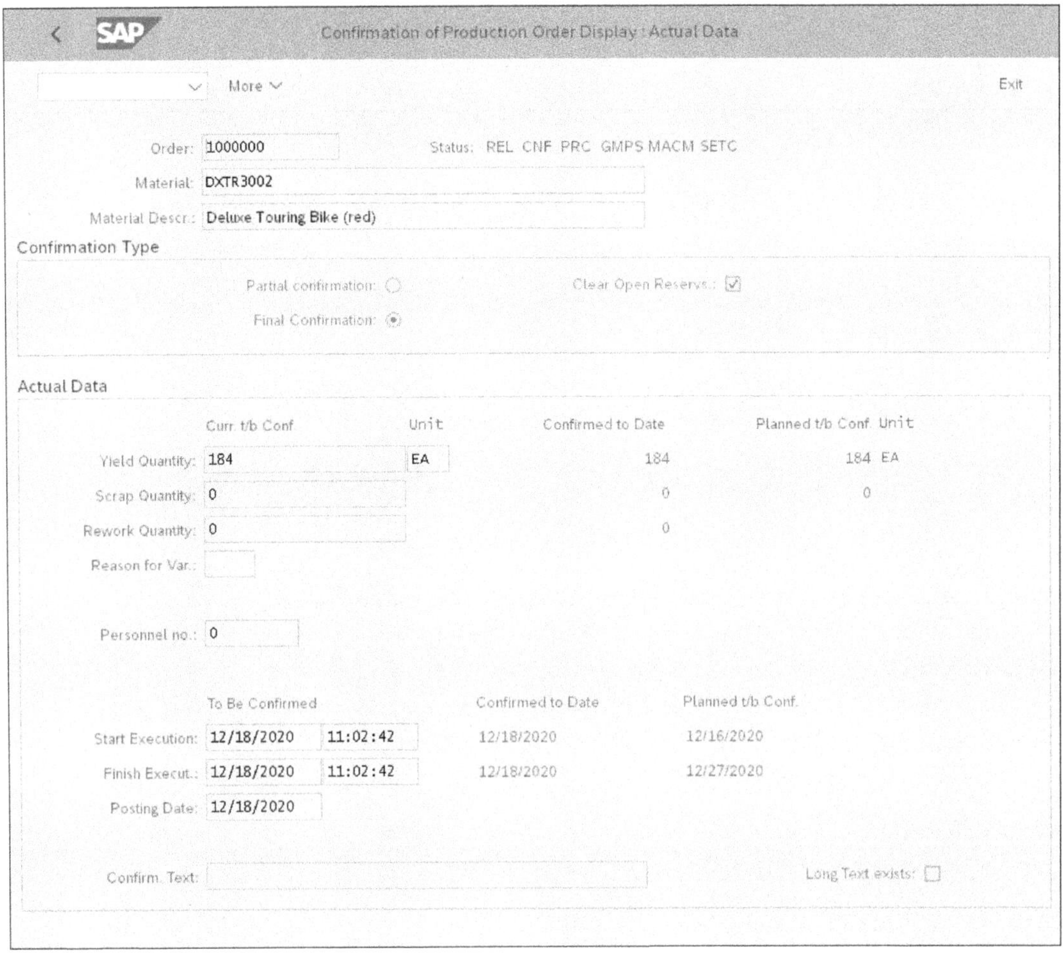

Figure 6.32 Final Confirmation for a Production Order

- **Personnel**
  You can confirm the employees who actually performed the operations.
- **Work center**
  You can enter and confirm the work centers that were actually used in operations.
- **Reasons for variance or deviation**
  Confirmed values can be different than planned values. You can confirm reasons for variance or deviations by entering a key documenting their cause.
- **Goods movements**
  For each operation, you can enter planned and unplanned goods movements. For instance, if the control key for the operation is set to automatic goods receipt, the system automatically generates goods receipt upon saving confirmation.
- **WIP batches**
  You can create WIP batches in the confirmation for an operation.

When you save the confirmation, the system can carry out the following actions:

- Depending on settings, an automatic goods receipt can be created when the last operation is confirmed.
- For the material components that have the backflushing indicator set, an automatic goods issue is created, called a *backflush goods issue*. For these materials, the goods issue posting is delayed until you confirm the corresponding operation.
- If the system is integrated with SAP EWM, the system can create an inbound delivery to trigger the putaway of confirmed quantities. In this case, a user posts the receipt of the finished goods in SAP EWM.
- Capacities requirements are reduced at the work center.
- The production order is updated for actual quantities, activities, dates, and status, and the order assigned a confirmed status (CNF).
- The production order is debited for further actual costs for confirmed quantities and labor.
- HR data is transferred.
- Statistical data in the logistics information system (LIS) and business warehouse (BW) are updated.

Goods Receipt for Finished Product

To record the receipt of the finished good produced by the order into stock, you must post the receipt of the goods. You'll need to enter the quantities received, storage location, and movement type. As mentioned before, saving confirmations can trigger the automatic posting of goods receipts. The system carries out the following actions when posting a goods receipt for a finished product:

- A material document is created to document the goods movement.
- Total stock quantities are increased by delivered quantity in the material master record.
- Delivered quantities and the order status are updated in the production order.
- The inventory account for finished goods is debited, and the manufacturing output settlement account is credited with target costs in financial accounting. A financial accounting document is created to document these updates, as shown in Figure 6.33.

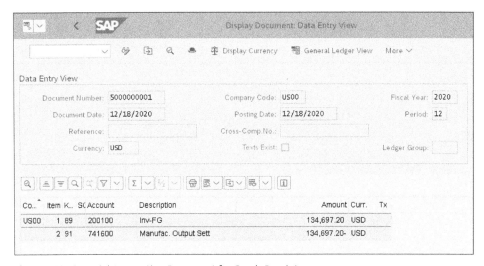

Figure 6.33 Financial Accounting Document for Goods Receipt

- The total value of the stock is updated in the material master. A Material Ledger document is created, shown in Figure 6.34, to document this increase in the value and level of the stock.

Figure 6.34 Material Ledger Document for the Receipt of Finished Goods

- The production order is credited with the target costs. The target cost is the planned cost of the actual quantities produced and is calculated over the released standard cost estimate.
- A controlling document is created to document credit updates in the order.
- If the finished good is managed at the warehouse, a transfer requirement is created for putaway.

Period-End Closing

When you release a production order, it starts collecting costs. From a cost point of view, the following actions are carried out in the system:

- During the material withdrawal, the order is debited for the material costs.
- Goods receipt postings and invoice verification for external procurement of nonstock items and externally processed operations also debit the order.
- Confirmation determines the actual quantities produced and the actual costs of the operations base on operations; this task calculates the target costs and the actual labor costs of production.
- A goods receipt posting credits the order with the target costs and updates the manufacturing output settlement account and inventory account (for finished goods) with the target costs.

You can calculate all further debits in period-end closing and calculate the difference between debits and the credits posted to an order with goods receipt postings.

During period-end closing, the following activities are carried out:

- **Overhead calculation**
  Overhead costs are indirect costs that are not directly related to production (e.g., rent on a machine that you pay whether you produce or not). Planned overhead costs are calculated during the preliminary costing of the manufacturing order. However, actual overhead costs (accumulated in costs centers) are calculated during period-end closing and applied to the production order as a further actual cost. In that case, the cost center is credited.
- **WIP calculation**
  If the order is not fully delivered but released (status **REL**), you can calculate WIP to evaluate unfinished products in manufacturing. WIP is the difference between the debit and credit of an order that has not been fully delivered. During settlement, the positive WIP is transferred to financial accounting and capitalized in the balance sheet under unfinished goods inventory.
- **Variance calculation**
  The variance is the difference between control costs (which can be the same as the net-actual costs) and the production order's target costs. You can calculate

the variance only for fully delivered (status **DEL**) or technically completed (status **TECO**) production orders. Thus, you can either calculate WIP or variance, but not both at the same time.

- **Settlement**
  Settlement transfers the WIP calculation or variance calculation to receivers by crediting the order with the settled costs. A prerequisite for the settlement is that you define the following settlement parameters in the system:
  – Settlement profile
  – Settlement structure
  – Settlement rule

  If the order is not completely delivered, the settlement posts only WIP to the general ledger (financial accounting). If the order is fully delivered, settlement posts the variance to the settlement receivers defined in the settlement rule. The settlement rule includes one or more distribution rules defining settlement receiver, settlement share, and settlement type. Depending on the following production scenarios, some possible settlement receivers include a material, cost center, internal order, sales order, project, network, or fixed asset:

  – The manufacturing output settlement account (debited) and the manufacturing settlement variance account (credited) are updated with the variance. An accounting document is created to document these updates in financial accounting.
  – The production cost centers are updated, and the order is credited with the variance. The order balance becomes zero. A controlling document is created to document these updates in management accounting.
  – The variances are also settled to profitability analysis as variance categories.

- **Technical completion**
  Let's say the order cannot be executed in the required manner. In this case, you can technically complete the order to delete its related reservations, capacity requirements, and purchase requisitions and finalize the order from a logistics point of view. Upon technical completion, the order is assigned the **TECO** status.

- **Closing the order**
  Let's say, however, that the order is released or technically completed, the order balance is zero, and no open purchase requisitions, purchase orders, or commitments exist for the order. In this case, you can close the order. You cannot change the orders that have been closed.

Figure 6.35 shows the financial accounting document ❶ and controlling document ❷ that result from settlement.

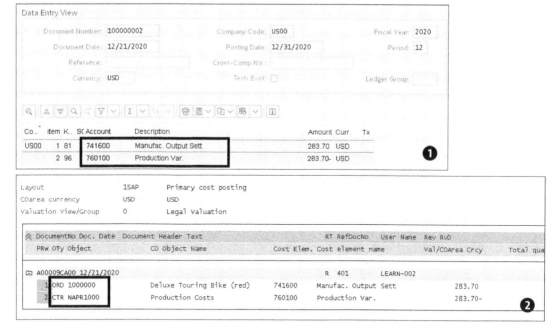

Figure 6.35 Financial Accounting Document and Controlling Document

6.4 Integration with Other Modules

In this section, we explain the touchpoints of integration between design-to-operate processing and other system modules. You can organize cross-module integrations into two categories:

- Integrations via cross-module data assignments
- Integrations via transactions

6.4.1 Integration via Cross-Module Data Assignments

Cross-module data assignments in the system connect the business processes in SAP S/4HANA and lead to data flows between the system's components. Some examples of cross-module data assignments include the following:

- **Management accounting**
  Cost center is master data in cost center accounting (controlling). A work center is assigned to a cost center in its master record, as shown in Figure 6.36. The activity types for which prices are planned for the cost center can be linked to standard values used in formulas.

- **Financial accounting**
  A profit center is a master record in profit center accounting (if active) or in financial accounting. A material is a master record in production. A finished product can be assigned to a profit center in its master record, thus integrating profit centers with production.

- **Human resources**
  A work center can be assigned to an HR organizational unit in its master record, thus integrating HR with production.

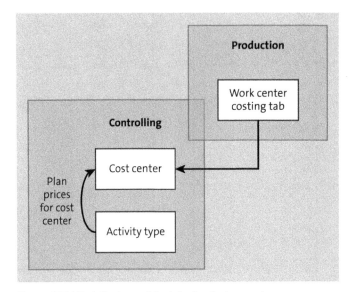

Figure 6.36 Work Center and Cost Center Assignment

6.4.2 Integration via Transactions

The production module is tightly integrated with other system modules via transactions, as shown in Figure 6.37. Some examples of transactions that lead to cross-module integration include the following:

- **Strategic planning**
  Strategic planning in production uses past data from profitability analysis and from sales information systems (SISs) to forecast future demand, thus integrating production planning with sales and distribution and profitability analysis.

- **Product cost planning**
  In product cost planning based on quantity structure, the system uses BOM and routing master records in production to create a standard cost estimate. Released cost estimates can then be used in the valuation of goods movements and preliminary costing of orders in production, thus integrating production with controlling.

- **Demand management**
  Demand management generates a demand program that differentiates PIRs from strategic planning and CIRs (current sales orders) from sales and distribution, thus integrating production with sales and distribution.

- **Detailed planning**
  Detailed planning tools like MPS, MRP, MRP Live, or PP-DS determine material shortages and can generate purchase requisitions for externally procured items, thus integrating production with materials management (purchasing and inventory management).

- **Production order creation or release**
  Production orders can be assigned to WBS elements, sales orders, and profit centers in their master records, thus integrating the production order with those corresponding processes. The system generates reservations for stock items in the components list when you create or release the order (based on the order settings), thus integrating production with inventory management. If the components are managed in a warehouse, automatic transfer requirements are created. Order creation or release may also generate and purchase requisitions for externally processed operations and nonstock items in the components list. Purchase requisitions are then converted to production orders to start a standard procurement process.

- **Material withdrawal and material staging**
  After order release, you can withdraw the necessary materials. Material staging can be managed via warehouse activities. Thus, warehouse management integration can occur. A material withdrawal (for stock items) is documented by posting a goods issue, which triggers postings to financial accounting and controlling. (Financial accounting and controlling documents are created.) Posting a goods issue creates a cross-module integration between production, inventory management, financial accounting, and controlling.

- **External procurement**
  Goods receipt postings and invoice verifications for externally processed operations (as specified in the routing) or externally procured materials (as specified in the components list) lead to debit postings to the production order, thus integrating production with purchasing.

- **Order confirmation**
  Confirmations can generate backflush goods issues (inventory management) and inbound deliveries (if the system is integrated with SAP EWM). HR data can be transferred. Furthermore, statistical data can be updated in the LIS.

- **Settlement**
  Settlement can transfer manufacturing variances to several receivers, such as a cost center, internal order, sales order, project, network, profitability segment, or fixed asset. The settlement process also triggers postings to manufacturing settlement accounts in financial accounting. If a WIP balance exists on the order, settlement leads to financial accounting and controlling postings.

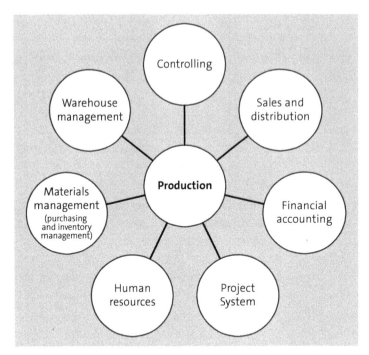

Figure 6.37 Modules Integrating with Production

6.5 Important Terminology

In this chapter, the following terminology relevant to design-to-operate is important to know for the exam:

- **Advanced planning**
  The planning of material requirements with exact times and dates. This feature is based on an SAP APO tool, called production planning and detailed scheduling (PP-DS), recently embedded into SAP S/4HANA. Materials are marked for advanced planning in their master records.

- **Bill of materials (BOM)**
  A master record consisting of a structured list of components necessary for manufacturing a product.

- **Confirmation**
  A transaction in manufacturing execution that confirms actual quantities, dates, times, variances, and persons that take place in the production.

- **Customer independent requirements (CIRs)**
  The requirements (required quantities) in the current sales orders in sales and distribution.

- **Demand management**
  An interface between strategic planning and detailed planning that aligns PIRs with CIRs.

- **Dependent requirements**
  The quantities of components required to produce the finished product or the assembly. These requirements are determined by exploding the BOM in detailed planning.
- **Design-to-operate**
  An intelligent end-to-end process on SAP's intelligent enterprise suite. This process includes the plan-to-produce business process as a subprocess.
- **Detailed planning**
  A planning process concerned with determining dependent requirements based on independent requirements from demand management. This capability provides several planning tools (e.g., MPS, MRP Live, and advanced planning) to guarantee material availability in the manufacturing execution phase of plan-to-produce.
- **Master production scheduling (MPS)**
  Single level BOM planning of critical items for which changes in the master production plan dramatically influences the entire production cycle.
- **MRP Live**
  A new MRP tool that leverages the massive computation potential of SAP HANA. This tool reacts to critical material shortages in planning more quickly than traditional MRP.
- **Planned independent requirements (PIRs)**
  Forecasted stock requirements derived from future demand and available capacities. PIRs are aligned with customer independent requirements (CIRs) in demand management and used in material requirements planning (MRP) to determine dependent requirements.
- **Procurement proposal**
  A planned order, purchase requisition, or schedule lines generated in detailed planning (by MRP or PP-DS) to cover material shortages identified in net requirements calculation.
- **Production resources and tools (PRTs)**
  A master record that represents a movable or nonstationary tool or resource used in production.
- **Production version**
  A master record in production that combines a material BOM and routing to define an alternative variant of production of a material.
- **Routing**
  A master record in production that describes operations, in terms of the sequence of steps, which operations are performed, and where operations are carried out to produce a material.
- **SAP Integrated Business Planning (SAP IBP)**
  A cloud-based planning tool for sales and operations planning (S&OP) and demand management. This tool provides end-to-end visibility in the supply chain and integrates with SAP Ariba.

- **Settlement**
  Period-end closing activity that transfers WIP to the general ledger (based on predefined rules) or variances to settlement receivers defined in the settlement rule.

- **Strategic planning**
  Aggregate level planning for sales and production based on historical data. This planning transfers forecast results in the form of independent requirements after disaggregation.

- **Target cost**
  The planned cost of actual quantities produced.

- **Variance**
  The difference between the control costs and the target costs transferred to financial accounting during the delivery of finished products. Calculated for orders with the delivered status.

- **Work center**
  A master record representing a location in a plant where routing operations are carried out. A work center master record includes standard values and formulas for the calculation of costs and capacities.

- **Work in process (WIP)**
  Calculated to evaluate unfinished products on a partially delivered order.

6.6 Practice Questions

These practice questions will help you evaluate your understanding of the topics covered in this chapter. The questions shown are similar to those found on the certification examination. Although none of these questions will be found on the exam itself, they will allow you to review your knowledge of the subject. Select the correct answers and then check the completeness of your answers in the next section. Remember that you must select all correct answers on the exam and select only correct answers to receive credit for the question.

1. Which of the following views of the material master record are directly relevant to production? (There are two correct answers.)

   ☐ A. Accounting
   ☐ B. MRP 1-4
   ☐ C. Advanced Planning
   ☐ D. Plant Data/Storage Loc.

2. Which of the following are organizational data in the design-to-operate business process? (There are two correct answers.)

☐ A. Cost center
☐ B. Work center
☐ C. Plant
☐ D. Storage location

3. Which of the following is master data in the design-to-operate business process? (There are three correct answers.)

☐ A. Activity types
☐ B. Standard values
☐ C. PRTs
☐ D. Production versions
☐ E. Routings

4. Which of the following are the areas of use for BOMs? (There are two correct answers.)

☐ A. Product cost planning
☐ B. Price update
☐ C. Inventory valuation
☐ D. Procurement

5. Which of the following item categories can be in BOM components? (There are two correct answers.)

☐ A. Standard items
☐ B. Variable-size items
☐ C. Document items
☐ D. Consumption items

6. Which of the following statements are correct about material BOMs? (There are three correct answers.)

☐ A. BOMs are plant specific
☐ B. BOM is multilevel
☐ C. BOM header includes a base quantity and a BOM usage key
☐ D. BOMs are assigned to routings and production versions in their master records
☐ E. A material BOM is defined at the client level

7. Which of the following describes the production of a material? (There are two correct answers.)

☐ A. Material BOM
☐ B. Work center
☐ C. Material master
☐ D. Routing

8. Which of the following can be found in the routing master record? (There are three correct answers.)

☐ A. Sequence
☐ B. Costs
☐ C. Work center
☐ D. Cost center
☐ E. Material

9. Which of the following are elements of quantity structure in product cost planning?

☐ A. Standard price
☐ B. Material BOM and routing
☐ C. Cost center
☐ D. Moving average price

10. Which of the following data assignments are correct in production? (There are three correct answers.)

☐ A. Activity type is assigned to a work center
☐ B. Work center is assigned to a cost center
☐ C. Component is assigned to a routing operation
☐ D. Production resource or tool us assigned to BOM component
☐ E. Work center is created in a plant

11. Which of the following data in the work center master record is used for scheduling, calculation of costs, and capacity requirements?

☐ A. Standard values
☐ B. Operations
☐ C. Material BOMs
☐ D. Routings

12. Which of the following statements are correct about MRP? (There are three correct answers.)

☐ A. Concerned with determining independent requirements
☐ B. Performs a net requirements calculation to determine material shortage
☐ C. Generates purchase orders
☐ D. Creates procurement proposals
☐ E. Determines dependent requirements

13. Which of the following are demand elements in the net requirements calculation? (There are two correct answers.)

☐ A. Purchase orders
☐ B. Firmed procurement proposals
☐ C. Safety stock
☐ D. Dependent requirements

14. Which of the following statements are correct about MRP Live? (There are two correct answers.)

☐ A. Faster and less manually intensive than classic MRP
☐ B. Explodes full computation potential of SAP HANA
☐ C. Plans with exact times in hours and minutes
☐ D. All stock items must be planned with MRP Live

15. Which of the following are procurement proposals generated by MRP? (There are two correct answers.)

☐ A. MRP lists
☐ B. Planned orders
☐ C. Purchase orders
☐ D. Purchase requisitions

16. Where can you see the most up-to-date requirements in a plant?

☐ A. Stock overview
☐ B. Stock requirements
☐ C. MRP list
☐ D. Planned order

17. Which of the following are processing keys in MRP? (There are two correct answers.)

    ☐ A. Regenerative planning
    ☐ B. Net change planning in the total horizon
    ☐ C. Net change planning in the planning horizon
    ☐ D. Total planning

18. Which of the following production master data is integrated with resources master data in advanced planning?

    ☐ A. Material master data
    ☐ B. Production version
    ☐ C. Work center and capacities
    ☐ D. Storage location

19. Which of the following steps of manufacturing control and execution can be automated in Customizing? (There are three correct answers.)

    ☐ A. Order release
    ☐ B. WIP calculation
    ☐ C. Material staging
    ☐ D. Goods receipt for finished products
    ☐ E. Availability check

20. Which of the following can be converted into a production order?

    ☐ A. Purchase order
    ☐ B. Planned order
    ☐ C. Maintenance order
    ☐ D. Scheduling agreement

21. Which of the following can be found in a production order? (There are three correct answers.)

    ☐ A. Operations and sequences
    ☐ B. Previous price
    ☐ C. Planned costs
    ☐ D. Future price
    ☐ E. Settlement rule

22. Which of the following are not possible before the release of the order? (There are two correct answers.)

☐ A. Printing the order
☐ B. Reservations
☐ C. Availability check
☐ D. Material withdrawal

23. Which of the following can link a production order to purchasing?

☐ A. Release order with a nonstock item as a component
☐ B. Settle the order
☐ C. MRP
☐ D. Material withdrawal for reserved components

24. Which of the following are the points of integration between production and warehouse management? (There are two correct answers.)

☐ A. Order creation
☐ B. Material staging
☐ C. Goods receipt
☐ D. Settlement

25. Which of the following is a point of integration between production and HCM?

☐ A. Order release
☐ B. Confirmation
☐ C. Goods issue posting
☐ D. WIP calculation

26. Which of the following steps of manufacturing execution trigger debit posting to production order? (There are two correct answers.)

☐ A. Saving the order
☐ B. Goods receipt for the finished products
☐ C. Confirmation
☐ D. Goods receipt posting for the delivery of nonstock items in the component list

27. Which of the following steps of manufacturing execution generates a financial accounting document? (There are two correct answers.)

    ☐ A. Settlement
    ☐ B. Confirmation
    ☐ C. Goods issue posting
    ☐ D. WIP calculation

28. What can you settle in the settlement? (There are two correct answers.)

    ☐ A. WIP
    ☐ B. Target costs
    ☐ C. Variances
    ☐ D. Actual costs

29. Which of the following *cannot* be a settlement receiver? (There are two correct answers.)

    ☐ A. Profit center
    ☐ B. Work center
    ☐ C. Cost center
    ☐ D. Profitability segment

6.7 Practice Question Answers and Explanations

1. Correct answers: **B and C**

   The **MRP 1-4** views include data necessary for MRP and external procurement tasks in production. You must maintain data in the **Advanced Planning** view if the material is planned with the PP-DS tool. The **Plant Data/Storage Loc.** view includes data relevant to inventory management, such as storage locations and shelf life. The **Accounting** view includes accounting-relevant data such as valuation class and prices/values used for the valuation of stock.

2. Correct answers: **C and D**

   A work center is master data in production. A cost center is master data in controlling. Clients, company codes, plants, and storage locations are organizational data used in manufacturing, which is part of the design-to-operate business process.

3. Correct answers: **C, D, and E**

   An activity type is master data in controlling. Activity types are planned for the cost centers that are assigned to work centers, which are master data in production. In this case, you can link activity types with the standard values in the work center master record. Note that standard values are part of work center master data but not standalone master data in production. PRTs, production versions, routings, materials, and material BOMs are other master data in the design-to-operate business process.

4. Correct answers: **A and D**

   Material BOMs and routings are used as a basis for quantity structures in product cost planning. BOMs are also used in purchasing to determine requirements. Price updates and inventory valuations are not directly relevant to material BOMs.

5. Correct answers: **B and C**

   Variable-size items, stock items, nonstock items, class items, text items, comparable units, and document items are some examples of item categories you can use as BOM components. The other options are not item categories in the BOM master record.

6. Correct answers: **A, C, and D**

   To create a material BOM, you must first enter the key specifying the plant. Thus, BOMs are plant specific. BOMs are single level. However, you can enter another BOM (for a semifinished product or assembly) in the component list of a material BOM to define multilevel products. In the header details of a BOM, you can enter the base quantity, which is a quantity to which all components in a BOM relate, and a BOM usage key specifying where BOM can be used (e.g., in production, design, or engineering).

7. Correct answers: **A and D**

   A material master record describes a material and includes data specifying how the material is planned, stored, evaluated, procured, and sold. However, it does not describe the production process. A work center is master data that represents the location in a plant where operations are carried out. However, it does not define the production process of a specific product. A material BOM is a list of components used in production, and a routing is a list of tasks carried out in production. BOMs and routings are assigned to a specific material, and they together describe the production of a product.

8. Correct answers: **A, C, and E**

   A routing is assigned to a material at the header level. A sequence is an ordered list of tasks (operations) in a routing. Work centers are assigned to routing operations. However, the routing master record does not include costs or cost centers.

9. Correct answer: **B**

   A material BOM and a routing is a basis for quantity structures in product cost planning, which generates a standard cost estimate. The standard price is updated when the standard cost estimate is released, but is not part of the quantity structure. The moving average price can be used in inventory valuation or in the evaluation of goods movements.

10. Correct answers: **B, C, and E**

    Activity types are not directly assigned to the work center but to the cost center in activity planning. When you assign a work center to that cost center, you can then link activity types to standard values in the work center. Components and PRTs can be assigned to operations in routing. PRTs are not assigned to BOM components. Work centers are created and planned at the plant level. A plant may have several work centers.

11. Correct answer: **A**

    The work center master record does not include any material-relevant information such as operations, routings, or BOMs. It includes some data, such as standard values, formulas, cost center assignments, which are necessary for scheduling, capacity planning, and cost calculation.

12. Correct answers: **B, D, and E**

    PIRs are transferred from strategic planning to demand management, where they are aligned with CIRs, which MRP uses as a basis to identify dependent requirements. MRP performs net requirements calculations to determine material shortages and generates procurement proposals for in-house production or external procurement to cover the shortages. Depending on the material's procurement type, planned orders or purchase requisitions are created as procurement proposals. Purchase requisitions are then converted to orders, but MRP does not directly create purchase orders.

13. Correct answers: **C and D**

    Purchase orders, current stock, goods receipts, and firmed procurement proposals are supply elements in net requirements calculation, while safety stock, sales orders, independent requirements, and dependent requirements are considered demand elements.

14. Correct answers: **A and B**

    MRP Live does not plan with exact times in hours and minutes, but PP-DS does. MRP Live uses the massive computation potential of SAP HANA and is significantly faster than classic MRP. Some stock items in the system can be planned by advanced planning and classic MRP.

15. Correct answers: **B and D**

    MRP generates procurement proposals (planned orders, purchase requisitions, or schedule lines) to cover material shortages identified in net requirements calculation. Dependent requirements are listed in the procurement proposals. Optionally, an MRP list can also be created, in which you can find the procurement proposals and independent requirements. However, an MRP list is not a procurement proposal. MRP does not directly generate production orders.

16. Correct answer: **A**

    The MRP list is static, and its data remains the same until the next MRP run. However, the stock requirements list is dynamic and includes the most recent information about the requirements in the plant.

17. Correct answers: **A and B**

    Regenerative planning (NEUPL) and net change planning in the total horizon (NETCH) are MRP processing keys in SAP S/4HANA. However, unlike classic SAP ERP, SAP S/4HANA does not provide the processing key for net change planning in the planning horizon (i.e., NETPL). Total planning is not a processing key but a planning mode you would select at the beginning of planning.

18. Correct answer: **C**

    Advanced planning has its own master data, including location, product, production data structure, and resources. To use advanced planning, you must integrate the master data in the production module with advanced planning. In this framework, resource master data is integrated with work centers and their capacities.

19. Correct answers: **A, D, and E**

    Order release, goods receipt postings for the delivery of finished products, and availability checks during order creation can be automated in Customizing. The transactions in the other options can be executed through background processing.

20. Correct answer: **B**

    You can create production orders by converting planned orders. In this case, data (dates, quantities, BOM routings) from the planned order is copied to the production order, which makes the data entry process easier and faster.

21. Correct answers: **A, C, and E**

    A production order includes all data necessary for executing the subsequent steps of manufacturing. Operations, sequences, BOM components, times/dates, and work centers are some examples of operational data in the order. From a controlling point of view, the production order is a cost collector. It includes planned costs, target costs, and actual costs of the material, labor, and overhead. The settlement rule includes distribution rules defining how production variances are settled. Previous and future prices are the types of standard prices that you can find in the material master record but not in the production order.

22. Correct answers: **A and D**

    Depending on system settings, you can generate reservations when you save the order. An availability check can be automatically carried out during production order creation. However, to execute the next steps in manufacturing, you must release the order. Printing out order or shop floor papers, material withdrawal or staging, confirmation, delivery of finished goods, and settlement are not possible before the release of the order.

23. Correct answer: **A**

    A nonstock item in the order's component list is directly linked to the external procurement process. When you release such an order, the system generates a purchase requisition, which is a request to the procurement department for purchasing. The purchasing department can convert the request to a purchase order to initiate a standard procurement procedure with an external vendor.

24. Correct answers: **B and C**
You can manage the staging of product components or inbound delivery of finished goods (goods receipt) using warehouse activities. Order creation or settlement do not trigger any warehouse tasks.

25. Correct answer: **B**
In the confirmation step of manufacturing execution, you confirm actual times and persons who carried out the operations. HR data is then transferred upon saving the confirmation, thus integrating production with HCM.

26. Correct answers: **C and D**
An order starts receiving debits when you release it. A goods receipt posting for finished products credits the order with the target costs. Order confirmations and receiving nonstock items for the production order debits the production order.

27. Correct answers: **A and C**
Settlement and goods issue postings trigger updates in general ledger accounts. These updates are documented by generating financial accounting documents.

28. Correct answers: **A and C**
You can settle WIP or production variances during settlement. A variance is the difference between control costs (which might be the same as the actual cost) and the target costs. Target costs are transferred to financial accounting during the goods receipt posting, crediting the order.

29. Correct answers: **A and B**
Materials, cost centers, profitability segments, materials, cost objects, or other real controlling objects can be settlement receivers. Work centers cannot be cost receivers in production, while profit centers can only receive information on costs statistically.

6.8 Test Takeaway

In this chapter, you learned the key topics of design-to-operate processing, which is a seamlessly integrated intelligent business process in SAP's intelligent enterprise suite. For the certification, we limited our focus to its subprocess called plan-to-produce processing in SAP S/4HANA. SAP S/4HANA's production module supports the strategic planning, detailed planning, and manufacturing execution phases of plan-to-produce.

A production-relevant enterprise structure is mapped into the system using client, company code, plant, and storage location organizational data in the production module. The system supports transactions in production with the following master data: material master, BOMs, routings, production versions, PRTs, and work centers. Work centers perform operations in production and can be assigned to cost centers for cost allocation in controlling.

SAP S/4HANA supports several manufacturing types. In this chapter, we focused on discrete manufacturing, which is based on the production order. You can perform strategic planning and detailed planning before creating a production order, which is necessary to plan the future demand and supply in the company. PIRs are a basis for MRP in detailed planning, which identifies dependent requirements and creates procurement proposals to cover material shortages. Planned orders are converted to production orders. You must release an order to carry out subsequent manufacturing execution steps, such as a material withdrawal, confirmation, delivery of finished goods, or settlement. The production module integrates with financial accounting, controlling, warehouse management, and materials management at these steps. From a controlling point of view, the production order is a cost collector that receives debit and credit updates after the order is released. During period-end closing, you can calculate overhead costs, WIP, and variances. The settlement is the final transaction or period-end closing at which variances are settled, and the order has a zero balance.

We've now covered the key topics of the design-to-operate process with SAP S/4HANA. The next chapter covers enterprise asset management business processes and the plant maintenance module of SAP S/4HANA.

Chapter 7
Enterprise Asset Management

Techniques You'll Master

- Understand the key topics of the enterprise asset management business process and the plant maintenance module in SAP S/4HANA
- Describe the phases of corrective maintenance and perform system transactions for planning, controlling, and executing corrective maintenance
- Explain the master and organizational data in the plant maintenance module
- Understand strategic and detailed planning tasks for manufacturing and execute transactions in production
- Identify the touchpoints of integration between the plant maintenance module in SAP S/4HANA and other system modules

This chapter covers all certification-relevant topics of the enterprise asset management business process in SAP S/4HANA. We'll describe the master data, organizational data, and the system transactions supporting maintenance planning, control, and execution in SAP S/4HANA and explain potential integration scenarios.

Enterprise asset management is a business process to maintain and control your company's fixed assets and operational systems to take full advantage of these resources during their lifecycle by minimizing operational costs, increasing efficiency, and keeping these assets in good running order. SAP S/4HANA provides technical objects to structure your company's technical systems, and the plant maintenance module supports inspections, preventive maintenance, and repair tasks on these technical objects.

> **Real-World Scenario**
>
> A company's physical assets and operational systems are generally deployed in all business processes across several departments, facilities, and geographical locations. So, managing their lifecycle, as well as optimizing their quality, performance, and utilization, can play a critical role in carrying out complex business operations seamlessly.
>
> Planning, control, and execution of maintenance processes must be performed considering their impacts on other business processes. By nature, the plant maintenance process is connected to materials planning, inventory management, warehouse management, procurement, capacity planning, management accounting, and financial accounting.
>
> As an SAP consultant, you should understand how a company's technical systems can be structured in the system, how malfunctions or damage can be reported, how maintenance activities can be planned and executed with integration to other system modules, and how maintenance costs can be accurately settled to their real originators in SAP S/4HANA.

7.1 Objectives of This Portion of the Test

This portion of the certification aims to test your knowledge of the key topics of plant maintenance that supports the enterprise asset management business process in SAP S/4HANA. The certification exam includes questions about the organizational data, master data, and system transactions for maintenance planning, control, execution, and completion. SAP consultants are expected to understand all integrations between the plant maintenance module and other system modules.

For the certification exam, business process integration consultants must have a good understanding of the following topics:

- The organizational structure and technical objects used in enterprise asset management
- Key tasks in preventive and corrective maintenance processes
- The relationship between fixed asset accounting and enterprise management
- Touchpoints of integration between plant maintenance and other system modules

> **Note**
> The topic of enterprise asset management covers 8%–12% of the questions in the certification exam.

7.2 Data Structures for Enterprise Asset Management

SAP S/4HANA provides a fully integrated plant maintenance module to support enterprise asset management tasks. In this section, we'll explain the certification-relevant concepts of enterprise asset management. In particular, we introduce you to the organizational data and master data supporting system transactions in plant maintenance. We'll also discuss the database relationships that exist between organizational and master data.

7.2.1 Organizational Data

The following organizational data is used to map the company's organizational structure for enterprise asset management into the system:

- Client
- Company code
- Plant
- Maintenance plant
  - Location
  - Maintenance work center
- Maintenance planning plant
  - Maintenance planning groups

In previous chapters, we described this general organizational data, including client, company code, and plant in more detail; thus, we'll avoid further discussion in this chapter.

Your company's technical systems can be structured through technical objects (i.e., functional location, equipment, or equipment at a functional location).

Depending on where the technical objects are installed or planned for maintenance, two types of plants are relevant for maintenance:

- **Maintenance plant**
A technical object's maintenance plant is a plant where the object is installed. In other words, the maintenance plant is the plant where the company's operational systems are installed.

    A location represents a subdivision of a maintenance plant and the place where a functional object is installed in a plant section. In this way, a plant is subdivided by location-based criteria, such as buildings and coordinates.

    Work centers are used in production, plant maintenance, and Project System. You can create work center categories in Customizing, as shown in Figure 7.1. The maintenance work center is the work center in charge of performing a maintenance task. This work center might represent a workshop in the maintenance plant where the maintenance tasks are carried out. Maintenance work centers are assigned to maintenance plants and cost centers in their master records.

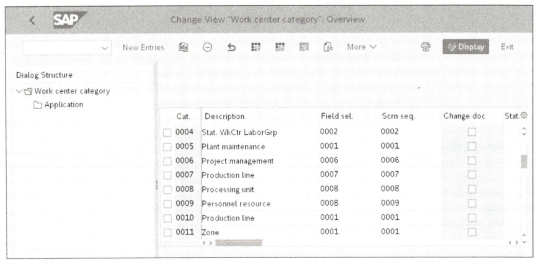

Figure 7.1 Work Center Categories in Customizing

- **Maintenance planning plant**
A maintenance planning plant for a technical object is a plant with maintenance planning groups responsible for planning and preparing maintenance tasks. The maintenance planning plant is in charge of creating maintenance notifications and executing maintenance orders for the maintenance plant's technical objects. Material planning and external procurement based on bills of materials (BOMs) are carried out in the maintenance planning plant.

A maintenance plant can perform planning for its own technical objects, which is called *decentralized planning* or *plant-specific planning*. In this case, the maintenance plant is indicated as a maintenance planning plant in the system. Other planning preferences may be required depending on the company's structure, such as centralized planning (cross-plant planning) or partially centralized planning. In centralized or partially centralized planning, another plant is responsible for planning and preparing maintenance activities in the maintenance plants. The maintenance plant itself does not plan maintenance for its own technical object and must be assigned to a maintenance planning plant. Note that maintenance planning plants are defined and created in the enterprise structure in Customizing.

Table 7.1 illustrates the three planning approaches in plant maintenance.

Planning Methods	Plants	Maintenance Plants	Maintenance Planning Plants	Plants Assigned to Maintenance Planning Plant
Decentralized planning	1000, 2000, 3000, 4000	1000, 2000, 3000, 4000	1000, 2000, 3000, 4000	All plants are indicated as planning plants in Customizing
Centralized planning	1000, 2000, 3000, 4000	1000, 2000, 3000, 4000	1000	2000, 3000, 4000
Partially centralized planning	1000, 2000, 3000, 4000	1000, 2000, 3000, 4000	1000, 2000	3000, 4000

Table 7.1 Planning Methods in Plant Maintenance

7.2.2 Master Data

The following master data can be used for planning and execution of plant maintenance tasks in the system:

- Technical objects
  - Functional location
  - Equipment
- Serial numbers
- Maintenance BOMs *Bill of Materials*
- Material

We'll walk through each in the following sections.

Technical Objects

Functional locations and equipment are master data and technical objects in plant maintenance. A functional location represents the site where you carry out a technical task, while equipment is an object used to perform the technical task. Technical objects are assigned to maintenance plants, maintenance planning plants, planning groups, and maintenance work centers in their master records.

Technical objects in the system create a basis for structuring the company's technical systems subject to maintenance. By structuring your technical systems, you can simplify maintenance processing and have more detailed data to monitor and evaluate your technical systems. From a technical point of view, you can choose between the following options for structuring the technical objects in the system:

- **Functional structuring (only functional locations)**
  In this structuring, the company's technical objects are subdivided into functional locations.
- **Object-related structuring (only equipment)**
  In this structuring, the company's technical objects are subdivided into pieces of equipment.
- **Function and object-related structuring (pieces of equipment installed at functional locations)**
  In this structuring, the company's technical objects are subdivided into pieces of equipment installed at functional locations.

You can also structure technical objects from an accounting perspective by assigning technical systems and their objects to cost centers and fixed assets. In the following sections, we'll describe technical objects and their use cases in more detail.

Functional Location

Functional locations are elements of the company's technical structure and master data in plant maintenance. You can create functional locations in a hierarchical structure based on the following criteria:

- Technical (e.g., press frame, press hydraulics)
- Spatial (e.g., building A, storeroom)
- Functional or process-oriented (pumping station, power station)

You may consider implementing functional locations if one of the following applies:

- You need to perform maintenance tasks for the individual areas of your technical system or operational structure.
- You want to keep records of the maintenance tasks performed for the individual areas of your technical system or operational structure.
- You need to collect and evaluate technical data over long periods for the individual areas of your technical system or operational structure.

- You want to monitor the costs of maintenance tasks for the individual areas of your technical system or operational structure.
- You want to analyze the influence of usage conditions on the damage susceptibility of the installed equipment.
- You need to use different views of a location structure.

When you create a functional location, you must enter a structure indicator key, which is necessary to create a functional location within a hierarchy. Structure indicator keys are created in Customizing, and as shown in Figure 7.2, they define coding templates for labeling the functional location ❶ and hierarchy levels determining the number of levels in the functional location hierarchy ❷.

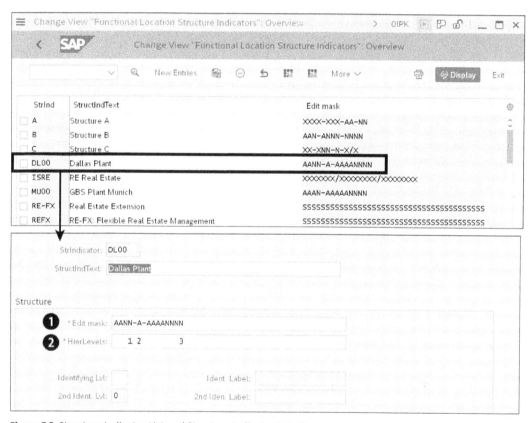

Figure 7.2 Structure Indicator List and Structure Indicator Details

Functional location master data is structured into views, such as the **General**, **Location**, **Organization**, and **Structure** views, as shown in Figure 7.3. You can integrate a functional location with asset accounting or cost accounting in the **Organization** view by assigning the functional location to a fixed asset or a cost center, as shown in Figure 7.3. Maintenance planning plant, planning group, and maintenance work center assignments can also be made in the **Organization** view. You can view the superior functional location or the pieces of equipment installed at the functional location in the **Structure** view.

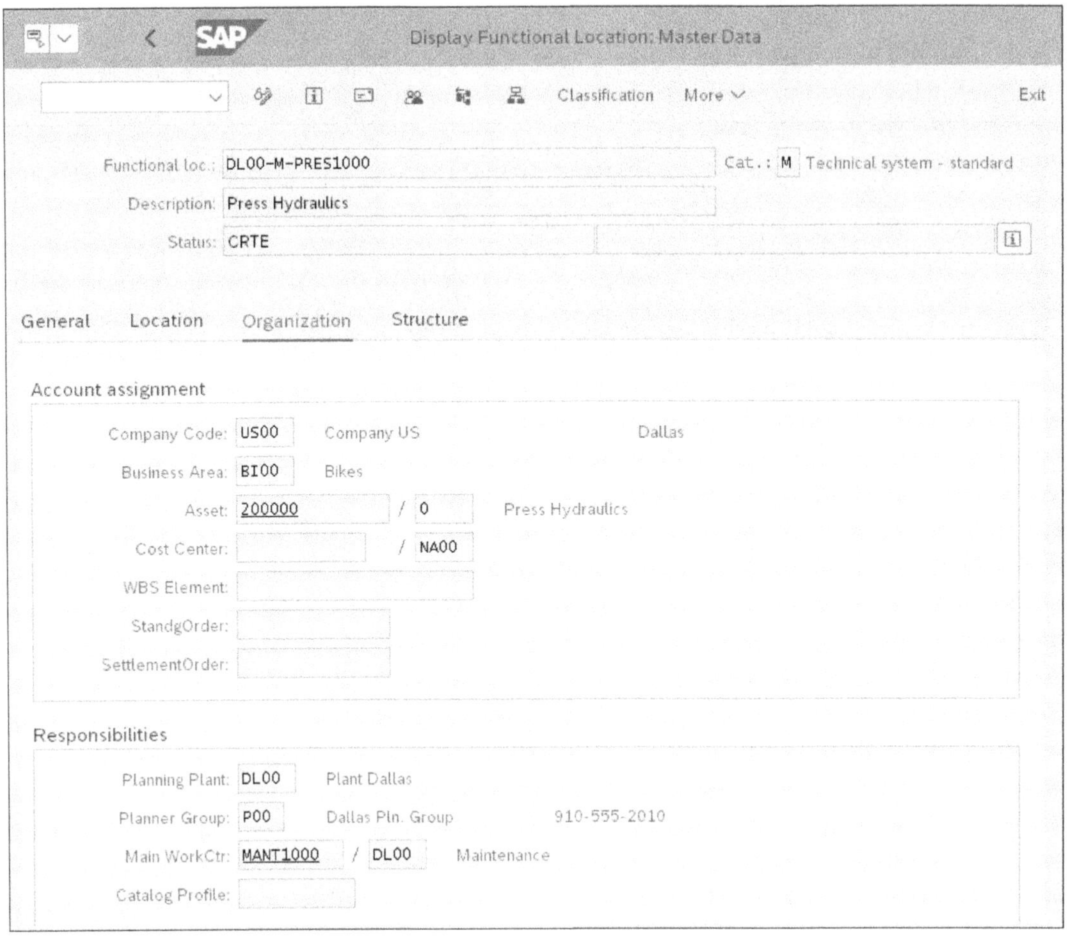

Figure 7.3 Functional Location Master Data

Equipment

Equipment is a technical object used in business operations and master data in plant maintenance. This object represents an individual physical object that is maintained independently of other objects. You can structure pieces of equipment as standalone (single) objects, which is called *object-related structuring*, or installed objects at a functional location, which is called *function and object-related structuring*. As a result, you don't have to define a piece of equipment specifically as an installed object at a functional location.

Some examples of pieces of equipment used in several enterprise resource planning (ERP) areas include the following:

- Test equipment in quality management
- Production resources and tools (PRTs) in production planning and control
- Serialized material in materials management

- Customer devices in sales and distribution
- Buildings, property, or vehicles in fixed asset management

By structuring your technical systems with equipment master records, you can perform the following tasks:

- Manage individual data for the objects
- Carry out maintenance tasks for the individual objects, either regular, planned, or resulting from damage
- Keep records of the maintenance tasks performed for individual objects
- Collect technical data on objects and evaluate equipment over a long period of time
- Monitor the costs of maintenance tasks for individual objects
- Record the usage times at functional locations for individual objects

When you create an equipment master record, you must specify an equipment category (e.g., asset, machine, PRT, test equipment, or customer equipment). Equipment categories can be defined in Customizing. Like functional location master data, equipment master data is structured into views, including the **General**, **Location**, **Organization**, and **Structure** views. You can define the maintenance plant for the piece of equipment in the **Location** view. You can maintain account assignments. such as asset, cost center, and company code, in the **Organization** view. In the **Structure** view, you can view the superior equipment in the equipment hierarchy (if this piece of equipment is assigned to a superior equipment) and the functional location where the equipment is installed (if the equipment is assigned to a functional location), as shown in Figure 7.4.

Depending on the equipment category, you may see additional views. For instance, customer equipment may include a **Warranty** view for warranty data and a **Sales and Distribution** view where you can assign a piece of equipment to a sales area. A master record for a PRT or test equipment will include a **PRT** view. You can activate additional views by using the **View Selection** function.

> **Note**
>
> You can assign a piece of equipment to an asset in the **Organization** view of the equipment master record. In the new system, several pieces of equipment can be assigned to an asset. However, a piece of equipment can belong to only one asset. The system allows you to ensure the integration between asset accounting and plant maintenance by setting up the system to synchronously create (or update) equipment master records whenever you create asset master records.
>
> Internal orders can be used to collect the maintenance costs of pieces of equipment. When you settle the internal order, the system transfers these costs to the master record of an asset.

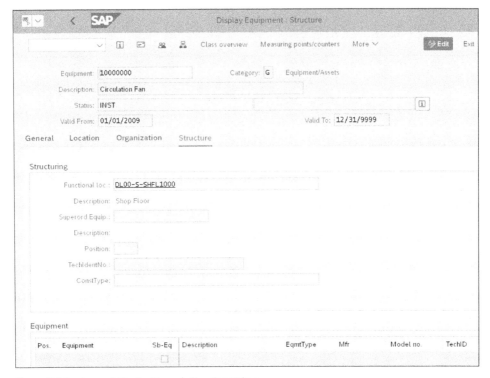

Figure 7.4 Equipment Master Record: Structure View

Maintenance Bills of Materials

A maintenance BOM is master data in plant maintenance. You can create maintenance BOMs for materials or technical objects (functional locations and equipment) in the system. Creating maintenance BOMs for objects or materials in maintenance is not mandatory. However, using maintenance BOMs in plant maintenance enables you to perform the following tasks:

- Clearly describe the structure of a technical object so that you can specifically address the components for which maintenance tasks should be carried out.
- Assign spare parts to a technical object so that you can plan the spare parts in maintenance orders or the tasks lists in preventive maintenance.

When you create a maintenance BOM for a technical object or material, you must enter the number of the technical object or material for which you want to create a maintenance BOM.

Using a material BOM in plant maintenance serves a particular purpose: You create material BOM to unify the BOMs of several similarly constructed technical objects in the system, as shown in Figure 7.5. This approach helps you avoid redundant records in the database. You must create a material before creating a material BOM in the plant maintenance module. Then, you must assign the material BOM to technical objects by maintaining the construction type (**ConstType** field) in the **Structure** view of their master records, as shown earlier in Figure 7.4.

Data Structures for Enterprise Asset Management — Section 7.2

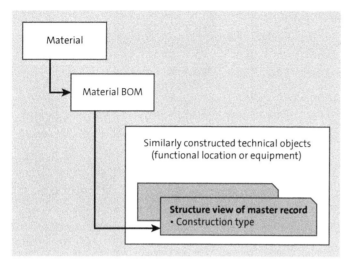

Figure 7.5 Procedure for Assigning a Material BOM to Similarly Constructed Technical Objects

Serial Numbers

Serialization is a procedure to assign a serial number to a piece of equipment. Serialization makes a piece of equipment available for inventory management (i.e., inventory monitoring and tracking).

Assigning a serial number to a piece of equipment can be done manually or automatically. With automatic serialization, the system creates a serial number and equipment master record synchronously during a goods movement, for instance, a goods receipt.

For manual serialization, you can use the following procedure:

1. Create serial number profiles for equipment categories and define their serializing procedures, as shown Figure 7.6, in Customizing.

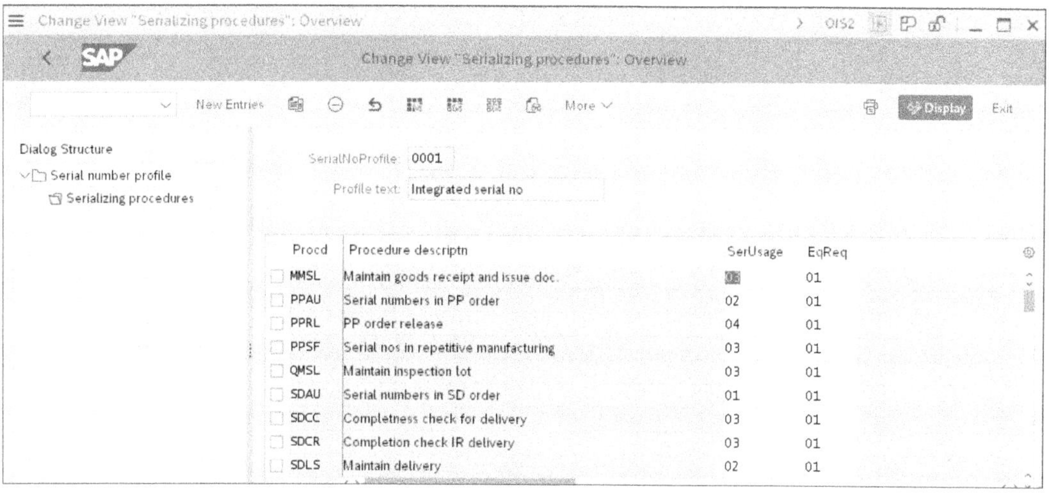

Figure 7.6 Maintaining Serial Number Procedures for Serial Number Profiles in Customizing

2. Create a material master record and assign a serial number profile in one of the following views of the material master record:
   - Sales: General/Plant Data
   - Plant Data/Storage 2
3. Create a serial number master record for a combination of material and equipment if you want to use a pool of serial numbers (optional) for a particular piece of equipment assigned to this material. You can follow this approach if no serial number profile has been entered into the material master record.
4. Perform material and serial number assignment in serialization data of the equipment master record. You can display the **SerData** (serialization data) view by using the **View Selection** function in the equipment master record, or in Customizing, you can set up the system to display the **SerData** view automatically for particular equipment categories.
5. In the **SerData** view of the equipment master record, you'll see the last serial number assigned to the equipment (if assigned before), as shown in Figure 7.7. You can use **Change Serial No** to link a new serial number to the last serial number.

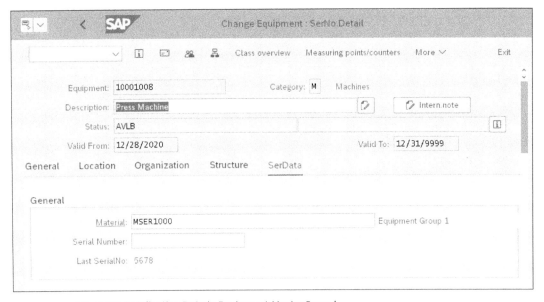

Figure 7.7 Serialization Data in Equipment Master Record

Figure 7.8 shows the procedure for a faulty piece of equipment that needs to be dismantled and transferred to a warehouse for refurbishment. The serialization of the piece of equipment before removal enables inventory management and tracking during warehouse processes and guarantees the right equipment is installed.

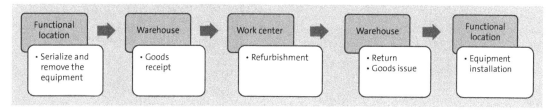

Figure 7.8 Processing Refurbishment of a Serialized Material

7.2.3 Data Assignments

The relationships between organizational and master data of plant maintenance can be outlined in the following way:

- A maintenance plant can plan its own maintenance. In this case, this plant is indicated as a maintenance planning plant. Otherwise, the plant can be assigned to a maintenance planning plant.
- Several maintenance plants can be assigned to a maintenance planning plant.
- Several plants can be assigned to a company code. A plant can be assigned to only one company code.
- Several technical objects (functional locations and pieces of equipment) can be assigned to maintenance plants and maintenance planning plants in their master records. A technical object can be assigned to only one combination of maintenance plant and maintenance planning plant.
- Functional location BOMs and equipment BOMs are uniquely assigned to the corresponding technical object.
- For similarly constructed objects, you can create a material and a material BOM, then assign the material to the objects via the construction type field in their master records. This procedure assigns the material BOM to similarly constructed technical objects.
- A serial number master record can be created uniquely for a combination of one piece of equipment and one material.

Figure 7.9 shows the relationships between organizational and master data in the plant maintenance module.

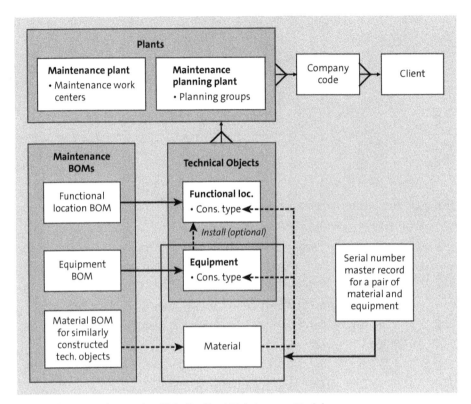

Figure 7.9 Data Assignments within the Plant Maintenance Module

7.3 Key Processes of Enterprise Asset Management

The enterprise asset management business process and corresponding plant maintenance module in SAP S/4HANA support the following key maintenance activities:

- **Inspection**
  To check actual working conditions of the technical system
- **Preventive maintenance**
  To avoid potential breakdowns in the technical system
- **Repair**
  Two different repair processes are available, depending on the working conditions of the technical system:
  – Breakdown maintenance: To fix the technical system that stopped working
  – Corrective maintenance: To improve a technical system that is working but not properly

Predictive maintenance is the next generation of preventive maintenance. It takes device and sensor data into account to predict failures or create optimal maintenance and service schedules. To prepare for the certification exam, we'll focus on the preventative (or corrective) maintenance processing in SAP S/4HANA in this section. The corrective maintenance process consists of the following phases, which do not necessarily all have to be implemented in full:

- **Notification**
  - Create a maintenance notification
- **Planning**
  - Create a maintenance order (status **CRTD**)
- **Control**
  - Availability check
  - Capacity planning
  - Release the maintenance order (status **REL**)
- **Execution**
  - Material withdrawal (planned/unplanned)
  - External procurement (for nonstock items)
- **Completion**
  - Completion confirmations (status **CNF**)
    Confirmation of time, services, material, measurements and counter readings, and technical completion confirmation
  - Technical completion (status **TECO**)
  - Settlement of order
  - Business completion (status **CLSD**)

Tip
The acronyms next to the listed transactions indicate the order statuses assigned to the maintenance order upon completing the transactions.

Maintenance notification and maintenance order processing play a crucial role in the phases of corrective maintenance. In the following sections, we'll explain each of the key phases, starting with maintenance notification and its data structure.

7.3.1 Maintenance Notification

You can create a maintenance notification to describe a technical object's condition or to report a malfunction in a technical object and further request the maintenance department to repair the damage. When you create a maintenance notification, you must choose between the following notification types, as shown in Figure 7.10:

- **Maintenance request (no malfunction)**
  Typically used for investments, for instance, replacing all office computers in the administrative building and setting up a fast internet connection.

- **Malfunction report**
  Used for reporting damage or a malfunction that prevents a technical object from functioning properly.

- **Activity report (no malfunctions, only activities)**
  Used for reporting maintenance or service activities (e.g., filling up oil, checking pressure, tightening screws) already performed. An activity report does not usually include malfunctions or problems with technical objects.

- **User-specific notifications**
  Depending on your company's specific needs, you can create user-specific notifications in Customizing.

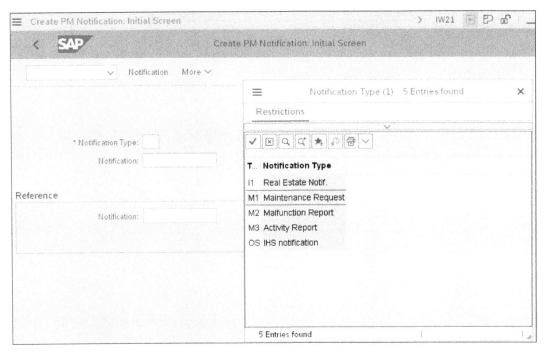

Figure 7.10 Create a Maintenance Notification Screen

Note
You can also use Transactions IW24, IW25, and IW26 to directly choose between malfunction reports, activity reports, and maintenance requests, respectively.

You can create notification types for the following reference objects:

- Functional location (with or without assembly)
- Piece of equipment (with or without assembly)
- Material with serial number
- Without reference object

A reference object is a technical object or assembly that is referred to by the notification. An assembly is not a technical object but is a part of a technical object. You can create malfunction reports or maintenance requests without a reference object if the object of interest has no object number in the system.

The data in a maintenance notification is structured into views. You can enter reference objects in the **Notification** view, as shown in Figure 7.11. You can change the reference object area's view using the **Reference object** view. In this case, you should not enter any number in the reference object area. Responsibilities (maintenance work center, planner group); malfunction data; and items (object parts) with damage can also be specified in the **Notification** view.

You can use the **Items** view if several parts of the reference object are to be maintained or more than one cause exists for a problem. You can plan the tasks, responsible persons, and start and end times in dates, hours, and minutes in the **Tasks** view. Completed tasks can be displayed in the **Activities** view.

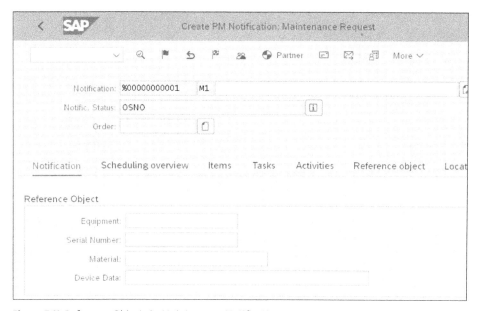

Figure 7.11 Reference Objects in Maintenance Notification

7.3.2 Maintenance Planning

Creating an order is an essential part of planning in plant maintenance. The plant maintenance module in the system provides the following order types to support the tasks in enterprise asset management:

- **Maintenance order**
  To plan, monitor, and execute maintenance tasks for the technical objects in the technical system. Relevant to materials planning, capacity planning, external procurement, project management, production, and controlling.
- **Service order**
  To plan, monitor, and execute service tasks and customer service tasks. Relevant to sales and distribution.

- **Investment order**
  To create new assets. Linked to asset accounting.

- **Calibration order**
  To test a piece of test equipment to see if it meets predefined performance criteria. Creates an inspection lot in quality management.

- **Refurbishment order**
  To refurbish repairable spare parts. To plan, monitor, and execute the process that includes uninstallation of the spare parts, goods movements in the warehouse, and reinstallation of refurbished spares in the maintenance plant.

To prepare for the certification exam, we'll limit our focus to maintenance orders (i.e., orders of type **PM1-3**), which support corrective, preventive, and breakdown maintenance processes, in the following sections.

Creating a Maintenance Order

You can create maintenance orders for maintenance notifications by using Transaction IW34. In this approach, you must choose an order type and enter a number of the notification for which you want to create an order, as shown in Figure 7.12.

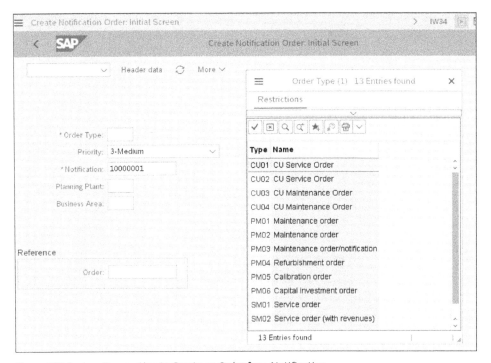

Figure 7.12 System Transaction to Create an Order for a Notification

Note that you do not need to use notifications to create a maintenance order. In general, creating a maintenance order involves one of the following scenarios:

- You can create an order directly without using a notification (for instance, a breakdown order can be created directly without a notification).
- You can combine several notifications in the object list of an order.
- An order can be automatically created from a maintenance item by maintenance plans.
- You can create an order and additional activity report (a notification type) subsequently.

Maintenance Order Structure

A maintenance order is a detailed document that includes all the necessary information for performing the subsequent steps of the corrective maintenance process. In general, a maintenance order consists of the following elements, structured into views:

- **Header data**
  Header data includes a notification number, responsibilities (person responsible, maintenance work center), basic dates (start and end date for the order), reference objects, malfunction data, and the first operation of the order.
- **Operation data**
  Operation data includes the list of operations to be performed. Each operation includes a work center and a control key. Operations can be processed internally or externally. For internally processed operations, you must enter a work center, activity type, person responsible, qualifications, standard times, and wage data. For externally processed operations, vendor and purchasing data must be maintained. Externally processed operations are relevant to external procurement. Each operation can be assigned the following data:
  - **Material list**
    You can assign several components (e.g., spare parts, consumption materials) to an operation. Assigned components are listed in the material list. A material list can include materials with the following item categories: stock item, nonstock item, variable-size item, text item. Nonstock items are relevant to external procurement. You can view the materials assigned to operations in the **Components** view of the order. Each material in the material list has an indicator that specifies when reservations for stock materials are relevant to MRP or when purchase requisitions for nonstock materials are generated. This indicator provides three options: immediately, from the release, and never.
  - **PRTs**
    You can assign several PRTs to operations in a maintenance order. An overview of the assigned PRTs can be viewed in the PRT list in the **Operations** view.
- **Cost data**
  Cost data includes estimated costs, plan costs, and actual costs by value categories. You can overview order costs in the **Costs** view of the maintenance order.

- **Object data**
  Object data includes an object list for the technical objects to be processed by the maintenance order. You can use the object list to combine multiple notifications into the maintenance order or assign several technical objects to the order. An overview of the reference objects assigned to a maintenance order can be viewed in the **Objects** view of the maintenance order.

- **Settlement rule**
  This rule includes distribution rules defining what proportion of the costs collected on the order must be transferred to which settlement receiver. Order types determine potential settlement receivers. By default, the settlement rule is proposed from the account assignment data in the master record of the technical object (if it exists). You can change the proposed settlement rule when you create the order. Depending on these settings, you must specify the settlement rule when the order is released or when the order is technically completed.

In the **Additional Data** and **Location** views of a maintenance order, you can assign the order to the following items, as shown in Figure 7.13:

- Profit center
- Cost center
- Work breakdown structure (WBS) element (project)
- Asset

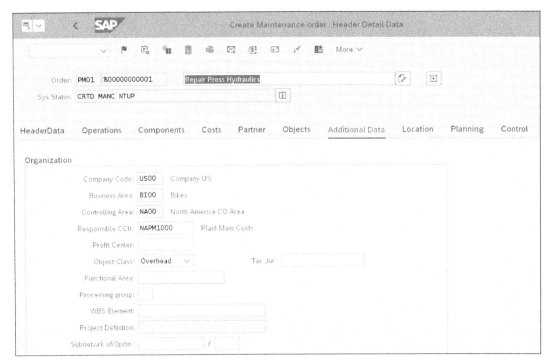

Figure 7.13 Additional Data View of a Maintenance Order

7.3.3 Maintenance Control

In this phase of corrective maintenance, you can perform detailed planning for an order. Control of a maintenance order includes the following tasks:

- Material availability check (for components assigned to operations)
- Availability check (for PRTs assigned to operations)
- Capacity planning (for work centers assigned to order and operations)
- Order release
- Printing order and shop floor papers

To prepare for the certification exam, we'll focus on two main tasks in the following sections: the availability check and the order release.

Availability Check

An availability check is a maintenance control task to check the availability of the materials, PRTs, and capacities necessary to execute operations specified in the maintenance order. Depending on your settings in Customizing, the system automatically checks the availability of materials, PRTs, and capacities when you release the order. You can also check availability manually by using the availability functions under **Order Functions**.

After saving the order, you can call the availability list to see the availability of planned material in the order, as shown in Figure 7.14. The system displays information (reserved or withdrawn quantities) about stock material in the availability list once an availability check for stock materials is performed. You can call a manual availability check for stock materials in the header data screen using the **Stock Material** function. The system displays availability information (required or received quantities) about the nonstock material in the availability list once a purchase requisition is created for the nonstock material.

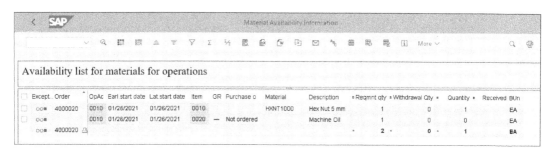

Figure 7.14 Availability List for a Maintenance Order

Depending on your settings in the order (or in Customizing), the system carries out the following actions either when you save or release the order:

- Reservations are generated for planned stock items.
- Purchase requisitions are generated for nonstock stock items.

Note
When you attempt to release a maintenance order, the system performs an automatic availability check. Depending on your system settings in Customizing, the system may or may not allow you to release the maintenance order if there is no availability.

Maintenance Order Release

After completing the maintenance order planning, with all entries and necessary availability checks, you can release the order. Maintenance orders for notifications and maintenance orders generated from maintenance items can be automatically released when created. You should make the necessary settings in Customizing for the automatic release of the maintenance orders.

You can perform the following steps with the maintenance order to perform corrective maintenance:

- Print order and shop floor papers
- Withdraw material
- Post goods receipts
- Create time confirmations
- Complete tasks

When you release a maintenance order, it is assigned a released status (**REL**), and the system performs availability checks for materials, PRTs, and capacities required to execute order operations. Depending on your settings, reservations and purchase requisitions are generated.

7.3.4 Maintenance Execution

In this phase of the corrective maintenance process, you enter goods movements for the materials necessary to execute operations specified in a released maintenance order. Depending on the item category (stock item/nonstock item) of the required material, one of the following tasks are carried out:

- **Planned or unplanned withdrawal of stock material**
  A planned withdrawal is the withdrawal of stock material planned in the maintenance order. The system generates reservations for planned stock materials when you save or release the order. You can carry out a planned withdrawal by posting a goods issue with reference to the maintenance order and effective reservations. Stock materials that are not planned in the maintenance order can also be withdrawn from stock. You can perform an unplanned withdrawal by posting a goods issue for the maintenance order with the movement type 261 (consumption for order from warehouse). You can use Transaction IW13 (Material Where-Used List) to check which withdrawals for a material were planned or unplanned.

In both cases, a material document is created documenting the goods movement. Available stock is reduced by the withdrawn quantity. The system updates the inventory and expense accounts in financial accounting and debits the order by the value of withdrawn materials, which increases the order's actual costs. Accounting and controlling documents are created documenting these updates. A Material Ledger document is created documenting the change in the total value of the stock.

- **External procurement of nonstock material**
  Nonstock material is a material not kept in stock and must be purchased externally. When you save or release the maintenance order, an automatic purchase requisition is generated for each nonstock item planned in the order. An external procurement process is initiated by creating a purchase order from that purchase requisition with an account assignment to the maintenance order. The system debits the maintenance order with the value of purchased items when you enter a goods receipt for the purchase order. Expense accounts (in general ledger accounting) are updated with the value of the purchased item. Accounting and controlling documents are created documenting these updates.

You can see the quantities for withdrawn stock materials and received nonstock materials in the availability list of the maintenance order, as shown in Figure 7.15.

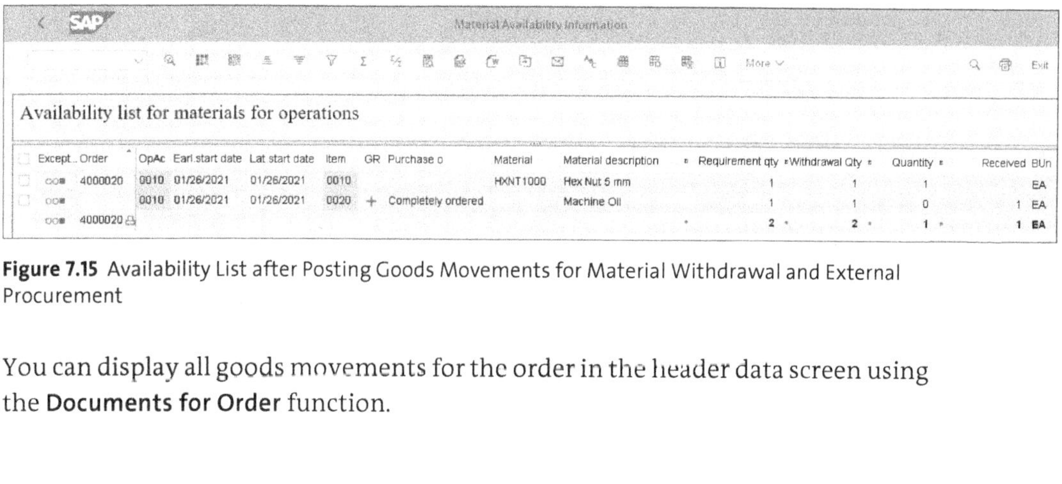

Figure 7.15 Availability List after Posting Goods Movements for Material Withdrawal and External Procurement

You can display all goods movements for the order in the header data screen using the **Documents for Order** function.

7.3.5 Maintenance Completion

The following tasks are carried out in the completion phase of corrective maintenance:

- Entering completion confirmations
- Technical completion of the order
- Settlement
- Business completion of the order

We'll discuss the exam-relevant topic of order completion tasks in detail in the following subsections.

Completion Confirmations

The order must be released to be able to execute the tasks in this phase. The completion confirmation component in plant maintenance provides several applications to enter confirmations, including by individual entry, by collective entry, by overall completion, and by cross-application time sheet (CATS). For instance, on the **Overall Completion Confirmation** screen (Transaction IW42), shown in Figure 7.16, you can confirm the following data collectively for a maintenance order operation or suboperation:

- Times
- Services
- Materials used
- Causes
- Tasks
- Activities
- Measurements/counter readings

Figure 7.16 Overall Completion Confirmation for a Maintenance Order

When you enter completion confirmations for all operations or suboperations of a maintenance order, the order is assigned a finally confirmed status (**CNF**).

Entering a time completion confirmation for the order leads to an internal activity allocation between the order and the costs centers assigned to the work centers where the order operations are carried out. That allocation debits the order and credits the relevant costs centers with the actual costs, thus integrating controlling with plant maintenance. Other integrations can be activated in the following ways:

- Entering times can transfer data to the time management component in human resources (HR).
- Confirming materials used can transfer data to inventory management. You can also enter the return of unused material to the warehouse, thus integrating plant maintenance with warehouse management.
- Confirmation of external services and external material by entering goods receipts integrates plant maintenance with purchasing. A goods receipt posting debits the maintenance order. Additional cost changes that arise during invoice verification are also settled to the maintenance order.

You can monitor the progress of the corrective maintenance process and confirmation status in the document flow of the maintenance order, as shown in Figure 7.17.

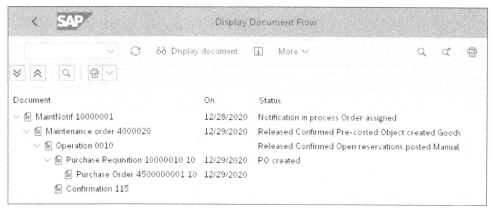

Figure 7.17 Document Flow of a Maintenance Order

Technical Completion

Technical completion is a transaction indicating that all planned operations in the maintenance order have been performed. After the technical completion, all technical data in the order is fixed and cannot be changed. As shown in Figure 7.18, in the header data screen, you can click the **Complete Technically** icon ❶ to technically complete a maintenance order in the technical completion screen ❷. At this step, you need to enter the reference data and reference time.

For technical completion, all relevant data in the order must be available and correct, and order operations must be completed. You can select the **Complete notifctns** (complete notifications) checkbox ❸ to complete the maintenance order with the assigned notification. The notification should not have the outstanding tasks status (**OSTS**) and all notification data must be complete and correct to be eligible for completion together with the order. A prerequisite to perform a technical completion for a maintenance order is to specify a settlement rule. The system can create a settlement rule automatically if all necessary data is available on the maintenance order. Otherwise, you'll need to specify the settlement rule manually to perform technical completion.

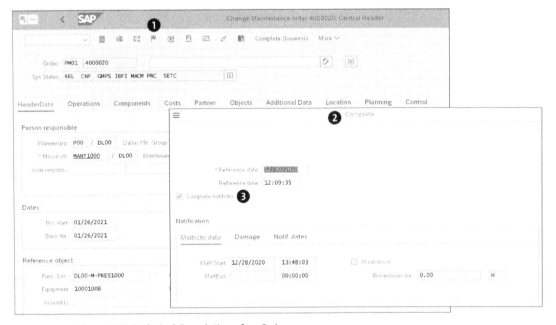

Figure 7.18 Technical Completion of an Order

A technical completion of the order has the following impacts:

- The maintenance order is assigned the technically completed status (**TECO**).
- The system flags all the existing purchase requisitions for the maintenance order for deletion.
- The system deletes all existing reservations for the maintenance order.
- The system clears all outstanding capacities scheduled for the order.

A technically completed maintenance order has limited ability for changes. When assigned the **TECO** status, the order can still collect actual costs from new confirmations, outstanding goods receipt postings, and invoice receipts. You can set a deletion flag, change the order's settlement rule, and lock and unlock an order with the status **TECO**. If you would like to perform significant changes to an order, you can reverse the technical completion. In this case, all the impacts of technical completion mentioned earlier are reversed.

You can display the **Action Log** in the **Documents for Order** function for an overview of all the changes made during the processing of the maintenance order. The action log can show you who made the changes, when changes were made, and which data fields in the maintenance order have been changed.

Settlement

After releasing a maintenance order, goods movements, material withdrawals, confirmations, and IRs debit the order with actual costs. The settlement is a period-end closing transaction that transfers the collected (actual) costs on the released order to settlement receivers based on the settlement rule. The order must have a settlement rule created status (**SETC**) to be eligible for settlement.

You can use Transaction KO88 to settle a maintenance order. You must specify a controlling area, the fiscal year, and a settlement period, as shown in Figure 7.19.

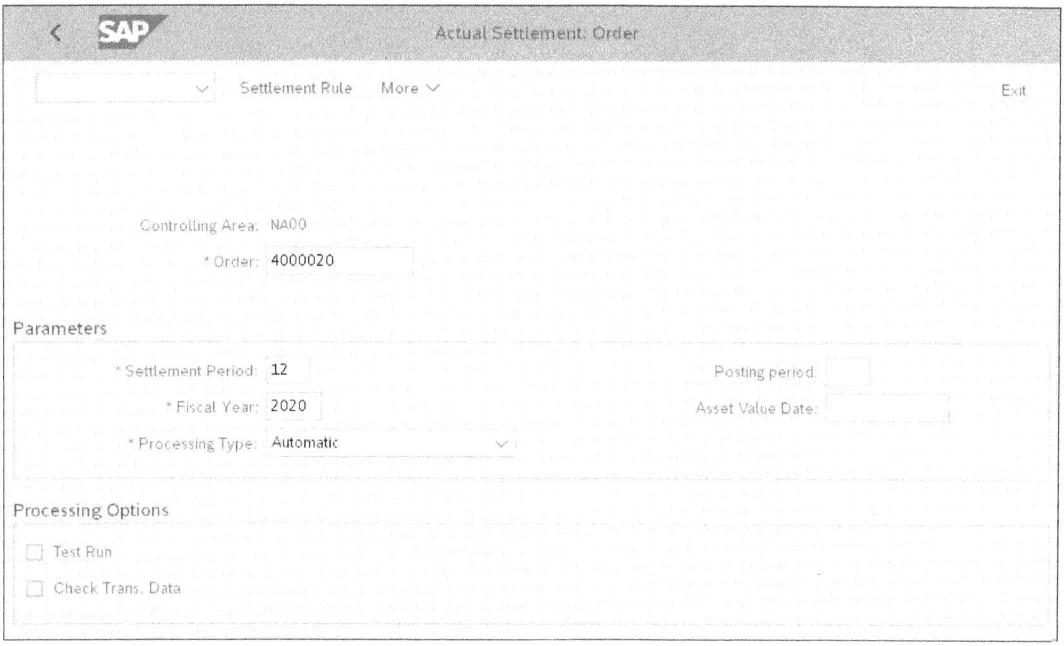

Figure 7.19 Settlement Transaction for a Maintenance Order

A settlement has the following impacts on the system:

- The collected (actual) costs on the maintenance are usually settled to the cost center of technical objects referenced in the maintenance order; this activity credits the order and debits the corresponding cost center. A controlling document is created documenting updates in the cost center and on the order.
- The balance of actual costs becomes zero after settlement. You can see the balance of actual costs in the **Plan/Actual Comparison** report in the **Costs** view of the maintenance order, as shown in Figure 7.20.
- Maintenance settlement accounts (secondary cost elements) in financial accounting are updated with the amount of settlement. An accounting document is created documenting these updates.

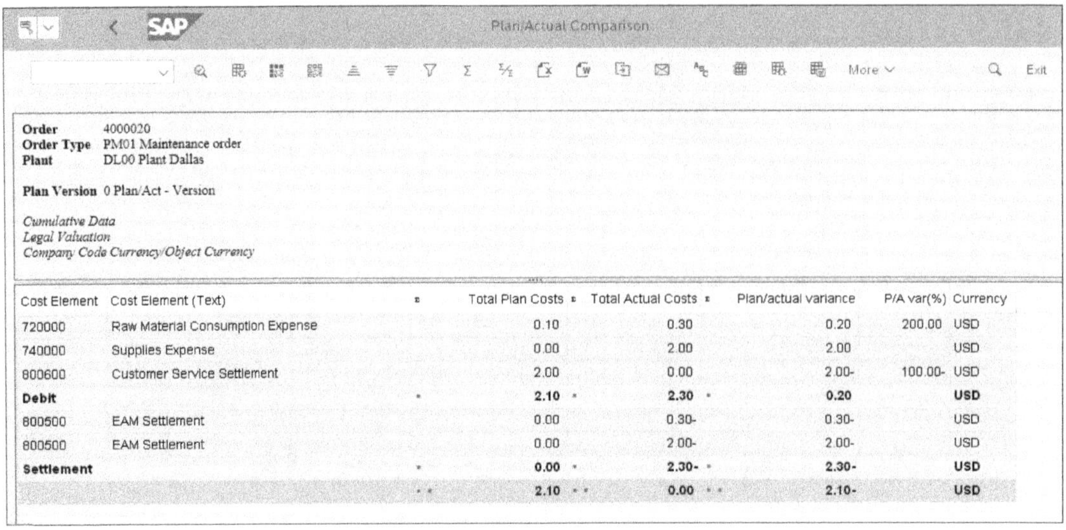

Plan/Actual Comparison
More
Exit
Order 4000020
Order Type PM01 Maintenance order
Plant DL00 Plant Dallas
Plan Version 0 Plan/Act - Version
Cumulative Data
Legal Valuation
Company Code Currency/Object Currency
Cost Element | Cost Element (Text) | Total Plan Costs | Total Actual Costs | Plan/actual variance | P/A var(%) | Currency
720000 | Raw Material Consumption Expense | 0.10 | 0.30 | 0.20 | 200.00 | USD
740000 | Supplies Expense | 0.00 | 2.00 | 2.00 | | USD
800600 | Customer Service Settlement | 2.00 | 0.00 | 2.00- | 100.00- | USD
Debit | | 2.10 | 2.30 | 0.20 | | USD
800500 | EAM Settlement | 0.00 | 0.30- | 0.30- | | USD
800500 | EAM Settlement | 0.00 | 2.00- | 2.00- | | USD
Settlement | | 0.00 | 2.30- | 2.30- | | USD
| | 2.10 | 0.00 | 2.10- | | USD

Figure 7.20 Plan/Actual Comparison Report for a Maintenance Order

Business Completion of an Order

After settlement, the order can still collect further costs to settle in the next settlement period. Let's say, however, you're not expecting additional costs to be posted to the maintenance order. In this case, you can perform business completion by clicking the **Complete (Business)** button in the header data screen of the order. The order must be released, settled, and have a zero balance to be eligible for business completion. After business completion, the order is assigned a closed status (**CLSD**). An order with the status **CLSD** cannot be posted costs or settled in future settlement periods.

7.4 Integration with Other Modules

In this section, we explain the touchpoints of integration between plant maintenance and other system modules. We can organize cross-module integrations into two categories:

- Integrations via cross-module data assignments
- Integrations via transactions

7.4.1 Integration via Cross-Module Data Assignments

Cross-module data assignments in the system connect the business processes in SAP S/4HANA and lead to data flows between the system's components. Some examples of cross-module data assignments include the following:

- **Management accounting**
  A cost center is master data in cost center accounting (controlling). A maintenance work center in the maintenance plant is assigned to a cost center in its master record. Technical objects (i.e., functional location, and equipment) are assigned to a cost center in their master records, thus integrating plant maintenance with controlling. Internal orders are master data in controlling. They can be used to collect the maintenance costs of pieces of equipment. When you settle the internal order, the system transfers these costs to the asset master record of equipment.

- **Project System and materials management**
  Technical objects are master data in plant maintenance that can be assigned to a project WBS element or material in their master records. A serial number master record can be assigned to a combination of material and equipment. Serialization is a procedure to assign a serial number to a piece of equipment. Serialization makes a piece of equipment available for inventory management (i.e., inventory monitoring and tracking).

- **Asset accounting**
  Technical objects can be assigned to assets in their master records.

- **Human resources**
  A work center can be assigned to an HR organizational unit in its master record, thus integrating plant maintenance with HR.

7.4.2 Integration via Transactions

The plant maintenance module is tightly integrated with other system modules via transactions. Some examples of transactions that lead to cross-module integration include the following:

- **Maintenance planning**
  A maintenance order can be assigned to a profit center, cost center, WBS element (project), or an asset. Maintenance order operations can be assigned nonstock materials linked to procurement and PRTs linked to production. You must maintain purchasing data (purchasing organization, purchasing group, and account assignment for consumption) for the externally processed operations or nonstock materials assigned to operations.

- **Maintenance control**
  Availability checks link the maintenance order to materials planning and inventory management. Availability checks or maintenance order releases generate reservations (for stock materials) and purchase requisitions (for nonstock materials) assigned to maintenance order operations.

- **Execution of maintenance order**
  Goods movements for material withdrawals or external procurements connect the maintenance order to inventory management, purchasing, controlling, and

financial accounting by generating material, accounting, and controlling documents.

- **Completion of order**
  Time, service (external), material, goods movement, and activity confirmations integrate the maintenance order with inventory management, HR, warehouse management (for returning unused materials), procurement, and controlling (via internal activity allocation). Maintenance order settlement triggers postings to cost centers and cost elements, thus connecting the order to controlling and financial accounting.

Figure 7.21 shows integration with other modules activated by transactions in maintenance order processing.

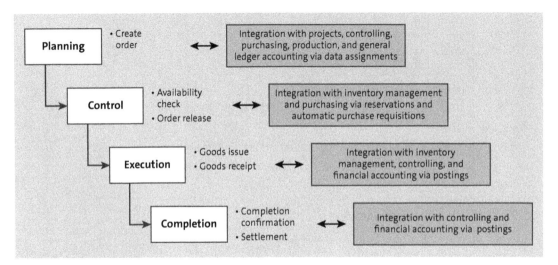

Figure 7.21 Cross-Module Integrations in Maintenance Order Processing

7.5 Important Terminology

In this chapter, the following terminology relevant to enterprise asset management is important to know for the exam:

- **Activities and tasks in a notification**
  A task in a notification represents the work that is planned to perform maintenance. An activity in a notification represents the work that has been already performed.

- **Availability list**
  A list provided my maintenance order that shows the required, available, withdrawn, and received quantities for the materials assigned to maintenance operations.

- **Confirmation**
  A transaction in the completion phase of maintenance order processing. This

transaction is used to confirm actual values of times and quantities, services, materials used, and measurements/counter readings during the maintenance of a technical object.

- **Equipment**
A technical object that represents an autonomous physical object maintained independently.

- **Functional location**
A technical object that represents the site where you carry out the technical tasks.

- **Maintenance planning plant**
A plant where maintenance tasks are planned and prepared for maintenance plants. A maintenance plant is indicated as a maintenance planning plant if it plans its own maintenance activities.

- **Maintenance plant**
A plant where operational systems are installed.

- **Maintenance work center**
A work center responsible for performing maintenance tasks.

- **Notification**
A request for the maintenance order that can represent a malfunction report, activity report, or maintenance request.

- **Object list**
The list of reference objects in a maintenance order. Object lists are used to combine several notifications into a single order.

- **Operations**
Operations represent the planned individual maintenance tasks in the maintenance order. Each operation determines the work centers, the person responsible, activities, materials, and production resources and tools (PRTs) necessary to execute maintenance tasks. Operations create a basis for the calculation of costs on a maintenance order.

- **Order release**
Order release is a transaction in the control phase of maintenance order processing. This transaction authorizes the execution of the order. You can withdraw materials; post goods movements; and confirm, complete, and settle the order only after the order is release.

- **Plan cost and the actual cost**
A plan cost is the expected cost of a maintenance order based on planned operations. An actual cost is a real cost incurred during the execution of maintenance activities.

- **Reference object**
A technical object with or without assembly, or a material with a serial number referenced by a maintenance notification or the maintenance order.

- **Settlement**
  A transaction in the completion phase of maintenance order processing. This transaction is a period-end closing transaction that transfers the collected costs on the released order to settlement receivers (e.g., a cost center) based on the settlement rule.

- **Technical completion**
  A transaction in the completion phase of maintenance order processing. This transaction is used to approve that all planned tasks specified in the maintenance order are complete. **TECO** status is assigned to the order after technical completion.

- **Technical object**
  Technical objects are master data in plant maintenance. Functional locations and pieces of equipment are technical objects creating a basis for structuring the company's technical systems.

7.6 Practice Questions

These practice questions will help you evaluate your understanding of the topics covered in this chapter. The questions shown are similar to those found on the certification examination. Although none of these questions will be found on the exam itself, they will allow you to review your knowledge of the subject. Select the correct answers and then check the completeness of your answers in the next section. Remember that you must select all correct answers on the exam and select only correct answers to receive credit for the question.

1. Which of the following are technical objects in plant maintenance? (There are two correct answers.)
   - ☐ A. Equipment
   - ☐ B. Material BOM
   - ☐ C. Functional location
   - ☐ D. Work center

2. Which of the following represents the organizational unit where operational systems are installed?
   - ☐ A. Company code
   - ☐ B. Maintenance work center
   - ☐ C. Maintenance plant
   - ☐ D. Maintenance planning plant

3. Which of the following statements are correct about the maintenance planning plant?

☐ A. It is a plant where maintenance activities are carried out
☐ B. Every maintenance plant is a maintenance planning plant
☐ C. It is a plant that plans and prepares maintenance activities
☐ D. It plans maintenance activities in all maintenance plans

4. Which of the following are criteria for structuring functional locations? (There are two correct answers.)

☐ A. Spatial
☐ B. Sectional
☐ C. Plant-specific
☐ D. Functional

5. Which of the following statements is *not* correct about a piece of equipment?

☐ A. It is an autonomous object maintained independently
☐ B. It must be installed at a functional location
☐ C. It can be serialized
☐ D. It can be assigned a material

6. Which of the following is used to link similarly constructed pieces of equipment to a material BOM?

☐ A. Superior equipment field
☐ B. Structure indicator
☐ C. Construction type field
☐ D. Equipment BOM

7. Which of the following enables a piece of equipment for inventory monitoring and tracking?

☐ A. Serialization
☐ B. Material BOM
☐ C. Installing it at a functional location
☐ D. Maintaining the **Sales: General/Plant Data** view

8. Which of the following are notification types in plant maintenance? (There are two correct answers.)

    ☐ A. Activity report
    ☐ B. Maintenance order
    ☐ C. Malfunction report
    ☐ D. Maintenance report

9. Which of the following can be reference objects in a notification or order? (There are two correct answers.)

    ☐ A. Maintenance work center
    ☐ B. A material with serial number
    ☐ C. Finished product
    ☐ D. An equipment with or without assembly

10. Which of the following can be found in a maintenance notification? (There are two correct answers.)

    ☐ A. Settlement rule
    ☐ B. Activities and tasks
    ☐ C. Plan costs
    ☐ D. Malfunction data

11. Which of the following are key maintenance activities in plant maintenance? (There are two correct answers.)

    ☐ A. Inspection
    ☐ B. Preventive maintenance
    ☐ C. Regular maintenance
    ☐ D. Procurement

12. Which of the following are *not* elements of the maintenance order structure? (There are two correct answers.)

    ☐ A. Routings
    ☐ B. Operations
    ☐ C. Objects
    ☐ D. Sequences

13. Which of the following makes a maintenance order relevant to procurement? (There are two correct answers.)

    ☐ A. Internally processed operation
    ☐ B. Externally processed operation
    ☐ C. Stock material assigned to an operation
    ☐ D. Nonstock material assigned to an operation

14. Which of the following are correct about maintenance order creation? (There are two correct answers.)

    ☐ A. You must use a maintenance notification
    ☐ B. Only one notification can be used to create an order
    ☐ C. Multiple notifications can be combined into an order
    ☐ D. It can be automatically created from a maintenance plan

15. Which of the following are activities in maintenance control? (There are two correct answers.)

    ☐ A. Order release
    ☐ B. Availability check
    ☐ C. Confirmation
    ☐ D. Business completion

16. Where can you see the results of an availability check (e.g., quantities)?

    ☐ A. Action log
    ☐ B. Document flow
    ☐ C. Availability list
    ☐ D. Order history

17. Which of the following *cannot* be done before an order release? (There are two correct answers.)

    ☐ A. Availability check
    ☐ B. Printing order
    ☐ C. Posting goods receipts
    ☐ D. Reservations

18. For which of the following can you post a goods issue in maintenance order execution?

    ☐ A. Withdrawal of stock material
    ☐ B. Withdrawal of nonstock material
    ☐ C. Receipt of stock material
    ☐ D. Receipt of nonstock material

19. Which of the following triggers an internal activity allocation between the maintenance order and cost centers?

    ☐ A. Order release
    ☐ B. Technical completion
    ☐ C. Business completion
    ☐ D. Time completion confirmation

20. Which of the following generates a Material Ledger document?

    ☐ A. Goods receipt posting for nonstock material
    ☐ B. Material withdrawal for stock item
    ☐ C. Settlement
    ☐ D. Technical completion

21. Which of the following activities can be performed after technical completion? (There are two correct answers.)

    ☐ A. Change the technical data in the order
    ☐ B. Goods receipt posting for order
    ☐ C. Enter new confirmations
    ☐ D. Process existing purchase requisitions for the order

22. Which of the following transactions in plant maintenance triggers postings to financial accounting?

    ☐ A. Technical completion
    ☐ B. Posting goods movements for an order
    ☐ C. Time confirmations
    ☐ D. Order release

23. Which of the following statements summarize the impacts of settlement?

    ☐ A. Data is transferred to personnel time management
    ☐ B. The order balance becomes zero

☐ C. The balance of actual costs becomes zero
☐ D. Variances are transferred to the cost center

7.7 Practice Question Answers and Explanations

1. Correct answers: **A and C**

   Technical objects form a basis for structuring the company's technical systems in SAP S/4HANA. You can use functional locations or pieces of equipment as technical objects in functional or object-related structuring approaches in plant maintenance. A material BOM is not a technical object but master data in plant maintenance. A work center is a part of a maintenance plant but not a technical object.

2. Correct answer: **C**

   A maintenance plant is a plant where the company's operational systems are installed. A maintenance planning plant is to plan and prepare maintenance activities. A maintenance work center is responsible for the maintenance process of a technical object. From an asset accounting perspective, all physical assets belong to the company code.

3. Correct answer: **C**

   A maintenance planning plant is a plant that plans and prepares maintenance activities (only) for the maintenance plants assigned to it. Maintenance activities are performed in a maintenance plant. A maintenance plant may not plan its own maintenance activities and thus should be assigned to a maintenance planning plant.

4. Correct answers: **A and D**

   You can use functional locations to structure your technical systems for plant maintenance. Functional locations can be structured by using spatial, functional (or process-oriented), and technical criteria.

5. Correct answer: **B**

   In a functional and object-related structuring of technical systems, you can define a piece of equipment as an object installed at a functional location. However, this approach is not mandatory. You can also use object-related structuring where a company's technical systems are subdivided into standalone pieces of equipment, not necessarily installed at functional locations.

6. Correct answer: **C**

   Each technical object (functional location or equipment) in the system can be assigned a maintenance BOM. Alternatively, you can use a single material BOM for similarly constructed technical objects in the system. In this case, you'll create a material and a material BOM and assign the material to a technical object via the construction type field in its master record.

7. Correct answer: **A**

   The serialization of equipment enables its inventory monitoring and tracking during the maintenance process, which starts with the dismantling of damaged equipment, continues with moving it to the warehouse, and ends with the installation of repaired equipment at the maintenance plant.

8. Correct answers: **A and C**

   Plant maintenance provides the following notification types: activity reports, malfunction reports, and maintenance requests. A maintenance order is for planning, controlling, and executing maintenance activities; notifications form the basis for the creation of maintenance orders.

9. Correct answers: **B and D**

   A reference object is a technical object (with or without assembly) or a material with a serial number referenced by a maintenance notification or order. A maintenance work center is not a technical object.

10. Correct answers: **B and D**

    A maintenance notification is not a cost collector and thus is not settled. It includes neither a plan cost nor a settlement rule. However, a maintenance notification does include planned work (tasks) and the work that has already been performed (activities). It also includes malfunction data describing the problem with the reference object.

11. Correct answers: **A and B**

    Plant maintenance in SAP S/4HANA supports the following key activities: inspection, preventive maintenance, and repair. Corrective maintenance repairs malfunctioning objects, and breakdown maintenance repairs broken objects.

12. Correct answers: **A and D**

    A routing is master data in production. A sequence is an element of production order, but not of a maintenance order. In a maintenance order, you can find objects and operations that are planned to be carried out for objects.

13. Correct answers: **B and D**

    The operations in the maintenance order can be processed internally and externally. You can assign stock and nonstock materials to those operations. Depending on your Customizing (and order) settings, the system generates purchase requisitions for externally processed operations and nonstock materials, thus linking the maintenance order to purchasing.

14. Correct answers: **C and D**

    You can create maintenance orders directly without using a notification (e.g., breakdown order). You can use one or more notifications to create an order. A maintenance order's object list can be used to combine multiple orders into the order. A maintenance order can also be created automatically from a maintenance item by a maintenance plan.

15. Correct answers: **A and B**

    Availability checks, capacity planning, and order releases are control tasks in corrective maintenance. Confirmation and business completion are tasks in the order completion phase.

16. Correct answer: **C**

    In the availability list of an order, you'll see the reserved and withdrawn quantities for the stock materials and the requested and received quantities for nonstock materials. The document flow displays the progress in processing of the maintenance order. The action log can display what fields on the order has been changed and who changed them.

17. Correct answers: **B and C**

    An availability check is a control task that can be done before the release of the order. Based on your system settings, reservations can be generated when you save the order. However, you cannot print out the order or post goods movements (for the order) before the order release.

18. Correct answer: **A**

    First, note that a goods issue indicates that a material is leaving stock; it is not posted for the receipt of materials. In the order processing execution phase, you can perform (planned or unplanned) withdrawal of stock materials by posting a goods issue for the order. To receive the purchased nonstock materials, you'll post a goods receipt for the order.

19. Correct answer: **D**

    Time completion confirmation enters the actual activity times used in maintenance work centers, which leads to an internal activity allocation between cost centers (assigned work centers) and the maintenance order. As a result, the order is debited for further costs, and the cost centers are credited.

20. Correct answer: **B**

    The system usually generates a Material Ledger document when you post goods movements that lead to a change in the company's stock's total value. A material withdrawal for a stock item is carried out by posting a goods issue, which automatically generates a Material Ledger document.

21. Correct answers: **B and C**

    Technical completion of the order indicates that all planned operations in the order have been performed. In this case, the technical data is fixed on the order and cannot be changed. All outstanding capacities, existing reservations, and purchase orders are deleted. You cannot process deleted purchase requisitions. However, you can still enter new confirmations or post goods receipts for the purchased materials and services.

22. Correct answer: **B**

    Goods movements for maintenance orders are either for material withdrawal or receipt of purchased nonstock materials. In either case, a financial impact exists from posting the goods movements.

23. Correct answer: **C**

    Personnel time management data is transferred when you enter completion confirmations, not in settlement. Unlike the settlement process in production, the settlement of a maintenance order transfers the actual costs (not variances) to the settlement receivers. In this case, the total balance of actual costs in the maintenance order becomes zero. Recall that an order balance is a function of the production order.

7.8 Test Takeaway

In this chapter, you learned key topics in the enterprise asset management business process and how SAP S/4HANA's plant maintenance module supports enterprise asset management tasks. Your company's enterprise asset management-relevant organizational structure can be mapped into the system using client, company code, maintenance plant, and maintenance planning plant organizational data. Maintenance planning can be performed centrally for all plants, or some plants can plan their own maintenance activities (decentrally). The system supports plant maintenance transactions with technical objects (functional location and piece of equipment), serial numbers, and maintenance BOM master data.

The corrective maintenance process is planned and executed through maintenance orders. A notification is created to report a malfunction or to request maintenance. An order can be created by using notifications or directly without notifications. Maintenance order release plays a crucial role in the execution of the order. In the execution phase, material withdrawal of stock items or external procurement of nonstock items is carried out. The plant maintenance module integrates with inventory management, purchasing, controlling, and financial accounting during the execution phase.

Completion confirmations confirm the actual work performed, materials consumed, and services used during maintenance. Confirmations trigger an internal activity allocation between the order and cost centers assigned to work centers where the maintenance operations are performed. With technical completion, you approve that all planned maintenance tasks are done. All existing reservations, purchase requisitions, and outstanding capacities are deleted, and a settlement rule is created if not already maintained. Settlement is a period-end closing task that transfers the actual costs collected on the order to the settlement receivers (cost centers). This transaction debits the settlement receivers and credits the order. The balance of actual costs on the order becomes zero.

We've now completed our discussion of the enterprise asset management business process. The next chapter covers the key topics of the warehouse management business process in SAP S/4HANA.

Chapter 8
Inventory, Warehouse, and Transportation Management

Techniques You'll Master

- Understand the key topics of inventory management, warehouse management, and transportation management in SAP S/4HANA

- Describe the organizational structure, key tasks, and goods movements in inventory management

- Understand SAP S/4HANA's warehouse solutions supporting businesses with various warehouse requirements

- Explain the warehouse organizational structure in SAP S/4HANA, its connections, and the differences between warehouse management and inventory management

- Describe the phases of a transportation project and perform the system transactions for planning, executing, and settling freight documents

- Identify the touchpoints of integration between the inventory, warehouse, and transportation management components and other system modules in SAP S/4HANA

Chapter 8 Inventory, Warehouse, and Transportation Management

This chapter of the book covers all certification-relevant topics of the inventory, warehouse, and transportation management processes in SAP S/4HANA. We'll describe the organizational structure and key tasks in these business processes and explains the system transactions supporting business process tasks. In compliance with the certification scope, this chapter also highlights potential integration scenarios.

SAP S/4HANA provides the inventory management, logistics execution, extended warehouse management (EWM), and transportation management components to support inventory management, warehouse management, and transportation management processes in a company.

> **Real-World Scenario**
>
> Inventory management, warehouse management, and transportation management are three critical business processes that guarantee on-time material availability in all logistics process operations. Accurate planning and efficient execution of tasks in these processes is crucial for customer satisfaction and productivity.
>
> Based on the lines of business (LoBs) and its organizational structure, a company must manage various categories of material stocks (raw materials, trading goods) at several organizational levels. Management of internal stock movements between the company's locations or external stock movements between the company and business partners is key to inventory management processes. Value-based inventory management is vital for external reporting purposes, while quantity-based inventory is essential for material planning, inventory replenishment, and monitoring consumption.
>
> Some small businesses do not require a separate warehouse management process while managing their inventory in a single location or in a few storage locations. However, companies with a diverse inventory of materials need to manage their stocks at the storage bin level in their warehouse complexes. Management of internal traffic within the warehouse, automation of goods movements, yard and labor management, value-added services, and seamless integration with inventory management and other business processes are among the priorities companies expect from a warehouse management system (WMS).
>
> Inventory management is concerned with recording logical and physical goods movements affecting financials and warehouse management. Warehouse management covers the physical movements of materials within the warehouse and has no controls on the external transportation process. Inventory management and warehouse management provide no tools for

carrier selection, load planning, or route optimization in goods' transportation. A business needs a comprehensive transportation management system to plan, optimize, execute, and monitor materials' physical transportation process in collaboration with business partners and logistics service providers.

As an SAP consultant, you must understand SAP S/4HANA's solutions for inventory management, warehouse management, and transportation management to provide your clients with a holistic software implementation creating cost-efficient and seamlessly integrated logistics processes in their enterprises.

8.1 Objectives of This Portion of the Test

This portion of the certification aims to test your knowledge of key topics in the inventory management, warehouse management, and transportation management processes in SAP S/4HANA. The certification exam includes questions about stock types and goods movements in inventory management and the impact of goods movement impacts on financial accounting. Relevant to warehouse management, you'll encounter questions about warehouse structures, movements, and solutions. The phases of transportation management in which system transactions are carried out is also a noteworthy topic that you must understand for certification.

SAP consultants are expected to know potential integration scenarios for the inventory management, logistics execution, EWM, and transportation components in the system.

For the certification exam, business process integration consultants must have a good understanding of the following topics:

- The organizational structure of inventory management, warehouse management, and EWM
- Goods movements and documents for goods movements
- Differences between warehouse processes
- Transactions in warehouse management and EWM
- Key tasks in transportation management and the role of transportation management in purchasing and sales
- Touchpoints of integration between inventory management, warehouse management, EWM, transportation management, and other system modules

Note
The topics in this chapter cover about 8%–10% of the questions in the certification exam.

8.2 Inventory Management

Inventory consists of all goods and materials in a company's stock at a particular time. SAP S/4HANA provides the inventory management component as a part of materials management to support the following key tasks:

- **Management of inventory on a quantity basis**
  The inventory management component in SAP S/4HANA tightly integrates with all other system modules during business processes affecting inventory quantities. For example, all business processes involving goods movements (e.g., goods receipt and goods issue) and reservations lead to a change in stock recorded in real time by inventory management. You can use the stock overview application to view the on-hand stock for a particular material by several organizational levels and stock types. Stock requirements lists allow you to monitor stock requirements determined in procurement proposals, such as planned orders and purchase requisitions.

- **Management of inventory on a value basis**
  Some materials are inventory managed only on a quantity basis; these materials are called *nonvaluated materials*. For example, for some consumables, those not subject to inventory valuation, you might want to track consumption on a quantity basis. Some materials (e.g., stock materials) are inventory managed not only on a quantity basis but also on a value basis. When you post goods movements for those items, the system automatically updates the stock quantity and value for inventory management, updates the account assignment for cost accounting, and updates the general ledger accounts for financial accounting.

- **Management of goods movements**
  This task is concerned with planning, posting, and documenting all goods movements, such as goods receipts, goods issues, stock transfers, and transfer postings. For each goods movement, several documents (material document, accounting document, controlling document, Material Ledger document) are created to document the goods movement and its impacts on financial accounting, controlling, and the Material Ledger.

- **Physical inventory**
  Physical inventory is concerned with counting stocks physically, matching the results with the inventory records, and posting inventory differences.

In this section, we'll walk you through the organizational data, goods movements processes, and documents that are important to know for the exam.

8.2.1 Organizational Data

A company's inventory management-relevant organizational structure can be mapped into the system by using the following organizational data:

- Client
- Company code

- Plant
- Storage location

You manage physical inventory at the storage location level. Storage locations allow you to distinguish between several physical storage characteristics or various material stocks in your plant. An inventory valuation can be carried out either at the plant level or at the company code level.

8.2.2 Goods Movements

A goods movement is a transaction that leads to a change in the stock levels or results in the consumption of a material. In logistics processes, you can post goods movements for the following stock types:

- **Unrestricted-use stock**
  Unrestricted-use stock includes the valuated stock of a company without any usage restriction.
- **Quality inspection stock**
  Quality inspection stock includes material retained for quality inspection. This stock cannot be consumed.
- **Blocked stock**
  Blocked stock includes a company's valuated stock that has been rejected due to poor quality. This stock type is regarded as "not available" in the availability check and cannot be classified as unrestricted-use stock.

The stock overview (Transaction MMBE) can display an overview of the stocks for a particular material across the several organizational levels of inventory management, as shown in Figure 8.1.

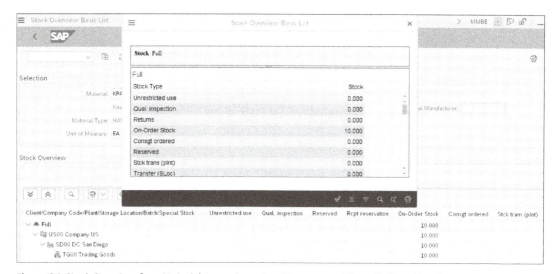

Figure 8.1 Stock Overview for a Material across Inventory Management Organizational Levels

Some goods movements can also be carried out for nonstock materials and services (without service specifications).

SAP S/4HANA's inventory management component supports the following categories of goods movements in logistics processes:

- Goods receipts
- Goods issues
- Transfer postings
- Stock transfers

In the following sections, we'll describe these categories of goods movements and their impacts on other system modules.

Goods Receipts

A goods receipt is a goods movement transaction used to initiate a material's receipt into inventory or to confirm the receipt of purchased services. For instance, you can post a goods receipt for a purchase order to receive the purchased materials (or services) in procurement. You can post a goods receipt for a production order to deliver finished products to stock in production. You can also post a goods receipt for customer returns in sales and distribution. In plant maintenance, a warehouse posts a goods receipt to confirm the receipt of serialized equipment that was dismantled for refurbishment. With a goods receipt posting, you can move materials to one of the stock types in a storage location.

For materials subject to inventory management on a quantity basis, a goods receipt posting always increases stock quantities. A goods receipt posting for materials subject to inventory management on a value basis changes the stock's total value and the material's value in the material master record. You can also post goods receipts to receive consumables that are not subject to inventory management on a quantity or value basis. In this case, only the account assignment is updated for consumption. In both cases, an accounting document is created documenting the impact on financial accounting. Note that some goods receipt postings (e.g., receiving a consignment material from a vendor) do not impact financial accounting and only lead to updates in stock quantities, not the value of the stock.

Goods Issues

A goods issue indicates the removal of material from stock. Unlike a goods receipt, a goods issue decreases the stock level and the total value of the stock. You can post goods issues for sales orders (via Transaction MIGO) as a part of the shipping process in sales and distribution. You can post goods issues for production orders, maintenance orders, or project networks to perform planned/unplanned material withdrawals for internal consumption from the stock. In most cases, a goods issue posting impacts financial accounting and controlling. You can only issue materials from unrestricted-use stock in an outbound delivery.

Transfer Postings

A transfer posting is a category of internal goods movement that does not necessarily involve a physical transfer of materials. You can use transfer postings (via Transaction MIGO_TR) to change the stock type, material number, or batch number of a material in stock. Using the corresponding movement type, you can execute the following types of transfer postings:

- **Stock-to-stock**
  To change the stock type of material.
- **Material-to-material**
  To change the material number of a material processed or changed over time (pharmaceutical or chemical industry).
- **Consignment-to-warehouse**
  To transfer a consignment material into the company's own stock.

Stock Transfers

A stock transfer is a category of internal goods movements that involve a physical transfer of materials from one location to another within the company. You can perform stock transfers between storage locations, plants, or company codes via transfer postings using one-step or two-step procedures or stock transport orders.

Stock transfers using a one-step procedure can be executed via a single transaction (i.e., stock removal). However, stock transfers using a two-step procedure include an additional step for placing material into storage. Until you enter the material placement at the receiving location, the issued stock appears in the receiving location's stock-in-transit stock. You can enter a material placement with or without reference to a stock removal document; the latter approach transfers the material from the stock-in-transit stock to the unrestricted-use stock of the receiving plant.

The following stock transfers can only be executed from unrestricted-use stock:

- Storage location-to-storage location with a two-step procedure
- Plant-to-plant with any procedure
- Company code-to-company code with any procedure

In contrast, stock transfers with a one-step procedure between storage locations can be carried out from any stock type in the issuing storage location to the same stock type in the receiving location.

You can specify the stock transfer procedure by selecting an appropriate movement type in the transfer posting transaction (Transaction MIGO_TR, shown in

Figure 8.2). Alternatively, you can transfer stocks between plants via stock transport orders (Transaction ME21N, shown in Figure 8.3) using a two-step procedure.

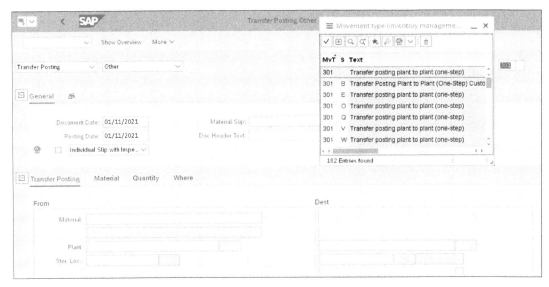

Figure 8.2 Stock Transfer via Transfer Posting

Figure 8.3 Stock Transfer via Stock Transport Order

Tip

In compliance with the certification exam, we use the term "transfer posting" to categorize transfer postings without physical movement and the term "stock transfer" to categorize transfer postings involving physical movement. You must use the transaction called *transfer posting* (Transaction MIGO_TR) to execute stock transfers between storage locations, plants, and company codes. The system has no separate transaction called *stock transfer*. You differentiate stock transfers from transfer postings (without physical movement) by choosing the appropriate movement type and maintaining the location data in Transaction MIGO_TR. The goods movements in the category that we call stock transfer in this section corresponds to transfer postings involving physical movements.

Now, let's walk through the procedures for stock transfers:

- **One-step procedure**

    The one-step procedure can be used by specifying the movement type in Transaction MIGO_TR (Transfer Posting). In the one-step procedure, the material is transferred from an issuing location (i.e., storage location, plant, or company code) to the same type of receiving location. This procedure decreases the stock levels at the issuing location and the receiving location simultaneously. You can apply the one-step procedure with or without reservations.

    Reservations are intended for the one-step procedure only and cannot be used in the two-step procedure. The issuing location can use the reservations as a basis for planning the materials' issue (via transfer posting with reference to reservations). In the one-step procedure, the system creates a single material document with two line items: one line item for the removal of the stock at the issuing location and one line item for the placement of the stock into storage at the receiving location, as shown in Figure 8.4.

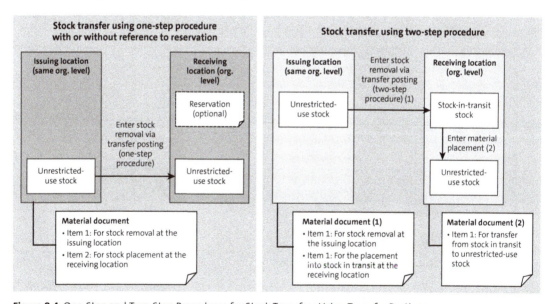

Figure 8.4 One-Step and Two-Step Procedures for Stock Transfers Using Transfer Postings

- **Two-step procedure**

    The two-step procedure can be used by specifying the movement type Transaction MIGO_TR. You can control the stocks' actual receipt in the two-step procedure using an intermediate stock called *stock-in-transit* stock. With this procedure, you can only transfer material from the unrestricted-use stock at the issuing location to the same stock type at the receiving location. The unrestricted-use stock level is decreased at the issuing location upon the removal of stock via transfer posting at the issuing plant. The transferred quantities appear in the receiving plant's stock-in-transit stock during the physical transfer of material, not unrestricted-use stock. When the receiving location enters the material placement, the issued material is transferred from stock-in-transit stock to unrestricted-use stock.

You may prefer the two-step procedure if significant time is required to complete the stock's actual receipt at the receiving location, which might be physically distant from the issuing location. In the two-step procedure, the system creates two material documents: The first material document removes the stock and has two line items for each material: one line item for removing the stock at the issuing location and one line item for placing the stock into stock-in-transit at the receiving location. The second material document has one item for each material: to document the transfer of the material from stock-in-transit stock to unrestricted-use stock, as shown in Figure 8.4.

- **Stock transport order (with or without delivery)**
A stock transport order is a particular purchase order used for (long-distance) stock transfers in internal procurement. This kind of order supports the transfer of unrestricted-use stock between plants or company codes. A stock transfer using a stock transport order is an internal procurement process between a supplying (issuing) plant and a receiving plant (buyer).

This stock transfer procedure can be executed by using Transaction ME21N (Create Purchase Order) in purchasing and creating a stock transport order. This procedure includes a goods issue posting at the supplying plant and a goods receipt posting at the receiving plant. The issued materials appear in the receiving plant's stock-in-transit stock until posting the receiving plant's goods receipt.

Note
The one-step procedure is not supported in stock transfers with stock transport orders.

After receiving the stock transport order from the requesting plant, the issuing plant can execute the shipping process by creating a delivery document, as shown in Figure 8.5. This delivery document is used to plan, control, and monitor picking and packing processes at the issuing plant before the goods issue posting. Alternatively, the issuing plant can directly start the shipping process without creating a delivery document.

You may prefer this type of stock transfer between plants to take advantage of the functions of purchase orders, such as triggering the stock transfer by creating purchase requisitions from material requirements planning (MRP), tracking the stock transfer by using the purchase order history, planning the receipt of the stock at the receiving plant, negotiating prices for the transferred stock, posting goods receipts directly to consumption (in maintenance, production, or projects), performing availability check for the stock transport order, entering delivery costs to stock transport order, or triggering a billing process at the issuing plant (supplying plant).

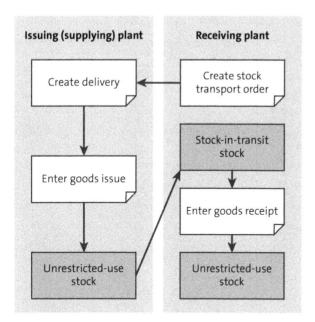

Figure 8.5 Stock Transfer Using Stock Transport Order and Delivery

SAP S/4HANA's inventory management component supports the following types of stock transfers:

- **Storage location-to-storage-location stock transfer (in a plant)**
  In this type of stock transfer, the material is moved from one storage location to another within the same plant using a one-step or a two-step procedure. In this type of stock transfer, the one-step procedure can be used for any stock type. In contrast, the two-step procedure must be carried out from unrestricted-use stock. A material document is created to document the goods movement. This type of stock transfer only changes the stock quantity in the storage location and does not change stock quantity in the plant. However, using a one-step procedure can change stocks' distribution to various stock types in the plant (i.e., unrestricted-use, quality inspection, or blocked stock). A stock transfer between storage locations does not affect financial accounting since the stock level is still in the same valuation area (i.e., plant). No accounting document is created for this type of stock transfer.

- **Plant-to-plant stock transfer (in a company code)**
  In this type of stock transfer, the material is moved from one plant to another within the same company code using a one-step or a two-step procedure. You can only transfer unrestricted-use stock between the plants. Unlike the stock transfer between storage locations, stock transfers between two plants with different valuation areas impact financial accounting. The system valuates the transfer posting at the valuation price of the material at the issuing plant. An accounting document is created upon goods issue posting in addition to a material document.

- **Company code-to-company code stock transfer**
  With this particular type of plant-to-plant stock transfer, the issuing and receiving plants belong to different company codes. Like stock transfers between plants, you can use this type of stock transfer using one-step or two-step procedures. However, in a company code-to-company code stock transfer, two accounting documents are created for the transfer posting when the goods issue is posted. One accounting document captures the removal of the stock at the issuing company code, and one accounting document captures the placement of the stock into storage at the receiving company code. The accounting document includes an offsetting line item for company code clearing accounts.

8.2.3 Documents for Goods Movements

When you post a goods movement, you must enter the movement type. A movement type is a key that classifies the movement and determines how accounts in financial accounting should be posted and how stock fields in the material master record will be updated. All data changes originated from the goods movement are recorded in documents. In all goods movement postings, a material document is created as proof of the goods movement. If the movement is relevant to financial accounting, an accounting document is also created. The system also updates stock quantities and stock values (if necessary) due to the goods movement.

Let's review goods movements and the documents created for them:

- **Goods receipt and goods issue**
  The following documents are created:
  - Material document (documenting the goods movement)
  - Accounting document (updating stock accounts, account assignment, goods receipt/invoice receipt account, or cost of goods sold [COGS] account)
  - Controlling document (updating controlling objects, such as cost centers and cost objects)
  - Material Ledger document (documenting the change in the stock's value)
- **Transfer postings**
  The following documents are created:
  - Stock-to-stock: Only one material document is created
  - Material-to-material: Material and accounting documents are created
  - Consignment-to-material: Material and accounting documents are created
- **Stock transfers (via transfer postings) between storage locations**
  No accounting document is created, but depending on the procedure, the following documents are created:
  - One-step procedure: One material document
  - Two-step procedure: Two material documents

- **Stock transfers (via transfer postings) between plants**
  In addition to an accounting document, the following documents are created:
  - One-step procedure: One material document
  - Two-step procedure: Two material documents
- **Stock transfers (via transfer postings) between company codes**
  In addition to two accounting documents, the following documents are created:
  - One-step procedure: One material document
  - Two-step procedure: Two material documents
- **Stock transfer using a stock transport order**
  Stock transport orders can be used for the stock transfers between plants within the same company code or between plants in different company codes. If the supplying and receiving plants are in the same company code, the system creates only one accounting document when the goods issue is posted. If the supplying and receiving plants belong to different company codes, the system creates two accounting documents when the goods issue is posted.

8.3 Warehouse Management

Inventory management is concerned with tracking changes in stock on both a quantity and a value basis. Physical inventory is managed at the storage location level. Although it supports the goods movements between the locations, inventory management is not intended to track inventory at the bin level or to manage internal stock movement traffic within the warehouse complex. SAP's WMS enables you to track warehouse stock quantities at the storage bin level and track storage bin locations while supporting the management of internal stock movements within a warehouse. You'll find all WMS transactions in the logistics execution module via the SAP GUI.

> **Note**
> The WMS is not a replacement for the inventory management component. The WMS provides additional and enhanced tools for efficient storage, internal movement (e.g., putaway and picking), and inventory control at a more granular organizational level in a warehouse, called *storage bins*. You still need inventory management for material planning and valuation of the stocks at the plant level. WMS fully integrates with the inventory management component, so the inventory balances in inventory management are always the same as inventory balances in warehouse stock.

Based on your company's warehouse requirements, you can choose between the following options relevant for warehouse processes in SAP S/4HANA:

- No warehouse management
- Lean warehouse management (for fixed bin warehouses)

- Warehouse management (for small or medium-sized warehouses)
- EWM (for medium- or large-sized warehouses)

Choosing no warehouse management means you want to manage your inventory only on a quantity and value basis at the storage locations without requiring warehouse functions supporting bin-level inventory management and inbound or outbound movements within the warehouse complex. This option may be suitable for businesses with simple inventories, managed in only a few storage locations.

Your company may have several warehouses that manage their inventories at different organizational units, such as storage locations and storage bins. Your company may also use non-SAP solutions for warehouse management. You may implement lean warehouse management if your company manages a warehouse's inventory at the storage location level with a fixed bin strategy. Still, you may want to keep warehouse processes compliant with other warehouses managing their inventories at the storage bin level. SAP's lean warehouse management solution can also integrate a non-SAP WMS with SAP S/4HANA.

To prepare for the certification exam, we'll focus on warehouse management and EWM processes.

WMS supports warehouse management processes that manage inventory quantities at the storage bin level. You can choose between the following deployment options:

- Centralized WMS
- Decentralized WMS

A centralized WMS is the WMS embedded in SAP S/4HANA. A decentralized WMS is a standalone system that runs on a different machine than the one where SAP S/4HANA runs. A decentralized WMS may be the approach of choice for high throughput warehouses that must be available 24 hours a day; these warehouses need to minimize downtime due to system problems and updates in SAP S/4HANA. Note that no integration with transportation management systems is possible with a decentralized WMS.

Now, let's walk through the organizational data and warehouse movements for a centralized WMS, before we take a closer look at a decentralized WMS.

8.3.1 Organizational Data

The WMS provides the following organizational data to map physical warehouse structures into the system, as shown in Figure 8.6:

- **Warehouse number**
  A warehouse number uniquely identifies the warehouse complex in the system. Each warehouse complex must be assigned a unique warehouse number in the system. The warehouse structure is mapped into a storage location by assigning the warehouse number to a plant's storage location; every warehouse

number must be assigned to at least one storage location. You can assign a warehouse number to several storage locations in a plant. However, you can manage stock for several plants in the same warehouse. In this case, you can assign a single warehouse to several storage locations in several plants (see the one-to-many relationship represented by the dashed line shown in Figure 8.6). A storage location may have only one warehouse number. In the system, you may have some storage locations without a warehouse number, which may be preferred if you prefer managing inventory at the storage location level.

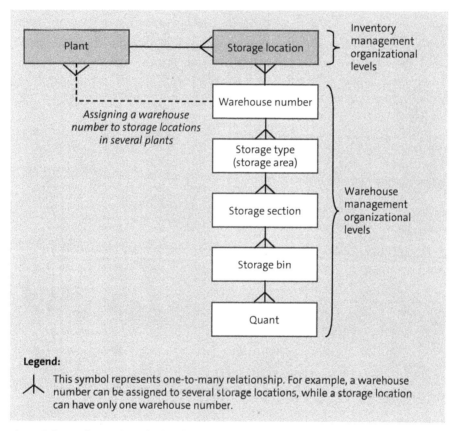

Figure 8.6 Warehouse Organizational Structure

- **Storage type**
  A storage type is a subdivision of a warehouse number that represents a storage area or physical or logical subdivision of a warehouse complex. Storage types are defined based on their spatial, functional, or organizational characteristics. Higher rack storage areas and lower rack storage areas are examples of storage types. Goods receipt areas, goods issue areas, and picking areas are some other examples of storage types.

- **Storage sections**
  A storage section is an organizational subdivision of a storage type that represents a group of storage bins with similar characteristics for putaway tasks. In

the higher rack storage area, you can use the front section as a storage section of the bins, including fast-moving items, and the rear section for slow-moving items.

- **Storage bin**
  A storage bin is the smallest organizational unit in the warehouse structure and represents the smallest storage space in the warehouse complex. You must assign each storage bin to a combination of warehouse number, storage type, and storage section. This assignment is crucial to define the location of the storage bin in the warehouse complex.

- **Quant**
  A quant represents a quantity or batch of material with similar characteristics (e.g., material number, batch number, plant, and stock category) in a storage bin. The system creates different quants for different batches of the same material in a storage bin. Quants enable you to perform inventory management of a stock of material at the storage bin.

Figure 8.7 shows two different quants in a warehouse storage bin.

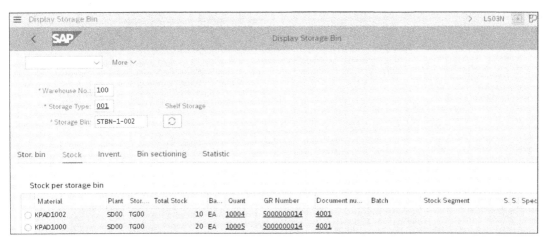

Figure 8.7 Quants in a Warehouse Storage Bin

8.3.2 Centralized Warehouse Management

In a centralized WMS, warehouse movements are requested, planned, and executed by the following two documents:

- **Transfer requirement**
  The transfer requirement is a planning basis for goods movements in the warehouse and requests for transfer orders. The transfer requirement data describes the materials and quantities planned to be moved and the planned movement time. Transfer requirements can be automatically created when you post a goods movement (e.g., a goods receipt) in inventory management or request material using a production planning system (e.g., release a production order with a component managed at the warehouse). You can also create transfer

requirements manually with reference to a material document or a production order, or without reference. The transfer requirement's status enables you to monitor the warehouse request's progress; when you create a transfer order for the transfer requirement or confirm the transfer order, the transfer requirement's status is updated. You can see status information in the header details of the transfer requirement, as shown in Figure 8.8.

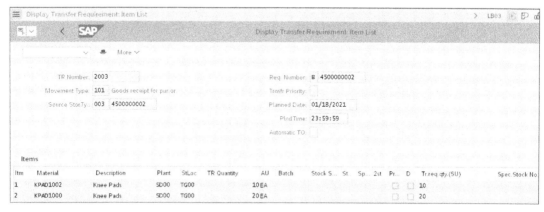

Figure 8.8 Transfer Requirement Automatically Generated by a Goods Receipt Posting

- **Transfer order**
  All physical goods movements (e.g., picking and putaway) in the warehouse are executed using a transfer order. You can create a transfer order with reference to a transfer requirement, delivery document (outbound or inbound), or material document. You can see the source document number in the header details of a transfer order. The transfer order line items include all data necessary for warehouse movement execution, as shown in Figure 8.9.

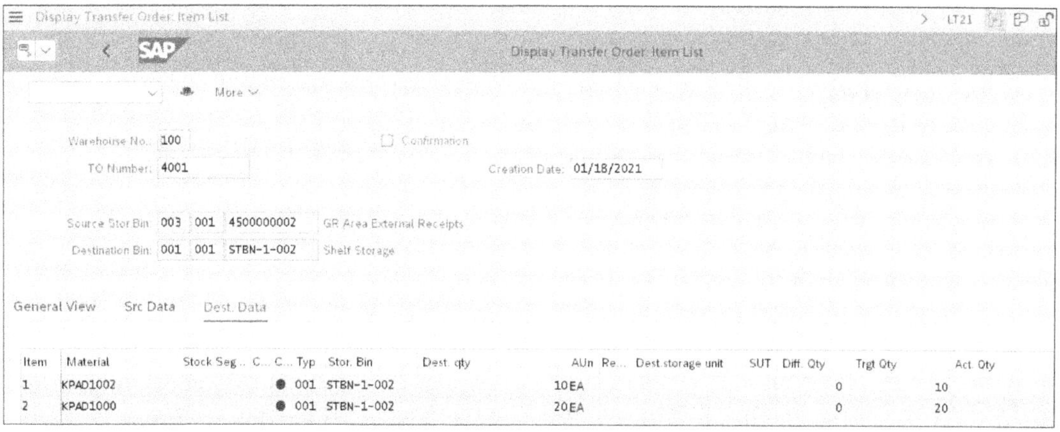

Figure 8.9 Transfer Order for the Transfer of Materials from the Goods Receipt Area to a Storage Bin

The transfer order confirmation is to inform the system that the goods have arrived at the planned destination. The WMS updates the warehouse stock upon confirming the transfer order. The transfer order confirmation informs the system that the material has arrived at the warehouse's planned destination. To document physical receipt and physical removal of goods at the warehouse, WMS supports posting goods receipts and goods issues with reference to transfer requirements or (inbound/outbound) deliveries.

Figure 8.10 shows the standard inventory management and warehouse management transactions for goods movements in purchasing and fulfillment. In purchasing, the goods receipt posting is followed by the transfer requirement, which serves as a connecting document between inventory management and warehouse management transfer orders. In sales and distribution, the outbound delivery document plays that role.

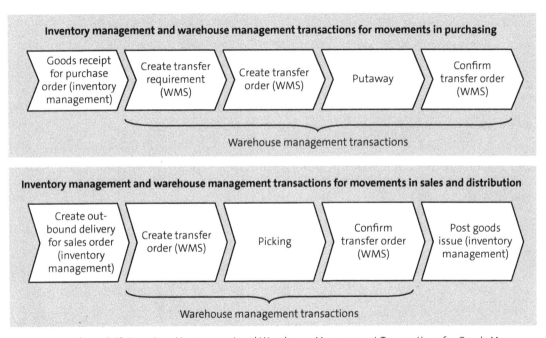

Figure 8.10 Inventory Management and Warehouse Management Transactions for Goods Movements in Purchasing and Sales and Distribution

8.3.3 Decentralized Warehouse Management

In a decentralized warehouse management scenario, warehouse activities are triggered by inbound and outbound deliveries created in inventory management. The system passes these documents to the decentralized WMS; the inbound/outbound deliveries are replicated to decentralized WMS via business application programming interfaces (BAPIs). Inbound and outbound deliveries serve as communication documents between a decentralized WMS and SAP S/4HANA.

In a decentralized warehouse management scenario, inventory postings (e.g., goods receipts and goods issues) are not immediately carried out in inventory management using one integrated step. You must initiate inbound or outbound deliveries in inventory management to prepare the system for inventory postings. For instance, when you create a purchase order (or scheduling agreement) in purchasing, a goods receiving point is determined. Then, an inbound delivery is created automatically or manually (depends on system settings). An inbound delivery document is a request to put material away into the warehouse. A transfer order is created for the inbound delivery to execute the required warehouse activities, such as repacking and putaway. The last step is to post a goods receipt for inbound delivery. In this case, the material's warehouse quantity is increased by the delivery quantity, and value changes are posted to inventory accounting.

Figure 8.11 shows a goods receipt process with an inbound delivery.

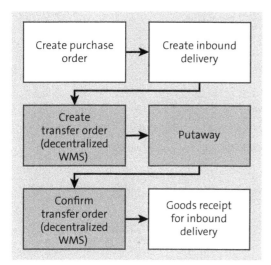

Figure 8.11 Goods Receipt with Inbound Delivery for Decentralized WMS

8.4 Extended Warehouse Management

EWM is recommended for medium-sized and large companies that need automated support for processing goods movements in their warehouses. Like WMS, EWM tightly integrates with inventory management and delivery processing in logistics processes, such as procurement, sales and distribution, plant maintenance, production, and project management.

For EWM, you have the following deployment options:

- Centralized EWM (fully embedded in SAP S/4HANA)
- Decentralized SAP Extended Warehouse Management (SAP EWM) based on SAP S/4HANA

Similar to a decentralized WMS, a decentralized SAP EWM system has its own advantages, which we discussed in the previous section. Unlike a WMS, however, there are no transfer requirements or transfer orders in SAP EWM processes. The following documents play a central role in the planning and execution of inbound and outbound delivery processes in EWM:

- Inbound delivery document (for putaway)
- Outbound delivery order (for picking)

Warehouse tasks control physical movements (e.g., picking and putaway) in EWM. You can monitor the processing of all goods movements with the warehouse activity monitor. EWM also supports connecting customized external systems (e.g., automated WMS) or integrated radio frequency solutions.

The organizational structure of EWM is the same as warehouse management. EWM provides activity areas to define bin sorting and group storage bins across storage types logically. EWM allows you to define activity areas for each activity, such as picking, putaway, and physical inventory. Storage bins, activity areas, storage sections, and storage types are structured and joined under an EWM warehouse number. You must assign an EWM warehouse number to an SAP S/4HANA warehouse number assigned to a plant's storage location; this step is necessary since EWM warehouse numbers are usually longer than SAP S/4HANA warehouse numbers. Unlike WMS storage bins, EWM storage bins include more detailed information about the storage bin, such as geographical coordinates, as shown in Figure 8.12.

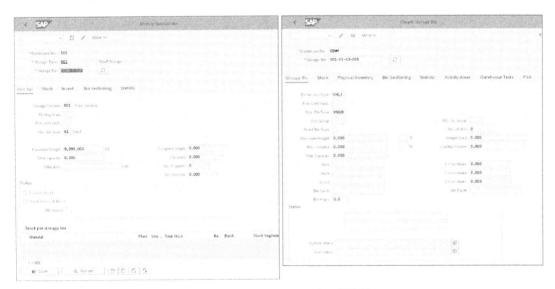

Figure 8.12 Storage Bins in Warehouse Management and EWM

In addition to standard warehouse functions (e.g., storage bin management, yard management, replenishment, and placement/removal strategies), EWM provides the following functions to enhance warehouse processes:

- Expected goods receipts
- Value-added services

- Opportunistic cross-docking
- Loading and unloading transfer units
- Deconsolidation
- Labor management
- Slotting and rearrangement
- Task and resource management

8.5 Transportation Management

SAP Transportation Management (SAP TM) supports all activities for transporting goods and products between locations that belong to your company or to your business partners (e.g., vendors or customers). You can use transportation management as an embedded component of SAP S/4HANA or deploy SAP TM decentrally.

SAP TM's integration with orders (in materials management and sales and distribution) and deliveries (in logistics execution for warehouse management) enables you to plan and execute transportation activities based on orders and deliveries. A typical transportation process is shown in Figure 8.13.

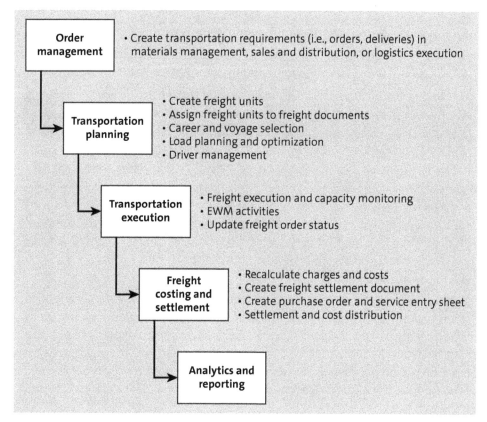

Figure 8.13 Transportation Process

Let's walk through the key phases of the process:

- **Order management**

  In the order management phase, you can create a transportation requirement in materials management, sales and distribution, or logistics execution. A transportation requirement is a basis for transportation planning and execution. The following orders and deliveries are regarded as requiring transportation planning in transportation management:
  - Sales orders
  - Customer returns
  - Purchase orders
  - Scheduling agreements
  - Stock transport orders
  - Returns purchase orders
  - Returns stock transport orders
  - Inbound and outbound deliveries

- **Transportation planning**

  Transportation planning is carried out based on freight units. A *freight unit* is the smallest set of goods or products that can be transported together. Freight units enable you to merge items in several transportation requirements (orders and deliveries). Transportation units (e.g., containers, trailers, railcars, packages) are used to consolidate freight units.

  In the planning phase, you can create freight units and assign them to capacity documents, such as freight documents (e.g., freight order or freight booking) and transportation units. Freight units are created based on transportation requirements. Based on your system settings, freight units can be automatically created when you save or change a transportation requirement (e.g., sales order or purchase order). In the planning phase, you can select and assign drivers to freight documents and perform load planning. You can perform manual and automatic planning in the planning phase. Automatic planning supports vehicle scheduling and routing optimization, load consolidation, and load planning. Package building, scheduling, and carrier selection are other tasks that take place in transportation planning.

- **Transportation execution**

  In this phase, freight orders or freight bookings are executed. A *freight order* is a transportation management order whose execution is planned by a carrier or the shipper; a *freight booking* is a specific transportation management order whose execution is planned by a carrier, for example, a shipowner. A freight order includes a plan for logistical processing, departure times for vehicles, and execution data, while a freight booking only includes a plan for logistical processing.

  Transportation management can integrate with logistics execution or EWM for execution. For instance, during loading/unloading, receipt, or arrival/departure of transportation units, all changes are recorded on freight documents via integration between EWM and transportation management. Moreover, the integration between transportation management and EWM supports order-/delivery-based planning and execution, cost settlement, and changing freight documents from departure to arrival.

- **Freight costing and settlement**
  In this phase, you'll perform the following tasks:
  - Recalculate the charges and the distributed costs on the freight order and freight booking
  - Create a freight settlement document (FSD)
  - Cost distribution
  - Freight settlement

The FSD is a basis for the cost distribution (which involves postings to profitability analysis or material valuation) and freight settlement (which involves verifying the invoice for transportation services provided to you by a carrier).

A cost distribution distributes costs over order (delivery) items in the FSD, as shown in Figure 8.14. A cost distribution is carried out based on predefined cost distribution parameters, such as the distribution method (direct or hierarchical), distribution rule (based on criteria such as gross weight or net weight), and distribution level.

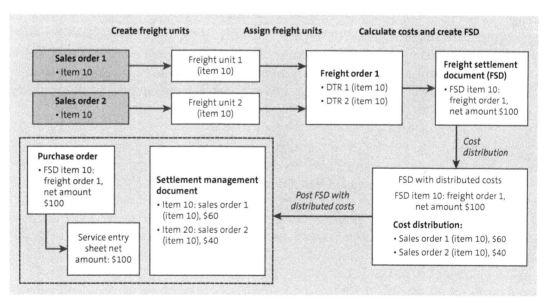

Figure 8.14 Processing FSD with Cost Distributions

Cost distribution is essential for recording delivery costs on the material (used for material valuation) and recording the delivery cost of sales orders/returns (used to calculate customer and/or product profitability).

An FSD represents costs from transportation management to materials management. In the freight settlement process, you post the FSD to materials management. In this case, a purchase order is created for services, and a service entry sheet is created with the values from transportation management. This integration between transportation management and materials management is essential for subsequent processes in financials. The final step in freight settlement is invoice verification.

8.6 Integration with Other Modules

In this section, we explain the touchpoints of integration between inventory, warehouse, and transportation management and other system modules. We can organize cross-module integrations into two categories:

- Integrations via cross-module data assignments
- Integrations via transactions

8.6.1 Integration via Cross-Module Data Assignments

Cross-module data assignments in the system connect the business processes in SAP S/4HANA and lead to data flows between the system's components. Some examples of integrations via data assignments include the following:

- **Plant maintenance**
  A serial number is a master record in plant maintenance that can be assigned to a combination of material and equipment. Serialization makes a piece of equipment available for inventory management (i.e., inventory monitoring and tracking).

- **Warehouse management**
  A storage location is organizational data in inventory management. A warehouse number is organizational data in warehouse management and EWM. A warehouse management warehouse number is assigned to a storage location to map the warehouse structure into the storage location. This assignment integrates the inventory management and logistics execution (warehouse management) components of SAP S/4HANA.

8.6.2 Integration via Transactions

The inventory management, logistics execution (warehouse management), EWM, and transportation management components of SAP S/4HANA are tightly integrated with other system modules via transactions. Some examples of transactions that lead to cross-module integration include the following:

- **Material availability checks**
  Material availability checks for orders (e.g., sales orders, production orders, maintenance orders); projects; or outbound deliveries integrate inventory management with the corresponding system modules.

- **Reservations**
  A reservation is a touchpoint of integration between inventory management (or warehouse management) and other system modules. A reservation is a request to the warehouse to keep materials ready for withdrawal at a requested time. When you save (or release) an order (e.g., a purchase or maintenance order); a network; or a project, the system automatically creates reservations for material components from which future goods issues will withdraw. If the material is managed under the WMS, transfer requirements or outbound deliveries are created. The system also creates automatic stock transfer reservations for replenishment quantities when the available stock level for a material arrives at a reorder point. As a result of reservation entry, the system creates a reservation document, and the requested quantity increases the reserved stock in inventory management. Still, the unrestricted-use stock quantity remains the same until the goods issue posting. Reserved quantities are reflected in the available stock for MRP. You can also create reservations manually for account assignment objects, such as cost centers, assets, and orders.

- **Goods movements**
  Goods movements play a crucial role in the integration of inventory management with other logistics processes. For instance, goods issue postings to issue materials for orders or projects (i.e., planned/unplanned withdrawals for production orders, maintenance orders, stock transport orders, or deliveries of sales orders) and goods receipt postings to receive materials for orders and projects create integration between inventory management and other system modules, such as purchasing, sales and distribution, production, plant maintenance, and Project System. Entering goods movements in inventory management also triggers warehouse activities, thus integrating inventory management with logistics execution.

- **Material staging in production**
  You can perform material staging for a production order with the order's warehouse management or EWM functionalities and initiate materials requiring transport to production storage bins, which integrates production orders with the corresponding modules.

- **Confirmations**
  Confirmations in production, plant maintenance, and Project System can result in transferring unused items to the warehouse and in backflush goods issue postings, thus integrating inventory management (and warehouse management) with the corresponding modules.

- **Order and deliveries**
  Transportation management integrates with orders and deliveries in the system. When you create orders or deliveries, freight units are created in transportation management. Freight units are the basis for transportation planning and execution. Transportation management also integrates with EWM and materials management (i.e., purchasing and inventory management) during the execution and settlement of freight documents, such as freight orders and freight bookings. Creating inbound and outbound deliveries for orders with materials managed in a decentralized WMS (or EWM) also triggers an integration between orders (e.g., purchase orders and sales orders) and corresponding WMSs.

8.7 Important Terminology

In this chapter, the following terminology we use is important to know for the exam:

- **Activity area**
  An organizational data element in the EWM structure. Activity areas are used to define bin sorting and group storage bins across storage types logically.

- **Freight booking**
  A freight booking is a transportation management order whose execution is planned by the carrier.

- **Freight order**
  A freight order is a transportation management order whose execution is planned by the carrier or shipper. (The shipper is your company in sales and distribution.)

- **Freight settlement document (FSD)**
  An FSD is a document used in the freight costing and settlement phase of transportation management. This document forms a basis for cost distribution and freight settlement.

- **Freight unit**
  A freight unit is the smallest set of materials that can be transported together. This unit is a basis for transportation planning and execution.

- **Goods issue**
  This goods movement in inventory management or warehouse management indicates the reduction of stock due to the delivery of products or a withdrawal of the material.

- **Goods movement**
  The general name of all physical or logical movements of materials. Goods movements usually change stock levels or lead to material consumption. Goods receipts, goods issues, stock transfers, and transfer postings are examples of goods movements.

- **Goods receipt**
  A goods movement in inventory management or warehouse management is used to receive materials and services in several logistics processes. A goods receipt for a stock material (for the stock) increases the stock level and updates the stock accounts in financial accounting.
- **Inbound/outbound delivery order**
  In EWM, no transfer order exists. Instead, all physical movements in the warehouse are planned and executed by inbound/outbound delivery orders.
- **Inventory**
  All goods and materials in a company's stock at a particular time.
- **Movement type**
  This key classifies a goods movement in inventory management. Its value determines the procedure used in the movement and what accounts in financial accounting are updated as a result of the goods movement.
- **Nonstock material**
  Material that you purchase when you need it. You can process nonstock materials in the system without having a material master record.
- **Quant**
  A quant is a quantity or batch of material with similar characteristics (e.g., material number, batch number, plant, and stock category) in a storage bin. Quants are used for inventory management of materials in the storage bin.
- **Stock material**
  The material you constantly keep in stock. All stock materials must have a material master record in the system.
- **Stock transfer**
  A goods movement that involves a physical transfer of stock from one location to another. A stock transfer can be executed, in either a one-step or two-step procedure, between storage locations, between plants, or between company codes.
- **Stock transport order**
  This particular purchase order can be used for internal procurement (i.e., for stock transfers between plants or company codes). You can also process stock transport orders with or without delivery. The one-step procedure is not supported for stock transport orders.
- **Stock type**
  A stock type subdivides stock in a storage location and defines a material's usability in business transactions. Three stock types are available in the system: unrestricted-use stock, quality inspection stock, and blocked stock.
- **Storage bin**
  A storage bin is the smallest physical storage space in the warehouse structure and organizational data in the WMS.

- **Storage location**
  A storage location is organizational data in inventory management. Physical inventory is managed at the storage location level.
- **Storage section**
  A storage section is an organizational subdivision of a storage type that represents a group of storage bins with similar characteristics for putaway tasks.
- **Storage type**
  A storage type is a subdivision of the warehouse number. This storage area can represent either a physical or a logical subdivision of the warehouse complex.
- **Transfer order**
  A warehouse management order that forms a basis for the planning and execution of all physical movements (e.g., picking, putaway) in the warehouse complex.
- **Transfer posting**
  This goods movement changes a material number, batch number, or stock type. A transfer posting does not necessarily involve the physical movement of a material. Three transfer posting categories are available in the system: material-to-material, stock-to-stock, and consignment-to-stock.
- **Transfer requirement**
  A transfer requirement is a request for a transfer order in warehouse management.
- **Transportation unit**
  You can use transportation units to consolidate freight units in transportation planning. You can assign transportation units to freight orders.
- **Warehouse number**
  A warehouse number is the highest organizational level in the warehouse structure, represents a physical warehouse complex, and must be assigned to a storage location.

8.8 Practice Questions

These practice questions will help you evaluate your understanding of the topics covered in this chapter. The questions shown are similar to those found on the certification examination. Although none of these questions will be found on the exam itself, they will allow you to review your knowledge of the subject. Select the correct answers and then check the completeness of your answers in the next section. Remember that you must select all correct answers on the exam and select only correct answers to receive credit for the question.

1. Which of the following are the key tasks of inventory management? (There are three correct answers.)

- [x] A. Management of inventory on a quantity basis
- [ ] B. Management of inventory on a location basis at storage bins
- [x] C. Management of goods movements
- [x] D. Physical inventory
- [ ] E. Management of internal traffic within the warehouse complex

2. Which of the following are organizational data in the WMS? (There are two correct answers.)

- [ ] A. Storage location
- [x] B. Storage type
- [ ] C. Warehouse complex
- [x] D. Warehouse number

3. Which of the following are stock types that you can use in goods movements? (There are two correct answers.)

- [x] A. Quality inspection stock
- [ ] B. Restricted stock
- [ ] C. Free stock
- [x] D. Blocked stock

4. Which of the following are organizational data in inventory management? (There are two correct answers.)

- [x] A. Storage locations
- [ ] B. Storage areas
- [ ] C. Plants
- [x] D. Storage sections

5. Which of the following are transfer postings in inventory management? (There are two correct answers.)

- [ ] A. Storage location-to-storage location
- [ ] B. Stock transport order
- [x] C. Consignment-to-warehouse stock
- [x] D. Material-to-material

6. Which of the following statements are correct about the goods movements in inventory management? (There are three correct answers.)

☐ A. Transfer postings must involve a physical movement of materials
☒ B. Stock transfers can be executed via a one-step or two-step procedure
☐ C. In the two-step procedure, the stock immediately appears in the unrestricted-use stock of the receiving location when the materials are issued
☒ D. You can use stock transport orders for stock transfers to take advantage of purchase orders in stock transfers
☒ E. A material document is created upon entering a goods movement

7. What are the advantages of using stock transport orders? (There are three correct answers.)

☒ A. You can plan the goods receipts
☒ B. You can trigger stock transfers via purchase requisitions
☐ C. It is only executed by using a one-step procedure
☒ D. Cost of delivery can be recorded for the material valuation
☐ E. It simplifies material-to-material transfer postings

8. Which of the following goods movements result in an accounting document? (There are two correct answers.)

☐ A. Stock-to-stock transfer postings
☒ B. Stock transfers between company codes
☐ C. Stock transfers between storage locations
☒ D. Transfer postings to change the material number

9. Which of the following goods movements is used for planned or unplanned material withdrawal in production?

☐ A. Stock transfers
☐ B. Transfer postings
☒ C. Goods issues
☐ D. Goods receipts

10. Which of the following goods movements can increase the unrestricted-use stock in a plant? (There are two correct answers.)

☐ A. Goods issue
☒ B. Goods receipt

- ☒ C. Transfer postings between stock types
- ☐ D. Two-step stock transfers between storage locations

11. Which of the following warehouse management documents can be triggered by other business processes in SAP S/4HANA to request the physical movement of materials in a warehouse complex?

- ☐ A. Outbound delivery orders
- ☒ B. Transfer requirements
- ☒ C. Transfer orders
- ☐ D. Transport orders

12. How can you create a transfer requirement? (There are two correct answers.)

- ☒ A. Automatically from the release of a production order
- ☐ B. Manually with reference to outbound delivery
- ☒ C. Manually with reference to a material document
- ☐ D. Automatically by generating a material document

13. Which of the following is a recommended solution for companies using fixed bin strategy or non-SAP solutions for warehouse management?

- ☒ A. Lean warehouse management
- ☐ B. Warehouse management
- ☐ C. EWM
- ☐ D. Decentralized warehouse management

14. Which of the following is a recommended solution for large warehouses that require automated warehouse movements?

- ☐ A. Lean warehouse management
- ☐ B. Warehouse management
- ☒ C. EWM
- ☐ D. No warehouse management

15. Which of the following represents a batch of a material putaway in a storage bin with the same warehouse movement?

- ☒ A. Quant
- ☐ B. Material group
- ☐ C. Product group
- ☐ D. Storage unit

16. Which of the following can be used to execute picking in EWM?
    - ☒ A. Outbound delivery order
    - ☐ B. Transfer order
    - ☐ C. Inbound delivery document
    - ☐ D. Transfer requirement

17. Which of the following is the smallest set of materials transportable together?
    - ☐ A. Package unit
    - ☐ B. Transportation unit
    - ☐ C. Container unit
    - ☒ D. Freight unit

18. Which of the following freight documents are executed in transportation management? (There are two correct answers.)
    - ☒ A. Freight order
    - ☐ B. Freight request
    - ☒ C. Freight booking
    - ☐ D. Stock transport order

19. Which of the following are transportation requirements in transportation management? (There are three correct answers.)
    - ☒ A. Sales orders
    - ☐ B. Transfer requirements
    - ☒ C. Purchase orders
    - ☐ D. Transfer postings
    - ☒ E. Inbound/outbound deliveries

20. Which of the following documents are created in the costing and settlement phase of transportation management? (There are three correct answers.)
    - ☒ A. Purchase order
    - ☐ B. Freight booking
    - ☒ C. FSD
    - ☒ D. Service entry sheet
    - ☐ E. Freight order

21. Which of the following transfers costs from transportation management to materials management?

    ☐ A. Purchase order
    ☐ B. Material document
    ☒ C. FSD
    ☐ D. Invoice

22. Which of the following are the touchpoints of integration between inventory management and sales and distribution? (There are two correct answers.)

    ☒ A. Goods issue posting
    ☐ B. Billing
    ☒ C. Availability check
    ☐ D. Goods receipt posting

23. Which of the following are the touchpoints of integration between warehouse management and production? (There are two correct answers.)

    ☐ A. Settlement
    ☒ B. Order release
    ☐ C. Sales and operations planning (S&OP)
    ☒ D. Material staging

24. Which of the following are used to trigger warehouse movements in decentralized warehouse management? (There are two correct answers.)

    ☒ A. Inbound delivery
    ☐ B. Goods issue
    ☐ C. Transfer requirement
    ☒ D. Outbound delivery

25. Which of the following makes a goods movement relevant to financial accounting?

    ☒ A. Movement type
    ☐ B. Stock type
    ☐ C. Item category
    ☐ D. Material number

8.9 Practice Question Answers and Explanations

1. Correct answers: **A, C, and D**
   The key tasks of inventory management are managing inventory on a quantity basis, managing inventory on a value basis, managing goods movements, and physical inventory. Management of inventory at the storage bin level and management of movement traffic within the warehouse complex are tasks of warehouse management.

2. Correct answers: **B and D**
   The warehouse number is the highest organizational level in the WMS. It is assigned to at least one storage location to map the physical warehouse complex into the system. A storage location is organizational data in inventory management. A storage type is organizational data in warehouse management and a subdivision of a warehouse number and represents a storage area or a physical or logical subdivision of a warehouse complex.

3. Correct answers: **A and D**
   The following are stock types can be used in goods movements: unrestricted-use stock, quality inspection stock, and blocked stock. Unrestricted-use stock can be used in all business transactions. Quality inspection stock includes stock materials reserved for quality inspection purposes. You cannot issue stocks in quality inspection stock or in blocked stock. MRP can consider quality inspection stock, but blocked stock counts are not available in the availability check.

4. Correct answers: **A and C**
   Clients, company codes, plants, and storage locations are organizational data in inventory management. A storage type (storage area) is organizational data in the WMS. A storage section is an organizational subdivision of a storage type.

5. Correct answers: **C and D**
   On the certification exam, a transfer posting is a category of goods movements without physical movements, such as material-to-material, consignment-to-own stock, or stock-to-stock movements. A stock transport order is used for stock transfers in internal procurement (between plants or company codes).

6. Correct answers: **B, D, and E**
   On the certification exam, a transfer posting is a category of goods movements without physical movements. Stock transfers involve physical movements of stock between locations, and they can be executed via one-step or two-step procedures. The two-step procedure enables the recording of the material's actual receipt at the receiving location (by posting a goods receipt). Until the goods receipt is posted, the issued stock appears in stock called *stock-in-transit*. All goods movements posted in the system are documented through automatically generated material documents.

7. Correct answers: **A, B, and D**

   A stock transport order is a particular purchase order used for (long-distance) stock transfers in internal procurement processes between plants or company codes. You may prefer this type of stock transfer between plants to take advantage of the purchase order's functions, such as triggering the stock transfer by creating purchase requisitions from MRP; tracking the stock transfer by using the purchase order history; planning the receipt of the stock at the receiving plant; negotiating prices for the transferred stock; posting goods receipts directly to consumption (in maintenance, production, or projects); or taking the delivery cost of transferred stock into account. Materials in a stock transport order can be issued by creating a delivery or without a delivery. A material-to-material posting is a transfer posting without physical movement. Stock transport orders are not used for transfer postings.

8. Correct answers: **B and D**

   Stock-to-stock transfer postings and stock transfers between the storage locations have no impact on financial accounting. Thus, no accounting document is created for these types of goods movements. However, a stock transfer between company codes decreases the stock at the issuing company code and increases the stock at the receiving company code, which means the movement leads to a change in the total stock value.

9. Correct answer: **C**

   A goods issue is the type of goods movement you must use for material withdrawals in production. A planned material withdrawal can be made by using a goods issue against reservations generated when you save or release the production order. An unplanned withdrawal is executed by using a goods issue against the production order.

10. Correct answers: **B and C**

    Goods receipts against purchase orders for stock materials increase the unrestricted-use stock. The two-step stock transfer between storage locations (in the same plant) does not change the plant's unrestricted-use stock. A goods issue leads to a decrease in the stock, not an increase. Transfer postings move stock between stock types, for instance, from quality inspection stock to unrestricted-use stock and can change the total unrestricted-use stock in a plant.

11. Correct answer: **B**

    When you post a goods movement in inventory management (e.g., a goods receipt against a purchase order for a material managed at the warehouse), the system automatically creates a transfer requirement to request the material putaway into a storage bin. The physical movement is carried out with a transfer order created against the transfer requirement. You can create transfer orders in the WMS with reference to several source documents, including transfer requirements, inbound/outbound deliveries, and material documents.

12. Correct answers: **A and C**

    The system automatically creates a transfer requirement when you post a goods movement or release a production order with a component managed at a warehouse. You can also manually create transfer requirements with reference to a material document. Transfer orders (not transfer requirements) are created against inbound/outbound deliveries.

13. Correct answer: **A**

    Lean warehouse management is recommended for businesses using a fixed bin warehouse. It is also recommended if your company uses a non-SAP solution for warehouse management and wants the processes for warehouse management to be uniform in the system.

14. Correct answer: **C**

    EWM is a recommended solution for medium-sized or large warehouses that require the automation of warehouse movements. A regular WMS is a suitable solution for small and medium-sized warehouses.

15. Correct answer: **A**

    A quant represents a quantity or batch of material with similar characteristics in a storage bin. The system creates different quants for different batches of the same material in a storage bin. Quants enable you to perform inventory management of a stock of material at the storage bin level.

16. Correct answer: **A**

    Outbound delivery orders can be used to execute the picking of materials from storage bins in EWM. Transfer orders are not used in an EWM system but (for picking/putaway) in a regular WMS.

17. Correct answer: **D**

    A freight unit is the smallest set of materials transportable together and forms a basis for transportation planning. They are created from transportation requirements. In planning, you can assign freight units to freight documents, such as freight orders.

18. Correct answers: **A and C**

    Freight orders and freight bookings are executed in the transportation execution phase of transportation management. Stock transport orders can only be used as a transportation requirement (in the order management phase), not a document executed in transportation management.

19. Correct answers: **A, C, and E**

    In the order management phase of transportation management, the system regards sales orders, purchase orders, returns, (inbound/outbound) deliveries, and stock transport orders as transportation requirements. Freight units are created from transportation requirements.

20. **Correct answers: A, C, and D**

In the freight costing and settlement phase of transportation management, you calculate the costs and charges and create an FSD. This FSD is then posted to materials management, where a purchase order and a service entry sheet are created. Freight orders and freight bookings are created in the planning phase of transportation management.

21. **Correct answer: C**

Related to the previous question, an FSD forms a basis for cost distribution and the transfer of transportation management costs to materials management. In materials management, purchase orders and service entry sheets are created for the carrier's transportation services provided to you.

22. **Correct answers: A and C**

A goods issue posting decreases in inventory quantities and values. In the availability check, the sales order integrates with inventory management to check for the available stock for a saleable material. A goods receipt posting is a part of purchasing, not sales and distribution. Billing passes the sales process to financial accounting and is not involved with inventory management.

23. **Correct answers: B and D**

When you release a production order with a warehouse-managed material component, a transfer requirement is created automatically to request a warehouse movement for the material withdrawal. You can also use warehouse management or EWM activities for material staging to transfer materials to production bins.

24. **Correct answers: A and D**

In decentralized warehouse management, there is no transfer requirement. You trigger and control warehouse movements via inbound/outbound deliveries. A goods issue posting can be the final step of an outbound delivery process.

25. **Correct answer: A**

When you enter a goods movement, you must choose a movement type. The movement type plays a critical role in classifying the goods movement, specifying movement procedures (one-step or two-step procedures) and determining the accounts in financial accounting that are updated upon entry of the goods movement. Updates in financial accounting are documented in the automatically generated accounting documents triggered by the goods movement.

8.10 Test Takeaway

In this chapter, you learned the key tasks related to inventory management, warehouse management, and transportation management in SAP S/4HANA.

Inventory management is concerned with managing stocks on a quantity and value basis, managing goods movements in logistics processes, and physical inventory. A physical inventory takes place at the storage location level. Goods receipts, Goods issues, stock transfers, and transfer postings are goods movements managed in inventory management. A movement type is an essential key for classifying a goods movement, specifying the movement's procedures and determining the accounts updated by the goods movement. Inventory management integrates with other logistics modules, such as purchasing, sales and distribution, production, plant maintenance, and Project System through various goods movements.

Warehouse management is concerned with location-based inventory management at the storage bin level and managing internal stock movements within the warehouse complex. You need to create a warehouse number and assign it to a storage location to map your warehouse complex into the system. The storage bin is the smallest storage space in the warehouse. SAP S/4HANA supports using a WMS centrally or decentrally. Transfer requirements (requests for transfer orders) and transfer orders are essential documents in warehouse management for requesting, planning, and executing physical movements in a warehouse. A transfer order executes all physical movements (e.g., picking and putaway) in the warehouse complex.

SAP EWM has been recently embedded into SAP S/4HANA and supports medium and large warehouses that require automated goods movements and enhanced optimization tools for planning and executing warehouse tasks. EWM uses inbound delivery and outbound delivery orders for the planning and execution of warehouse movements. Warehouse management and EWM are both tightly integrated with inventory management and other system modules (production, purchasing, sales and distribution, plant maintenance, Project System) during business transactions.

SAP TM supports all activities during the physical transportation of materials from one location to another. This solution is integrated with orders and deliveries in logistics processes (e.g., purchasing and fulfillment) to support seamless transportation planning to transport the materials in business processes. Freight units, the smallest set of materials that can be transported together, are assigned to freight orders and freight bookings, playing a pivotal role in planning, executing, and monitoring end-to-end transportation processes. The FSD transfers costs in transportation management to materials management, where you create a purchase order (for the services provided to you by the carrier). The FSD forms a basis for freight settlement and cost distribution.

We've now completed our review of topics relevant to inventory management, warehouse management, and transportation management. The next chapter covers the key topics related to SAP S/4HANA's Project System module.

Chapter 9
Project System

Techniques You'll Master

- Understand the key topics of Project System in SAP S/4HANA
- Describe the characteristics of a project and the project structuring elements in Project System
- Explain the phases of a project and perform system transactions for planning, budgeting, execution, and closing projects
- Identify the touchpoints of integration between the Project System module in SAP S/4HANA and other system modules

This chapter of the book covers all certification-relevant topics of the Project System module in SAP S/4HANA. We'll describe project structuring elements; explain the system transactions supporting planning, budget, execution, and period-end closing phases of a project in SAP S/4HANA; and highlight potential integration scenarios.

Project management is a business process that involves planning and organizing a company's internal and external resources to accomplish a unique goal with specific quality requirements under particular time, capacity, budget, and resource constraints. SAP S/4HANA provides project structuring elements to map your company's projects into the system. The Project System module in SAP S/4HANA supports planning, budgeting, monitoring, execution, and closing tasks for project structuring elements.

> **Real-World Scenario**
>
> By nature, projects are cross-departmental, unique, complex; they are of strategic importance; and they involve a high degree of risk. Projects usually have specific quality requirements and particular constraints, such as time, capacity, resources, and budget limitations. Project tasks are typically relevant to several business processes such as procurement, materials planning, production, plant maintenance, human resources (HR), financial accounting, and controlling.
>
> To achieve the precise targets of a project with the desired quality requirements, the planning, budgeting, execution, and closing tasks of a project must be performed integrated with all relevant business processes.
>
> As an SAP consultant, you should understand how a company's projects can be structured in the system, how project tasks can be accurately planned and successfully executed under the given constraints with integrations to other system modules, and how project costs and revenues can be settled to relevant receivers in SAP S/4HANA.

9.1 Objectives of This Portion of the Test

This portion of the certification aims to test your knowledge of the key topics of Project System that support the planning, control, and execution of projects in SAP S/4HANA integrated with other business processes. The certification exam includes questions about the project structures, project characteristics, and system transactions in project planning, control, execution, and period-end closing. SAP consultants are expected to understand all integrations between the Project System module and other system modules.

For the certification exam, business process integration consultants must have a good understanding of the following topics:

- Characteristics of projects
- Project structuring elements and their assignments to master and organizational data in other modules
- Phases of projects
- Touchpoints of integration between Project System and other business processes

Note
Topics related to Project System cover 8%–12% of the questions in the certification exam.

9.2 Data Structures for Project System

SAP S/4HANA provides the fully integrated Project System module to support planning and implementation tasks for internally and externally financed projects. In this section, we explain certification-relevant concepts related to Project System. In particular, we introduce you to the elements of a project structure and explain the relationships between project structuring elements and other system modules.

9.2.1 Project Structuring Elements

A *project* is a structured and complex set of tasks planned to be implemented to achieve a unique goal, with specific quality requirements under certain time, capacity, budget, and resource constraints, as shown in Figure 9.1.

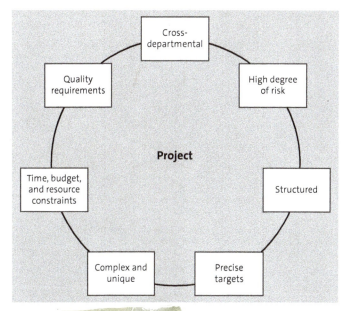

Figure 9.1 Characteristics of Projects

The Project System module provides project structuring elements that enable you to map a company's projects into the system. In the framework of structuring a project, you must answer the following two questions under the given project constraints (e.g., time, quality, budget, and capacity):

- **How is the project organized? (Responsibility-oriented structure)**
  A work breakdown structure (WBS) is a hierarchical model that organizes project tasks and defines responsibilities. The WBS is also used for evaluating aggregate data and allocating budgets. A WBS consists of hierarchically structured WBS elements, forming the basis for planning (process, costs, scheduling, capacity); costing; and control. Figure 9.2 shows the hierarchy graphic of a WBS in a project.

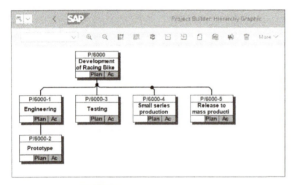

Figure 9.2 WBS in a Project Hierarchy Graphic

- **How is the project processed? (Process-oriented structure)**
  A network is a set of activities linked to each other by relationships, as shown in Figure 9.3. You can use one or more project networks to plan, control, and monitor the processing of project activities.

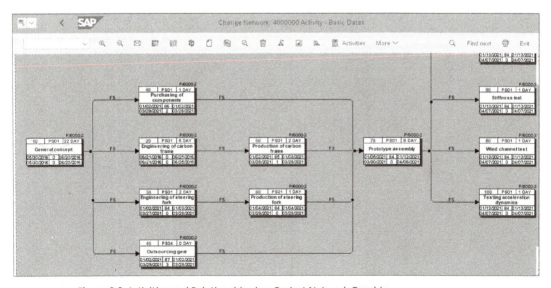

Figure 9.3 Activities and Relationships in a Project Network Graphic

You can use the Project Builder (Transaction CJ20N) to create, edit, and display the project, as shown in Figure 9.2 and Figure 9.3 for responsibility-oriented structures (WBS) and process-oriented structures (network), respectively, in a project.

The Project System module provides the following project structuring elements:

- The project definition
- WBS elements
  - Planning elements
  - Account assignment elements
  - Billing elements
- Networks
- Activities
  - Internally processed activities
  - Externally processed activities
  - General cost activities
- Material components
- Relationships
- Milestones

In the following sections, we describe these project structuring elements and show you how to maintain them in the Project Builder.

Project Definition

A project definition, shown in Figure 9.4 in the Project Builder, uniquely identifies the project in the system. This element includes dates, control data, and organizational information valid for the entire project structure. When you create WBS elements, the default values in the project definition are copied to the WBS elements. For instance, when you select the statistical indicator in the **Control** view of project definition, this setting will be transferred to all new WBS elements in the project. A statistical WBS element does not carry actual costs (or revenues) and it cannot be settled. You can define a project currency and assign the entire project to a controlling area, company code, business area, plant, or profit center in the project definition.

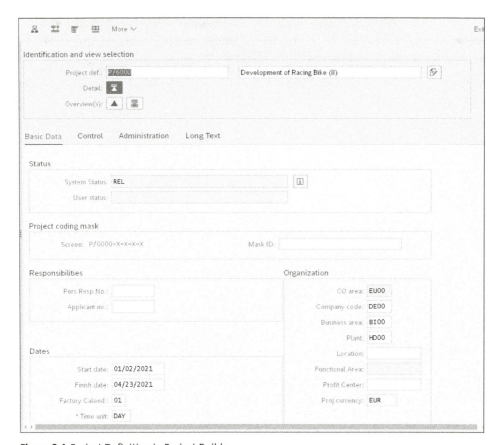

Figure 9.4 Project Definition in Project Builder

WBS Elements

A WBS element is a structural element in the project's WBS. A WBS element can represent a task, a partial task, or a work package in a project. WBS element master data is structured into views, such as **Basic Data**, **Dates**, **Assignments**, **Control**, **Progress**, **Documents**, and **Settlement Rule**. Three types of WBS elements are available in the system:

- **Planning element**
  A WBS element included in cost planning.
- **Account assignment element**
  A WBS element to which you can make actual postings and commitment postings.
- **Billing element**
  A WBS element that can be billed and can have revenues posted to it.

You can use operative indicators in the **Basic Data** view for determining the type of the WBS element. In the **Control** view, select the **Statistical** indicator checkbox to specify that the WBS element is only for statistical purposes and does not carry actual costs.

WBS elements carrying actual costs can be settled, so you can enter a settlement rule for these WBS elements. You cannot settle statistical WBS elements.

You can assign a WBS element to a responsible cost center, profit center, plant, company code, business area, plant, or technical object in the **Assignments** view, as shown in Figure 9.5. Note that WBS elements in a project can be assigned to different company codes assigned to the same controlling area.

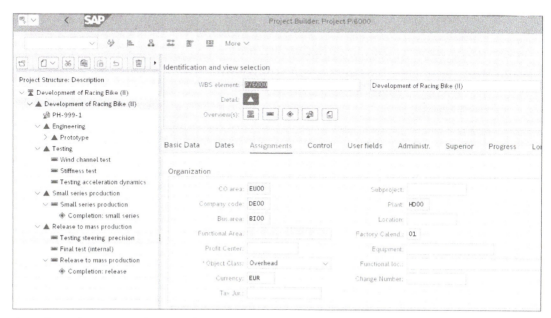

Figure 9.5 Assignment Data in a WBS Element

In the WBS element header, in the activity overview, you can define the project activities and assign them to the WBS element, as shown in Figure 9.6.

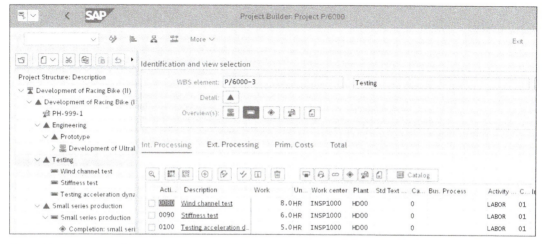

Figure 9.6 Project Activities Assigned to a WBS Element

You can also create new WBS elements, networks, and milestones and assign them to a WBS element by using the other overviews. Using the document overview, you can see document info records assigned to WBS elements. Note that document info records can also be assigned to activities.

Networks

A network is a set of activities connected with relationships; you must define activities, activity elements, and relationships to create a network. Networks enable you to structure the flow of a project or task. You create a network at the plant level, and the corresponding company code and controlling area are assigned to the network at the header level. You can also assign a network to a business area, profit center, and responsible cost center at the header level.

Network header data is structured into several views, such as the **Scheduling**, **Assignments**, **Control**, **Administr.** (administrative data), and **LongText** views. In the **Assignments** view, shown in Figure 9.7, you can assign the network to a WBS element or a sales order to determine where the network is settled.

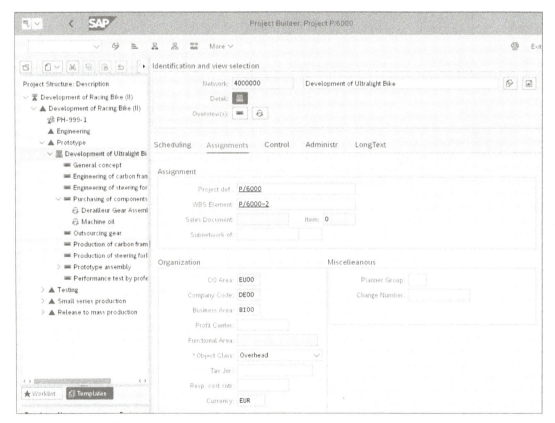

Figure 9.7 Assignments Data in a Network Header

A settlement rule can be defined for the network if no account has been assigned. If you assign a network to a WBS element, the plant for the WBS element must be the same as the plant for the network (and the network's activities).

Using the activity and relationships overviews in the network header screen, as shown in Figure 9.8, you can create activities in the network ❶ and define relationships between network activities ❷.

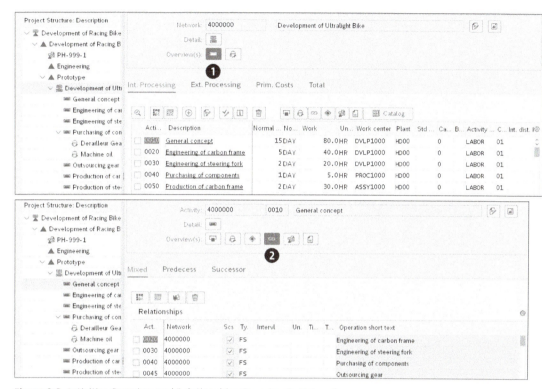

Figure 9.8 Activities Overview and Relationships Overview in Network

Activities

Activities enable you to define the process components in a project by maintaining the following data:

- Duration
- Work center or purchasing data
- Activity type
- Start and finish times
- Resources to execute the activity
- Costs
- Material requirements

Activities master data is structured into views, with header data in the **Internal** and **Extnl** (external) as well as the **Dates**, **Assignments**, and **Progress** views. Several organizational data assignments are possible in the activity data. When you assign an activity to a network, the controlling area, business area, company code, and plant assignments are inherited from the network header. You can also assign the activity to a profit center.

In the header data, you must maintain the control key that determines the activity category, which determines which business transactions must be executed for the activity. Four categories of activities exist in Project System:

- **Internally processed activity**
  For planning and executing activities at work centers.
- **Externally processed activity**
  For planning and procuring external services.
- **Service activity**
  For planning and procuring external services by using service specifications (e.g., service entry, receipt of service via service entry sheet, and acceptance of service).
- **General cost activity**
  For planning and assigning primary costs.

Work centers and their capacities are used for internally processed activities. For capacity planning, scheduling, and costing of an internally processed activity, you must enter a work center number, duration, dates, and activity type, as shown in Figure 9.9.

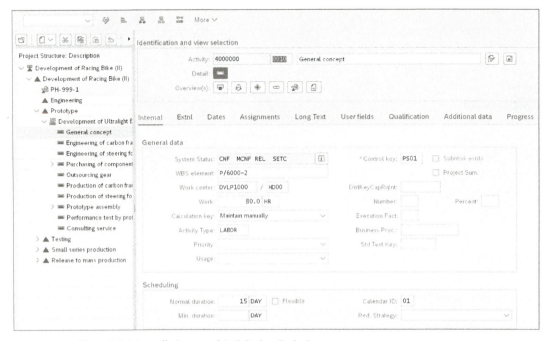

Figure 9.9 Internally Processed Activity in a Project

Externally processed and service activities are linked to procurement. You must maintain purchasing data (e.g., vendor, purchasing organization, and purchasing group) for these activity categories. Purchase requisitions are generated to initiate an external procurement process for externally processed and service activities. Based on project settings, the system generates purchase requisitions either upon saving or releasing the project. You can see the generated purchase requisition in the activity master record, as shown in Figure 9.10.

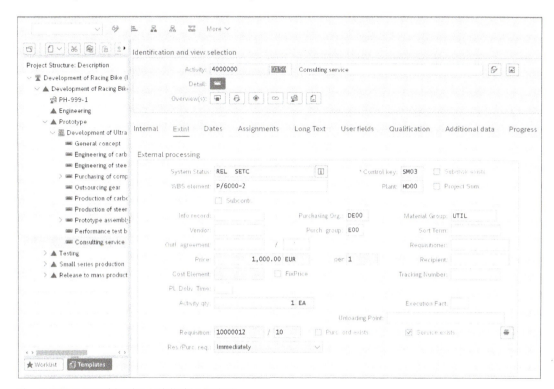

Figure 9.10 External Service Activity in a Project

General cost activities are linked to cost elements, as shown in Figure 9.11. This category of activities is used to collect travel and other types of costs in a project. You must enter the primary cost element in its master data. You can enter a settlement rule for a general cost element.

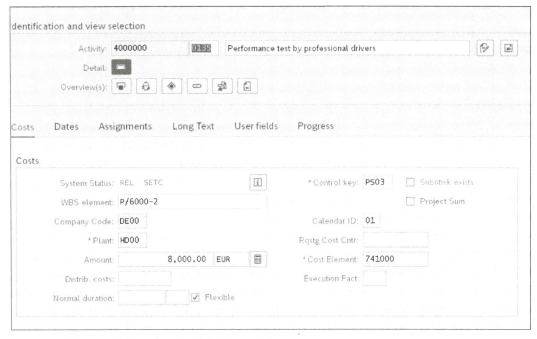

Figure 9.11 General Cost Activity in a Project

Material Components

You can use the components overview to assign material components to an activity, as shown in Figure 9.12.

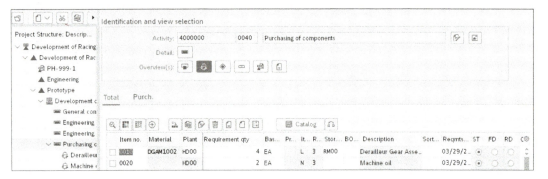

Figure 9.12 Material Components Assigned to a Network Activity

You can assign the following categories of materials to a project activity:

- Stock item
- Nonstock item
- Variable-size item
- Text item

The system generates reservations for stock items and purchase requisitions for nonstock items; the material component assignment links a network (or project) activity to materials management. You can see the purchase requisition number for nonstock material components in the component master record, as shown in Figure 9.13.

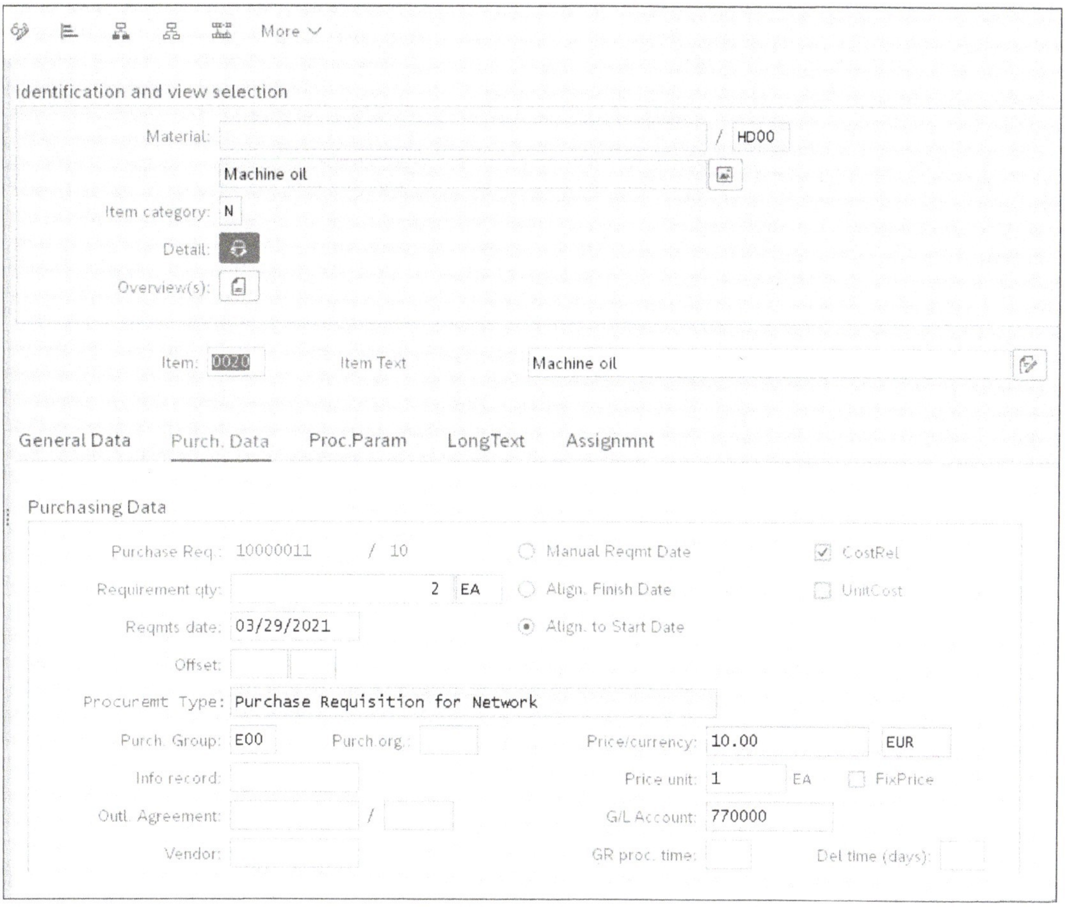

Figure 9.13 Nonstock Material Component Assigned to a Network Activity

You can use the activity elements overview to breakdown an activity into activity elements.

Relationships

Relationships enable you to define a chronological sequence of network activities. In the relationship overview of an activity header, you can define relationships between the current activity and other network activities, as shown in Figure 9.14. You must use the following procedure to define a relationship between two activities:

- Determine which activity is the predecessor and which activity is the successor
- Determine the type of relationship between predecessor and successor

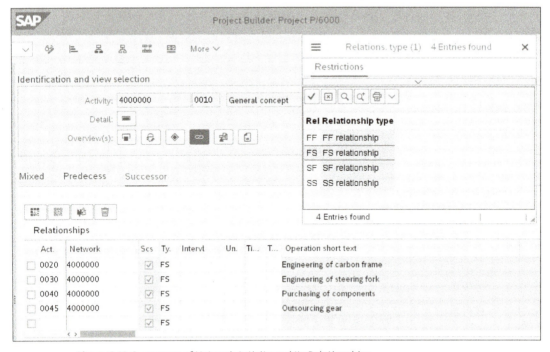

Figure 9.14 Successors of Network Activity and Its Relationships

Four types of relationships between are possible between predecessor and successor activities in a network:

- FS (finish-start relationship)
- SS (start-start relationship)
- FF (finish-finish relationship)
- SF (start-finish relationship)

Milestones

You can use milestones to mark the following events:

- Events of strategic importance
- Transitions between phases of a project
- Completion of a stage

Milestones can be assigned to WBS elements or activities. Depending on where a milestone is assigned, different use cases are available. For instance, milestones can be used to copy the actual date of the milestone into the billing plan in sales and distribution or to trigger predefined milestone functions. You define the usage of a milestone in its master record.

You can create and assign milestones in the milestones overview of WBS elements or activities, as shown in Figure 9.15.

Figure 9.15 Basic Data of a Milestone in a Project

9.2.2 Data Assignments

The Project System module does not have project-specific organizational data. You can create projects and their structuring elements at different levels of the company's organizational structure. Project structuring elements can be assigned to each other based on the following rules, as shown in Figure 9.16:

- Several WBS elements can be assigned to a project definition.
- You can assign WBS elements to other WBS elements to create a multilevel WBS hierarchy.
- Several networks can be assigned to a WBS element.
- Several activities can be assigned to a WBS element. An activity can be assigned to only one WBS element.
- Several activities can be assigned to a network. An activity can be assigned to only one network. Activities assigned to different WBS elements can be assigned to a network.
- Activities assigned to a network must be connected via relationships.
- An activity may have several activity elements and material components.
- Several milestones can be assigned to a WBS element or activity.

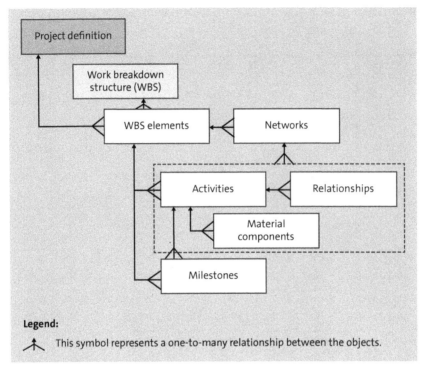

Figure 9.16 Data Assignments between Project Structuring Elements

9.3 Key Processes of Project System

Figure 9.17 shows the phases of a project and the Project System functions used in project phases, from planning to budgeting to execution to period-end closing.

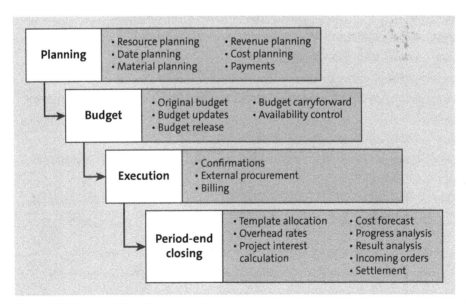

Figure 9.17 Phases and Functions of a Project

9.3.1 Project Planning

Project System provides the Project Builder (Transaction CJ2ON) and Project Planning Board (Transaction CJ27) to support project planning tasks. The Project Planning Board provides a graphic overview (e.g., Gantt charts) of your project's structure and progress, as shown in Figure 9.18. The Project Planning Board displays the interrelationships of project elements in the project's organization and the schedule. By simplifying planning, controlling, and monitoring tasks for the project, with the Project Planning Board, you can easily create, change, and display projects.

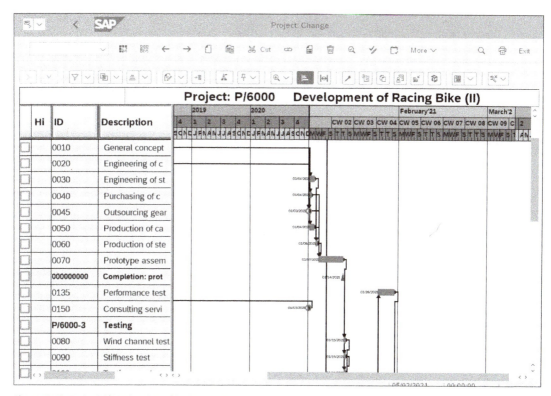

Figure 9.18 Project Planning Board in Project System

Once you finish structuring your project by defining its WBS structure, networks, and activities, you can plan the following facets of a project:

- Dates
- Resources
- Materials
- Revenues
- Cost planning
- Payments

To prepare for the certification exam, we'll explain some of these planning processes in the following subsections.

Scheduling

You can use WBS scheduling or network scheduling to plan the dates. In WBS scheduling, you can use bottom-up planning or top-down planning scenarios; other dates in the hierarchy are calculated by extrapolation. In the bottom-up planning scenario, network activities are scheduled based on the planned dates in the network header, and the scheduled dates are assigned to WBS elements. In the top-down scenario, you manually enter the dates of the WBS element, and the scheduling of assigned activities is performed based on the planned dates of the WBS element. In network scheduling, all activities of a network are scheduled based on backward or forward scheduling. You can also perform overall network scheduling to schedule several networks linked via external relationships.

Resource Planning

In resource planning, you can plan the internal and external resources you can use to execute the project's activities. Figure 9.19 shows the work center, duration, and activity type for an internally processed activity. Capacity planning with work centers, workforce planning, capacity leveling, planning for services, or externally processed activities (creating purchase requisitions) are the tasks that can be carried out in resource planning.

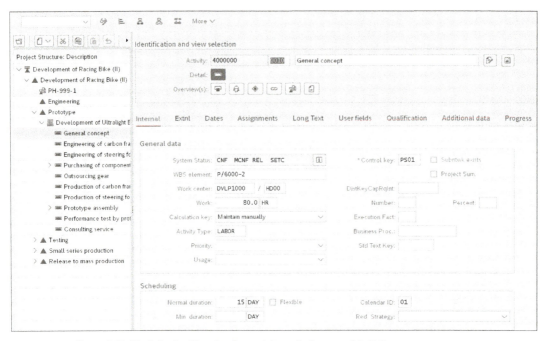

Figure 9.19 Work Center Planning for an Internally Processed Activity

Material Planning

In material planning, you plan the materials required for project activities. The first step is to assign material components to activities, as shown in Figure 9.20. The system generates reservations or purchase requisitions for the material components based on the item category (stock or nonstock) material. The material withdrawal (for stock materials) and delivery (of nonstock materials services) are also planned in material planning.

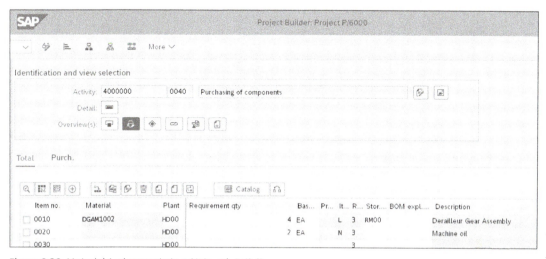

Figure 9.20 Material Assignments to a Network Activity

Cost Planning

In cost planning, you plan the costs you expect to incur during the execution of project activities. The system provides the following cost planning options:

- **Network costing**
  The system automatically calculates the planned costs (for procurement, consumption of resources, and material) based on dates, resource, and material planning results, as shown in Figure 9.21.
- **Planning costs at the WBS level** *Work Breakdown Structures*
  In this type of planning, you plan costs at the WBS element level. You may prefer this approach if you map your project into the system by using only WBS elements. You can choose between the following options:
  - Cost element-based cost planning (e.g., unit costing, detailed planning, and easy cost planning)
  - Period based cost planning (e.g., detailed planning)
  - Structure-oriented (hierarchical) cost planning (e.g., planning costs for each WBS element and breaking down totals by fiscal year)

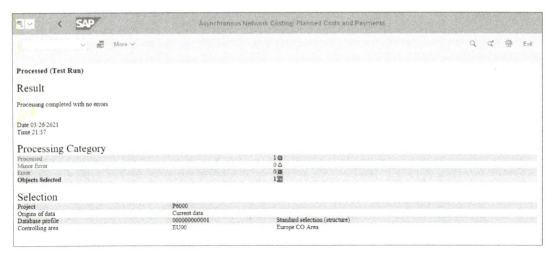

Figure 9.21 Network Costing in Project System

9.3.2 Project Budgeting

In cost planning, you calculate the planned costs of WBS elements and the project's overall plan value; in the budget phase, you transfer values from cost planning and request funds for the project in the form of a budget. In Project System, a project budget is defined as the project's approved cost structure. Once the budget is approved, you distribute the allocated budget to WBS elements (or orders assigned to the WBS element) using a top-down approach, as shown in Figure 9.22.

E...	Lev	WBS Element	Budget	Tran...	Current budget	Distributed	Distributable	Planned total Ver...	Cumulative	Remainder	Release
	1	P/6000	37,570.00	EUR	37,570.00	28,950.00	8,620.00	35,570.00		37,570.00	
	2	P/6000-1		EUR							
	2	P/6000-2	21,000.00	EUR	21,000.00		21,000.00	26,570.00		21,000.00	
	2	P/6000-3	950.00	EUR	950.00		950.00	950.00		950.00	
	2	P/6000-4	5,000.00	EUR	5,000.00		5,000.00	5,000.00		5,000.00	
	2	P/6000-5		EUR	2,000.00		2,000.00	3,050.00		2,000.00	

Figure 9.22 Project Budget

Project networks are not budgeted. The following budget types are available:

- **Original budget**
  Originally allocated budget.
- **Budget updates**
  Adjustments (i.e., transfers, supplements, and returns) in the original budget due to unforeseen events in the project.

- **Current budget**
  The current budget after updates.

You can then release the current budget at the project level or WBS element level to make funds available for a fiscal year. Project System offers a budget carryforward function that enables you to transfer unused funds in a fiscal year to a new fiscal year. The availability control component supports monitoring and controlling project costs by generating warning and error messages when costs occur. This component checks budget releases against the current (assigned) budget.

9.3.3 Project Execution

In the execution phase of the project, the following tasks are carried out:

- Internal and external resources are involved in executing the activities.
- Orders assigned to WBS elements are processed.
- Materials and services are purchased.
- In-house production is performed.
- Goods movements are posted.
- Invoices for procurement are entered.
- Customer invoices are sent.
- Internal cost allocations are made.

Material assignments in material planning play a distinctive role in the determination of tasks in project execution. Next, we discuss how stock and nonstock material assignments impact the workflow in project execution.

Processing Material Components Assigned to Activities

In the planning phase, you assign material components to activities. Depending on the type of the assigned material (stock/nonstock material), different tasks are carried out to execute the project activity. Figure 9.23 shows the different procedures for processing stock and nonstock material components assigned to a project activity.

Stock materials are materials that are kept in stock. Material withdrawal for assigned stock materials is performed by posting a goods issue. Material requirements for some stock materials (finished goods, saleable assemblies) may be covered by in-house production. Based on quantities and dates for these independent requirements, a material bill of materials (BOM) is exploded, and a planned order is scheduled, triggering the creation of a production order. In the execution phase, the production of finished goods or saleable items is followed by sending the produced item to stock (via a goods receipt) and posting a goods issue for the original reservation (withdrawal).

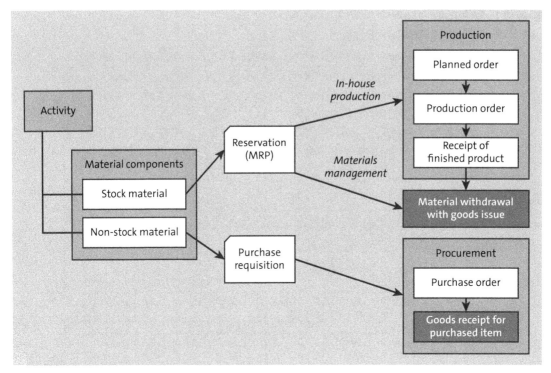

Figure 9.23 Processing Material Components Assigned to Activities

Nonstock materials are not kept in stock. Nonstock material assignments trigger the external procurement process initiated by a purchase requisition. An external procurement process is carried out via a purchase order based on the purchase requisition in the execution phase. This purchase order has an account assignment to the activity's WBS element or network. When purchased items are delivered, a goods receipt is posted. Nonstock items are not sent to stock but to an activity when delivered. The direct consumption of nonstock items is performed by a network activity. The system updates the activity's actual costs by the value of purchased items upon posting the goods receipt. Actuals costs are also updated through invoice verification if a price difference exists between the order and the invoice.

Processing Activities

Another distinctive factor in the execution of a project is the type of activity to be processed. Internal activities are processed in-house at work centers, while externally processed activities or services are purchased from vendors. Internally processed activities require actual time and work confirmation. Externally processed activities require a procurement process updating project costs via invoice verification, as shown in Figure 9.24. Some differences between the purchasing processes for externally processed activities and services include the following:

- Externally processed activities are received by posting goods receipts.
- Services are received by service entry sheets.
- You need to accept services after receiving them.

Figure 9.24 shows the in-house and external procurement processes for three types of activities.

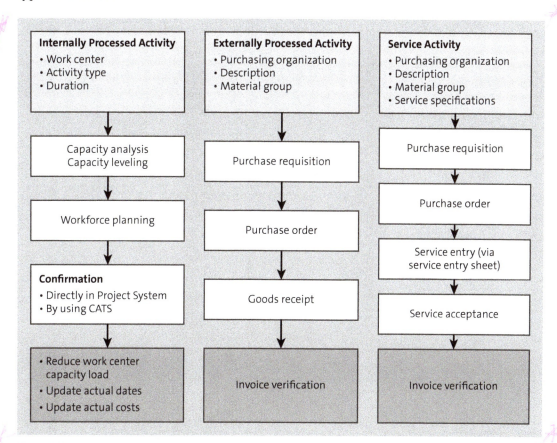

Figure 9.24 In-House Processing and External Procurement for Project Activities

Confirmation

In this phase, you make confirmations to document the state of processing for activities and activity elements in a network. You can make partial or final confirmations (statuses **PCNF** and **CNF**) for activities or activity elements. Entering confirmations for network activities will lock the network.

You have two options to enter confirmations:

- Directly in Project System
- By using the cross-application time sheet (CATS)

Chapter 9 Project System

The following data can be entered during confirmations, as shown in Figure 9.25:

- Actual dates
- Actual durations
- Work done
- Reason for variance
- Forecast values for the remaining work and the remaining duration
- The confirmation status

Figure 9.25 Entering Activity Confirmations in Project System

Saving a confirmation has the following potential impacts:

- Work center capacity load is reduced.
- Actual costs are updated based on confirmed data.

- Actual times and dates are updated.
- Duration, work, and status data are updated in the network.
- Functions in project milestones are activated.
- Goods issues for backflushed materials are posted.
- Personnel administration data is transferred for the calculation of wages.

Entering confirmations for the actual times leads to internal activity allocations between the activity and the cost centers assigned to activity work centers. In this case, the actual cost of the confirmed work is calculated, the cost centers are credited, and the project activity is debited.

Note
You cannot trigger milestone functions by entering confirmations via CATS. Entering actual working hours via CATS provides the following processes with the actual time data:
- Controlling (for internal cost allocations)
- Plant maintenance
- HR
- Customer services
- Project System (for confirmation of activities)

9.3.4 Period-End Closing

In the period-end closing phase, you perform a series of transactions to make sure that all the financial data of a period is finalized and accurately available for enterprise control.

You can use the following period-end closing functions in Project System:

- **Template allocation**
  To distribute overhead from cost centers and activity types.
- **Overhead**
  To calculate the project's overhead on a quantity basis or percentage basis.
- **Interest calculation**
  To evaluate fund commitments based on costs, revenues, and payments.
- **Cost forecast**
  To calculate cost-to-complete based on planned, actual, and forecast data.
- **Progress analysis**
  To compare the actual project status to planned progress values.
- **Result analysis**
  To periodically evaluate the costs and revenues for your project.

- **Incoming orders**
  To determine the outstanding costs and revenues from closed or changed orders assigned to WBS elements.
- **Settlement**
  To settle the actual costs and revenues in projects to settlement receivers based on settlement rules.

Settlement is the key piece of period-end closing. Project objects collect revenues (e.g., billing elements) and costs (e.g., account assignment elements) via material withdrawals, goods receipts, invoices (customer/vendor), activity allocations, distributions, overheads, order settlements, and confirmations. You can settle the actual costs and revenues for projects, WBS elements, networks, or activities, as shown in Figure 9.26. Some projects may require the settlement of WBS elements to a higher-level element directly and then to an external cost object (cost center, profitability segment).

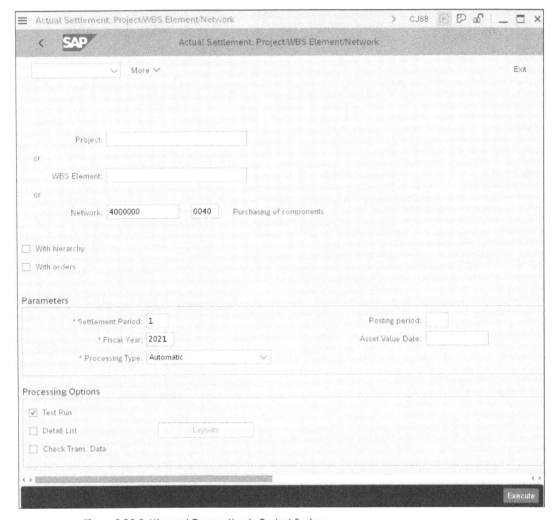

Figure 9.26 Settlement Transaction in Project System

You must define a settlement rule to execute settlements. A settlement rule consists of one or more distribution rules determining the settlement receiver and settlement parameters. Depending on the type of the project, the following settlement receivers can receive costs via settlement:

- General ledger accounts
- Fixed assets
- Orders
- Cost centers
- Profitability segments
- Project objects, including WBS elements, networks, and activities

9.4 Integration with Other Modules

In this section, we explain the touchpoints of integration between Project System and other system modules. We can organize cross-module integrations into two categories:

- Integrations via cross-module data assignments
- Integrations via transactions

9.4.1 Integration via Cross-Module Data Assignments

Cross-module data assignments in the system connect business processes in SAP S/4HANA and lead to data flows between the system's components.

You can assign project structuring elements to the organizational/master data of other modules to incorporate the project into other business processes' organizational structures. Table 9.1 lists potential data assignments for project structuring elements.

Project Element	Organizational/Master Data
Project definition	- Controlling area - Company code - Business area, profit center, plant
WBS elements	- Company code - Business area, profit center, plant - Technical object (functional location/equipment) - Responsible cost center
Networks	- Business area, profit center, plant - Responsible cost center - Sales document

Table 9.1 Project Structuring Elements and Potential Data Assignments

Project Element	Organizational/Master Data
Internally processed activities	- Business area, profit center, plant - Work center
Externally processed activities	- Business area, profit center, plant - Purchasing organization - Purchasing group
Service activities	- Business area, profit center, plant - Purchasing organization - Purchasing group
General cost activities	- Business area, profit center, plant - Cost element
Material components	- Purchasing organization - Purchasing group - Plant - Storage location

Table 9.1 Project Structuring Elements and Potential Data Assignments (Cont.)

These elements play key roles in the following business processes:

- **Management accounting**
  A cost center is a master data in cost center accounting (controlling). WBS elements and networks can be assigned to a responsible cost center in their master records. Projects, WBS elements, networks, and activities can be assigned to profit centers, thus integrating a project with controlling.

- **Plant maintenance**
  Technical objects (functional locations and equipment) are master data in plant maintenance. These objects can be assigned to a project WBS element in their master records, thus integrating a project with plant maintenance.

- **Purchasing**
  Externally processed activities and service activities are assigned to purchasing organizations and purchasing groups (organizational data in purchasing), thus integrating a project with purchasing. Material components are assigned to project activities, which integrates a project with materials management.

- **Financial accounting**
  Project structuring elements can be assigned to company codes and business areas, thus integrating a project with financial accounting.

9.4.2 Integration via Transactions

The Project System module tightly integrates with other system modules via transactions. Some examples of transactions that lead to cross-module integration include the following:

- **Planning**
  In the planning phase, you plan resources (workforces, capacities, external activities, and services); materials; costs; and revenues. In planning transactions, Project System uses data from controlling, materials management, production, and sales and distribution. You can assign sales documents to billing elements (revenue planning) and schedule planned orders for the in-house production of finished products assigned to activities. You assign stock or nonstock materials to activities and trigger the generation of reservations and purchase requisitions for material components. In cost planning, the system calculates the planned cost of activities based on durations, materials, activity types and prices, and orders assigned to WBS elements or networks. Procurement and delivery of materials, services, and externally processed activities are planned. These planning tasks create integration between the project and corresponding system components, such as orders, purchasing, HR, controlling, sales and distribution, inventory management, and production.

- **Execution**
  In the execution phase, internal and external resources are used to execute the activities. Materials are withdrawn, purchased, or produced. Inventory updates (for stock materials), cost element updates, and financial accounting integrations occur. You post goods movements or make service entries to issue the materials and receive services, thus integrating a project with other modules, such as materials management, financial accounting, and controlling. Actual costs are posted to the project. Confirmations trigger data transfers to HR and internal activity allocations between cost centers and the activities. Confirmation can also trigger good issues for backflush materials, thus integrating a project with materials management.

- **Period-end closing**
  In period-end closing, overhead is calculated and distributed. Actual costs and revenues on the project and project objects are settled to settlement receivers, such as general ledger accounts; assets; orders (production order, maintenance order, internal order, sales order); cost centers; and profitability segments, thus integrating a project with corresponding modules.

- **Orders**
  You can assign WBS elements to internal orders, production orders, maintenance orders, and sales orders as account assignment objects. Goods movements, confirmations, and settlements for these orders can trigger cost postings to WBS elements.

- **General ledger postings, distributions, and assessments**
  WBS element is a true controlling object (not just statistical) and thus can be used as an account assignment object when you post to primary cost elements. WBS elements can also receive costs from distributions and assessments.

9.5 Important Terminology

In this chapter, the following terminology related to Project System is important to know for the exam:

- **Activity**
  Activities form an operative basis for a project. Using activities, you can define process components of a project, such as activity types, work center durations, start and finish times, external/internal resources, and material requirements. Four types of activities exist: internally processed activities, externally processed activities, services, and general cost activities.

- **Budget**
  A project's approved cost structure.

- **Milestone**
  Used to mark events of strategic importance, transitions between phases of a project, and the completion of a stage.

- **Network**
  Representing a project's process-based structure, a network consists of activities connected via relationships.

- **Project structuring elements**
  The data you must maintain to create and plan a project, such as the project definition, work breakdown structure (WBS) elements, activities, networks, relationships, milestones, and material components are all elements of a project's structure.

- **Relationship**
  Used to define a chronological sequence of network activities.

- **Settlement**
  A period-end closing transaction that transfers costs and revenues from project elements to settlement receivers based on the distribution rules specified in settlement rules. You can settle a project, WBS element, network, or activity.

- **WBS element**
  An element in a WBS hierarchy. This element can represent a task, a partial task, or a work package in a project. Three types of WBS elements exist: planning elements, account assignment elements, and billing elements.

- **Work breakdown structure (WBS)**
  A hierarchical model of a project that organizes the project's tasks and responsibilities.

9.6 Practice Questions

These practice questions will help you evaluate your understanding of the topics covered in this chapter. The questions shown are similar to those found on the certification examination. Although none of these questions will be found on the exam itself, they will allow you to review your knowledge of the subject. Select the correct answers and then check the completeness of your answers in the next section. Remember that you must select all correct answers on the exam and select only correct answers to receive credit for the question.

1. Which of the following are project structuring elements in Project System? (There are two correct answers.)
   - ☐ A. Purchase requisition
   - ☐ B. Project definition
   - ☐ C. Network
   - ☐ D. Budget

2. Which of the following defines the category of a WBS element in Project System?
   - ☐ A. Control key
   - ☐ B. Construction type
   - ☐ C. Structure indicator
   - ☐ D. Operative indicators

3. Which of the following WBS elements can receive revenue postings?
   - ☐ A. Revenue element
   - ☐ B. Account assignment element
   - ☐ C. Planning element
   - ☐ D. Billing element

4. Which of the following forms an operative basis for a project?
   - ☐ A. Activities
   - ☐ B. WBS elements
   - ☐ C. Milestones
   - ☐ D. Project definition

5. Which of the following forms a hierarchical model and a planning basis for a project?

   ☐ A. Network
   ☐ B. Activities and relationships
   ☐ C. WBS
   ☐ D. Budget

6. Which of the following can be assigned to a WBS element? (There are three correct answers.)

   ☐ A. Milestones
   ☐ B. Relationships
   ☐ C. Activities
   ☐ D. Networks
   ☐ E. Materials

7. Which of the following activity types are assigned to a purchasing organization? (There are two correct answers.)

   ☐ A. Internally processed activity
   ☐ B. Externally processed activity
   ☐ C. Service activity
   ☐ D. General cost activity

8. What can be found in the data for an internally processed activity? (There are two correct answers.)

   ☐ A. Work center
   ☐ B. Purchasing group
   ☐ C. Vendor
   ☐ D. Activity type

9. Which of the following project structure elements trigger automatic purchase requisitions? (There are three correct answers.)

   ☐ A. Billing element
   ☐ B. Service activity
   ☐ C. Material component with item category as the nonstock item
   ☐ D. Network
   ☐ E. Externally processed activity

10. Which of the following item categories for material components can trigger an in-house production?

☐ A. Stock item
☐ B. Nonstock item
☐ C. Variable-size item
☐ D. Text item

11. Which of the following defines the chronological sequence of network activities?

☐ A. Activity types
☐ B. Operations
☐ C. WBS elements
☐ D. Relationships

12. Which of the following are the phases of a project? (There are two correct answers.)

☐ A. Budget
☐ B. Control
☐ C. Period-end closing
☐ D. Completion

13. Which of the following are period-end closing activities for a project? (There are three correct answers.)

☐ A. Interest calculation
☐ B. Confirmation
☐ C. Template allocation
☐ D. Settlement
☐ E. Budget approval

14. Which of the following are integration points between Project System and controlling? (There are two correct answers.)

☐ A. Cost planning
☐ B. Material planning
☐ C. Date planning
☐ D. Confirmation

15. Which of the following budgeting functions can be used in Project System? (There are two correct answers.)

    ☐ A. Budget carryforward
    ☐ B. Availability control
    ☐ C. Confirmation
    ☐ D. Cost forecasting

16. Which of the following statements are correct about issuing materials and receiving services in the execution phase? (There are two correct answers.)

    ☐ A. Services are received by posting a goods receipt
    ☐ B. A goods issue is posted for nonstock materials
    ☐ C. A goods receipt is posted to receive externally processed activities
    ☐ D. Material withdrawal for stock items is carried out via goods issues

17. In which of the following phases does a project collect actual costs? (There are two correct answers.)

    ☐ A. Period-end closing
    ☐ B. Planning
    ☐ C. Execution
    ☐ D. Budget

18. Which of the following objects can be settled? (There are three correct answers.)

    ☐ A. Statistical WBS elements
    ☐ B. Activities
    ☐ C. Projects
    ☐ D. Networks
    ☐ E. Milestones

19. What do you settle in period-end closing? (There are two correct answers.)

    ☐ A. Revenues
    ☐ B. Variances
    ☐ C. Actual costs
    ☐ D. Plan costs

20. Which of the following can be assigned a responsible cost center? (There are two correct answers.)

☐ A. WBS elements
☐ B. Activities
☐ C. Networks
☐ D. Milestones

21. Which of the following can be assigned to a WBS element? (There are three correct answers.)

☐ A. Production orders
☐ B. General ledger accounts
☐ C. Work centers
☐ D. Internal orders
☐ E. Maintenance orders

22. Which of the following triggers and internal activity allocation between a project and cost centers?

☐ A. Confirmation
☐ B. Budget release
☐ C. Goods receipt
☐ D. Material withdrawal

23. Which of the following can transfer costs to a WBS element? (There are three correct answers.)

☐ A. Confirmations
☐ B. Order settlements
☐ C. Assessments and distributions in controlling
☐ D. Scheduling planned orders
☐ E. Creating purchase orders for project reservations

9.7 Practice Question Answers and Explanations

1. Correct answers: **B and C**

   Project definitions, WBS elements, networks, activities, relationships, milestones, and material components are the project structuring elements in Project System. The budget is the approved cost structure of a project, but not a project structuring element. Purchase requisitions can be generated when you create (or release) some activities and material components, but a purchase requisition is not a project structuring element.

2. **Correct answer: D**
Using the operative indicators in WBS master data, you can categorize a WBS element. Structure indicators and construction types are part of functional location master data in plant maintenance and have no relationship with the WBS element. A control key is part of activity data.

3. **Correct answer: D**
A billing element is a WBS element that can be billed and posted on revenues. A revenue element is a general ledger account and has nothing to do with a WBS element. A planning element is a WBS element considered in cost planning. An account assignment element is a WBS element that can be posted actual costs and commitments.

4. **Correct answer: A**
Activities and relationships form an operative basis for a project. WBS elements are used to create a WBS of a project. Milestones trigger some functions, and they are used to mark some strategic events in a project. The project definition uniquely identifies a project in the system and includes information valid for the entire project structure.

5. **Correct answer: C**
A WBS defines the responsibility-oriented structure of a project in the form of a hierarchical model and serves as a planning basis for a project. A network forms the process-oriented structure of a project and consists of activities connected via relationships.

6. **Correct answers: A, C, and D**
You can assign networks, activities, and milestones to WBS elements. Materials are assigned to activities, while relationships define the chronological sequence of activities in a network.

7. **Correct answers: B and C**
Externally processed activities and service activities are performed by external vendors and are relevant to external procurement. Purchase requisitions are created to initiate the purchasing process for these activities. Internally processed activities are carried out in-house at work centers. General cost activities are relevant to a cost element and carry actual costs.

8. **Correct answers: A and D**
Internal activities are carried out in-house at work centers. For capacity planning and scheduling, you must specify the necessary data, such as work center, activity type, and duration. You must maintain vendor and purchasing group data for activities relevant to procurement, such as externally processed activities and service activities.

9. Correct answers: **B, C, and E**

   Some project structuring elements are linked to procurement. For instance, nonstock materials (assigned to activities as material components), service activities, and externally processed activities are relevant to procurement; automatic purchase requisitions are created when you create or release these project elements.

10. Correct answer: **A**

    For stock items assigned to activities, the system generates reservations. A reservation is a request to MRP. If the assigned stock item is a finished product not available in stock, you can cover the requirement by producing it by scheduling a planned order, which triggers the generation of a production order.

11. Correct answer: **D**

    You can use relationships to define the chronological sequence of activities. A relationship is defined between a pair of successor and predecessor activities. No operations data exists in a project. An activity type is master data in controlling and determines the category of work that must be done at the work center.

12. Correct answers: **A and C**

    The following are project phases: planning, budget, execution, and period-end closing. Control and completion are phases of maintenance order processing in plant maintenance.

13. Correct answers: **A, C, and D**

    You can perform interest calculations, template allocations, and settlements in the period-end closing phase. Confirmation is a transaction in the execution phase, while budget approval is a part of the budget phase of a project.

14. Correct answers: **A and D**

    In cost planning, the system calculates the costs of activities assigned to WBS elements or networks. Project System integrates with controlling to transfer the necessary data for cost planning, such as activity types and activity prices for cost centers. You'll enter the actual dates and durations during confirmation, which triggers an internal activity allocation between the project and the costs centers assigned to the activity's work center.

15. Correct answers: **A and B**

    You can use the budget carryforward function to transfer unused funds in a fiscal year to a new fiscal year. The availability control component supports monitoring and controlling project costs by generating warning and error messages when costs occur. This capability checks the budget releases against the current (assigned) budget. Confirmation and cost forecasting are not budget functions.

16. Correct answer: **C and D**

    You use a service entry sheet (not goods receipt) to receive a service. Nonstock materials and externally processed activities are received by posting goods receipts. You withdraw stock materials by posting goods issues.

17. Correct answers: **A and C**

    In the period-end closing phase, overhead costs and costs from incoming orders can flow into the project. In the execution phase, the project collects actual costs in several ways, such as withdrawing, purchasing, or producing materials assigned to activities, receiving services, and external activities.

18. Correct answers: **B, C, and D**

    You can settle the entire project or the project objects, such as WBS elements, network, orders, or activities. Statistical WBS elements or statistical projects are for information purposes only. They don't carry actual costs, so they are not settled. A milestone is not an object that can carry costs and is not settled.

19. Correct answers: **A and C**

    During the execution and period-end closing phases, a project collects actual costs and revenues, which are transferred to receivers in the settlement phase. Variances are settled in production.

20. Correct answer: **A and C**

    Project WBS elements and networks can be assigned to a responsible cost center, which also determines the responsible area for carrying out the WBS element or network.

21. Correct answers: **A, D, and E**

    You can assign orders to WBS elements as an account assignment object. Production orders, sales orders, internal orders, and maintenance orders can have WBS elements as account assignments. You can also assign a responsible cost center to WBS elements in their master records. Work centers and cost elements (general ledger accounts) are assigned to activities, not WBS elements.

22. Correct answer: **A**

    During confirmation, you'll enter confirmations for actual durations, based on which internal activity allocations are carried out between project activities and cost centers. Cost centers are credited, and project activities are debited with the actual costs. Material withdrawals and goods receipts also lead to actual cost updates (for materials and services) in a project, but not to internal activity allocations.

23. Correct answers: **A, B, and C**

    Confirmations can update the actual costs of activities. Settling orders assigned to WBS elements can trigger actual cost transfers to WBS elements. WBS elements can be receivers of assessments and distributions in controlling, which would lead to increases in WBS elements' actual costs.

9.8 Test Takeaway

In this chapter, you learned key topics related to SAP S/4HANA's Project System module, which supports project management tasks. A real-world project can be mapped to the system using project structuring elements, such as the project definition, WBS elements, networks, activities, milestones, and material components. A WBS is a hierarchical model of a project and determines responsibilities. By creating WBS elements and assigning them other structuring objects, you form a planning basis for a project. A network determines the process-based structure of a project. Defining activities, linking them via relationships, assigning them material components, you create an operative basis for the project in the system. You create the cost structure of a project based on WBS elements and networks.

The Project System module in SAP S/4HANA is not just a project planning tool. Project System provides several tools (e.g., Project Builder and Project Planning Board) to control, trigger, and monitor all project-related transactions in the system, such as procurement, manufacturing, billing, and goods movements. During the planning, execution, budget, and period-end closing phases of a project, Project System fully integrates with other system components by generating documents and transferring data.

Thus concludes our discussion of key topics related to Project System. The next chapter covers key topics related to hire-to-retire processing with human experience management (HXM) in SAP S/4HANA using SAP SuccessFactors.

Chapter 10
Hire-to-Retire Processing

Techniques You'll Master

- Explain the key tasks of SAP SuccessFactors' hire-to-retire process
- Understand the key differences between human capital management (HCM) and human experience management (HXM)
- Identify the SAP solutions supporting HCM and HXM
- Describe the elements of HXM structures and their roles in HXM processes
- Understand the cloud transition scenarios for human resources (HR) processes and explain the underlying technologies in cloud transition
- Explain the structure of employee master records and infotypes
- Define the system transactions for employee master data maintenance and edit, delete, and create employee master records
- Identify the touchpoints of integration between HR and other system modules in SAP S/4HANA

This chapter of the book covers all certification-relevant topics related to hire-to-retire processing. We'll outline the key differences between HXM and HCM processes and describe the SAP solutions supporting these processes. This chapter describes HXM structures, the structure of employee master records, and their maintenance in the system. In compliance with the certification scope, this chapter also highlights potential integration and cloud transition scenarios.

SAP provides SAP SuccessFactors HXM Suite and the HR application module, called SAP Human Capital Management for SAP S/4HANA (SAP HCM for SAP S/4HANA), to support HXM and classic HCM processes involving key tasks of hire-to-retire processing.

> **Real-World Scenario**
>
> Human experience in a company has a direct impact on workforce performance and business outcomes. Business processes within a company and across companies are connected to each other through people who are planning, managing, and executing business operations. Considering how employees feel about the different kinds of experiences is of critical importance for retaining employees and the reputation of the company in the job market. For instance, *task experience* is about ease of use and the challenges of tasks being performed, while *social experience* is about the social relationships between people working together, and *fulfillment experience* is about employee satisfaction and their expectations of work.
>
> HCM primarily focuses on a company's needs from the workforce and treats the human experience as a secondary purpose. HXM takes the employee's experiences and the company's goals into account simultaneously and aims to develop better work experiences for employees aligned with the company's business goals.
>
> As an SAP consultant, you must understand SAP solutions supporting business experience management and core HR processes. You must know how SAP technologies provided to managers and employees enable them to perform their jobs effectively and efficiently. Understanding how SAP's HXM solutions enable the synchronization of operational data (O-Data) and experience data (X-Data) for management decisions and business practices is critical. You should be able to technically explain cloud transition scenarios, how experience management and core HR processes can be mapped into SAP systems, and how these processes can be integrated with other logistics and accounting processes running on the system.

10.1 Objectives of This Portion of the Test

This portion of the certification aims to test your knowledge of key topics related to hire-to-retire processing with HXM and SAP solutions supporting HXM processes. The certification exam includes questions about HXM organizational structures, the employee master record structure and its maintenance in the system, HR self-service tools, and SAP's HXM solutions, such as SAP SuccessFactors Employee Central. The key differences between HCM and HXM are essential topics that you must understand for certification.

SAP consultants are expected to know cloud transition scenarios and potential integration scenarios between HXM and other system components. For the certification exam, business process integration consultants must have a good understanding of the following topics:

- Key tasks of hire-to-retire processing
- HXM organizational structures
- Infotypes and master data maintenance in HXM
- Integration between SAP SuccessFactors and SAP S/4HANA
- Employee and manager self-service tools
- Touchpoints of integration between HXM and other business processes

Note
The topics in this chapter cover about 8% of the questions in the certification exam.

10.2 Data Structures for Hire-to-Retire

SAP redefined HCM with a new employee-centered mindset, and the classic HCM process has evolved into an HXM process with the new approach. This section defines the HXM structures that you can use to map a company's HR-relevant organizational structure into the system and determine employee positions in the business organization. Transactions for HXM master data maintenance are also covered at the end of this section.

10.2.1 Organizational Structures

You can use HXM organizational structures to map your company's HR-relevant organizational levels into the system. An employee is a master record in HXM and must be assigned to the following HXM structures to define the employee's position within the business organization, as shown in Figure 10.1:

- **Enterprise structure**
An enterprise structure includes elements that define the structure of a company in personnel administration. By assigning an employee to an enterprise

structure, you define the employee's position in the company structure according to personnel administration.

- **Administrative personnel structure**
An administrative personnel structure includes elements that define the personnel structure from an administrative perspective. By assigning an employee to an administrative personnel structure, you define an employee's position in the company's personnel structure from an administrative perspective.

- **Organizational personnel structure**
An organizational personnel structure includes elements that define the personnel structure from an organizational perspective. By assigning an employee to an organizational personnel structure, you define an employee's position in the company's personnel structure from an organizational assignment perspective.

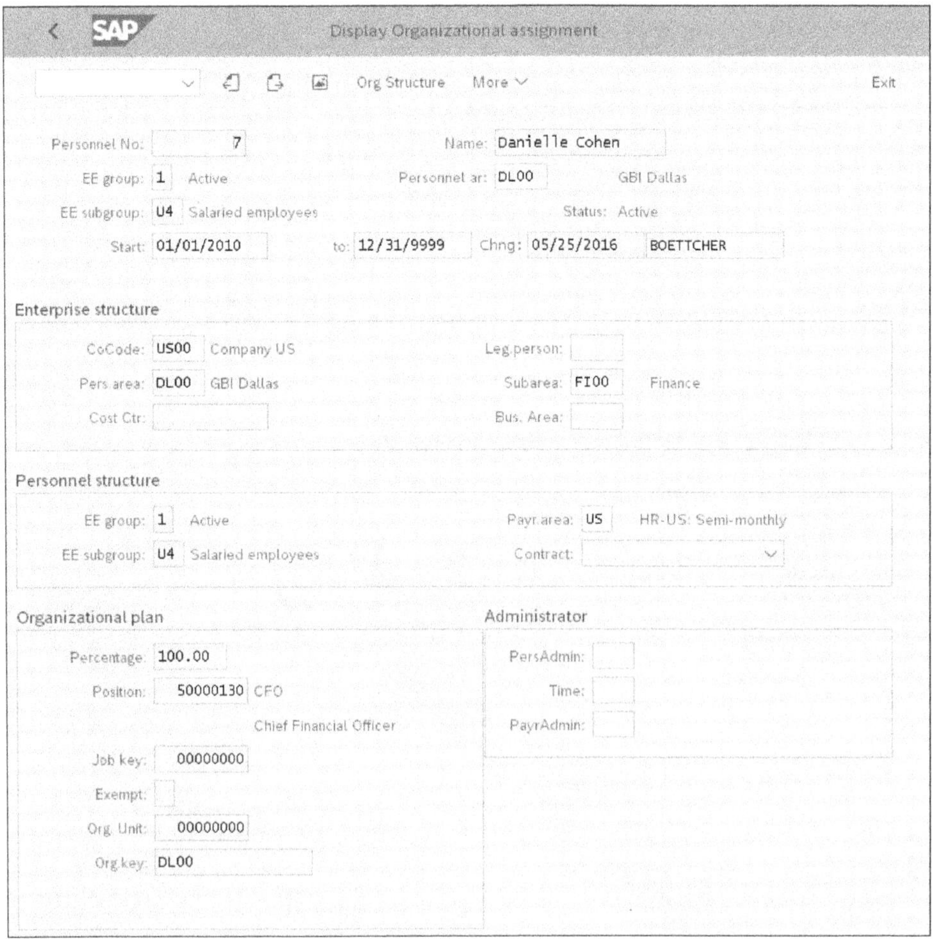

Figure 10.1 Organizational Assignment Infotype for Employee Master Record

In the following sections, we'll take a closer look at these HXM structures.

Enterprise Structure

The enterprise structure consists of the following elements that you can create in Customizing:

- **Client**
  Represents the highest organizational level in the enterprise structure and keeps the master records and the tables separate from other clients. A client can have several company codes.
- **Company code**
  The company code represents the smallest organizational unit in external accounting. A company code can belong to only one client.
- **Personnel area**
  A personnel area is uniquely defined in each client and represents a subdivision of company code in personnel administration. A personnel area defines an enterprise area from personnel administrative, time management, and payroll aspects. Each personnel area is assigned to only one company code in Customizing.
- **Personnel subarea**
  A personnel subarea is a subdivision of the personnel area and specifies the personnel groups for time management and defines subarea-specific wage types for the personnel area. The personnel subarea is a selection criterion for personnel evaluations.

Figure 10.2 shows the data assignments and the relationships between the elements of the HXM enterprise structure.

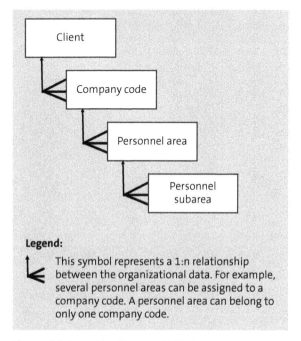

Figure 10.2 Enterprise Structure in HXM

Administrative Personnel Structure

The administrative personnel structure consists of the following elements that you can create in Customizing:

- **Employee group**
  An employee group is a general division of employees. You can use employee groups to generate default values for data entry in the payroll area related to the employee's basic pay. An employee group can be used as a selection criterion for reporting. External employees, active employees, retirees, and pensioners are some examples of employee groups, as shown in Figure 10.3.
- **Employee subgroup**
  An employee subgroup represents a subdivision of an employee group. Salaried employees, trainees, and nonpayscale employees are some example employee subgroups.
- **Payroll area**
  A payroll area is an organizational unit in which you plan and execute payroll. Employees accounted simultaneously in the payroll are assigned to the same payroll area in the organizational assignment infotype. You can define payroll areas in personnel administration in Customizing, as shown in Figure 10.4.
- **Organizational key**
  An organizational key is a 14-character field that consists of a part of personnel and enterprise structures. This key is used for authorization checks.

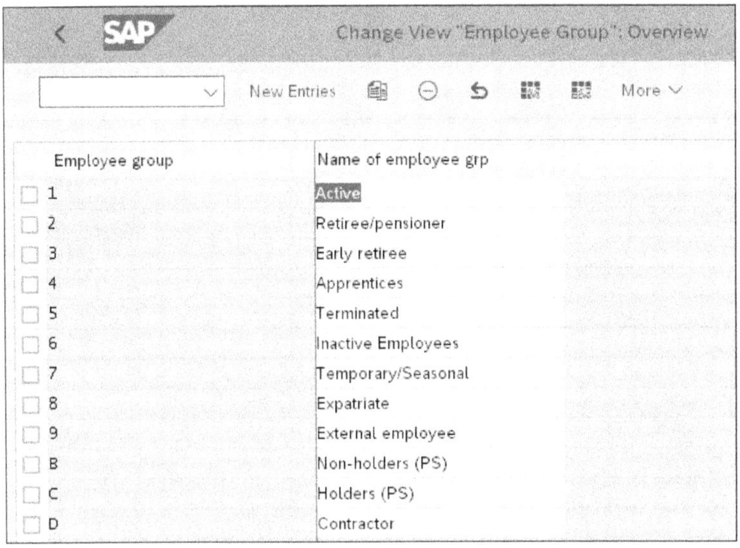
Change View "Employee Group": Overview
New Entries
More
Employee group
Name of employee grp
1
Active
2
Retiree/pensioner
3
Early retiree
4
Apprentices
5
Terminated
6
Inactive Employees
7
Temporary/Seasonal
8
Expatriate
9
External employee
B
Non-holders (PS)
C
Holders (PS)
D
Contractor

Figure 10.3 Employee Groups in Customizing

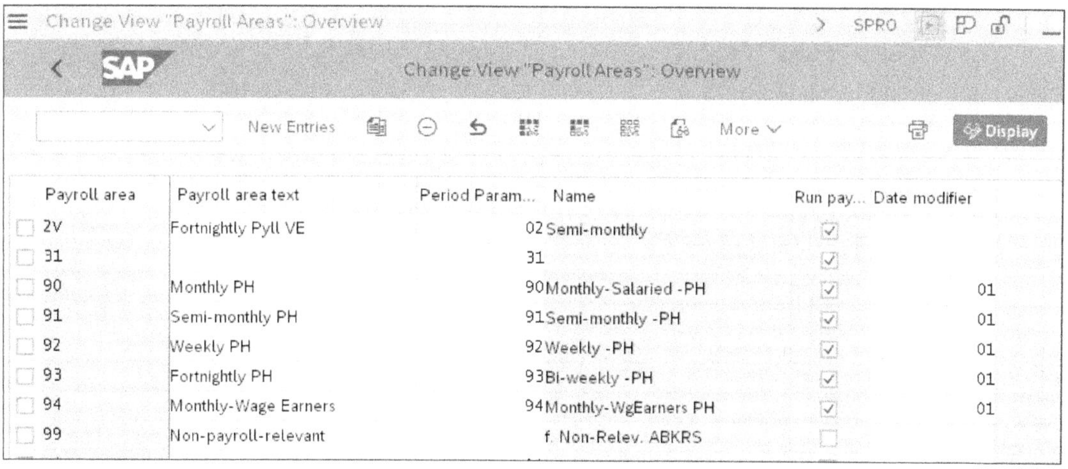

Payroll area	Payroll area text	Period Param...	Name	Run pay...	Date modifier
2V	Fortnightly Pyll VE	02	Semi-monthly	✓	
31		31		✓	
90	Monthly PH	90	Monthly-Salaried -PH	✓	01
91	Semi-monthly PH	91	Semi-monthly -PH	✓	01
92	Weekly PH	92	Weekly -PH	✓	01
93	Fortnightly PH	93	Bi-weekly -PH	✓	01
94	Monthly-Wage Earners	94	Monthly-WgEarners PH	✓	01
99	Non-payroll-relevant	f.	Non-Relev. ABKRS		

Figure 10.4 Payroll Areas in Customizing

Organizational Personnel Structure

An organizational personnel structure consists of the following elements that you can create either in Customizing or in organizational management by using Transaction PPOCE (Organization and Staffing):

- **Organizational unit**
  An organizational unit defines a functional unit in an enterprise. An organizational unit is represented by the object type **O** in the system. Based on your company's task structure, an organizational unit can represent a department (e.g., marketing, finance); a group (e.g., executive board); or a project team (e.g., research and development [R&D]). The organizational structure of an enterprise is defined by assigning organizational units to each other in a hierarchy. An organizational unit can be assigned to a company code, business area, personnel area, and personnel subarea. You can also assign an organizational unit to a cost center represented by the system object type **K**. The cost center assigned to an organizational unit is inherited by the positions belonging to the organizational unit. You can classify organizational units in the system based on functional or regional criteria.

- **Position**
  In the system, you create positions for organizational units to define existing or required personnel capacities in organizational units—for example, the chief financial officer position in financials department (organizational unit). A position is represented by the object type **S** in the system. You can create positions either in Customizing or in organization management. When you create a position, you can assign it to a job, as shown in Figure 10.5. A task is represented by the object type **T** in the system. Note that you can define additional tasks for a position without assigning the position to a job.

Positions can be assigned to enterprise structure (e.g., company code, personnel area/subarea) and administrative personnel structure (e.g., employee group and employee subgroup) in the organizational management by using Transaction PPOCE.

Employees (persons) occupy (holds) the positions. The system allows you to define several employees to occupy a single position. In this case, you must define the percentages of the employees occupying the position. A position can be assigned a job, which describes the tasks of a position. You can assign a cost center to a position in its master record. Positions also inherit the costs centers assigned to their organizational units.

- **Job**
  You can define jobs for a general classification of task areas in your company (e.g., manager). Several positions can be assigned to a job (e.g., sales manager, purchasing manager, plant manager). When positions are assigned to a job, they inherit the tasks of a job. A job is represented by the object type **P** in the system.

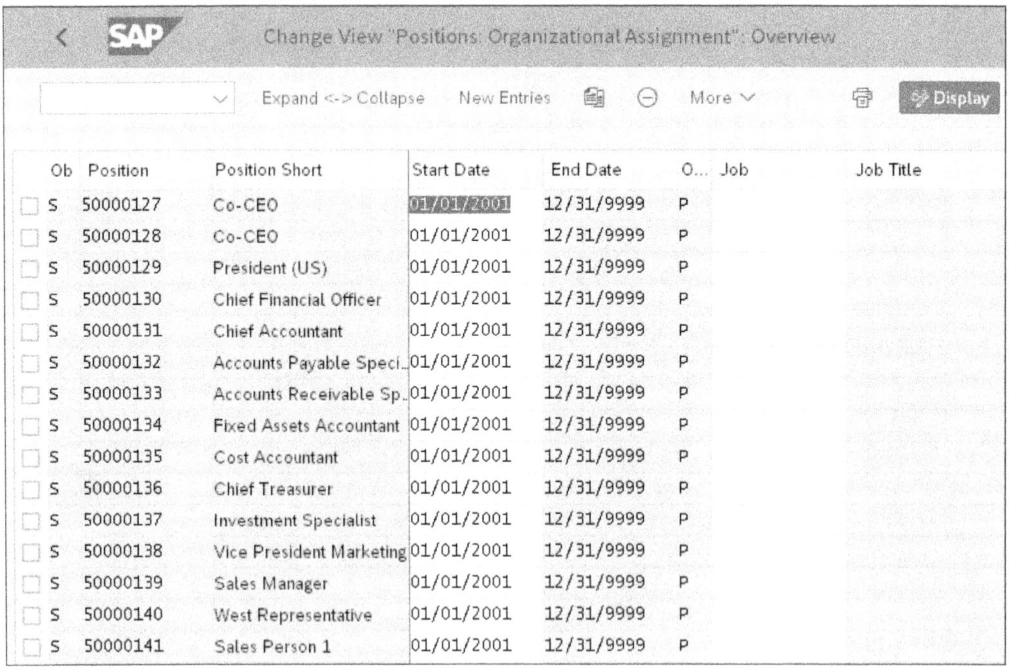

Ob	Position	Position Short	Start Date	End Date	O...	Job	Job Title
S	50000127	Co-CEO	01/01/2001	12/31/9999	P		
S	50000128	Co-CEO	01/01/2001	12/31/9999	P		
S	50000129	President (US)	01/01/2001	12/31/9999	P		
S	50000130	Chief Financial Officer	01/01/2001	12/31/9999	P		
S	50000131	Chief Accountant	01/01/2001	12/31/9999	P		
S	50000132	Accounts Payable Speci..	01/01/2001	12/31/9999	P		
S	50000133	Accounts Receivable Sp..	01/01/2001	12/31/9999	P		
S	50000134	Fixed Assets Accountant	01/01/2001	12/31/9999	P		
S	50000135	Cost Accountant	01/01/2001	12/31/9999	P		
S	50000136	Chief Treasurer	01/01/2001	12/31/9999	P		
S	50000137	Investment Specialist	01/01/2001	12/31/9999	P		
S	50000138	Vice President Marketing	01/01/2001	12/31/9999	P		
S	50000139	Sales Manager	01/01/2001	12/31/9999	P		
S	50000140	West Representative	01/01/2001	12/31/9999	P		
S	50000141	Sales Person 1	01/01/2001	12/31/9999	P		

Figure 10.5 Positions in Customizing

Figure 10.6 shows the organizational plan in the US company code. In the organizational plan, organizational units, positions, and persons are linked to each other in a hierarchical structure.

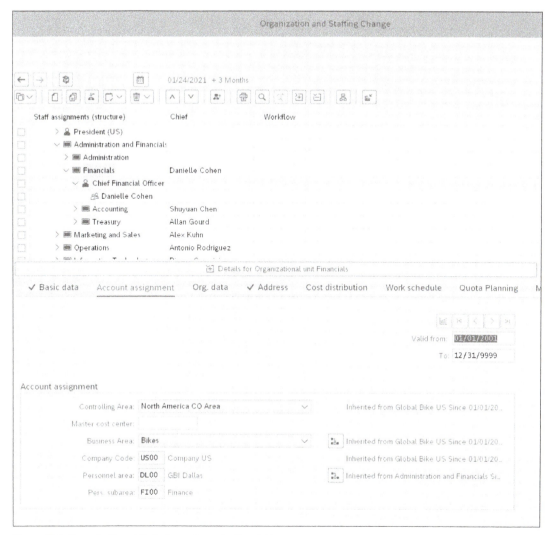

Figure 10.6 Organizational Units in an Organizational Plan

10.2.2 Master Data

An employee is a master record in HXM. The employee master record is stored in infotypes. An *infotype* is a group of data fields that logically belong to some content (e.g., addresses, basic pay, bank details, organizational assignment, personal data). For instance, a personal data infotype, shown in Figure 10.7, includes data not relevant to the organization but to the person, such as a title (Mr. or Mrs.), a name, a birthdate, a Social Security Number, a language, a nationality, a marital status, and a gender. An organizational assignment infotype includes data relevant to the employee's assignment to HXM structures (i.e., enterprise, organizational, and administrative personnel structures). Infotypes are valid between the start and end dates (i.e., validity period) defined in their master record.

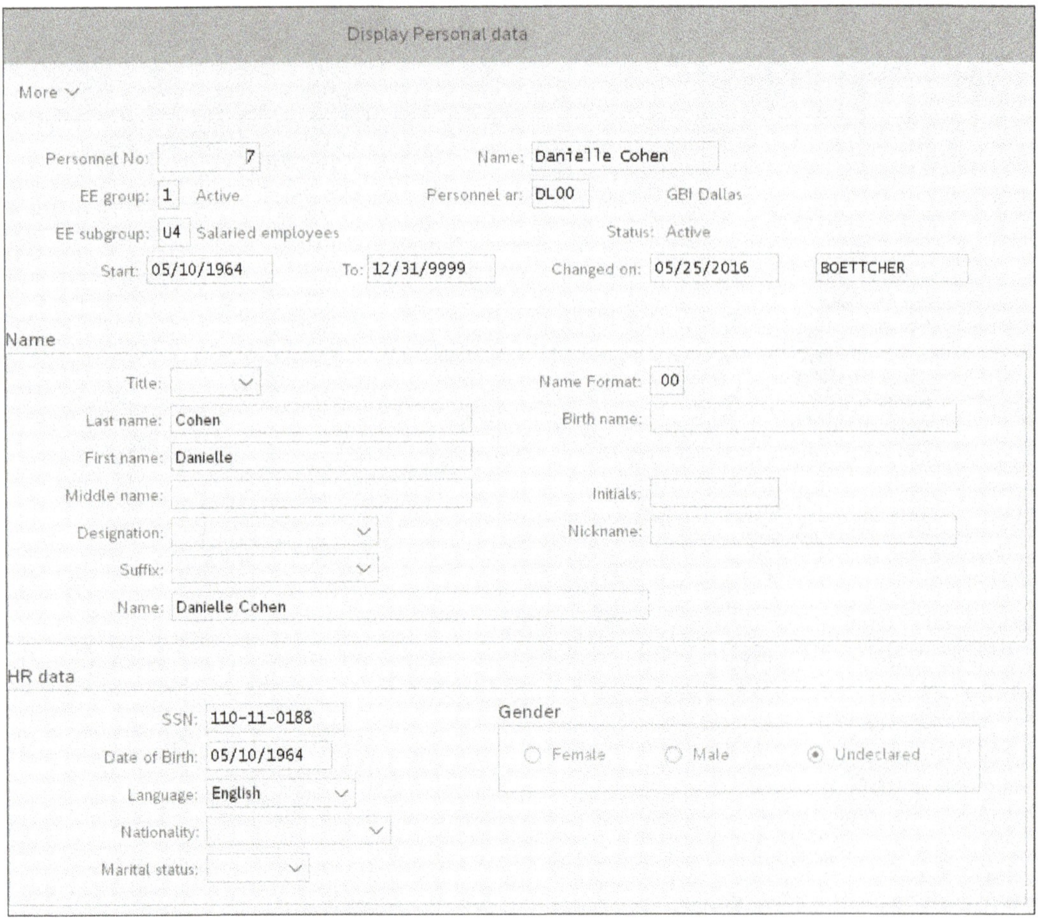

Figure 10.7 Personal Data Infotype

In the system, you can maintain (create, change, and edit) infotypes in three different ways:

- **Single screen maintenance (to maintain a single infotype applied to a single person)**
  You can perform a single screen maintenance with Transaction PA30 (Maintain HR Master Data) to add a new infotype to an existing employee master record or change an employee's existing infotype. To run the single infotype maintenance transaction, you must enter a personnel number and select the infotype you want to maintain, as shown in Figure 10.8.

- **Personnel actions (to maintain multiple infotypes applied a single person)**
  In personnel actions, you can maintain (add, change, or delete) several infotypes of a single employee master record for a reason (e.g., hiring, leaving, retirement, or organizational reassignment) you must specify at the beginning of the transaction (Transaction PA40), as shown in Figure 10.9. Depending on the reason (action type) you select, the system may let you maintain a series of infotypes on the employee master record.

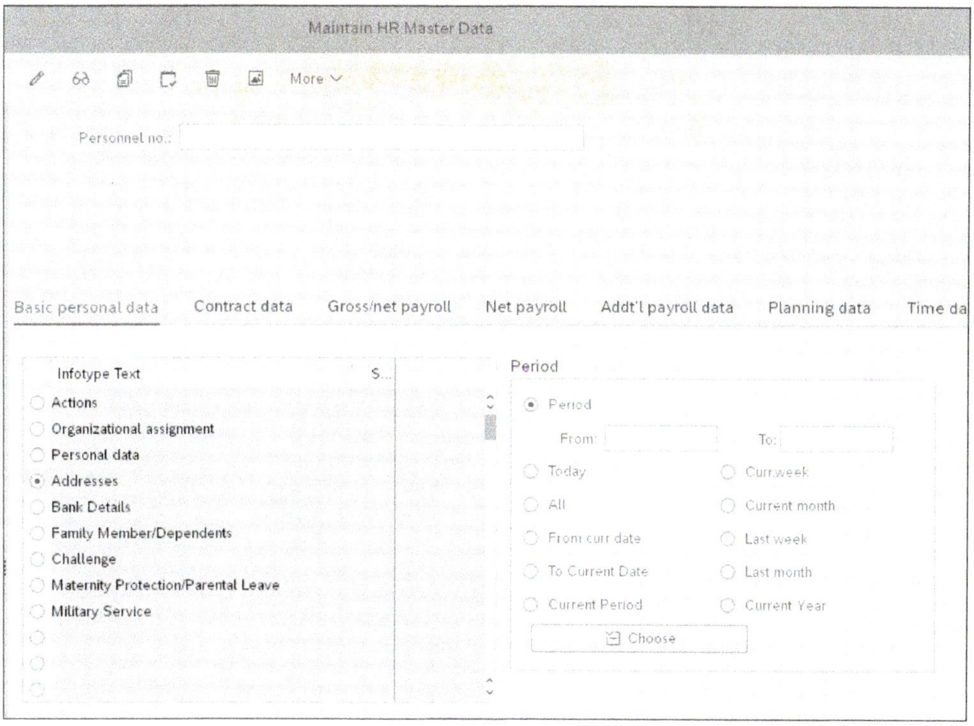

Figure 10.8 Infotypes in Single Infotype Maintenance

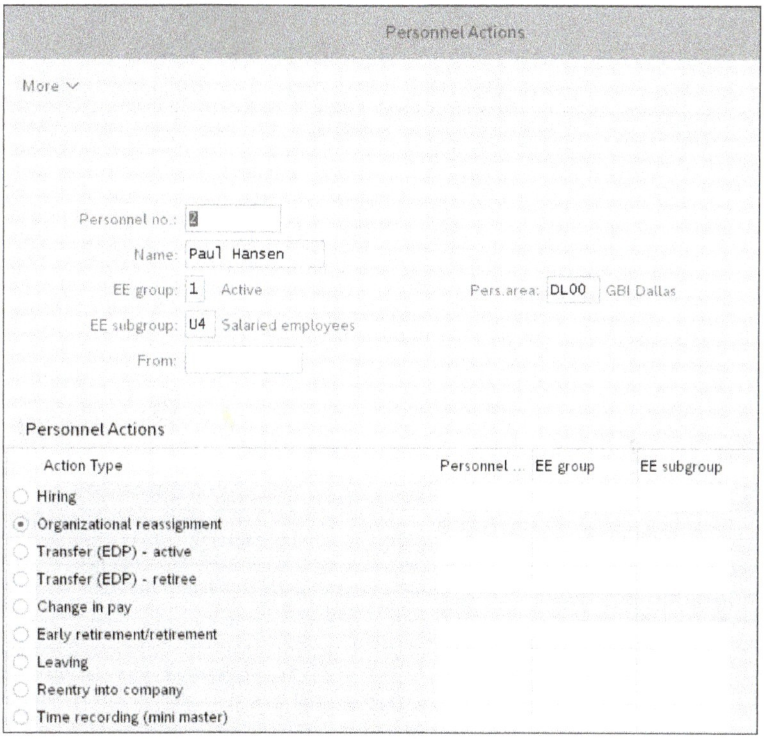

Figure 10.9 Action Types in Personnel Actions (Multiple Infotype Maintenance)

- **Fast entry (to maintain a single infotype applied to multiple persons)**
  The fast entry transaction (Transaction PA70) enables you to create, edit, or delete a single infotype for several employees simultaneously, as shown in Figure 10.10. You can select the employees for whom you need to maintain default infotypes such as recurring payments/deductions, additional payments, fiscal data, child allowances, and other transaction data.

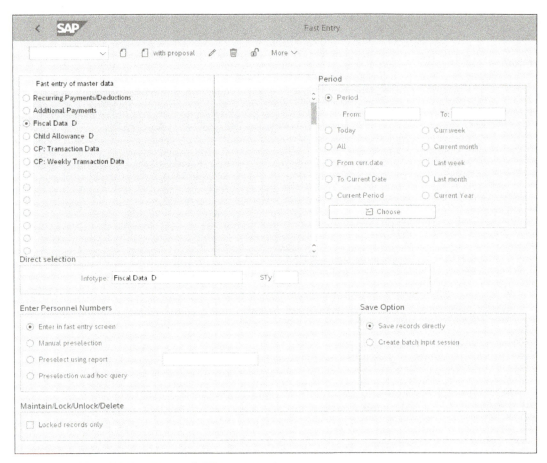

Figure 10.10 Fast Entry of HR Master Data Screen

You can display employee records in several ways in the system. The personnel file transaction (Transaction PA10) is one method that lists all existing infotypes (e.g., actions, organizational assignments, personal data) of an employee master record. The personnel file represents a collection of all recorded infotypes for an employee in the system. Using the navigation buttons on top, you can navigate to the infotype you would like to display, as shown in Figure 10.11.

Figure 10.11 Displaying Infotypes Using Personnel File

10.2.3 Data Assignments

Some examples of data relationships available in HXM include the following:

- Each person has a unique employee master record stored in infotypes.
- An employee is assigned to HXM structures (i.e., enterprise structure, administrative personnel structure, and organizational personnel structure) in the organizational assignment infotype of its master record.
- Organizational units can be assigned to each other to create an organizational plan.
- Several organizational units can be assigned to an enterprise structure (i.e., personnel area and personnel subarea) in their data in organizational management.
- Several positions can be assigned (or belong) to an organizational unit.
- Several positions can be assigned to a job.
- Several positions can be assigned to an enterprise structure (company code, personnel area, and personnel subarea) and an administrative personnel structure (employee group and employee subgroup).
- A job describes the tasks in a position.
- Positions and organizational units can be assigned to a cost center.
- Several personnel areas can be assigned to a company code.

Figure 10.12 shows the relationships between objects and structures in HXM.

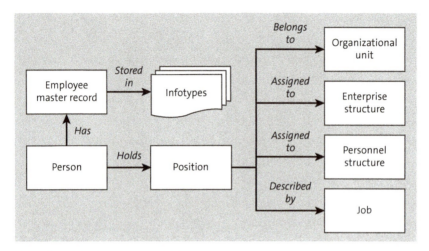

Figure 10.12 Data Assignments in HXM

10.3 Key Processes of Hire-to-Retire

In this section, we'll walk through the key tasks of the hire-to-retire business process and HXM processes involved in hire-to-retire processing in SAP S/4HANA and SAP SuccessFactors. We'll begin with an overview of the hire-to-retire business process. Then we'll continue with a comparative overview of HXM and HCM before walking through the key solutions and features.

10.3.1 Hire-to-Retire Tasks

Hire-to-retire processing consists of the following HXM tasks:

- **Recruit-to-onboard**
  - Workforce analytics and planning
  - Position management
  - Recruitment management
  - Onboarding
- **Manage workforce and retirement**
  - Manage employee data
  - Performance management
  - Career development
  - Retirement and offboarding
- **Time management**
  - Recording attendance or absence via time sheets
- **Payroll and reimbursement**
  - Monitoring costs and margins
  - Handling supplier invoices for contingent workforce
  - Processing payroll
- **Invoice-to-pay**
  - Payment of payroll
  - Payment of external workforce invoices

10.3.2 Human Capital Management versus Human Experience Management

In recent years, SAP has reinvented HCM by putting employees' experience at the center of everything, resulting in HXM, which focuses on three types of experiences that influence employees' feelings, expectations, perceptions, and needs:

- Task experience
- Social experience
- Fulfillment experience

A company's decisions result in employee reactions, and an employee's experience determines the employee's behavior, possibly directly or negatively affecting workforce performance. Business outcomes depend entirely on workforce performance. Considering human experience and business goals synchronously in management decisions is critical for achieving the best business outcomes. For this purpose, HXM incorporates X-Data into HR processes and synchronizes the X-Data with its (transactional) O-Data for decision-making. Figure 10.13 shows the interaction between a company's decisions, human experiences, and business outcomes. The following technologies support the intelligent enterprise when you are dealing with X-Data and O-Data in HXM:

1. Conversational AI
2. Robotic process automation (RPA) and monitoring
3. Machine learning
4. Voice and feedback

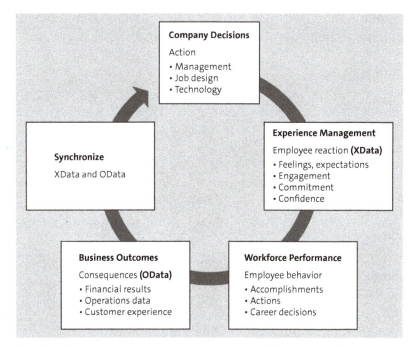

Figure 10.13 Synchronization of X-Data and O-Data in Management Decisions

HXM's employee-centered strategy is of critical importance for creating agile and high-performing companies. Both HCM and HXM are concerned with getting employees to do the things aligned with the company's business strategies. HXM adopts an inspiring and engaging approach that simultaneously focuses on employees' experiences and the company's needs. In contrast, HCM has a more transactional mindset that focuses primarily on the company's needs and treats the employee experience secondarily. HXM aims to harmonize O-Data and X-Data to support leadership decisions, while HCM is based only on the enterprise resource planning (ERP) of system operational data related to HR.

SAP distinguishes between HCM and HXM processes in the following way:

- **Human capital management**
  Methods for hiring, managing, developing, and retaining employees that support company goals.

- **Human experience management**
  Methods for creating work experiences that align employee wants, needs, and expectations with company goals.

SAP GUI includes the HR module (i.e., SAP HCM for SAP S/4HANA), as shown in Figure 10.14, to support the following core HCM processes:

- **Organizational management**
  Concerned with modeling organizational structures (e.g., department hierarchy) and reporting structures, creating and analyzing organizational plans, and managing workflows. This component includes the organizational plan in which you can create objects like organizational units, positions, and jobs and perform assignments between the objects.

- **Time management**
  Concerned with time recording, attendance, time schedule, shift management, etc.

- **Personnel administration**
  Concerned with managing personal administration tasks, processing employee-related data in infotypes, maintaining organizational structures, integration with time and payroll, etc.

- **Payroll**
  Concerned with payroll activities with payroll types, payroll group configuration, primary and secondary wages, gross pay, bonus, etc.

- **Recruitment**
  Concerned with hiring an employee, maintaining HR master data, etc.

- **Training and event management**
  Concerned with planning and managing business events, determining training needs, scheduling training, training cost management, etc.

- **Travel management**
  Concerned with planning and managing official trips, cost management for travel, travel expenses, etc. This component integrates with payroll and financial accounting.

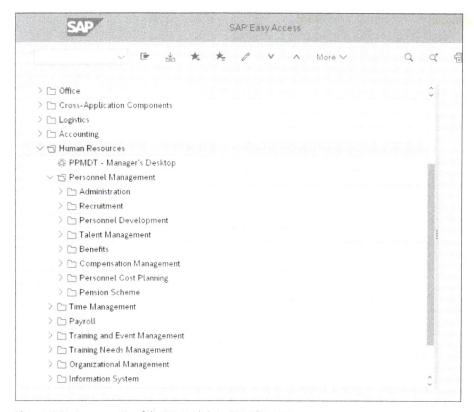

Figure 10.14 Components of the HR Module in SAP S/4HANA

SAP also provides a cloud-based HXM solution called SAP SuccessFactors HXM Suite, which consists of fully integrated software with the following solutions:

- **Employee experience management software**
  Includes the following solutions:
  - SAP Qualtrics Employee Engagement
  - Qualtrics EmployeeXM for IT
  - SAP Qualtrics Employee Lifecycle
  - SAP Qualtrics 360 Feedback
  - SAP Qualtrics Employee Benefits Optimizer
- **Core HR and payroll software**
  Includes the following solutions:
  - SAP SuccessFactors Employee Central
  - SAP SuccessFactors Employee Central Payroll
  - SAP SuccessFactors Employee Central Service Center
  - SAP SuccessFactors Visa and Permits Management
  - SAP SuccessFactors Document Management Core by OpenText
  - SAP Work Zone for HR

- **Talent management software**
  Includes the following solutions:
  - **Recruiting solutions**
    - SAP SuccessFactors Recruiting
    - SAP Fieldglass Contingent Workforce Management
  - **Onboarding solutions**
    - SAP SuccessFactors Onboarding
    - SAP Signature Management by DocuSign
  - **Performance management solutions**
    - SAP SuccessFactors Performance & Goals
  - **Compensation management solutions**
    - SAP SuccessFactors Compensation
  - **Learning management solutions**
    - SAP SuccessFactors Learning
    - SAP Jam Collaboration (for social collaboration)
    - SAP Enable Now
  - **Succession and development solutions**
    - SAP SuccessFactors Succession & Development
- **HR analytics and workforce planning software**
  Includes the following solutions:
  - **Workforce analytics solutions**
    - SAP SuccessFactors Workforce Analytics
    - SAP Digital Boardroom
  - **Workforce planning**
    - SAP SuccessFactors Workforce Planning

Based on your company's business needs, you can fully or partially transfer your HR processes to the cloud. SAP SuccessFactors HXM Suite supports transitioning your HR processes to the cloud in the following scenarios:

- **Talent hybrid**
  Use talent analytics on the cloud.
- **Side-by-side**
  Use talent analytics, personnel administration, and organizational management on the cloud.
- **Core hybrid**
  Use talent solutions, workforce analytics, personnel administration, and organizational management on the cloud.
- **Full cloud**
  Use payroll, talent solutions, workforce analytics, personnel administration, and organizational management on the cloud.

10.3.3 SAP SuccessFactors Employee Central

SAP SuccessFactors Employee Central, shown in Figure 10.15, is the cloud-based HR information system and the central data repository for all employee data and serves as a foundation for the other SAP SuccessFactors HXM Suite solutions, such as recruitment, onboarding, payroll, and talent management.

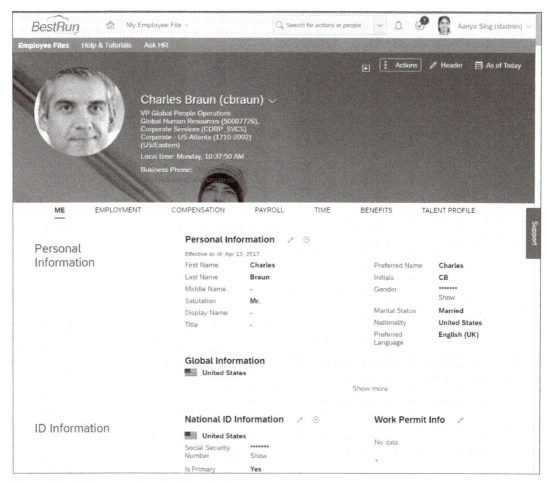

Figure 10.15 SAP SuccessFactors Employee Central

The functions of Employee Central include the following capabilities:

- Houses all HR data for all employees in the company (e.g., employment data, compensation data, payroll data, time management data, benefits, talent profiles)
- Includes foundation objects (e.g., organization, job, payment) that allow a company to define its corporate structure (i.e., organization management), which helps organize employee information
- Enables SAP SuccessFactors Employee Central Payroll, which offers the same the same features and benefits of payroll as on-premise SAP S/4HANA

- Keeps HR data up to date by recording all HR transactions and updates
- Enables analytics with HR data to meet compliance requirements and perform business analysis
- Integrates HR data with other systems through a cloud-based platform
- Provides downstream systems with HR information
- Supports built-in employee self-service (ESS) and manager self-service (MSS) tools to empower employees and managers

10.3.4 Self-Service Tools

ESS and MSS tools were built into Employee Central. Companies using only SAP HCM for SAP S/4HANA must deploy SAP Enterprise Portal or SAP Business Client to make web-based self-service interfaces available for their employees and managers.

Employees of a company can use the intuitive HTML-based ESS interface to perform the following activities:

- Submit travel expenses
- View the calendar
- Search who's who
- Update their own personal data
- Enter work times
- Enroll in benefits
- Update banking info
- Enroll in a training course

ESS supports well-informed employee decisions, reduces administrative costs and the HR department's workload, shortens process cycle times, and enables up-to-date employee records.

MSS also has a web-based interface that supports managers' daily administrative tasks with the following functions:

- Gather information
- Recruitment
- Monitoring
- Compensation planning
- Cost control
- Budget management and head counting

Managers can also use the **Manager's Desktop** (Transaction PPMDT), shown in Figure 10.16, in SAP S/4HANA to have immediate access to cross-application administrative functions besides financial accounting and controlling data.

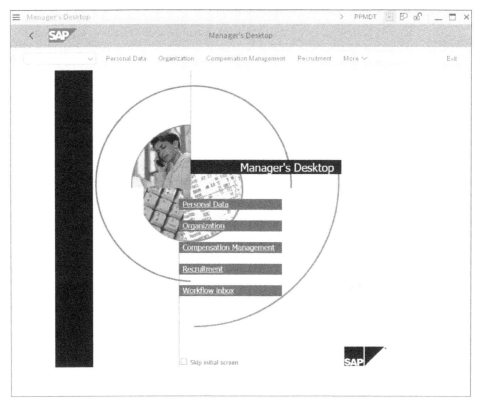

Figure 10.16 Manager's Desktop in HR Module

10.4 Integration with Other Modules

In this section, we explain the touchpoints of integration between HXM and other system modules. We can organize cross-module integrations into two categories:

- Integrations via cross-module data assignments
- Integrations via transactions

10.4.1 Integration via Cross-Module Data Assignments

Cross-module data assignments in the system connect the business processes in SAP S/4HANA and lead to data flows between the system's components. Some examples of integrations via data assignments include the following:

- **Management accounting**
  A cost center is a master data in controlling. Positions and organizational units can be assigned cost centers in their records. An employee master record can also be assigned a cost center, thus integrating the HR module with the controlling module.

- **Production and plant maintenance**
  A work center is a master data in production. A maintenance work center is also a part of the maintenance plant in enterprise asset management. An organizational unit is an object in the organizational plan and organizational personnel structure in HXM. A work center can be assigned to an organizational unit in its master record, which creates an integration between corresponding modules and SAP HCM for SAP S/4HANA.

10.4.2 Integration via Transactions

SAP HCM for SAP S/4HANA integrates with other system modules via transactions. Some examples of transactions that lead to cross-module integration include the following:

- **Confirmations**
  Time confirmations for production orders, maintenance orders, and projects initiate data transfers to HR, thus integrating HR with other system modules.
- **Payroll**
  The payroll process triggers data transfers, thus integrating HR with financial accounting and controlling.
- **Training and event management**
  Internal charges for employee training or events are transferred from HR to the cost center assigned to the employee, thus integrating HR with controlling. Training and event management can also trigger an integration with sales and distribution when a customer is invoiced for the costs of the organization's internal training events.

10.5 Important Terminology

In this chapter, the following terminology we use is important to know for the exam:

- **Employee Central**
  SAP SuccessFactors Employee Central stores HR data and foundational objects to map the organizational structure into SAP SuccessFactors HXM Suite. Employee Central is the foundation of all applications in SAP SuccessFactors HXM Suite and also provides self-service tools.
- **Employee group**
  An employee group is a part of the administrative personnel structure and represents a general division of employees.
- **Employee self-service (ESS)**
  ESS is an HTML-based interface that enables employees to maintain their personal data and execute employee-relevant transactions, such as enrolling in a benefit or a training course and submitting travel expenses.

- **Employee subgroup**
  An employee subgroup is a part of the administrative personnel structure and represents a subdivision of an employee group.
- **Fast entry**
  A transaction in which you can maintain a single infotype for a series of employees simultaneously.
- **HXM structures**
  HXM structures are used to map HR-relevant enterprise and personnel structures into the system. Each employee in the system is assigned to HXM structures, including enterprise structures, organizational personnel structures, and administrative personnel structures.
- **Infotype**
  Employee master records are stored in the infotypes. An infotype is a group of data fields that logically belong to a content (e.g., addresses, basic pay, bank details, organizational assignment, and personal data).
- **Job**
  A job is a part of the organizational personnel structure and classifies the tasks in a position. Several positions with similar tasks and features can be assigned to a job.
- **Manager self-service (MSS)**
  MSS is an interface that supports the daily administrative tasks of managers, such as obtaining personnel information, recruitment, monitoring, compensation management, and cost control.
- **Organizational unit**
  An organizational unit is a part of the organizational personnel structure and defines a functional unit in an enterprise. The organizational structure of an enterprise is defined by assigning organizational units to each other in a hierarchy.
- **Payroll area**
  A payroll area is an organizational unit in which you plan and execute payroll. The system defines two pieces of information based on payroll: the number of employees for whom payroll is to be run and the payroll dates.
- **Personnel action**
  A transaction in which you can maintain several infotypes of an employee for a reason, such as hiring, retirement, or leave of absence.
- **Personnel area**
  A personnel area is a part of the enterprise structure and represents a subdivision of a company code in personnel administration.
- **Personnel subarea**
  A personnel subarea is a part of the enterprise structure and represents a subdivision of a personnel area. It specifies the personnel groups for time management and defines subarea-specific wage types in a personnel area.

- **Position**
  A position is a part of the organizational personnel structure. Employees hold positions in the system. A position defines an existing or required personnel capacity in an organizational unit where it belongs to. Positions are used to create reporting structures.
- **Single screen maintenance**
  A transaction to maintain a single infotype for an employee.

10.6 Practice Questions

These practice questions will help you evaluate your understanding of the topics covered in this chapter. The questions shown are similar to those found on the certification examination. Although none of these questions will be found on the exam itself, they will allow you to review your knowledge of the subject. Select the correct answers and then check the completeness of your answers in the next section. Remember that you must select all correct answers on the exam and select only correct answers to receive credit for the question.

1. Which of the following are elements of administrative personnel structures in HXM? (There are two correct answers.)

    ☐ A. Employee groups
    ☐ B. Personnel areas
    ☐ C. Payroll areas
    ☐ D. Company codes

2. Which of the following are elements of enterprise structures in HXM? (There are two correct answers.)

    ☐ A. Personnel subareas
    ☐ B. Organizational units
    ☐ C. Employee subgroups
    ☐ D. Client

3. Which of the following can be assigned to a company code?

    ☐ A. Payroll areas
    ☐ B. Employee groups
    ☐ C. Positions
    ☐ D. Personnel areas

4. Which of the following can be assigned a cost center? (There are two correct answers.)

☐ A. Personnel areas
☐ B. Organizational units
☐ C. Payroll areas
☐ D. Positions

5. Which of the following system objects stores the employee master record?

☐ A. InfoCubes
☐ B. Infostructures
☐ C. Infotypes
☐ D. Info sets

6. Which of the following describes the tasks in positions?

☐ A. Organizational units
☐ B. Personnel areas
☐ C. Jobs
☐ D. Task areas

7. Which of the following relationships are correct in HXM? (There are three correct answers.)

☐ A. Persons occupy jobs
☐ B. Positions belong to organizational units
☐ C. Organizational units are assigned to personnel areas
☐ D. A position is assigned to a job
☐ E. Organizational unit is assigned to an employee area

8. Which of the following are methods to maintain infotypes in HXM? (There are two correct answers.)

☐ A. Personnel maintenance
☐ B. Single screen maintenance
☐ C. Fast entry
☐ D. Collective action

9. Which of the following transactions can be used to create an employee master record for a new hire employee?

- ☐ A. Personnel action
- ☐ B. Fast entry
- ☐ C. Personnel file
- ☐ D. ESS

10. Which of the following are elements of HCM? (There are three correct answers.)

- ☐ A. Time management
- ☐ B. Work center planning
- ☐ C. Task allotment
- ☐ D. Organizational management
- ☐ E. Payroll

11. Which of the following statements are correct about HXM? (There are two correct answers.)

- ☐ A. Focuses an enterprise's goals primarily and treats employees' experiences secondarily
- ☐ B. Harmonizes X-Data and O-Data for leadership decisions
- ☐ C. Based only on O-Data from ERP systems
- ☐ D. Involves methods for creating work experiences that align employees' wants, needs, and expectations with company goals

12. Which of the following statements are correct about Employee Central? (There are two correct answers.)

- ☐ A. Embedded in SAP S/4HANA Enterprise Management
- ☐ B. It is a foundation for SAP SuccessFactors HXM Suite applications
- ☐ C. Central data repository for SAP SuccessFactors HXM Suite
- ☐ D. An alternative on-premise HCM software providing all HR functions in SAP S/4HANA

13. Which of the following are the functions of ESS? (There are two correct answers.)

- ☐ A. Obtain the personal data of other employees
- ☐ B. Compensation planning
- ☐ C. Search who's who
- ☐ D. Submit travel expenses

14. Which of the following are the functions of MSS? (There are two correct answers.)
  - ☐ A. Recruitment
  - ☐ B. Entering work times
  - ☐ C. Enrolling in benefits
  - ☐ D. Cost control

15. Which of the following can be assigned to an organizational unit in its master record? (There are two correct answers.)
  - ☐ A. Work center
  - ☐ B. Cost center
  - ☐ C. Employee
  - ☐ D. Profit center

16. Which of the following can lead to integration between HR and production?
  - ☐ A. MRP
  - ☐ B. Sales and operations planning (S&OP)
  - ☐ C. Confirmation
  - ☐ D. Settlement

10.7 Practice Question Answers and Explanations

1. Correct answers: **A and C**
   An administrative personnel structure describes the position of an employee from an administrative perspective and consists of the following elements: employee group, employee subgroup, payroll area, and organizational key. Company codes and personnel areas are elements of the enterprise structure.

2. Correct answers: **A and D**
   An enterprise structure in HXM describes the company's structure according to personnel administration, time management, and payroll aspects and consists of the following elements: client, company code, personnel area, and personnel subarea. An organizational unit is part of an organizational personnel structure.

3. Correct answer: **D**
   A personnel area represents a subdivision of the company code in personnel administration. A personnel area defines an enterprise area from personnel administrative, time management, and payroll aspects. Each personnel area is assigned to only one company code in Customizing. A company code can be assigned several personnel areas.

4. Correct answers: **B and D**

    An organizational unit can be assigned a cost center to enable the updating of costs incurred by the organizational unit. Positions are either assigned cost centers in their master records or inherit cost centers from the organizational units of the positions.

5. Correct answer: **C**

    The employee master record in HXM is stored in the infotypes, which are groups of data fields that logically belong together (e.g., addresses, basic pay, bank details, organizational assignment, personal data).

6. Correct answer: **C**

    A job is a part of an organizational personnel structure, and you can use jobs to describe the tasks and responsibilities conducted in the enterprise. Positions assigned to a job inherit the tasks described by the job. In addition to the tasks inherited from a job, you can also define additional tasks for a position.

7. Correct answers: **B, C, and D**

    Persons or employees do not occupy jobs; they occupy positions. Positions belong to organizational units and can be assigned to jobs. Organizational units are not assigned to employee areas but to the personnel areas or personnel subareas. Positions and the employees holding positions can be assigned to employee areas or employee subareas in their master data.

8. Correct answers: **B and C**

    You can maintain employee master records stored in infotypes in three different ways: through the single screen maintenance to maintain a single infotype of a single person, through personnel actions to maintain several infotypes of a single person, and through fast entry to maintain a single infotype for several persons.

9. Correct answer: **A**

    When you hire an employee, you must create an employee master record consisting of several infotypes. Thus, you must maintain several infotypes for a single person, which can be achieved by using the personnel actions transaction.

10. Correct answers: **A, D, and E**

    SAP S/4HANA supports the following HCM processes: organizational management, time management, personnel administration, payroll, recruitment, training and event management, and travel management.

11. Correct answers: **B and D**

    Unlike HCM, HXM focuses both on employee experiences (i.e., task experience, social experience, and fulfillment experience) and on an enterprise's goals simultaneously. The HXM approach uses X-Data and O-Data synchronously for structuring a company's decisions. HXM involves methods for creating work experiences that align employees' wants, needs, and expectations with company goals.

12. Correct answers: **B and C**

    Employee Central is a central data repository for SAP SuccessFactors HXM Suite applications. It includes HR data (e.g., employment data, compensation data, payroll data, time management data, benefits, talent profiles) and the foundation objects for the enterprise's organizational structure. Employee Central is a cloud-based (not on-premise) solution and is not embedded in SAP S/4HANA Enterprise Management.

13. Correct answers: **C and D**

    As an employee, you can use the HTML-based ESS interface to perform the following activities: submit travel expenses, view the calendar, search who's who, update their personal data, enter work times, enroll in benefits, update banking info, and enroll in training courses. Compensation planning or obtaining personal data of other employees are functions of MSS.

14. Correct answers: **A and D**

    As a manager, you can use the web-based MSS interface to perform your daily administrative tasks by using the following functions: gather information, recruitment, monitoring, compensation planning, cost control, budget management, and head counting.

15. Correct answers: **A and C**

    Work centers and employees can be assigned to an organizational unit in their master records. This assignment is necessary to determine the work center's or employee's position in the organizational structure of the enterprise.

16. Correct answer: **C**

    Time confirmations for a production order trigger an HR data transfer to the personnel administration component of SAP S/4HANA, thus integrating production with HR.

10.8 Test Takeaway

In this chapter, you learned the key topics of hire-to-retire processing and SAP's new HCM approach, called HXM.

SAP GUI for SAP S/4HANA provides the HR module supporting the core HCM processes, including organizational management, time management, personnel administration, payroll, recruitment, training and event management, travel management. SAP SuccessFactors HXM Suite supports the transition of HCM processes to the cloud in several scenarios, including talent hybrid, side-by-side, core hybrid, full cloud.

Based on years of experience, SAP redefined the HCM process with an employee-centric mindset that creates new work experiences that align employee wants, needs, and expectations with company goals. SAP SuccessFactors HXM Suite is the suite of various HXM applications that can be categorized in the following way:

employee experience management software, core HR and payroll software, talent management software, HR analytics, and workforce planning software.

The employee is an HXM master record stored in the infotypes in the system. The company's HR-relevant organizational and personnel structure is mapped into the system using HXM structures, including enterprise structures, administrative personnel structures, and organizational personnel structures. Each employee must be assigned to these structures in their master records.

Employee Center is a central data repository and the foundation for other SAP SuccessFactors HXM Suite software. It houses HR data (e.g., employment data, compensation data, payroll data, time management data, benefits, talent profile) and foundational objects created by replicating employee data and organizational data from SAP S/4HANA. It also provides built-in self-service tools for employees and managers.

ESS is a web-based interface that enables employees to maintain their own personal data and execute employee-relevant HR transactions, such as submitting travel expenses, enrolling in benefits and training, and searching a company directory. MSS is an interface supporting managers' administrative tasks with cross-application functions, enabling them to obtain personnel data and engage in recruitment, compensation planning, head-counting, monitoring, and cost control.

With this discussion of HXM with SAP S/4HANA, we've concluded our coverage of the core certification topics. We wish you the best of luck on exam day!

The Author

 **Dr. Murat Adivar** is a professor of business analytics and an SAP-certified consultant at Fayetteville State University. He is the founder of the ERP Concentration Program at Broadwell College of Business and Economics, SAP Next-Gen Lab at Fayetteville State University, and the ERP and Advanced Analytics Center at Fayetteville State University. He currently teaches data analytics courses at the MBA program and trains students for the TS410 business process integration exam. Dr. Adivar has the C_TERP10, C_TS410_1610, C_TS410_1809, C_TS410_1909, and C_TS410_2020 certifications.

Index

A

Account assignment category 207, 208, 227
Account assignment element 442
Account determination key 81, 100
Account group 85, 111
   profit and loss 90
Account-based profitability analysis 153
Accounting document 92, 96, 218, 220, 275, 280, 340
   display 95
Accounting principles 74, 82, 83
Accounts payable 98, 111
   asset postings 103
Accounts receivable 99, 111
Accrual order 148
Acquisition and production costs (APC) 105
Acquisition from an internal activity 104
Action log 384
Activities 388, 445, 451, 466
   master record 447
   processing 458
Activity allocation 166
Activity price 166
Activity type 131, 133, 139, 166
   master data 139
   planning 141
Activity unit 139
Activity-based costing 129, 146, 166
Actual cost 389
Actual costing 158
Adjustment posting 144
Administrative personnel
   structure 480, 482
Advanced planning 301, 324, 344
   options 325
Advanced shipping notification 248
Alert monitor 327
Allocation 140, 144
   BOM 305
Analytical applications 54
Application component 53, 58
Application development and
   integration 49
Application help 31
Application programming interface
   (API) 42
Application services 49
Ariba Network 47, 226
Assembly 374

Assessment 111, 145, 153, 163, 166
Asset account 78, 81
Asset accounting 99, 112
   acquisition 103
   cross-module assignments 387
   depreciation 104
   master data 100
   postings 102
   retirement 104
   segments 100
Asset acquisition 103, 110, 164
   reporting and monitoring 107
Asset class 100, 112
Asset explorer 104, 107, 112
Asset history sheet 102, 107, 112
Asset posting 102
Asset retirement 104
Automatic payment run 224, 227
Availability check 257, 279, 281, 332, 379, 423
   types 258
Availability control 259
Availability list 388
Available-to-promise (ATP) 258

B

Backflush goods issue 337
Backorder 264
Backorder processing (BOP) 264
Backward scheduling 257
Balance sheet 97, 112
Balance sheet account 76, 88, 112
Bank ledger accounting 112
Basic data view 192
Bill of materials (BOM) 224, 344
   component allocations 305
   explosion 317
   maintenance 368
   material 302, 305, 368
   usage key 303
Billing 111, 253, 275
   document 277, 281
   due list 275, 276
   element 442
   impact 278
   settlement 276
Bill-to party 247
Blocked stock 403
Budget 456, 466

Business application programming
  interfaces (BAPIs) 416
Business area 75, 80, 112
  cross-module assignments 162
Business completion 386
Business partner 78
  approach 194
  categories 78, 112, 194
  customers 246
  general role 79
  groupings 80, 112
  number 80
  roles 79, 195, 197, 203, 246, 251
Business process 61, 146, 166
  integration 61
  master record 146
Business roles 51

C

C_TS410 certification exam 19, 21, 34
  resources 27
  tips 32
  ways to learn 23
Calibration order 376
Capacities 312
Central procurement 42
Centralized warehouse
  management 412, 414
Certification exam 20
  preparation tips 32
  question types 21
  resources 27
  test-taking tips 33
  ways to learn 23
Certification Hub 21, 33
Characteristics 152, 166
Chart of accounts 81, 84, 85, 112
  segment 87, 88
  types 85
Client 57, 74, 80, 128, 186, 227, 481
Cloud 38, 43
  platform 49
Collective billing document 276
Commitment 212, 219, 225
  objects 214
Commitment management 129, 149, 212,
  215, 225
Company code 74, 80, 82, 87, 187, 202, 227,
  250, 481
  assign to chart of accounts 85
  assign to controlling area 128
  cost centers 139
  cross-module assignments 162

Company code (Cont.)
  currency 129
  segment 87, 89
  stock transfer 410
Completion confirmation 165, 382
Component data 331
Conditions 201, 227
  master record 247, 249, 251, 262
  types 247
Confirmation 382, 388, 423, 459, 465, 498
Construction type 368
Consumption 301, 334
Consumption-based planning 299
Contact-to-lead 251
Contract 210
Contract accounts receivable and
  accounts payable 78
Controlling 76, 90, 126
  commitments 213
  cross-module assignments 108, 161
  data assignments 133
  data structures 127
  document 218, 221, 275
  integration 161, 279
  key processes 133
  master data 130
  objects 126, 142, 167
  organizational structures 128
Controlling area 108, 128, 133, 167
  cross-module assignments 161
  currency 129
  segment 90
Core data services (CDS) views 52
Corrective maintenance 373
Cost and revenue element 134
  accounting 167
Cost center 81, 95, 108, 131, 133, 136, 167,
  309, 341, 387, 497
  activity types 141
  category 137, 139, 167
  groups 137
  master data 137, 138
  production 340
Cost center accounting 136, 146, 167
Cost data 377
Cost distribution 421
Cost element 131, 134, 143, 447
  accounting 134
  allocation 140
  category 90, 167
Cost estimate 155
Cost forecast 461
Cost object 167
Cost object controlling 155, 157

Cost planning	455
Costing-based profitability analysis	153
Country-specific chart of accounts	85
Credit processing	248
Cross-application time sheet (CATS)	166, 461
Cross-company code cost accounting	108, 128, 161
Cross-module data assignment	61
design-to-operate	341
enterprise asset management	386
financial accounting	108
HXM	497
inventory, warehouse, and transportation management	422
lead-to-cash	279
management accounting	161
Project System	463
source-to-pay	224
Currency	82
company code	129
controlling area	129
cost center	138
Current price	156
Current tangible asset	99
Customer	74, 80, 99, 186, 245, 279, 281
account	78
invoice	281
master	245, 251
number	80
role	79, 246, 251
Customer independent requirements (CIRs)	316, 344
Customizing	55
Cut score	22
Cycle segment method	145

D

Data	55
cross-module assignments	61
design-to-operate	297
enterprise asset management	361
financial accounting	73
HXM	479
lead-to-cash	240
management accounting	127
Project System	439
source-to-pay	185
Data assignment	55, 61
controlling	133
design-to-operate	312
enterprise asset management	371
financial accounting	80
Data assignment (Cont.)	
HXM	489
lead-to-cash	249
Project System	451
source-to-pay	201
Data footprint	45
Data management	49
Database services	49
Decentralized extended warehouse management (EWM)	271
Decentralized planning	363
Decentralized warehouse management	412, 416
Decoupling	318
Delivery document	408
Delivery due list	265
Demand	319
Demand management	314, 316, 343, 344
Demand-driven material requirements planning (DDMRP)	318
Demand-driven replenishment	300, 318
Dependent requirement	317, 322, 345
Deployment	43, 63
Depreciation	104
posting run	110, 164
types	105
Depreciation area	100, 105
Depreciation key	106
Design phase	313
Design principles	51
Design-to-operate	47, 296, 345
data assignments	312, 341
integration	341, 342
key processes	313
master data	298
organizational data	298
Detailed planning	317, 343, 345
Determination of requirements	205
Developers	51
Digital badge	23
Digital core	39
Direct activity allocation	167
Discrete manufacturing	327
Display Asset Master Worklist app	108
Distribution	111, 145, 163, 167
rules	151
Distribution channel	242, 250, 282
Division	242, 250, 282
Document	59, 332
accounting	92, 218, 275, 340
billing	276
cross-module	61
delivery	408
display	273

Document (Cont.)
flow 272, 282
general ledger accounts 92
goods movements 410
goods receipt 220
integrated asset acquisition 103
item 303
material 217, 275
Material Ledger 338
outbound delivery 265, 268
PRT 307
reference 257
sales 243
type 93

Document splitting 75, 94, 113
method 95
rules 95

E

Embedded analytics 45, 49
Employee 485, 489
group 482, 498
subgroup 482, 499
Employee experience management
software 493
Employee self-service (ESS) 496, 498
Enterprise asset management 360
data 56
data assignments 371
integration 386
key processes 372
master data 363
organizational data 361
Enterprise management 40
Enterprise resource planning (ERP) 37
Enterprise structure 479, 481, 489
Equipment 307, 364, 366, 371, 389
categories 367
master records 367
Exclusive free goods 262
Execution phase 465
Expense and revenue account 134
Experience 491
Experience data (X-Data) 478, 491
Expert users 51
Extended warehouse management
(EWM) 337, 417
functions 418
organizational structure 418
External acquisition 103
External procurement 326, 335, 343
nonstock material 381
Externally processed activity 446, 447, 458

F

Fact sheet applications 54
Fast entry 488, 499
FI Customer role 79, 246, 251
FI Vendor role 79, 196, 203
Field status 86
Financial accounting 72
business transactions 109
cross-module assignments 108, 161, 342
customer role 79, 246, 251
data 56
data assignments 80
goods receipt 217
integration 163, 225, 280, 464
key processes 81
master data 75
organizational structures 73
vendor role 79, 196, 203
Financial statement 75, 82, 97
document splitting 94
Financial statement version 97, 113
Fiscal year 82
Fiscal year variant 82, 128
Fixed assets 81, 100, 108
Fixed tangible asset 99
Flexible planning 314
Forecast-based planning 300
Forecasting 301, 314
Formula key 310
Free goods 261
Freight booking 420, 424
Freight order 420, 424
Freight settlement document (FSD) ... 421, 424
Freight unit 420, 424
Function and object-related structuring ... 366
Functional location 364, 371, 389
master data 365
Functional structuring 364
Functionality 53
Future price 156

G

General cost activity 446, 447
General ledger 81, 113
General ledger account 76, 80, 83, 85
cross-module assignments 161
integration 225
master data 87
post documents 92
type 88
General ledger accounting 81, 113
configuration 82

Index

General ledger accounting (Cont.)
  objects 83
Generally Accepted Accounting
  Principles (GAAP) 74
Glossary 30
Goods issue 110, 165, 269, 274, 279, 282, 334, 337, 404, 424
  documents 410
  posting 274
Goods movements 110, 333, 337, 402, 403, 424
  categories 404
  documents 410
  integration 423
Goods receipt 110, 164, 215, 227, 337, 404, 425
  accounting 218
  documents 220, 410
  impact 217, 219
  invoice verification 221
  master data 216
  outputs 220
Goods receipt/invoice receipt clearing 98
Group chart of accounts 85

H

Hierarchy area 138
Hire-to-retire processing 478
  key processes 490
Human capital management
  (HCM) 478, 491, 492
  data 57
Human experience management
  (HXM) 478, 492
  cross-module assignments 109, 163
  data assignments 489, 497
  integration 497
  key processes 490
  master data 485
  organizational structures 479, 499
Human resources (HR) 478, 492
  analytics and planning 494
  cloud 494
  cross-module assignments 342, 387
Hybrid deployment 44

I

Imputed costs 134
Imputed interest 105
Inbound delivery 417, 425
  document 418
Inclusive free goods 262

Income statement 97
  account 76, 89, 90, 113
Incompletion log 261
Incoterms 255
Individual billing document 277
Industry sector 189
Info record 198
Infotype 485, 499
  maintain 486
In-house production 301
In-memory database 38, 45
Inquiry 282
Inspection 372
Intangible assets 100
Integration 45
  design-to-operate 341, 342
  enterprise asset management 386
  financial accounting 108, 109
  HXM 497
  inventory, warehouse, and
    transportation management 422
  lead-to-cash 279
  management accounting 161, 163
  Project System 463
  SAP Ariba 226
  services 49
  source-to-pay 224
Intelligent enterprise 46, 62
Intelligent Spend Management 184
Intelligent suite 46, 62
  value chain 47
Intelligent technologies 46, 48, 49, 62
Interest calculation 461
Internal controlling posting 144
Internal order 108, 132, 133, 147, 167, 387
  cross-module assignments 161
  maintenance 367
  master data 148
  settlement 150, 163
Internal unit of measure 90
Internally processed activity 446, 458
International Financial Reporting
  Standards (IFRS) 74
Internet of Things (IoT) 38
Inventory 402, 425
Inventory management 217, 400, 402, 411
  integration 225, 279, 422
  organizational data 402
  stock transfers 409
Investment order 147, 376
Invoice 221, 227, 248, 275
  posting 222
  splitting 276

Invoice (Cont.)
  verification 164, 221
Item category 206, 303

J

Job 484, 489, 499

K

Kanban processing 327
Key performance indicator (KPI) 54

L

Lead 239, 251, 282
Leading ledger 82
Lead-to-cash 47, 238
  data assignments 249
  integration 279
  key processes 251
  master data 243, 250
  organizational data 249
  organizational structures 240
Lead-to-opportunity 251
Lean warehouse management 271, 412
Learning journey 25, 27
Learning resources 27
Learning room 27
Ledger 82
Line items 268
Line of business (LoB) solutions 41, 44, 62
  categories 42
  suite 42
List of all chart of accounts 83
Location 362
Logistics 108, 162
  execution 420

M

Maintenance bill of materials (BOM) 368
Maintenance completion 381
Maintenance control 379, 387
Maintenance execution 380
Maintenance notification 373
  views 375
Maintenance order 375, 376
  completion 388
  control 379
  execution 387
  release 380
  settlement 385
  structure 377

Maintenance order (Cont.)
  technically complete 384
Maintenance planning 375, 387
  plant 362, 371, 389
Maintenance plant 362, 371, 389
Maintenance request 373
Maintenance work center 389, 498
Make-to-order (MTO) 280, 326
Make-to-stock (MTS) 326
Malfunction report 374
Management accounting 72, 126
  cross-module assignments 108, 161, 341, 387, 497
  data 56
  data assignments 133
  integration 161, 163, 225, 279, 464
  key processes 133
  master data 130
  organizational structures 128
Manager self-service (MSS) 496, 499
Manager's Desktop 496
Manual actual posting 163
Manufacturing 296, 313
  control and execution 322, 327
  master data 298
  orders 325
  types 327
Margin analysis 154
Master data 55, 56
  assets 100
  design-to-operate 298
  enterprise asset management 363
  financial accounting 75, 80
  HXM 485
  lead-to-cash 243, 250
  maintenance 111
  management accounting 130
  source-to-pay 188, 203
Master production scheduling
  (MPS) 300, 317, 345
Material 162, 189, 194, 312
  assignment 204
  availability checks 423
  BOM 302, 303, 305, 312, 368
  classification 318
  components 448, 457
  consumption posting 334
  document 217, 220, 274, 275, 381
  list 377
  planning 455
  price 218
  processing 166
  PRT 307
  staging 343, 423

Index   515

Material (Cont.)
    types 189, 224, 244
    withdrawal 333, 343, 380, 457
Material determination list 263
Material exclusion list 262
Material Ledger 158
    document 217, 221, 275, 338
Material master 189, 227, 244, 279, 298
    advanced planning 324
    data 192
    goods receipt 217
    record 189, 190
    views 189, 191, 244, 299
Material processing 165
Material requirements planning
    (MRP) 300, 317
    area 300
    control parameters 320
    list 321, 322
    modes 320
    type 299
    views 299, 301
Materials management 155, 244, 402, 422
    commitments 213
Milestone 450, 451, 461, 466
Module 53, 57, 63
    core processes 58
Movement type 216, 410, 425
Moving average price 157
MRP Live 318, 321, 325, 345

N

Negative available stock 319
Net requirements calculation 299, 318
Network 440, 444, 451, 466
    activities 445
    costing 455
    scheduling 454
Neutral expenditures 134
Nonoperating expense account 89
Nonstock material 217, 244, 303, 381, 402, 425, 457, 458
Nonvaluated material 217, 402
Notification 389
Number range 86

O

Object data 378
Object list 389
Object-related structuring 364, 366
Occasional users 50
Onboard cache 38

One-step procedure 407, 408
Online analytical processing (OLAP) 49
Online training 24
Online transactional processing (OLTP) 49
On-premise 43
openSAP 31
Operate phase 313
Operating chart of accounts 85
Operating concern 128, 133, 151, 168
    definition 154
    master data 152
Operation 304, 313, 389
    data 330
Operational data (O-Data) 478, 491
Operational document 103
Operational expenditures 134
Operational process 40
Operative indicator 442
Opportunity 239, 282
Opportunity-to-quote 252
Order combination 266, 268
Order confirmation 248, 335, 337, 343, 344
Order management 420
Order manager 148
Order release 380, 389
Order type 149, 168
    settlement 151
Orders with revenue 148
Order-to-cash 99, 240, 252
    data 56
Ordinary depreciation 105
Organizational data 55, 56
    design-to-operate 298
    enterprise asset management 361
    financial accounting 73, 80
    inventory management 402
    lead-to-cash 240, 249
    management accounting 128
    source-to-pay 186, 202
    warehouse management 412
Organizational key 482
Organizational management 492
Organizational personnel structure ... 480, 483
Organizational unit 308, 483, 489, 498, 499
Outbound delivery 253, 265, 425
    activities 265
    document 265, 268, 282
    master data 266
    order 271, 282
    strategies 266
Outbound delivery order 418
Outline agreement 201, 209, 227
Output 60, 248, 263
    master record 248, 251

Overhead calculation 144, 339
Overhead cost controlling 129
Overhead costs 339
Overhead order 147

P

Packaging material 244
Parallel accounting 82, 113
Parallel ledger 82
Partial delivery 266
Partner function 247, 249, 259
Payer 247
Payment 111, 223, 253
Payroll 492, 493, 498
   areas 482, 499
Period-end closing 144, 339, 461, 465
   internal orders 150
   methods 145
Periodic reposting 145, 168
Personnel actions 486, 499
Personnel administration 492
Personnel area 481, 499
Personnel file 488
Personnel subarea 481, 499
Physical inventory 402, 411
Picking 265, 269, 280
   activities 270
   list 269
Plan cost 389
Planned depreciation value 104
Planned independent requirements
   (PIRs) 315, 316, 345
Planned order 319, 322, 325, 329
Planned withdrawal 333
Planning 296, 317
   advanced 324
   cost 455
   integration 465
   material 455
   modes 320
   plant maintenance 363
   resource 454
   types 299
Planning element 442
Plant 187, 191, 202, 228, 241, 250, 312, 371
   cross-module assignments 163
   maintenance 362
   MRP areas 300
   stock transfer 409
Plant maintenance 360, 372
   cross-module assignments 109, 163, 422, 498
   data assignments 371

Plant maintenance (Cont.)
   integration 165, 225, 387, 464
Plan-to-deliver 313
Plan-to-produce 56, 313
   integration 164
Plant-specific planning 363
Position 483, 489, 500
Posting key 93, 102
Predictive material and resource
   planning (pMRP) 318
Preliminary costing 332
Preventive maintenance 372
Previous price 156
Price calculation 248
Price control 157
Price indicator 140
Price update 156
Pricing 259
Primary costs and revenue account 88, 90, 134, 168
   cross-module assignments 162
Private cloud 44
Process manufacturing 327
Processing key 320
Processing services 49
Procurement 186, 206, 209, 335
   activities 447
   proposals 322, 345
Procurement analytics 40
Procurement type key 301
Procure-to-pay 47, 184
Product allocation 258
Product cost accounting 155, 158
Product cost controlling 168
Product cost planning 155, 342
Product group 314
Production 162, 313, 325, 327
   cross-module assignments 498
   integration 164, 280
   processes 326
Production order 165, 319, 326, 328
   confirmation 335
   data categories 329
   integration 343
   management 328
   material withdrawal 333
   period-end closing 339
   release 333
Production planning and detailed
   scheduling (PP-DS) 301, 324–326, 344
   master data 325
Production planning and execution 296
Production resources and tools (PRTs) 306, 313, 345, 377

Index 517

Production version 302, 305, 313, 329, 345
Profit and loss (P&L) account 76, 113
Profit and loss (P&L) statement 97
Profit center 76, 80, 109, 113, 139, 158, 168, 342
    accounting 158, 168
    cross-module assignments 161
    master data 158
Profitability analysis ... 151, 155, 168, 275, 278
    integration 165, 279
    methods 153
Profitability segment 143, 152, 160, 168
Progress analysis 461
Project 438, 439
    budgeting 456
    definition 441
    execution 457
    planning 453
    structuring elements 441, 466
Project Builder 441, 453
Project management 438
Project Planning Board 453
Project System 438
    cross-module assignments 109, 163, 387
    data assignments 451, 463
    integration 166, 225, 281, 463, 465
    key processes 452
    period-end closing 461
    structuring elements 439, 441
Public cloud 43
Purchase order 198, 209, 211, 225, 228, 335
    commitments 214
    history 219
    invoice verification 221
    master data 212
    price 218
Purchase requisition 205, 225, 228, 319, 320, 335, 447
    commitments 214
    covert to purchase order 209
Purchase-to-pay 98
    data 56
    integration 164
Purchasing 109, 184, 195, 202, 204
    group 188
    integration 280, 464
    organization 187, 196, 202, 203
    view 192
Purchasing info record 198, 203, 228
    creation 199
    master data 200
    views 199

Q

Quality inspection stock 403
Quality management
    goods receipt 219
    integration 225, 280
Quant 414, 425
Quantity structure 155
Quotation 201, 228, 252, 256, 282
Quote-to-order 252, 256

R

Reconciliation account 76, 80, 90, 113, 197, 224
Recruitment 492
Reference document 257
Reference object 374, 389
Refurbishment order 376
Relationship 449, 451, 466
Reorder point planning 299
Repair 372
Repetitive manufacturing 327
Reporting standards 82
Reposting 144, 168
Request for quotation (RFQ) 210, 228
Reservation 380, 407, 423
Resource planning 454
Result analysis 461
Routing 303, 305, 312, 345

S

Sales and distribution 109, 155, 238, 240, 244, 253, 416
    documents 273
    integration 165
    profitability analysis 153
Sales and operations planning (S&OP) 280, 314, 316
Sales area 242, 245, 254, 282
Sales controlling 151
Sales document 243, 283
Sales information system 278
Sales item 283
Sales order 149, 253, 254, 261, 280, 283, 326
    alterations 261
    document flow 272
    functions 257
    master data 254, 255
Sales organization 241, 250, 283
Sales price 156
SAP Advanced Planning and Optimization (SAP APO) 324

Index

SAP Ariba 42, 62, 184, 226
SAP Business Suite 39
SAP Business Suite on SAP HANA 39
SAP Business Technology Platform
   (SAP BTP) 46, 48, 50, 62, 238
SAP Cloud Platform 50, 62
SAP Commerce Cloud 252
SAP Concur 43, 62
SAP Conversational AI 52
SAP Customer Data Cloud 252
SAP Customer Experience 43, 47, 62,
   238, 252
SAP Easy Access 57, 58
SAP Extended Warehouse Management
   (SAP EWM) 417
SAP Extension Suite 50
SAP Fieldglass 43, 63
SAP Fiori 40, 50, 63
   applications 54, 63
   design and dimensions 50
SAP Fiori launchpad 51–53, 57, 63
SAP Gateway 52
SAP GUI 50, 57
SAP HANA 39, 45, 49, 54, 63
SAP Help Portal 30
SAP Human Capital Management for
   SAP S/4HANA 478, 498
SAP Implementation Guide (IMG) 55
SAP Integrated Business Planning
   (SAP IBP) 316, 345
SAP Integration Suite 50
SAP Jam 316
SAP Learning Hub 24, 27
SAP Marketing Cloud 252
SAP Next-Gen 25
SAP S/4HANA 32, 36, 39
   business process integration 61
   characteristics 43, 44
   components 39
   deployment 43
   motivators and enablers 38
   suite 37, 63
   system-wide concepts 54
SAP S/4HANA Cloud 43
SAP S/4HANA Cloud, private edition 44
SAP S/4HANA Enterprise Management ... 39–
   41, 44, 63
SAP Sales Cloud 252
SAP Service Cloud 252
SAP SuccessFactors 43, 63, 478
SAP SuccessFactors Employee Central ... 495,
   498
SAP SuccessFactors HXM Suite 493
SAP Training and Adoption 20, 23, 26
SAP Transportation Management
   (SAP TM) 265, 419
SAP University Alliances 21, 25
SAPUI5 51
Scalability 44
Schedule line 255, 267, 283, 321
   categories 258
Scheduling 311, 321, 332, 454
Scheduling agreement 210, 283
Secondary cost account 89, 90
Secondary cost element 135, 169
Segment 74, 80, 113
   assets 100
   chart of accounts 88
   company code 89
   controlling area 90
   general ledger accounts 87
   profitability 152, 160
Self-service requisitioning 40, 46
Sequence 304
   data 330
Serial number 369, 371, 422
Serialization 369, 370, 387, 422
Service activity 446, 447
Service order 375
Services 244
Settlement 111, 150, 163, 169, 340, 346,
   390, 462, 466
   billing 276
   integration 343
   maintenance orders 385
   plant maintenance 165
   production 165
   Project System 166, 462
   receivers 151
   rules 151, 169, 340, 378, 463
Shipping point 243, 250, 267
Ship-to party 247, 254, 256, 267
Single screen maintenance 486, 500
Sold-to party 247, 254
Source determination 209
Source of supply 208
   determination 209
Source-to-pay 47, 184
   data assignments 201, 224
   integration with other modules 224
   key processes 204
   master data 188, 203
   organizational data 186, 202
   SAP Ariba 226
Sourcing 184, 209
Special depreciation 105
Standard cost estimate 155, 169
   release 156

Index

Standard hierarchy 137, 146, 169
Standard order 211
Standard planning 314
Standard price 156, 157
    types 156
Standard value 310
    key 309
Statistical key figure 132, 133, 141, 169
Statistical object 142, 169
Statistical order 150
Statistical posting 143
Stock item 217, 303
Stock material 379, 380, 425, 457
Stock overview 403
Stock requirement list 322
Stock transfer 110, 405, 425
    documents 410
    procedure 405, 407
    types 409
Stock transport order 211, 408, 411, 425
Stock type 216, 425
Stock-in-transit stock 407
Storage bin 411, 414, 425
    EWM 418
Storage location .... 187, 194, 202, 228, 413, 422, 426 [SLOC]
    MRP areas 300
    stock transfer 409
Storage section 413, 426
Storage type 413, 426
Strategic planning 314, 342, 346
Strategy group 301
Structure indicator 365
Subcontractor 301
Subledger account 76, 77, 80, 113
Supplier 301
Supply 319
System module 63

T

Table ACDOCA 162
Talent management 494
Target cost 339, 346
Tasks 375, 388
Technical clearing account 103
Technical completion 340, 383, 390
Technical object 364, 371, 387, 390
Technology enablers 37
Template allocation 145, 153, 461
Three-way match 221, 228
Time management 492
Time-phased planning 300
Top-down planning 454

Topic area 22
Tracing factor 139, 169
Trading goods 244
Training 23
Training and event management 492, 498
Transaction 57
    ABAON 104
    ABAVN 104
    ABZON 103
    AR02 .... 107, 112
    AW01N 104, 107
    CAT2 166
    CF01 307
    CJ2ON 441, 453
    CJ27 453
    cross-module 61
    currency 129
    CV01N 307
    F-90 103
    F-91 103
    F-92 104
    FB70 98
    IE01 307
    IW24 374
    IW25 374
    IW26 374
    IW34 376
    IW42 382
    K004 148
    KE91 160
    KO88 385
    KP26 141
    MD_MRP_FORCE_CLASSIC 317
    ME1L 198
    ME1M 198
    ME21N 406, 408
    ME49 211
    MIGO 215, 404
    MIGO_GR 215
    MIGO_TR 405, 407
    MIRO 221
    MM01 307
    MMBE 403
    OKENN 137
    PA10 488
    PA70 488
    PPMDT 496
    PPOCE 483
    S_ALR_87012333 84
    type 102
    VA01 254
    VF01 276
    VF04 276
    VF06 276

Transaction (Cont.)
 VL10A 265
 VL10C 265
Transactional applications 54
Transactional data 56
Transfer order 271, 272, 283, 415, 426
Transfer posting 110, 405, 406, 426
 documents 410
Transfer requirement 414, 426
Transmission medium 249
Transportation execution 420
Transportation management 400, 419
 integration 280, 422
Transportation planning 420
Transportation request 280
Transportation requirement 420
Transportation unit 420, 426
Travel management 492
True object 142, 143, 169
Two-step procedure 407

U

Universal Journal 162
Unplanned depreciation 105
Unplanned withdrawal 333
Unrestricted-use stock 403, 405
User experience (UX) 38, 45, 50, 51
User interface (UI) 51

V

Valuation class 224
Valuation document 103
Value chain 47, 63
Value fields 152
Value structure 155

Variable-size item 303
Variance calculation 339, 346
Vendor 79, 80, 98, 194, 224
 account 78
 invoices 98
 master 194, 197, 203, 228
 number 80
 payment 224
 role 80, 195, 203
 selection 211
View 191, 244

W

Warehouse management 400, 411
 cross-module assignments 279, 422
 goods receipt 220
 integration 225, 280, 422
 organizational data 412
Warehouse management system
 (WMS) 400, 411
 centralized 414
 decentralized 416
 organizational data 412
 picking 271
 types 412
Warehouse number 279, 412, 422, 426
Warehouse transfer request 225
Work breakdown structure (WBS) 440, 466
 elements 109, 442, 451, 466
 scheduling 454
Work center 308, 312, 313, 337, 342, 346,
 446, 498
 cross-module assignments 162
 maintenance 362
 master data 308
Work in process (WIP) 339, 346